FROM MARX
TO MISES

FROM MARX TO MISES

POST-CAPITALIST SOCIETY AND THE CHALLENGE OF ECONOMIC CALCULATION

DAVID RAMSAY STEELE

Open Court

La Salle, Illinois

OPEN COURT and the above logo are registered in the U.S.
Patent and Trademark Office.

© 1992 by Open Court Publishing Company

First printing 1992

Printed and bound in the United States of America.

The photograph used in the cover design is reproduced by
permission of the Ullstein Fotoarchiv. It shows socialists in
Berlin in 1918 demonstrating for "All Power to the Workers' and
Soldiers' Councils".

Library of Congress Cataloging-in-Publication Data

Steele, David Ramsay.
    From Marx to Mises : post-capitalist society and the challenge of
economic calculation / David Ramsay Steele.
        p.   cm.
    Includes bibliographical references and index.
    ISBN 0-87548-449-2 (cloth).—ISBN 0-8126-9016-8 (pbk.)
    1. Von Mises, Ludwig, 1881–1973. 2. Marx, Karl, 1818–1883.
    3. Economics—History. 4. Capitalism—History. 5. Post-communism.
I. Title.
HB101.V66S73 1992
330.9—dc20   92-35738
                                                    CIP

For Lisa

BRIEF TABLE OF CONTENTS

DETAILED TABLE OF CONTENTS

PREFACE

Karl Marx (1818–1883) and Ludwig von Mises (1881–1973) were economists of Jewish background, born and raised in German-speaking communities, who each resided for the final 33 years of their lives in the English-speaking world. At the times of their deaths, they each had a loyal and growing following but were outsiders, voices crying in the wilderness. After their deaths, the influence of their ideas began to spread with increasing rapidity.

Marx and Mises took the prevailing economic doctrines of their day, and developed these ideas in new ways, giving their own theories a distinctive cast which mainstream thinkers found unacceptable. In the final decade or so of their lives, they both tended to repeat their earlier views without fresh thinking, and seemed to be out of touch with contemporaneous discussions.

Marx and Mises combined erudition with a combative, frequently vituperative style of presentation, displaying in their writings little patience with critics. They presented economic theory as part of a much larger theoretical panorama, and advanced peculiar views on history and human behavior. They each became committed to unpopular political doctrines at a time when these doctrines were despised by conventional people, and therefore costly to embrace. They both helped to rescue their political causes from this pariah status, though in each case we can see with hindsight that those causes were already on the rise, a rise from which the posthumous reputations of Marx and Mises benefitted. They each attracted a small, industrious band of dedicated disciples prepared to brave— and reciprocate—the disdain of conventional thinkers.

As men and as thinkers, Marx and Mises could hardly have been more different. But a confrontation of their entire theoretical systems is far from being the purpose of this book. Rather, I am concerned to look at an argument, advanced by Mises against Marxism and other forms of socialism. The argument in question is the 'economic calculation argument', which I will often refer to as 'the Mises argument', deployed by Mises to support his seemingly preposterous claim that "socialism" is "impossible". Mises's argument began a vigorous debate, which is still going on in the sense that there is little agreement as to what the outcome was, though most of the essential points had been made by the end of the 1930s.

I try to explain Mises's argument from several angles, to give some notion of its historical background and impact, to explore some of the discussions it has provoked, and to look at a few of its broader ramifications. All my historical and theoretical discussions are related directly to my central theme of the Mises argument. For instance, although I examine some of the views of Karl Marx, and although these views are intrinsically fascinating, I don't attempt to present here a 'balanced picture' of Marx's theories, but only an accurate picture of some elements of his thought intimately related to economic calculation. The same goes for Mises's theories.

This work is designed to be completely comprehensible to a reader who begins with no knowledge of the economic calculation debate. I take an unorthodox view of some details of that debate, but I explain clearly what the alternative views are. This book can therefore be used as an introduction to the economic calculation issue, but I have taken the discussion a little further here and there. My interest in economic calculation is conceptual or philosophical rather than technical, and I am not attempting to contribute to economic theory.

While I was finishing this book, there occurred the disintegration of the Soviet bloc and the demise of 'state socialism' in Eastern Europe. Almost the only important repercussion for the text was that references to Soviet developments had to be shortened and changed from the future or present tenses to the past tense. This work is concerned with general issues inherent in attempts, usually called socialist, to replace or curtail the market. Although events in Russia have affected the course of the discussion of these issues, viewed from a general theoretical perspective, Soviet experience is only one of many sources of evidence. In all essentials, this book would be the same if the Soviet debacle had been completed in 1921, or if it had been delayed for another 20 years after 1989.

However, Soviet-bloc events may serve to illustrate the importance of this book's theme. Across Eastern Europe—indeed, across the world—state planners are putting the ax to state planning; they are encouraging private ownership of the means of production and financial markets such as stock exchanges. Sometimes they hesitate, and tinker with schemes to introduce some fragments of privatization and marketization, hedged about with controls to prevent them functioning as such, but such tinkerers are always in danger of being swept aside by more radical spirits. Practical policy-makers are faced with the apparent fact that, for some reason or other that they cannot fathom, tolerably high living standards for the masses require private property in the means of production, along with substantially free capital and money markets. Meanwhile, there are intellectuals who instruct students in the humanities and convey to successive generations the ruling ideas of this epoch. Overwhelmingly, these intellectuals, whether they consider themselves 'left' or 'right', are at a loss to give any serious explanation of the Soviet collapse. To them, what has happened still possesses a fairytale quality—and the first legend to congeal was that no one had expected the collapse. This book offers a thread by aid of which such intellectuals may hope to grope their way out of their labyrinth of confusion.

This work is a nonspecialist account of Mises's argument. It combines portions of the recognized corpus of economic theory with other considerations which are harder to classify, though perhaps many of them belong to philosophy. The portions of economic theory are elementary, and therefore not especially fascinating to economists, but remain unfamiliar to the typical intelligent, conventionally well-read non-economist. The economist may become exasperated by my belaboring of some fundamentals of economic principles and price theory, intermixed with assertions which he may well regard as more contentious. The non-economist may wrongly suppose that the issues being debated are such as economists have some special competence to judge. But this would be like going to physicists to enquire whether there is a God (In either case one *might*, of course, get a sensible answer). I have done my best to ensure that the purely theoretical bits of this book, elementary though they be, are not in dispute among economists. To put it another way, this book has been so designed that anyone who has read and understood it will be almost as competent as anyone else to evaluate those points in it which are likely to be seriously contested. It hardly needs saying that I roam over many areas in which I am not an expert, but I have tried never to fall below the level of a shrewd dilettante.

In the 1960s I was under the spell of Marx, though I had qualms about some elements of his system. In 1970, Mark Brady outlined to me Mises's economic calculation argument, and (though convinced that it must be wrong) I immediately recognized it as the most powerful objection that has been made to Marxian socialism. I am now less in agreement with Mises's theory, as a whole, than I came to be in the 1970s, but I still maintain that socialists have yet to face the challenge of economic calculation.

Among those who have helped me with their comments on various parts of this work in various stages of completion are: Dr. David Barker, Stephen H. Berry, Mark Brady, Dr. André W. Carus, Robin Cox, Professor James Dorn, Dr. David Gordon, Dr. John N. Gray, Professor Israel Kirzner, Professor Don T. Lavoie, Dr. J.C. Lester, David McDonagh, M.L. Rantala, James Sadowsky S.J., Dr. Jeremy Shearmur, Jeffrey A. Smith, Professor Sudha Shenoy, Dr. Eugenie Short, and Lisa Zimmerman. An anonymous reviewer for Open Court was helpful in demonstrating how completely some arguments, as they stood in an earlier draft, could be misunderstood. Professor Stephan Boehm, Professor Barry Smith, and Dr. Albert Zlabinger supplied me with copies of works difficult to obtain in the U.S. None of the above individuals is necessarily to be identified with my views on all matters, and one or two of them might consider it an affront to be identified with my views on anything.

Some years ago, near the beginning of the period in which I was intermittently preparing this book and pursuing other interests, I received two fellowships for which I am very grateful, one from the Institute for Humane Studies (now the Institute for Humane Studies at George Mason University), the other from the Center for Libertarian Studies.

I especially thank Leonard Liggio and Ivar Oxaal for strong encouragement and advice which made a big difference.

— 1 —

A QUICK LOOK AT THE MISES
ARGUMENT

i. A DEBATE ABOUT THE FEASIBILITY OF SOCIALISM

It turns out, of course, that Mises was right. (Heilbroner 1990, 92)

In 1920 an Austrian economist named Ludwig von Mises[1] published a short article in which he claimed that socialism was not a practical possibility (Mises 1920). Two years later this article was incorporated in a book (Mises 1922) which became widely read and much debated on the European continent. At that time socialism still appeared to be in the ascendant. Its recent disappointments in Germany, Austria, and Hungary seemed temporary setbacks, and the construction of a completely new economic order was triumphantly under way in, of all places, Russia. To many observers of socialism, friendly, apprehensive, or hostile, its eventual triumph appeared inescapable. Yet Mises contended that, however powerful the socialist movement might become, and no matter how many people wanted socialism, howsoever ardently, they would always be powerless to bring socialism into being, because socialism was inherently unfeasible.

There was nothing new in the assertion that socialism could not work in practice. Malthus's 1798 *Essay on the Principle of Population* was written primarily to show that Godwin's socialism (a form of agrarian anarchocommunism) was impossible. A passage in Marx's *Civil War in France* shows him bristling at the charge, evidently a tired old cliché by 1871, that "communism" was "impossible" (MECW v22, 335). What *was* new to Mises's readers was his specific argument for the impossibility of socialism. Most earlier arguments had rested either on an appeal to human nature (especially the alleged need for appropriate material incentives) or on the Malthusian population theory. Arguments from human nature or motivation suffer from weaknesses which render them rather ineffective, and the

Malthusian argument, though it was extraordinarily effective for a century, was eventually recognized to be unsound. Mises's argument against the practical feasibility of what he calls "socialism" does not hinge upon questions of motivation, but rather claims that, with the best will in the world, humans *are not able* to operate a society on 'socialist' lines, because modern industry cannot be successfully guided or administered without the information provided by market prices of factors of production. Mises claims that even where there's a will, there's no way. It is part of Mises's definition of socialism that factors of production are not exchanged on the market, so that under socialism there cannot be market prices of factors of production. Whether this really is integral to socialism is one of the questions I consider later. Mises's argument, known as the *Wirtschaftsrechnung* or 'economic calculation' argument, had been proposed by several earlier writers (summarized in Chapter 4 below), but little notice was taken, and no serious debate ensued until 1920.

In the 1920s and 1930s the Mises argument was celebrated. Many articles and quite a few books were written attacking and defending Mises. Well-informed socialists felt they had at least to mention Mises and economic calculation in passing. By the end of the Second World War the opinion had become widely accepted that Mises had been refuted. Socialists stopped paying any attention to Mises; anti-socialists mostly argued that socialism would inevitably be brutal and despotic, a claim which, as several socialists correctly observed, contradicted the Misesian claim that socialism was unattainable, and looked like a retreat from that position. New generations of socialists arose who had never heard of the Mises argument, but if they did get to hear of it, they had no difficulty in finding assurances by distinguished scholars that Mises had been decisively answered. When I began reading about economic calculation in 1970 the dominant view was that Mises was a nonentity whose simple-minded criticism of socialism had been deservedly buried. In theory, Mises had been refuted by Lange, and in practice by the Sputnik. Among mainstream economists it was the rule, when making an occasional passing reference to the debate over the Mises argument, to state that Mises was wrong, perhaps obviously wrong, and possibly so obviously wrong as to approach silliness.[2] There were a few economists who championed Mises, the most distinguished being F. A. Hayek, but they often held other views which put them out of the mainstream, and Hayek himself gave up doing economics during the 1950s and 1960s.

In the 1980s the volume of references to the Mises argument grew rapidly. The references were often favorable and in some cases simply averred that Mises was right.[3] The tide may have already turned when Lavoie's book (1985) began to convince an ever-widening circle of readers that the heretofore standard account of the economic calculation debate was wrong. These re-appraisals reflected the new groundswell of antisocialist, pro-market opinion, which could trace its lineage by various branches back to Mises. In 1989 there occurred the spectacular events in Eastern Europe which resulted from the indisputable, chronic, and comprehensive failure of Soviet-style socialism. The well-known Polish economist Włodzimierz Brus, whose earlier writings had been thoroughly socialist, stated that "the Mises/Hayek type of charge against orthodox socialism" had "prove[d] correct" (Brus and Laski 1989, 151). Brus and Laski also note the striking congruence between Mises's writings on socialism and recent practical debates among Eastern European economists. In 1990 the economist, socialist sympathizer, and popular writer, Robert L. Heilbroner, who had earlier dismissed the Mises argument (Heilbroner 1970, 87–90) candidly proclaimed his conversion with the words: "It turns out, of course, that Mises was right" (Heilbroner 1990, 92).

The Mises argument raises many fascinating questions. To me, the most intriguing is: 'How can it conceivably be the case that humans can achieve an intricately structured and highly desirable outcome *only* by leaving individuals alone, within limits, to do what they like, and are bound to fail to achieve the same outcome if they try to attain it by deliberate organization or conscious planning?' Later chapters of this book explore this and other issues in a nontechnical but I hope passably intelligent way. In this chapter I attempt to convey an understanding of the gist of the Mises argument. It's not my purpose at this point to evaluate the argument, but only to explain clearly what Mises was driving at.

ii. What the Mises Argument Claims to Show

The broad conclusion of the Mises argument can be stated in this form: the productive achievements of modern industrial civilization depend upon the existence of a functioning market. If this be true, then we cannot hope to maintain the living standards of the mass of the people at their present level, let alone increase these living standards, if we abolish the market. Some readers may at first find this claim uninteresting, since nowadays not many socialists still demand the complete abolition of the market. But there is more to it. In Chapter 11 below I look a little more closely at what is meant by 'market'; at this point we can get along by saying that 'market' means trade, commerce, buying and selling. By a *functioning* market I mean a market which need not be 'perfect' nor even 'free', but one which does actually function as a market, because individuals (or small groups of individuals) are permitted sufficient autonomy to trade, and do in fact trade. A functioning market might also be termed a 'genuine' market. The insistence on a functioning market is important because there can be a functioning market where official or conventional descriptions indicate the absence of a market, and conversely, there can be the absence of a functioning market where official or conventional reports imply a market.

The Mises argument goes further: not only must there be a functioning market, but this functioning market must extend to 'factors of production'. Factors of production include hours of carpentry, hours of systems analysis, ounces of platinum, barrels of petroleum, square meters of land, BTUs of electricity, all kinds of machines, planks, bricks, nuts and bolts, and all the other things which are used (and, often but not always, used up) in making the goods people want. The terms 'factor of production', 'factor', 'resource', 'asset', and 'input' all mean more or less the same, and are used interchangeably throughout this book.

If the economic calculation argument were correct, it would follow that many forms of 'socialism' would have to be judged unfeasible, namely: all those forms of socialism which proposed to give people living standards at least as high as could be attained within a market economy, and at the same time proposed (explicitly or implicitly) to do without a functioning market in factors of production. I call these forms of socialism 'non-factor-market socialism' (NFM socialism).

Socialist systems which envisage markets in consumer goods but require the absence of markets in all or most factors have been commonly proposed and widely embraced. Socialist systems which call for markets in factors but not in consumer goods are virtually unknown.[4] Mises equates 'socialism' with NFM socialism, a definition highly consonant with 1920 usage, but less so with more recent usage. Mises also takes the view that functioning markets in factors require private property in those factors, though he does not argue for this at length. This view seems to have been widely shared by socialists and nonsocialists prior to the 1930s, but since then many socialists have rejected it.

In a new twist to his argument, responding to the 'market socialist' proposals of the 1920s, Mises later claimed (Mises 1932) that even factor markets, such as might conceivably exist among commonly-owned or publicly-owned enterprises in a completely socialized economy, would not be enough to make a socialist industrial order practicable. Financial markets, notably markets in stocks, bonds, and loanable funds, were also essential. This important extension of Mises's position has been largely ignored. Although I discuss it in subsequent chapters, I take the classic Misesian challenge of 1920 as my point of departure.

In order to present Mises's argument clearly, I now proceed in two stages: 1. I give a highly simplified (and therefore unrealistic) illustration to bring out the essence of the economic calculation problem; 2. I discuss some of the qualifications and complications needed to bring this simplified story closer to reality.

iii. A SIMPLIFIED ILLUSTRATION

Imagine that there are no market prices but there is a complex and intricate 'advanced' industrial structure. Suppose that we are in charge of a local unit of production, for example, a factory. We will call such a local production organization an 'enterprise'.[5] I make no assumptions about the structure of this enterprise; nor do I make any assumption about who 'we' are: 'we' can be an individual manager appointed by a socialist industrial administration, a committee or board appointed by that administration, a committee or board appointed by all the people who work in the enterprise or in a confederation of enterprises, or by all the members of the local community, or 'we' can even be all those workpeople or community members, supposing managerial decisions to be made by vote of the entire workforce or community. *Someone* has to make the sort of decision we are now going to consider, and it does not affect the statement of the problem who that someone might be.

Our problem is this. It has been decided to make useful products which we will call 'widgets'. We are informed by our engineering and design experts—our technologists—that there are three different ways of making widgets, three technical processes of production or recipes, which I will call methods A, B, and C. All three methods require inputs of rubber and wood, but in different quantities. To make one widget:

Method A requires 5 lbs of rubber and 5 lbs of wood.
Method B requires 5 lbs of rubber and 4 lbs of wood.
Method C requires 4 lbs of rubber and 5 lbs of wood.

Instead of rubber and wood, we could use bricks and cement, or paper and plastic, or—for the mathematically gifted—*x* and *y*. We can assume that rubber and wood are the only factors used up in making a widget, or (slightly more realistically) we could suppose that there were many other factors, but that these were identical for all three methods, so that the only differences lay in the amounts of rubber and wood required. We can also choose to assume that the products of the three processes (the widgets) are identical, or alternatively, that they are not identical, but that they are equally useful and desirable: there is nothing to choose between them, in terms of quality or utility. We have to choose *one* of these three processes, and we cannot decide by comparing the products: by our assumption, the widgets would be equally good made by any of the three methods. In other words, we have set up a problem where the only basis for choice between production processes is the different quantities of rubber and wood used up in production. We have devised an unrealistic imaginary situation to focus attention on the question of alternative production methods which differ *only* in the different quantities of factors they employ.

If we now look at our three methods, A, B, and C, and compare them, we at once perceive that *both Method B and Method C must be better than Method A*. Method A has to be rejected. Method A uses up more wood than Method B and more rubber than Method C, and Method A has no advantage which would make up for these disadvantages.

So we confidently eliminate Method A. We now have to choose between B and C. Here, all of a sudden, we face a perplexing difficulty. There seems to be no sensible reason for preferring B over C, or C over B. B uses up less wood than C, but then, B uses up more rubber than C. We can state our problem like this: We know that A costs more than either B or C, but we have no way of telling whether B costs more than C, or C costs more than B, or (a third possibility) whether B and C cost the same. Notice that this problem, which can be described as one of comparing production costs, has nothing essentially to do with money. When people talk about 'cost' within a market-oriented society, they are often thinking of sums of money expended. They may draw from this the conclusion that cost is a *result* of the money system, and that therefore without money we would no longer be bothered by cost. As we can see from our example, this is a mistake. In the choice among methods of production, the problem may arise of comparing costs, regardless of money.

Is our problem a bogus problem? There are two ways in which it might be contended that it is bogus: 1. that in this example, it doesn't really matter which method we pick, and 2. that choices like this don't arise in practice in the real world. You will find considerations relevant to 1. and 2. throughout this book, and in the literature of price theory (sometimes called micro-economics).[6] However, I will say something immediately about 1., and Section v. of this chapter is a brief preliminary counter to 2.

It is a good thing, when using up a certain amount of resources, to produce the maximum amount of goods for human enjoyment, and (to look at the same fact from a different angle) it is a good thing, when aiming to produce a certain amount of goods for human enjoyment, to do so by using up as few resources as possible. That is *economic efficiency*. If we have alternative ways of producing the same amount of something (in this case, widgets, which we assume to be a desirable product), it is preferable to choose the way which uses up the least resources. Why should this be good? Because it leaves over more resources to be used for other purposes, and therefore helps to maximize the total amount of all desirable goods available for people. In the choice between A, B, and C, if we pick a method which uses up more resources than necessary, then we are being wasteful, and people as a whole will be poorer. The total amount of desirable things available for people will be less than if we had made a different choice. (In "desirable things" are included leisure, pleasant working conditions, a wholesome environment, abatement of disease, and virtually all 'social goals'. All these may be restricted unnecessarily if resources are wasted.)

For the sake of efficiency (that is, for the sake of minimizing poverty, or making people as well off as possible), we must discard Method A. But someone might suggest that, while A has to be discarded, B and C are equally good, or alternatively, that we have no basis for supposing that any good reason for preferring one over the other can be found. Even on immediate reflection, the first of these is implausible, because what it amounts to is the claim that it is a matter of indifference whether 1 lb of rubber or 1 lb of wood is left over, and thus made available for other uses. The reason we prefer either B or C to A is that either rubber or wood can be left over, and used to make other things. The question then is whether the other things which can be made with 1 lb of rubber are more or less desirable than the other things which can be made with 1 lb of wood. (Since we are going to be mass-producing widgets every week, it is really a matter of, say, 10,000 lbs of rubber, or 10,000 lbs of wood, per week.) This is more complicated than you might at first think, because those other things, the making of which uses up rubber or wood, also involve the using up of *other* factors, probably thousands of other factors, and in deciding how much rubber or wood to use in making those other things, we may be faced by alternative methods, like methods A, B, and C. In that case, it seems we must *simultaneously decide* all the choices of production methods of all the different products—widgets and thousands of others. It appears unlikely that it is a matter of indifference to society whether 10,000 lbs of rubber are used up (and 10,000 lbs of wood not used up) per week, or alternatively 10,000 lbs of wood used up (and 10,000 lbs of rubber not used up) per week. What matters is the contribution to production of other things made by 10,000 lbs of rubber or 10,000 lbs of wood. These two contributions might happen to be identical, in their benefits to consumers, but there is no reason why they should be; that would be unlikely.

Except for an improbable coincidence, then, we know that one of the methods B and C is comparatively inefficient, comparatively wasteful, or if chosen, would make people poorer than if the other method were chosen. We know that both B and C are efficient compared with A, but we cannot tell, without further information, whether B is more efficient than C, or C more efficient than B. We call the comparative efficiency of B or C with respect to A *technical efficiency*. We call the efficiency of B with respect to C, or the efficiency of C with respect to B *economic efficiency*. (Economic efficiency can also be defined to include technical efficiency. So another way of making the point is to say that technical efficiency doesn't exhaust economic efficiency. From an economic point of view, the efficiency which is not merely technical is the more interesting.) A method of production is technically efficient if no other method can be found which uses no more of any factor and uses less of at least one factor. Thus, we can say that method A is not technically efficient, because we know that, for example, method B uses a smaller amount of one factor (wood), without using a larger amount of any other factor. Methods B and C are both technically efficient, on the assumption that only Methods A, B, and C are available. There is no reason why there should not be several alternative technically efficient methods for producing any given article; in fact, there is generally a vast number of alternative technically efficient methods—a virtual infinity of them. Someone acquainted only with technical processes—an engineer, technologist, or applied scientist—may be able to tell us whether one production method is technically more efficient than another. This will eliminate many possible methods as wasteful or inefficient, but it will leave many technically efficient methods to choose from. We need to know something which the engineer or scientist can't tell us.

This claim may surprise some readers: no matter how detailed our knowledge of technical facts, that would be insufficient for us to choose the best production methods. Ira Levin's novel, *This Perfect Day* (1970), depicts a future society in which money and trading have been eliminated, and production is administered entirely by technical and managerial expertise. (This is not given great emphasis in the story. It is a background fact, more or less taken for granted.) The society portrayed is horrifying. Yet it is a society in which modern industry is maintained and people's material needs are, in a sense, quite well catered for. It probably does not occur to one reader in a thousand, and very likely never occurred to the author, that such a system of industrial administration may be out of the question, may just not be capable of working, because in order to make efficient decisions in the administration of production, we need to know something which scientists, technicians, and administrators are powerless to tell us. And without knowing that something, production would have to contract, perhaps so much that the most elementary amenities of civilized life (plumbing, electric light, and so forth) could not be kept going. Such, at any rate, is what the economic calculation argument propounded by Mises may suggest.

What is the additional information which we need to know? In our example, we need to know how many pounds of wood are 'worth' one pound of rubber. We need some way of comparing amounts of wood and rubber by reducing both of them to a common unit. Once we have found this common measure of 'worth', we can make the choice without any difficulty. If a pound of rubber is equivalent to a pound of wood, then methods B and C are equally costly. Each is economically, as well as technically, efficient, and the choice between them is a matter of indifference. If a pound of wood is worth more (rated as more costly) than a pound of rubber, then Method B is preferable, and Method C is inefficient. If a pound of rubber is worth more than a pound of wood, then Method C is the one we should select, and Method B is wasteful.

Our problem, then, is this: *We want to economize, but we don't know how to.* Even perfect knowledge of the technology of widget-making would not enable us to make widgets in the most economical (least costly) way. After we have used up some resources in producing our widgets, we want to leave over for production of other things as many resources as possible, but we do not know what constitutes 'more' or 'less' resources, once we have eliminated technically inefficient methods. We cannot tell whether a pound of wood is more or less than a pound of rubber, whether a ton of coal is more or less than a ton of bauxite, whether an hour of secretarial work is more or less than an hour of computer time.

In this case, it so happens that it would be sufficient merely to know which was 'more' or 'less', but that's just an accident of the way I have set up the example. Generally, we should have to know exactly *how much* more or less. For instance, if the choice were between a method using 4 lbs of rubber and 5 lbs of wood, and a method using 5 lbs of rubber and 3 lbs of wood, it would not be enough to know that wood were more costly, by weight, than rubber; we should need to know *how much* more costly, at least within a certain range—and supposing a number of different contexts for comparing the cost of pounds of wood and rubber, with each other, or either with any other factors, that range would be narrowed until, with a very large number of production choices, we would need an exact equation of the form: 1 lb wood = (say) 1.38 lbs rubber.

But what is this 'worth' or 'cost' which we want to be able to measure? We have already answered this implicitly. In carrying out any productive project, such as making widgets at our widget factory, we use factors. These factors have other possible uses, but if these factors are employed in the project under consideration, they cannot be simultaneously employed in any of those other possible uses. Therefore, to make the decision to use these particular factors in this particular project means to deny these particular factors to all other projects for which they might have been allocated. To use a particular ton of steel to make car bodies at a particular car factory means that particular ton of steel cannot be used for any other purpose (at least until the cars' lives are over and the steel is recycled). To produce one thing is therefore always to deny the possibility of producing other things—usually, innumerable other possible things. This is sometimes difficult to see because, after all, no single other thing necessarily has to go unproduced because the steel is used in this particular way, so using the steel in this way does not strictly rule out the possibility of any given alternative. It is even more slippery, because in all likelihood, the use of that ton of steel in this particular way does not even mean that *any* other 'use' (in the sense of a whole type of use) is denied; it probably means that, of all the many hundreds of thousands of other possible 'uses' for that steel, a few hundred thousand of them will be slightly cut back—since we are talking about only a ton, *very* slightly cut back. Still, it is clear that there is only a certain amount of steel in existence at any time (More could be produced, but that would take time, and would entail the using up of other factors). If millions of tons of steel were to miraculously appear out of nowhere (conveniently located and in usable form), we would have no trouble finding uses for them. If, on the other hand, millions of tons of steel were miraculously to disappear, production of some things requiring steel would have to be cut back (or resources would have to be diverted from other uses to increase the supply of steel, so that production of things requiring those resources would have to be cut back). It is just the same with a single ton, though the expansion or cut-back would be small.

Any possible production project entails a corresponding reduction in production somewhere else—not necessarily a reduction compared with previously, but a reduction compared with what would be produced if the project in question had not been embarked upon. So all production carries with it a corresponding reduction in alternative kinds of production. It is this reduction in alternative kinds of production which is the 'cost' of any production project. Thus, the cost of using up a pound of rubber to make widgets is the reduction in production of other things because that pound of rubber is denied to the production of those other things. The total cost of producing anything is the total effect in reducing production of other things because of the factors used up. This, then, is what we mean by 'cost of production'. It is this that we always want to minimize when we produce anything.

This understanding enables us to recognize the essential continuity from technical efficiency to (nontechnical) economic efficiency. Both involve producing a certain amount at the least cost. Just as it is wasteful to use 2 lbs of rubber when we could use 1 lb of rubber and get exactly the same result, or as good a result—because this leaves over less rubber for other uses—so it is important to reduce costs by using *more* of one factor when this enables us to use sufficiently *less* of another factor—'more' and 'less' being defined in terms of reduction in other forms of production, or in terms of the lost contribution of these factors to other forms of production. Upon reflection, the same considerations which make us so sure that it is wasteful to use 2 lbs of rubber when we need to use only 1 lb of rubber indicate that we must know the cost ratio of rubber to wood in order not to be wasteful. In both cases, we want to produce widgets at the lowest possible cost in reduction of other forms of production.

Ultimately, the cost of any act of production is the *products* lost or foregone—the products which will not come to be, because this act of production (with its products) was selected. Factors are not valued, or ascribed a cost, for their own sake (if they are, then by definition they are consumer goods). Costs always derive ultimately from products, not means of production. But the ultimate product is always the benefit the consumers get from consumer goods. It follows that in order to measure costs we have to measure the 'worth' or 'cost' of consumer goods. In order to settle questions like whether a ton of coal is more or less costly than a barrel of petroleum, we would first have to settle questions like whether a typewriter is more or less costly (in the sense of how much we would value its loss or absence) than a radio. However, settling these questions for consumer goods would not be *sufficient* to settle them for factors.

It might occur to the reader that we are smuggling in somehow the assumption that people ought to be materialistic, that they ought to want production of as many things as possible. That might seem almost like a religion of production for production's sake. But this response would be based on a misunderstanding. A nature reserve may be considered as the site for a copper mine. If the copper is mined, that may destroy, temporarily or permanently, the nature reserve. The benefits of the nature reserve (being able to watch wildlife in a comparatively undisturbed environment, or just the feeling of satisfaction of knowing it's there even if you never go to watch it) are consumer goods. In order to produce these consumer goods, we need the factor: this area of land. Part of the cost of producing these consumer goods (the benefits of the nature reserve) is reduced production of things made with copper. Or, if the copper mine goes ahead, part of its cost is reduced production of the benefits of nature reserves. We make no assumption as to which is preferable; the same analysis holds in either case. Or consider the view that people ought to work shorter hours and spend much of their time meditating. Production of the consumer good, meditation, then has among its costs: the production of other things which people could have produced if they had worked longer hours. Again, the analysis involves no prejudice for one way of life or the other.

In our example of methods A, B, and C, we have been supposing that we were living in a world without any market prices. The problem would be similar, however, if we lived in a society which did have prices of consumer goods, but did not have prices of factors, such as rubber and wood.

If we now drop the assumption of no market prices of factors, then a method is available for choosing between B and C. We can look at the prices of rubber and wood. If, for example, a pound of wood costs $20 and a pound of rubber costs $40, then a widget made by Method B costs $280 and a widget made by Method C costs $260. In that case, we would choose Method C, because it is a cheaper way to get the same result. The existence of market prices and money has enabled us to make a choice.

We can now give a preliminary summary of the Mises argument. It is an *informational* argument about 'comparative institutions'. Mises contends: 1. that we need some way of comparing the production costs of alternative methods or techniques; 2. that market prices of factors give us an adequate way to do this; and 3. that no other adequate way exists. Therefore we need market prices of factors, and therefore factors (such as rubber and wood) have to be permitted to change hands among market traders. Therefore any proposed form of socialism which abolishes market exchange of factors of production will not be able to accurately compare the costs of alternative methods of production, and will therefore display inefficiency, or waste of resources, on a grand scale. Therefore, living standards in such a society will be considerably lower than the living standards made possible by a society which does have market exchange of factors of production. (If desired, we can eliminate the use of the term 'adequate' by saying merely that any alternative to market prices is a lot poorer at providing information about costs. We can also eliminate the term 'impracticable' or 'unfeasible' by simply saying that there will be inefficiency, hence lower output, in the absence of factor markets, and that the reduction in output will not be slight.)

Two lines of thought come together in the Mises argument, and it is important to comprehend them both: 1. There is the 'economic problem', allocating scarce resources to a variety of competing ends; 2. There is the comparison of institutions for their capacity to communicate information.[7] 1. has been very well known to the economics profession (and superbly well-elaborated theoretically) since the early decades of the twentieth century, but has been largely unknown to non-economists. 2. has been neglected by almost everyone, and mainstream economists have frequently stated that it has nothing to do with them (this has begun to change over the past

20 years). Of course, 2. can be viewed as a special case of 1., but it has generally not been so viewed.

iv. A MORE REALISTIC ELABORATION

The example of Methods A, B, and C for producing widgets had to be unrealistic to be simple, and to bring out the essential point clearly. I now consider some ways in which the example is unrealistic; we can then decide whether these affect the conclusions.

Nothing is made with only two factors: there are usually thousands. To make cars, for instance, might require several different kinds of metal and plastic, fabrics and rubber, hundreds of different kinds of labor, numerous machines, several buildings, power to heat and light the buildings and drive the machines, telephones, desks, stationery, lavatories and wash basins for the workers, and so forth. This does not change the essentials of the problem. It does make the problem trickier, because some measure of cost has to be found for all possible factors—thousands of them, and if we consider all lines of production, millions upon millions—not just two. Thus, a better idea of the sort of choice that might confront enterprise decision-makers would be between two production methods, where each method used, say, the same 1,000 factors in the same quantities, each method used a further 2,000 factors, the same kinds but in different quantities, and in addition, one method used 200 factors not employed at all in the other method, which used 350 factors not employed at all in the first method.

In our simplified widget example, we supposed that only the technical facts were known. Given these technical facts, we were faced with the problem of comparing costs. In real life, we usually don't first establish all the 'technical' facts and then subsequently apply 'economic' principles to estimate costs. Engineers already know that some materials are less costly than others. Technologists have a general background knowledge of market prices, and automatically reject some possibilities as too costly. Hardly ever would an engineer selecting a production method make purely technical calculations without the guidance of market prices.

In our references to the market, we gave the impression that enterprise decision-makers simply read off market prices, and in this way derived a verdict on the costs of production methods by straight calculation from technical facts plus market prices. It is sometimes useful, as a simplified illustrative model, preliminary to a more adequate explanation of the market, to assume that decision-makers do behave in this way, reacting to technical knowledge plus market prices. It is interesting and illuminating that the market process can be imagined to work, after a fashion, if enterprise decision-makers really did behave in this purely mechanical fashion. The actual process of judgment by decision-makers in the market is very different. They generally strive to find out the most relevant facts bearing upon future prices. I live in the Midwest and occasionally hear radio broadcasts intended for farmers. Among these broadcasts are quite detailed analyses of recent, current, and future weather conditions in agricultural areas all over the world—China is sometimes treated region by region, for instance. This information bears upon future crop prices, and helps to guide Midwestern farming decisions. Since all production decisions are about the future, and the future is always uncertain, decision-makers have to make guesses, take gambles, play hunches, and follow their experienced noses. Producers are always speculators. They must use their judgment and insight to estimate the outcomes of possible future production choices. It is commonplace for a project to encounter unforeseen difficulties, and the magnitude of these difficulties may determine whether or not the project has to be axed. But the reverse also occurs: after a new factory has been built and operating for a year or two, improvements are found, and some aspects of the work may turn out to be easier or less costly than was expected. Prices change all the time, and no one can know with confidence what the price of any factor will be, even a few days ahead. Estimating how things will turn out in production is like playing chess: exact calculation is important, but it takes you only so far; then you have to rely on a feeling for the position, to make a judgment which cannot be demonstrated at the time to be correct or incorrect, though we can say, looking back on different persons' playing records, that some folks have more of a knack for it than others.

Prices are uncertain. For some explanatory purposes, it simplifies matters to assume that people's behavior is guided by 'current' (recent) prices. In reality, people make decisions on the basis of what they expect future prices to be. In the 1970s many people made decisions based on the then fashionable theory that the politically-engendered 'energy crisis' was due to an absolute and technical 'energy shortage', and was the beginning of permanently higher energy prices. This theory was false, and the decisions it suggested were mistakes. When oil prices came tumbling down again, many people found that they had blundered badly. The prices that matter for decision-makers are estimated future prices. Even most of the magnitudes 'recorded' by book-keepers in financial statements are, surprising though this often is to those unused to the idea, based on estimates of future prices. People who act on the basis of unrevised recent prices are in effect testing the theory that future prices are going to be the same as recent prices. This theory is generally false, and is often found to be a poor rule-of-thumb. (In other words, there is no such thing as a 'parametric function of prices' in the real world, but only in simplified models, useful for elucidating aspects of the real world.)

For the benefit of readers whose experience of prices is confined mainly to consumer goods, it's worth pointing out that prices of factors fluctuate much more widely and frequently than prices of consumer goods. The price of copper fluctuates far more than the price of radios; the price of raw cocoa far more than the price of chocolate bars. There are two main reasons for this. One is that prices of all the factors which go into making a product are unlikely to move simultaneously in the same direction. A rise in price of one factor may well be offset by a fall in price of another factor, but even if prices of the other factors remain the same, a ten percent rise in the price of a factor which accounts for one-tenth of the cost of a product translates into only a one percent rise in the production cost of the product. The second reason is that if the price of a factor rises, enterprise decision-makers will seek ways to economize more stringently than heretofore on the use of that factor. They will use less of that factor and more of other factors.

Does the fact that production is actually guided by estimates of future prices, and not by reading off 'current' (recent) prices, destroy the force of the Mises argument? Apparently not, for two reasons: 1. past prices are a guide which helps people to make more accurate (though still fallible) estimates of future prices; and 2. people's estimates of future prices are eventually confirmed or refuted. There is an objective test of the accuracy of the estimates: profit and loss. (This objective test in its turn draws upon recent prices, so there may seem to be the danger of an infinite regress. The dangers of such a regress can be limited by provisionally accepting some theory which supports the judgment that market processes are most often swiftly self-correcting or 'equilibrating'. This theory can then be tested empirically.)

Two arbitrary features of my simplified example were chosen for expository reasons. First, methods B and C are two isolated combinations. In real life it would be common to find a continuous range of combinations of rubber and wood, so that a little bit less rubber could be employed with a little more wood, along a curve containing an infinite series of such combinations. Most people find a straight choice between two factor combinations easier to visualize. Second, I have assumed so far that the products are identical, or of equal utility; only the production methods differ. While this is by no means rare, it is not the most common case. Availability of a new cheap, strong plastic may, for instance, lead to more plastic and less steel in the components of a typewriter. The new design of typewriter will probably be slightly less or slightly more appreciated by typewriter users than the older model with more steel and less plastic. Either possibility, of course, will also be taken into account by the typewriter manufacturer, but in many cases such differences in product quality will be small compared with the opportunity for cost savings. A related point is that in the simplified example we assumed that we *were* going to produce widgets, whereas in real life it may turn out that cost calculations show that widgets, or this particular grade of widget, should not be made at all. I have found that it minimizes misunderstanding to approach the economic calculation argument by taking the less common case where product quality is unchanged, and by assuming for the sake of argument that we do want to produce the product in question. This approach emphasizes that the Mises argument is primarily about the possibility of an efficient organization of production. In other words, the argument cannot be dismissed by retorting that consumers' wants need not be accorded much respect by the socialist administration, for the argument casts doubt on the administration's capacity to pursue *its own* production goals efficiently.

It does appear that the fundamental ideas of our simplified widget example survive a somewhat more realistic elaboration. These fundamental ideas are: 1. that in choosing among alternative production methods, we need to know something which technicians or scientists cannot tell us, or in other words, that technical facts about production processes do not enable us to find the most economically efficient methods; and 2. that the information which we need to know has to come by way of being able to measure physically unlike factors in common units.

Numerous different lines of production compete for the use of limited stocks of factors. For simplicity, consider just two lines of production and one factor. Manufacturing TV sets and producing medical services both employ steel. This is a 'pre-institutional' fact confronting any society, whether or not there is rivalrous behavior by profit-seeking firms. Economic theory tells us that a condition for the best allocation is that a unit of steel should make the same contribution to output in making TV sets and in providing medical services. If a ton of steel currently makes a bigger contribution to providing medical services than it does to making TV sets, then tons of steel ought to be re-allocated from TV sets to medical services. The contribution of any ton of steel to TV sets will then rise and the contribution of any ton of steel to medical services will fall. This should be continued until they are equal. This is one of the important and non-obvious properties of an ideal allocation. Economic theory also tells us that a competitive market will carry out just such an adjustment, and even a not-fully competitive market will have a powerful tendency to adjust in some such way, and will normally come close to such an ideal adjustment. Theory also tells us of various imperfections which may arise in practice, leading to a departure from the best allocation, but theory does not tell us that we necessarily have good grounds for supposing that we can, independently of the market, find out what the best allocation is. Either way, whether we think the market will do better than any alternative, or whether we think we know some superior alternative, economic theory does not give us the same kind of rigorous and precise answers that it does when detailing the general properties of an ideal allocation (although progress has been made, partly under the impetus of the Mises argument, in developing good theories to compare the performance of alternative institutions).

We observe a factory in operation.[8] We know that trucks are leaving the factory every day with useful goods that people urgently desire, and that trucks are entering the factory with raw materials to be used for the production of those goods. We know that all the technical methods of production implemented at that factory are as efficient as current human knowledge permits, that the factory is superbly well managed, that all supplies and equipment are looked after carefully and not abused, and that the workers are all conscientious and capable. To keep things simple, suppose that we entirely approve of the consumers' desires for the products of this factory, that in no sense do we think there is anything bad about the consumers' wish to have these particular goods. Now, the question arises: Is this factory a net benefit to human beings, or is it an appalling waste of resources? The answer is that, with only the given information, we cannot tell. Furthermore, if we know nothing about the methods of economic calculation employed, and are not allowed to make inferences thereto (inferences of the sort: 'This is an industrial civilization, so it must have an adequate method of economic calculation, so that method is probably in force at this factory'), then it is *virtually certain that the factory is a terrible waste of resources.* This conclusion follows from the fact that there is an infinity of ways of running the factory wastefully under the stated conditions. In much the same way, if we start a car in Chicago and make purely random movements with the steering wheel, we can be morally certain that the car will not arrive in Saint Louis. In order to assess whether the factory is a net benefit or a horrible waste we must put prices (or some substitute measure of cost) on the factory's outputs and inputs. We then have to be able to determine whether the factory is making a 'profit' or a 'loss'—whether all the resources used in producing the output are greater or less than the value of that output. The question raised by Mises is whether we have available any practicable method for attributing the measure of cost, other than reliance on prices generated spontaneously in a functioning market.

v. Production Choices are Everywhere

Decisions among different methods fall into two broad categories, though there is not always a sharp division between them. There are choices among basic techniques, and adjustments within any one of these techniques. The factors used up in a nuclear power plant are different to the factors used up in a coal-fired plant, and different again to those used up in a hydro-electric plant. Yet the electricity produced by all three plants is identical. Even having decided upon a nuclear-powered plant, there are various choices to be made, broad design choices which will determine permanently the whole character of the plant—pressurized water reactor versus fast-neutron reactor, for example. In running an existing plant or factory, without any radical change of technique, numerous minor decisions have to be made every day. Here too comparisons of cost need to be made: whether it is worth immediately replacing some machine which is performing poorly, or whether it is better to wait until more use has been derived from that machine before it is scrapped and replaced with a new one; whether to make some adjustment which will reduce the consumption of some material input, yet require more energy; whether to send freight by rail, road, or barge. There are organizational choices, which also require a comparison of costs: notably, whether to get a certain job done by someone within the enterprise, or whether instead to request that this job be done by another enterprise. All of these choices require comparisons of costs, and therefore require prices, or some other measure of costs.

The influence of price on production methods is easily seen. If you read the labels on bottles of vegetable oil or coffee creamer, you will often find that alternative ingredients are cited—the producer will shift from one kind of oil to another as their relative prices change. The extent to which bricks are used in building construction is extremely variable. One would expect a rise in the price of bricks, or a fall in the price of alternatives like plasterboard, to lead to reduced use of bricks. If office space is comparatively cheap, modes of office organization that make lavish use of space will be adopted; if the price of office space rises, managers will reorganize offices to be more sparing with space (they will be more ready to adopt miniaturized filing systems, to farm out work to freelancers, and so forth). A fruit grower with an abundant supply of cheap labor will be less inclined to invest in costly mechanized picking equipment. A rise in the price of copper will cause some producers to substitute aluminum or silver in some electrical applications. A rise in the price of heating automatically causes more expenditure on building insulation.

Observation and reflection shows that the impact of price changes on production methods is profound and widely ramified, but this is often obscure to the casual onlooker. Since firms in the same industry copy one another, and especially copy the more successful firms, there will often appear to be just one way of doing something, and this way will mysteriously appear to be 'right'. The existence of numerous ways of achieving more or less the same outcome, ways that are now loss-making but would become profitable if prices were to change, may easily be overlooked. Hence one can thoughtlessly fall into the error of supposing that the 'best' way to do something is dictated by technology alone. Price changes cause producers to change production methods, but in practice such chains of events are intertwined with other changes, notably technological innovation. Thus, to a superficial glance, any change in methods may be attributed entirely to new technological discoveries.

This impression may be reinforced because it does seem, at first blush, that many production processes involve fixed physical ratios. A construction worker with whom I discussed economic calculation argued that the ratios of sand and cement vary only among specific purposes. For a given specific purpose, there is just one correct ratio. Let's assume this is true. It may seem at first that industry must be filled with such examples. The objection can be answered on a number of levels: 1. Even if it be true that some processes involve fixed inputs, there are *also* processes where the inputs are variable, and this is sufficient for the argument; 2. Even if, within a specific process, the ratios were unalterable, the question of whether to use that process or another would still be influenced by costs. Thus, whether to use cement at all is influenced by the comparative prices of cement and substitutes (lawns, fences, glass blocks, and so forth); 3. Even though the ratio of sand, cement, and water may be fixed, other inputs in the same process are not: the kinds of labor and equipment employed to mix cement may be varied according to their prices. These points are quite sufficient to answer the objection. But in fact it is satisfying to be able to point out that: 4. Even technical ratios apparently fixed by chemical or other constants are in practice always variable. This arises because of an unavoidable residue of wastage or spillage, and the need to store supplies, in all production processes. The costly labor and equipment deployed to combat such wastage will vary according to the cost of the input lost by spillage, damage in transit, material adhering to the insides of discarded containers, loss through botched attempts, and so forth. (To take an example from common experience, the ratio of balls to racquets in tennis, as actually played, appears absolutely fixed. But the number of balls lying around the court, kept in store, or lost in the nearby undergrowth because it's not worth looking for them, and the point at which the deterioration of balls and racquets is considered to warrant their replacement, mean that in practice the ratio of balls to racquets is extremely variable.) Empirically, then, virtually all industrial input ratios are variable according to the prices of the inputs.

vi. How To Refute Mises

No one can read through the literature on the economic calculation debate without being struck by the mutual irrelevance of much of the argument. Some of this shadow boxing arises from the failure, on both sides, to distinguish between a strict proof and a strong argument. Some of Mises's remarks to the contrary, Mises does not offer a strict proof or demonstration that NFM socialism cannot work. He makes the bold claim that it cannot work, which implies that no one will be able to explain how it could work—a corollary still unrefuted. His argument in support of this claim is strong, if questionable in places. Mises's opponents frequently seem to think that Mises is offering a strict proof that NFM socialism cannot work, and that their job is to show that such a proof doesn't hold. They often try to concoct a proof for Mises, refute it, then move rapidly from 1. 'Mises has not supplied a proof that NFM socialism can't work', to 2. 'There is no proof that NFM socialism can't work', then to 3. 'NFM socialism can work', and finally to 4. 'There is a proof that NFM socialism can work'. None of these statements follows from its predecessor. The reader should bear these distinctions in mind in the chapters ahead: there are passages where I exhibit the strengths of the Mises argument by showing that certain Misesian contentions *might conceivably* be true and that we have *some good reasons* to think they are true. It would not be a successful rebuttal to point out that I have not *demonstrated* them to be true.

My own view can be summarized by saying that, while Mises made some mistakes in the development of his argument, and expressed it in a way that helped to give rise to misunderstandings, there is a defensible core of his argument which has not yet been refuted. I don't see it as the task of this book to prove or disprove that NFM socialism is impracticable or inefficient, but to clarify what is meant by these claims in the context of the Marxian revolutionary program, and thus to show how seriously questionable is the feasibility of NFM socialism.

Mises is not only a foe of NFM socialism; he is also a laissez-faire liberal. Does the economic calculation argument lend support to free-market liberalism or libertarianism? It lends some inconclusive support. Contrary to what Mises and some of his followers have occasionally seemed to imply, it is perfectly reasonable for a welfare-statist or interventionist to accept the economic calculation argument in its entirety. No inconsistency is entailed in this.

The Mises argument's inconclusive support for free-market liberalism is of two kinds. First, the argument, if correct, narrows the range of feasible options. It supports the free market in the same sense that the proposition 'Our next convention will be in the Midwest' supports the proposition 'Our next convention will be in Chicago'. Once it's accepted that our next convention will be in the Midwest, it's illegitimate to argue against Chicago on the grounds that San Francisco has better scenery. Second, the economic calculation argument, if correct, gives a kind of general endorsement to the effectiveness of the market price system, a system which requires some measure of freedom from coercive interference in order to function at all. It is quite likely that someone who takes the trouble to follow the arguments sufficiently to understand the strength of the claim that factor markets cannot be dispensed with will then find herself inclined to approve a wider scope for the operation of the market price system. This will tend to move her closer to the libertarian position, but not necessarily very close.

Since the Mises argument draws upon price theory, one defense against Mises is to call into question the validity of price theory. Marxists sometimes dismiss the economic calculation argument out of hand on the grounds that it rests upon 'neoclassical' or 'bourgeois' economic theory. If this theory be found wanting, then anything that draws upon it is considered baseless, and of course, economic theory is, just like physics or set theory, replete with anomalies, absurdities, and cloudy areas. Misesians themselves would repudiate the connection with 'neoclassical' theory, but Marxists are liable to find that the neo-Austrian or 'praxeological' approach shares many suspect assumptions with neoclassical theory, and, insofar as it differs, is even more hopelessly bourgeois.

This response to the Mises argument evinces an oversimple view of the relation between specific arguments and a body of theory. Suppose that someone advanced an argument that a particular design of aircraft was inherently unsafe. The argument would be in engineering terms, and would rest upon principles drawn from Newtonian mechanics, a branch of physics, and from various empirically-established properties of materials, which might be framed in terms of molecular structure. Now suppose that someone else responded that this argument could be disregarded because physics as it stands is a bourgeois science, and proceeded to list some of the philosophical difficulties with the theory of relativity or to make nasty remarks about the Copenhagen interpretation of quantum theory. This response is inappropriate, because a body of theory that has emerged from a welter of controversy and criticism over many generations very likely contains much that would have to be incorporated into any alternative body of theory that might be pronounced superior. For example, let's suppose that economics is revolutionized tomorrow, and a new set of theories replaces neoclassical economics. That new set of theories will certainly *not* predict that storekeepers who want to clear out inventory quickly will raise the prices of their goods, nor that risky loans will have a lower interest-rate than safe loans, nor that a rise in interest rates will cause a rise in bond prices. Across a wide area of economic phenomena, the new set of theories must come up with substantially the same results as the old set, and numerous practical applications of theory will have to remain unchanged.

A common reaction to the Mises argument from socialists is to reply by denouncing the market. This, however, misses the point. The Mises argument does not imply that the market is fine and good, nor would it be in the least affected by a demonstration that the market was obscenely immoral, though if Mises were right, such a demonstration would face us with the painful choice between obscene immorality and general immiseration.

Even attacks on the market's efficiency do not necessarily touch the economic calculation argument, unless some more efficient alternative can be devised. Many economists believe that the unfettered market is inefficient in certain identifiable circumstances, and therefore call for government intervention to correct the market in these particulars. For instance, there may be general theoretical grounds for holding that a particular kind of price is too low, and the government may step in, by taxation or some other method, to make that price higher. Whatever we may think of such measures, they are piecemeal adjustments to the market process. They do not imply that the market process as a whole should or could be replaced by some other institutional system.

Naturally, if the Mises argument relied on some proposition in economic theory which could be refuted, then this would be a way to refute the Mises argument. But if the crucial claim of the Mises argument is ever to be refuted, it will have to be done by outlining how NFM socialism could work in practice, in other words: some method for replacing the system of market prices by performing the functions which that system now performs. As the following chapters make clear, such a workable outline has not yet been devised. This is the challenge of economic calculation.

— 2 —

THE ABOLITION OF THE MARKET

In communist society it will be easy to be informed about both production and consumption. Since we know how much, on the average, a person needs, it is easy to calculate how much is needed by a given number of individuals, and since production is no longer in the hands of private producers but in those of the community and its administrative bodies, it is a trifling matter *to regulate production according to needs*. (Engels MECW, v4, 246)

i. COMMODITY PRODUCTION AND PRODUCTION FOR USE

The essential features of Marx's conception of communist society did not change from the time he became a communist (1843) until his death (1883). Some of these aspects of communism are not central to the issues investigated in this book: communism would be world-wide, it would have no social classes, and no state. The important feature for my discussion is that Marxian communism necessarily entails the absence of any buying and selling. It follows that under communism as Marx envisages it there will be no money and no market prices. Not only does Marx explicitly state this, but his conception of communist society follows from his principle that the bourgeois 'anarchy of production' will be supplanted by 'conscious' direction of industry. Marx's view of what this means strictly requires (both in his judgment and in mine) the elimination of markets and therefore of money prices, in the realm of factors of production—though Marx ruled out the possibility of markets and prices for consumer goods as well. Marx completely understood and accepted the proposition later advanced by Neurath in the words: "every completely administered economy is a natural economy" (Neurath 1919, 216).

That there will be no markets or money in a communist society is fairly often stated by Marx in plain and straightforward language.

The *Communist Manifesto* speaks, for example, of "the Communistic abolition of buying and selling", making it clear by the context that this is what the authors favor (MECW v6, 500). However most of the passages where Marx implies the non-market nature of communism may be obscure until the reader grasps Marx's distinctive terminology, especially his employment of the word 'commodity'. A commodity, in the Marxian terminology, is something produced with a view to market exchange. Commodity production means production for sale. In Marx's German, the word is *Ware*, which like the English 'ware' (or 'merchandise') means something intended for sale.

In Engels's classic description of the coming "socialist" revolution:

> With the seizing of the means of production by society production of commodities is done away with and, simultaneously, the mastery of the product over the producer. Anarchy in social production is replaced by plan-conforming conscious organization. (Engels 1954, 392)

In the passage from which the above quotation is taken, and in other passages by Marx and by Engels, it is held that: 1. commodity production is inherently anarchic and cannot be planned; 2. commodity production is characterized by the apparent mastery of the product over the producer ('commodity fetishism'); 3. commodity production is less efficient than planned production; and 4. the introduction of planned production abolishes commodity production.

Chapter 1 of Volume 1 of Marx's *Capital*, is entitled 'Commodities'; in the second sentence of the first page, Marx commences to explain what a commodity is. A commodity must be useful—"by its properties" it "satisfies human wants of some sort or another" (I, 43)—but not every useful good is a commodity. The distinguishing mark of a commodity is that, as well as "use-value", it possesses "exchange-value" (44). Marx goes on to argue that exchange-value ("the proportion in which values in use of one sort are exchanged for those of another sort", or in the terminology of non-Marxist economists, price) is "only the mode of expression, the phenomenal form" (45) of an amount of labor-time (46–47). Useful goods are produced by human labor in all societies, but only in some societies are commodities produced. As examples of *non*-commodity production Marx here cites: 1. the marooned Robinson Crusoe; 2. medieval Europe with its "services in kind and payments in kind"; 3. production "for home use" by "the patriarchal industries of a peasant family"; and 4. the future communist society (81–83). In

Marx's terminology, both 'exchange-value' and 'value' have no place in post-capitalist society, for Marx defines 'value' in a special sense, to mean, not merely an amount of labor-time but this amount only as it manifests itself anarchically and therefore fetishistically in determining market prices.

In Marx's analysis, capitalist production is the most highly developed form of commodity production; capitalism *is* production for sale grown to fulfil its complete potential (conversely, any and all production for sale is embryonic capitalism); communist production will know nothing of 'commodities' and hence of 'exchange-value', 'value', 'prices', 'wages', or 'capital'. Capitalist production is the fullest flowering of production for the market; the onset of communism means the abolition of the market, and therefore the abolition of money and the price system. At the turn of the century, Marxists frequently referred to communism as 'production for use', as opposed to 'production for sale'. Under communism production will be directed, consciously and deliberately, towards the satisfaction of people's wants, instead of towards profitable sale.

The non-commodity nature of Marx's post-capitalist society is often disputed. One source is Robinson 1966, which supplies a doctored quotation from Marx suggesting that commodities will sell at their values under socialism (xviii, 23). Robert Freedman, for example, has produced at least three works on Marx, each relying on this mangled quotation to yield the same false interpretation (Freedman 1961, 263; 1968, 280; 1990, 119). In Marx's version (Capital III, 187–88) it's clear that the reference to communism is a parenthetical aside, contrasted with the material immediately before and after, which refers to commodities tending to exchange at their values under capitalism.

After Marx's death, the socialist movement grew rapidly and became increasingly dominated by Marx's ideas. It became a cliché of this movement that 'production for sale' would be replaced by 'production for use'. These phrases faithfully encapsulate Marx's standpoint. Yet the use of such terms may encourage a superficial view of the issue. The producer in the market doesn't normally aim to satisfy his customers' wants (the economic conception of 'use') independently of their ability and willingness to spend money. On the other hand, production for sale *is* production for use, in the sense that someone's willingness to buy is evidence of the product's perceived usefulness to her, in her judgement, at the time of purchase. Marx himself emphasizes that before an article can become a commodity, it must be able to satisfy a human want (I, 43).

For this reason, Marxists sometimes qualify 'production for use' with the adverb 'directly', to make clear that they intend to rule out any price or exchange relationship.

It may be said 1. that the producer for sale does not aim directly at use, but only at sale; and 2. that what is produced sometimes turns out not to be useful. However, the more fundamental distinction is between production for a use with which the producer is intimately acquainted (for instance, growing food for her family) and production for numerous unknown consumers—production for scattered strangers. The second kind of production is inseparable from modern industrial techniques: the producer of sugar, lathes, or bricks cannot be expected to know in detail the uses to which they will be put. In production for scattered strangers, if it were to be organized in any non-market way, production would also necessarily be not-for-use, in the sense that some abstract indicator of 'use' would have to be aimed at by producers. The indicator might be called 'plan fulfillment' or 'conformity with democratic directives' or 'maximization of social welfare points', or something else, but production for one of these would be just as much production not-for-use as is production for sale—at least, in the sense that the not-for-use quality of production for sale is immediately evident and uncontroversial. Furthermore, once we recognize that large-scale industrial production *cannot conceivably* be for 'direct use', it becomes clear that 'production for sale' has certain merits; for example, it encourages the producers to give the customers what they want: the most obvious contrast between 'making money' and 'making steel' is that producers could easily make steel that was inadequate for the users' purposes, since steel, like many products, has very many qualities relevant to the users' satisfaction. Marxists hold, of course, that some non-sale indicator would be a *better* indirect indicator of use than profitable sale, but that has to be argued for, and the need for such an argument tends to be swept from view by the phrase 'production for use'.

There are various identifiable reasons why the non-market nature of Marxian post-capitalist society has been so often obscured or denied. Chief among them are two related theories, held by most Marxists in one form or another: 1. that humankind is being borne towards communism by tremendous historical forces, independently of anyone's wishes, and 2. that it is 'premature' to 'discuss the details' of how communism will work. These convictions have meant that Marxists have often seen themselves advancing towards communism by pursuing 'the immediate struggle', and have even seen any talk of the ultimate goal as a distraction from that struggle. This became most marked in the Bolshevik wing of Marxism after 1921, when the Lenin-Trotsky government's attempt to move straight into communism had to be ignominiously abandoned. Thenceforth, any talk of abolishing money could constitute an objective example of counter-revolutionary ultra-leftism, best criticized by the blunt proletarian argument of a bullet in the head. Nonetheless, the commitment to the ultimate abolition of money was regularly reiterated in party textbooks and other canonical documents (Kuusinen et al. 1961, 860–64; Khudokormov et al. 1967, 280).

ii. MARX AND LABOR-VOUCHERS

a. The Function of Labor-Vouchers in Marxian Communism

A source of lingering confusion about Marx's conception of communism is the belief that he distinguished between two successive stages of society, 'socialism' and 'communism'. This makes it possible for superficial readers of Marx to accept his references to communism as commodityless and moneyless, yet retain the belief that Marx expected the market and money to persist for a long time after the socialist revolution. While this was until recently the standpoint of the Marxist-Leninist government of the Russian empire, it is not the standpoint of Marx, who always thinks of money and the price system as coming to an end simultaneously with the termination of capitalist production.

In interpreting Marx's own statements on the matter, the key points are: 1. that Marx does not distinguish between two stages called socialism and communism; 2. that he does distinguish between an early stage of communism and a later stage of communism; and 3. that the early stage, like the later stage, is a non-commodity (non-market) system.

Marx surmises that immediately communism appears, there may have to be a system of labor-vouchers (certificates, tickets, chits, notes, coupons, or checks) as advocated by Owen. But Marx insists that these vouchers must not be confused with money, which will disappear from the outset. Readers may at first be puzzled by the fact that in some places Marx appears to denounce labor-voucher proposals out of hand, whilst in other places he appears to recommend some such proposal for the intitial period of communism, though with a distinct lack of enthusiasm. The explanation is that Marx attacks the proposal to retain commodity production (with its organizational separation of the producers) and reform it by using labor-vouchers *as money*. Marx bitterly opposes all forms of socialism which involve some kind of reformed arrangement of market exchange and money, instead of their complete elimination. But he is prepared to consider the possibility of labor-vouchers as instruments for rationing out consumer goods within "directly associated labour" (communism). This helps to explain Marx's insistence that Owen's "labour-money" is not really money.

Marx is convinced that communism will engender an even more rapid progress in technology and output than has occurred within capitalism, and so the labor-vouchers will in time be abandoned, leading ultimately to voluntary work and free access—"From each according to his ability, to each according to his needs"—that is, in Marx's understanding of this phrase, all work to be done as a voluntary contribution without any reward being conditional upon it for the individual worker, and everyone to be free to take what they wish from the superabundant common store of goods. In the later stage of communism, individuals will work as much, or as little, as they please, and take as much, or as little, as they wish. I will call this 'free-access communism', to distinguish it from 'labor-voucher communism'. Marx doesn't imply that there will be no other stages intervening between the first stage of labor vouchers and the higher stage of free access (which he doesn't call the 'second' stage), but commentators have usually assumed this.

There may be room for doubt as to whether Marx ever actually believed that labor-voucher communism was desirable or would come about. His language suggests an illustration of what might conceivably occur, rather than a prediction of what would occur. He generally attaches to his fleeting references to labor-vouchers some disclaimer such as "for all it matters" (II, 362) or "We will assume . . . for the sake of a parallel" (I, 83). The longer discussion in the marginal comments on the Gotha Unity Program sounds more commital, but is followed by the statement that Marx has conducted the discussion solely to show the fallacies in slogans like "undiminished proceeds of labour" and "fair distribution", and that it is wrong to waste time considering the future system of distribution, which will sort itself out automatically once production becomes communist (MECW v24, 87–88).

It is surprising that Marx's comments on the Gotha Program are so frequently cited by those who claim that he envisages a lengthy transitional period between capitalism and communism, maintaining commodity production. For this text cannot be reconciled with any such transition. It tells us that "communist society . . . *emerges* from capitalist society, . . . still stamped with the birth-marks of the old society from whose womb it emerges" (85) and that "the first phase of communist society" emerges "after prolonged birth pangs from capitalist society" (87). There is no mention of a stage of society called 'socialism'. In the first period of communism, immediately following capitalism, "the producers do not exchange their products" and there is no "value" (85). They are, however, paid in labor-vouchers which they exchange for consumer goods.

b. Are Marx's Labor-Vouchers Money?

According to Marx, the labor-vouchers which might be used in the first days of post-capitalist society are not money. The question arises whether Marx was right. A variety of writers with different axes to grind have suggested that Marx's labor-vouchers are equivalent to money, or as near money as makes no difference. Kropotkin (1907, 203) makes the facetious comment: "After the Collectivist Revolution, instead of saying 'twopence worth of soap', we shall say 'five minutes worth of soap'." Kropotkin's point is that the situation of the worker is only superficially different from, and no better than, his lot under capitalism. Others more sympathetic to Marxism have suggested that since the labor-vouchers are so close to money, there is nothing anti-Marxian about a socialist economy which employs rubles or dollars.

Some writers have claimed that the system of labor-vouchers would not in practice work out as Marx envisaged, and that the vouchers would come to be used as money whether the communist administration intended this or not, in other words, that the vouchers would *turn into* money. I discuss this contention in the next section; it is not the same question as whether the labor-voucher system, operating as Marx conceived it, is a money system.

Surprisingly, Marxian labor-vouchers have often been interpreted as coupons entitling the holder to specified goods. Thus, the first half-hour's labor might entitle the voucher-holder to a pound of meat. This implies that all working individuals receive vouchers for the same goods, at least for the first few hours of the working day, corresponding to the working-day of those who work the shortest hours. If we depart from this notion, and suppose that all vouchers will be exchangeable for any of a range of goods, it becomes necessary to 'price' all such goods in vouchers, and the system begins to look a bit more like a market in consumer goods.

Marx states that Owen's labor-vouchers are no more to be considered as money than a theater ticket would be (Capital I, 97). The evident distinction between money and theater tickets becomes less definitive if we admit 'pricing' and consumers' choice of goods. The labor-vouchers then become something like the gift certificates issued by modern retail stores, but closer to money than those, for gift certificates are valued in terms of an independent unit, whereas under labor-voucher communism, all consumer goods would have to be 'priced' in labor-hours, and the only public embodiment of the labor-hours would be the vouchers themselves.

Despite these moneylike qualities of labor-vouchers, they have other features dramatically unlike anything normally considered money. Each voucher ends its life once it has been exchanged for goods. (This is not the same as a present-day check, which transfers ownership of a deposited sum. Although one physical check serves for a single transaction and then ends its life, an asset has been transferred to the payee, who can then transfer it to others. The check is not money, in the sense of what is paid over; the check serves to carry out and attest to the transfer of a deposit from one person's ownership to another's.) It is not intended that anyone other than the first recipient of a labor-voucher shall be able to exchange it for goods. It would be in the spirit of Marx's approach to make the vouchers non-transferable in the way that credit cards and library cards are often non-transferable. As Marx says: "These vouchers are not money. They do not circulate" (II, 362).

Marx conceives the matter in this way: 'Society' (the democratically-organized population) has to find some way of rationing out consumer goods, since communism has not yet reached the level of productivity that would permit people to take freely whatever they please. If it is decided to ration the goods in proportion to hours worked, then each person can be given a certificate for the number of hours they work. Thus, the whole scheme is an instrument of society-wide planning. It is the method by which 'society' rations out the goods, as 'society' decides. Leaving aside the question of whether the labor-vouchers conform to some non-Marxian definition of 'money', I conclude that they are very different from any money we know of, and that when Marx denied that they were money he was saying something coherent.

Marx seems to have given little thought to the labor-voucher scheme. For example, he asserts that society gives the worker "a certificate" declaring the number of hours worked. This might be cumbersome, because the certificate-holder might not want to spend all of the certificate in the same store on the same day. Of course, the store could accept the certificate and then keep a record of that worker's 'credit', but pursuing that argument, there might be no need for 'certificates' at all. Nothing in Marx's treatment suggests a serious attempt to devise a scheme that might work: the discussion is an incident in an argument, and is given no more attention than necessary for the argument. In the discussion of the Gotha Program the argument is about the slogan, "Undiminished proceeds of Labor"; elsewhere the argument is about the difference between commodity and non-commodity production, and the need for all societies to have a method of allocating labor-time.

Marx conceives of labor-voucher communism and free-access communism as variants of the same system, with the same kind of administration of production. (Labor-vouchers should not be confused with the labor-time planning proposal, which Marx apparently favors for all stages of communism. See Chapter 6 below.) The vouchers cannot be used analogously with wages in a true labor market, to attract workers to the appropriate jobs. This must be done by a different method, presumably the same method, whatever it may be, as would be used under free-access communism. It is clearly intended that no one will accumulate vouchers or speculate in them—and this would be easy to prevent, for example by making the vouchers expire after a short period. The stores are not to engage in competition; voucher prices are to be fixed, and there is to be no higgling. It seems from all this that Marx's statement that the vouchers are not money should be taken seriously, at least on one intelligible definition of money. Whether they would *become* money, by coming to be used in a manner quite different from that imagined by Marx, is a different question.

c. The Metamorphosis of Labor-Vouchers into Money

It was claimed by Pierson (1902) and by Mises (1920) that a labor-voucher system, once set up, would rapidly evolve into a market system. Mises interprets the voucher scheme as one in which individuals get allowances of specified goods. He contends that trade will emerge between consumers, much in the way that inmates of internment camps exchange portions of the contents of their Red Cross parcels (though Mises does not refer to this example, which had not yet appeared in the economics literature. See Radford 1945). The non-smoking opera-lover will swap her tobacco allowance for the opera tickets issued to the tone-deaf chain-smoker. This market will not necessarily affect output. The assortment of goods produced continues to be determined by the society-wide plan. Once that has been determined, the individual consumer has to take from what is available in the stores. The spontaneous and unintended emergence of a 'black market' re-arranges the allocations of consumer goods in a way that improves the wellbeing of the consumers, but it does not seriously affect the non-market character of the system, and it does not provide the industrial administration with a means of valuing factors of production, since factors do not enter into the market.

In that scenario, a market arises automatically, after individual consumers have collected their rations from the stores. The administration could instead arrange for a consumer goods market by allowing each voucher to be exchangeable in the stores for any goods. This would require that a price, in labor-vouchers, be set for all consumer goods. That would apparently enable consumers to acquire the goods they wanted by a more direct route. But now the pricing of goods becomes a difficult art for the administration. Underpriced goods would disappear quickly from the stores. One might expect overpriced goods to remain on the shelves, but if workers are paid just enough to purchase the weekly flow of all goods at the set prices, and if vouchers can be spent only on goods in the stores, and lose their legal purchasing power by expiration a short while after being issued, then (unless some goods are of no use to anyone, or close to it) all the goods will be cleared from the shelves. However, those who acquired the underpriced goods will now be in a position to exchange them for overpriced goods, at a more favorable ratio. If we suppose that the storekeepers cannot be bribed, and that goods are sold to the first taker, then those more ready to camp outside the stores will have higher gross real incomes than those less eager to do so. The inconvenience suffered by people camping outside stores is, of course, a cost to 'society' (that is, to all those individuals), and potentially a huge one, but it will be less the more accurate is the stores' pricing of the goods.

In order to encourage accurate pricing, it would help to give each local store management the freedom to set its own prices. But this would defeat its purpose if the store simply set all prices so low that the shelves were empty most of the time. An improvement would be (assuming each store's weekly intake of goods is fixed) for the store to pursue a policy of maximizing its weekly labor-voucher income, which ideally means pricing each good so that a week's supply exactly sells out in a week.

The best prices will clear the shelves for each good. In trying to set these prices, it would be an irrelevant distraction for stores to pay any attention to the labor-hours embodied in each good, even supposing these quantities could be known. The more inaccurate the stores in setting shelf-clearing prices, the more scope for private trading among consumers once they had gotten their hands on the goods. If such private trading is discouraged by the administration, inefficiency will result and people will effectively be poorer. If A has an orange and would prefer an apple, while B has an apple and would prefer an orange, then they can both gain if they are free to exchange the apple for the orange. (They can gain if the 'transactions costs' of making the exchange are not too high. If these costs are too high, then A and B will not execute the transaction, so they lose nothing by the freedom to exchange.) If such exchanges are effectively prohibited, then both A and B are made worse off. This is just as wasteful as if part of society's stock of apples and oranges were physically destroyed. It may therefore 'pay society' (make some people better off without making anyone worse off) to take some of the resources devoted to producing apples and oranges and devote them instead to shopkeeping and advertising. It is worth sacrificing some physical output of tangible goods to get those goods into the hands of the people who will value them most highly.

Any attempt to introduce a system of distribution by labor-vouchers will tend to lead to an actual distribution (after trading) which departs from one proportionate to hours worked. Rations of specific goods (whether proportionate to hours worked or not) will spontaneously lead to a market. Payment in vouchers and pricing of goods in vouchers will constitute a kind of market, though this will be spontaneously supplemented by a further 'unofficial' market, wherever the administration's stores fail to price goods at market prices. A point not explicitly noted by Pierson or Mises is that, although the vouchers might come to be used as money, if this were discouraged by making the vouchers non-transferable and expirable, then some other monetary medium would spontaneously arise—just as cigarettes have frequently emerged as money in prisons, internment camps, and hyperinflationary situations.

It has long been agreed, virtually unanimously by economists, that as long as consumer goods are not superabundant there has to be a market in consumer goods; attempts to suppress such a market will lead to inefficiency and will probably be unsuccessful (see Mandel

1968, 633). Once this is acknowledged, all that remains of the labor-voucher system is the proposal that individuals be paid proportionately to the hours they work. Labor-vouchers were frequently advocated by Marxists before the First World War, but have not played a major role in twentieth-century Marxism, perhaps because they were not espoused by Kautsky, and therefore not by his pupil, Lenin. The followers of De Leon are among the few Marxists to have continued to advocate the scheme.

The question of the distribution of consumer goods can be considered independently of the organization of production. Whether NFM socialism admits consumer goods markets is a fairly minor issue, with respect to the Mises argument. Once a consumer goods market is accepted, it naturally suggests that production will be adjusted to demand as expressed in that market, but this doesn't touch upon the Mises question, since there are still no factor markets. Yet there is a suggestive similarity: the administration requires consumer goods markets, ultimately because it is not possible for the administration to know every individual consumer's preferences. According to Mises, factor markets are necessary because the administration cannot know the production relationships known to every individual engaged in production.

iii. Post-Capitalist Society

a. Moore's Argument against Marxian Communism

Moore (1980) argues that Marx was mistaken to advocate moneyless communism: Marx erred in clinging to 'communism', because of a primitive, utopian strand in his thought, instead of opting for 'socialism' as the ultimate form of post-capitalist society, and not merely as a transitional stage towards communism. According to Moore, "communism" abolishes both exploitation and exchange, whereas "socialism" abolishes exploitation while maintaining exchange (63). Moore accepts Marx's view that capitalists necessarily exploit, and therefore favors a market system without capitalists. In Moore's opinion, Marx muddles the arguments for "socialism" with those for "communism", and gives no adequate reason why "communism" should be preferred to "socialism" (7, 27–31).

Moore tends to confuse matters by first classifying labor-voucher communism as a system of "exchange", contrary to Marx who classifies it as a non-commodity system. Then, Moore lumps together all collectivist systems involving "exchange" as "socialism". Thus, 1. the immediate measures proposed by Marx and Engels in the *Communist Manifesto*, and later repudiated by them (MECW v23, 174–75); 2. Proudhon's market socialism; and 3. labor-voucher communism, are discussed by Moore as variants of "socialism". From a Marxian standpoint, 1. is a kind of capitalism, reformed and under a working-class administration; 2. is an absurdity which can never materialize; and 3. is a form of communism. The Marxian classification is intelligible. In 1., production is immediately controlled by profit-seeking capitalists in an anarchic market environment (despite a co-existing sector operated by the workers' government under a "social plan"—and therefore not within the market). In 3., production is planned society-wide, without using markets or prices for this purpose. In 2. we have some of the features of commodity or market-oriented production, without other concomitants.

Marx considers capitalism to be inherent in commodity production; commodity exchange permitted to develop fully is capitalism, and will throw up capitalists. It is a fundamental assumption of Marx's that "exchange corresponds to the bourgeois organization of society" (Marx 1973, 134). It is beside the point to say, as some writers do, that commodity exchange occurs in societies other than capitalism, with the implication that from a Marxian standpoint there is nothing peculiarly capitalist about commodity exchange. In Marx, commodity exchange exists in undeveloped forms in pre-capitalist societies, but always contains the potential to develop into capitalism, and must do so if it develops fully. For Marx, all commodity production is at least embryonic capitalism.

Marx and Engels frequently attack non-communist forms of socialism, which involve the retention of buying and selling. Their insistence upon the total elimination of exchange-value and money is not casual nor unconsidered. In Marx's day some of the proposals for market socialism involved the view that capitalism was unjust because commodities did not sell at their labor-values. In socialism, it was thought, this would be put right, and commodities would be made to exchange in proportions governed by their labor-values. This was sometimes allied with the proposal that labor-time itself should be money, and some experimental communities did issue labor-time notes. Marx attacks such proposals by arguing that, in the market, it is not possible to know what labor-values are except by making inferences from the phenomena of competition. Moore claims that the same objection applies also to Marx's communism, which would be unable to determine the hours of socially-necessary labor-time associated with particular goods (See below, 6.v.).

Moore's argument does not touch Marx's criticism of Proudhon's scheme. If Marx's communism is unfeasible for the reason given by Moore, Proudhon's socialism might still be unfeasible for the reason given by Marx. Moore wants a "socialism" which combines society-wide planning with market competition. Marx would have regarded this as incoherent, and it seems that Marx is on this point correct. Marx writes: "It is just as pious as it is stupid to wish that exchange value would not develop into capital, nor labour which produces exchange value into wage labour" (Marx 1973, 249. By "capital" Marx understands means of production used to employ wage-labor. In his terminology, 'capital' is confined to commodity production). Marx insists that fully-developed capitalism, with its exploitation of wage-laborers by profit-crazy capitalists, is the natural flowering of commodity exchange. He doesn't argue for this very rigorously, and neither does he explain why the system could not be forcibly kept from its full flowering, indefinitely. But his arguments were probably adequate to defeat the market socialists he crossed swords with, and Proudhon was an anarchist, whose principles ruled out the kind of harsh authoritarian controls which would be required to attempt to prevent a developed market system from throwing up private capitalists.

A possible radical counterattack against Marx would take his own argument a stage further, by maintaining that any social relations which permitted advanced industry would have to evolve into commodity relations ('It is just as pious as it is stupid to wish that modern industry would not develop into production of exchange value', and so forth). Marx never discusses this, because he thinks he has strong grounds for believing that the market is holding back production, and that the advance of industry automatically tends to abolish the market.

There is also a lot to be said for Marx's view that the market tends to give rise to capitalists, and that therefore 'exchange without exploitation' is not an available option (if capitalists necessarily exploit). Any functioning market would have to be perpetually and very intrusively regulated to prevent the accumulation of private sums which could be used to employ factors and make a private profit. Perhaps Moore would contend that such regulation ought to be imposed, and it is true that Marx never takes any trouble to refute such a suggestion. If the inherent tendency of commodity production is to throw up exploiting capitalists, why not keep commodity production and thwart this tendency by particular state interventions? Again, there is an obvious answer: that each such intervention will cause inefficiency, so that the workers would be better off exploited than protected from exploitation ('protected' in the sense of being forcibly forbidden to sell their labor services to someone who would make it worth their while to be exploited).

b. Commodity-Fetishism

> . . . the cohesion of the aggregate production imposes itself as a blind law upon the agents of production, and not as a law which, being understood and hence controlled by their common mind, brings the productive process under their joint control. (Capital III, 257)

According to Moore, Marx's argument for communism is purely a moral one, harking back to his "philosophical communism" of the early 1840s. Moore maintains that historical materialism, which he seems to accept as correct, provides reasons why capitalism must give way to socialism, but no reasons why capitalism or socialism have to give way to communism (Moore 1980, 23–30, 89).

Moore's criticism loses sight of two key assumptions in Marx's analysis: the superiority of planned over anarchic production, and the inherently anarchic nature of the market. Moore seems to reject the second of these assumptions, but he offers no argument against it. If both assumptions are granted, historical materialism can seem to support communism, because historical materialism favors the triumph of systems of production yielding greater efficiency (higher output), which can be obtained, Marx believes, by replacing anarchy with planning.

Marx also expresses several moral grounds for preferring communism to commodity production (including Moore's "socialism", from Marx's standpoint an unfeasible proposal for a reformed capitalism). One moral reason is Marx's distaste for "commodity fetishism". Moore's discussion of commodity fetishism (59–62) proceeds as though this concept were little more than an exercise in flowery religious metaphors. The crucial idea of commodity fetishism is more straightforward. Commodity fetishism is the apparent domination of people by inanimate objects, actually the domination of people by their own social relationships which have gotten out of control.

For Marx, the most important feature of capitalism, by contrast with communism, is *the mutual independence of the producers at the level of conscious organization.* Each organizational entity, each firm, makes its own autonomous decisions. The mutual dependence of the producers, which is essential if society-wide production is not to be chaotic, is brought about in an indirect fashion, through the market. Separation of the producers means that production is a hit-and-miss undertaking in which producers' day-to-day decisions are evaluated by the market after production has taken place. According to Marx, this state of affairs ineluctably leads to commodity-fetishism, which is "inseparable from the production of commodities" (Capital I, 77).

Marx characterizes fetishism as the mystified manner in which a relation between persons appears as a relation between things. The exchange of commodities represents (Marx claims) a relation among social labor, but it appears to people (Marx claims) as a relation among physical objects (Capital I, 77–79). At times, Marx seems to argue as though commodity fetishism exists only when people do not understand the true underlying economic reasons for the dictates of prices, for instance, when they mistakenly suppose that the price of a commodity is something emanating from the physical commodity itself, apart from its social context (79). This would mean that commodity fetishism were an intellectual error which could be dispelled by learning economic theory. But some of Marx's statements seem to suggest that commodity fetishism exists even if people understand why commodity prices change (80).

For Marx, commodity fetishism is something which always arises automatically from the fact that the market is unplanned. And, although the point probably never crossed Marx's mind, his position implies that any uncentralized *non-market* system in which autonomous producer groups try to guess the demand for their products and subsequently receive some kind of feedback signal telling them how they should correct their plans, would also be objectionably 'fetishistic'. Anarchy of production (a spontaneous allocative process without conscious overall control) *always results in fetishism* and commodity fetishism can occur only where there is anarchy of production. Contrary to Moore (1980, 63–67) there is no puzzle about why commodity-fetishism is absent under labor-voucher communism, in which there are no autonomous or competing producer organizations. But could not a 'socialist' government, operating within a market economy, intervene consciously to achieve certain goals? Marx pays little attention to such questions. He sometimes welcomes particular interventionist measures, which he views as developments within capitalism that help to make capitalism ripe for the communist revolution. Marx's response is consistent: specific government interventions within a market system do not necessarily prevent the market from functioning, and consequently, do not prevent the great majority of allocations from being anarchic, and therefore in Marx's analysis, fetishistic.

One application of commodity-fetishism is Marx's treatment of industrial organization. We observe hundreds of workers congregating every day in a factory, co-operating closely in the production of useful articles. We observe that production of these articles is adjusted to society-wide demand and supply conditions. An unbriefed visitor from a distant planet might hastily conclude that the workers co-operate each day because they see the need for it, and fit their activities into the society-wide pattern because they perceive (presumably after consultation with workers in other factories) the need for such adjustments. As a second guess, the alien observer might surmise that some group or individual, after due analysis and deliberation, tells everyone else what to do. But what do we discover instead? The workers find their work meaningless, living only for evenings and weekends. They are arranged in the factory by an external authority, whose purposes are obscure to them, and under whose harsh discipline they chafe. They participate in order to get a wage. Instead of the workers employing the machines and other equipment, it appears, paradoxically, as if the equipment employs them, for its own ends. The capitalist, meanwhile, cares nothing for the society-wide adjustment of production to wants and supplies, but seeks only to get rich. The people we might suppose to be directing the whole process, the 'captains of industry' are only captains of their own little ships, tossed to and fro by the billows of the marketplace. From Marx's standpoint, this is all weird and fantastic, horribly and self-evidently evil, and hardly likely to last long. It is this absence of control by human beings of their individual and collective destinies which is the true source of the pathos of *Capital*. Readers impressed primarily by the documented physical deprivation and squalor have read it superficially. *Capital* is a saga of the mysterious, macabre adventures that befall people who have lost conscious control of their collective lives.

Although Marx's insistence on the inescapably anarchic nature of the market is sound, his indictment of commodity fetishism is not so convincing. Much of the time, Marx writes scathingly as if commodities themselves dominated humans, and ruled their lives. This, of course, is ironic and figurative. At other times, Marx writes as if humans, including economists, habitually committed the mistake of thinking that commodities exchange, have value, or perform their other stunts, in ways that are not merely the outcomes of human dealings. I have never met anyone, read anyone, or heard of anyone who believed this.

G.A. Cohen (1978, 115–125) maintains both 1. that commodity-fetishism is inseparable from the production of commodities, and 2. that commodity-fetishism involves an intellectual mistake or illusion of some kind. From this follows the evident falsehood that a population of individuals who shared Cohen's economic theories, and therefore did not make the mistakes or suffer the illusions he talks about, could not engage in the production of commodities. From Cohen's account, it's difficult to pin down what the specific "illusions" are. For instance, he asserts that things appear to have exchange-value autonomously but in reality do not have it autonomously (116). If a thing's having exchange-value autonomously is taken to be incompatible with the opinion that a thing's having exchange-value is dependent on such facts as that the thing is desired and that it is scarce or costly to produce, then who holds that things have exchange-value autonomously? Not many people, surely. It cannot be that Cohen thinks that a thing's having exchange-value autonomously is merely incompatible with Marxian price theory (the labor theory of value), for he does not accept Marxian price theory. If (as may be suggested by 116, n1) Cohen holds that a thing's having exchange-value autonomously is incompatible with a class of price theories, including Marx's and Sraffa's, but excluding, say, Marshall's or Wicksell's, then the principle of exclusion is obscure. And a market society could continue perfectly well with a population convinced of Marx's or Sraffa's price theory.

But what of the more fundamental idea that there is something insulting to human dignity in permitting our individual decisions to be guided by automatic, abstract signals like price changes, rather than by conscious collective decisions? This judgment rests implicitly on an implausible notion of what collective society-wide decision-making could be like. In any large-scale co-operation, the individual cannot know all the particular reasons why he is induced to behave in certain ways, to fit his actions into the vast interpersonal latticework of actions. The individual has to follow general, impersonal signals. In any really big, complicated organizational structure, the results bearing on the individual's behavior would be just as mysterious to him as those of the market, as some of Kafka's stories illustrate. The individual could know, in a *general* way, how his instructions had been arrived at, but so can he, in a general way, know what causes price changes. Struck by his perception that commodities are oddities, Marx never considers that the fetishism of commodities may be no odder than the fetishism of committees.

A counter to this might be that the sort of organization devised under communism would not be large-scale. An individual would have a voice in local, 'human-scale' organizations, which would then federate into a world structure. This line of argument is weak, because, on the one hand, the more *some* decisions are made locally, the more it must be the case that many important matters are determined by the spontaneous interaction of local bodies, or by the relationships of local bodies to a central body. On the other hand, the market also allows people to form local organizations, like firms, clubs, communes, churches, or co-operatives, and within limits such organizations enable groups of people to exercise some conscious and collective control over their destinies.

c. Usages of 'Socialism' and 'Communism'

The terms 'socialism' and 'communism' became current in the 1830s, and any general agreement about precisely what they meant was soon lost (see Müller 1967 for a detailed account). Quite early the word 'socialism' came to mean, in some quarters, almost any kind of reform intended to improve the lot of the less well-off. Even where that usage did not prevail, some writers treated 'socialism' and 'communism' as interchangeable, others viewed 'communism' as a variety of 'socialism', and yet others counterposed the two terms as mutually exclusive. Generally, 'communism' was defined as more extreme or thorough-going than 'socialism'. One widespread distinction was that socialism socialized production only, whereas communism socialized both production and consumption. At the time when Engels and Marx became 'communists', the absence of any markets or money was generally seen as a *sine qua non* of communism, as in the works of Weitling. It was often assumed that communism would be more barracks-like, more regimented, and less affluent, than socialism—a characterization later to be exactly reversed by the Leninist definitions of these terms.

In the 1840s, Engels and Marx described themselves as 'communist' and often tacitly defined 'socialists' as their opponents, confused advocates of a form of society distinct from communism. In their criticisms of each other, both Marx and Proudhon accepted that Marx was a 'communist', Proudhon a 'socialist', and that these were distinct. Later, Marx and Engels switched to using the term 'socialism', to signify exactly what they had earlier meant by 'communism'. Consequently, when, five years after Marx's death, Engels came to write a new preface to the *Manifesto of the Communist Party*, which he and Marx had composed in 1847, Engels felt it necessary to explain why they had employed the term 'communist' rather than 'socialist': it was because, said Engels, 'Socialism was, in 1847, a middle-class movement, Communism a working-class movement' (MECW v26, 516). (Here Engels uses 'middle-class' to characterize ideas in a sociologizing vein. In real life, Marx and Engels were capitalists, while Proudhon was a worker.)

By 1888, the term 'socialism' was in general use among Marxists, who had dropped 'communism', now considered an old-fashioned term meaning the same as 'socialism'. The more generally-accepted and moderate term was taken over and used to mean precisely what had formerly been meant by the less popular and narrower term.

Karl Kautsky's *Erfurt Program* of 1892 explained:

> The abolition of the present system of production means substituting production for use for production for sale . . . Such co-operative production for use is nothing less than communistic, or as it is called today, socialist production. Production for sale can be overcome only by such a system. Socialist production is the only system of production possible when production for sale becomes impossible. (Kautsky 1910, 95–97)

Thus, a 'communist' movement, or at least one led by 'communists', while it grew to become far bigger than any other 'communist' or 'socialist' movement, abandoned the term 'communism' and started referring to itself as 'socialist'. Meanwhile, non-Marxist socialists continued to talk about a distinction between socialism and communism, though not as successive stages (Tugan-Baranowsky 1966, 18). And meanwhile too, some Marxists, including eventually Kautsky himself, began to move further away from the kind of socialism which had once been called 'communism', in favor of a kind of socialism incorporating production for sale.

At the turn of the century, Marxists called themselves socialists, and some non-Marxists defined a difference between socialism and communism, as alternatives, not successive stages. No Marxist before 1917 used 'socialism' to denote a stage between capitalism and communism. The definition of socialism and communism as successive stages was introduced into Marxist theory by Lenin in 1917 (LCW v24, 84–85; v25, 475). It was a slight terminological change, but it paved the way for further innovations by Stalin and others. At the time, it merely established the two-stage idea more firmly, and widened the gulf between the stages, particularly since

Lenin also identified the "first stage'" with Marx's "dictatorship of the proletariat". (In Marx, the dictatorship of the proletariat *precedes* any phase of communist society.) The new distinction was helpful to Lenin in defending his party against the traditional Marxist criticism that the Russian empire was too backward for a socialist (that is, communist) revolution. Still, the distinction between socialism and communism did not become standard even among Bolsheviks until well into the 1920s.

As the Leninist orthodoxy developed, 'communism' became the name for an ever-receding future destination. 'Socialism' was identified, for the sake of the ideological pedigree, with Marx's 'first phase', but the labor-vouchers were replaced by rubles. The Soviet Union officially entered 'socialism' in 1936. Among Western journalists the term 'Communist' came to refer exclusively to regimes and movements associated with the Communist International and its offspring: regimes which insisted that they were not communist but socialist, and movements which were barely communist in any sense at all.

In this book I use 'socialism' as a broad category, the scope of which I will not attempt to circumscribe. 'Communism' is reserved for all forms of socialism in which there is no trade (no exchange of commodities, in the Marxian sense) and therefore no money. As we have seen, Marxian 'socialism' is a type of communism.

In 1920 Mises argued that socialism was not a practicable system *because it excluded the possibility of markets in factors of production.* Since 'socialism' is now sometimes employed to denote systems which *do* embrace factor markets, it's desirable to draw a clear distinction between these two kinds of socialism. I will therefore frequently refer to 'non-factor-market socialism' (NFM socialism). A socialist system may permit markets in some factors and not in others, but this need not hinder the discussion. Some systems involve markets for labor but not for other factors. These are classified as NFM systems. Some systems permit a small part of economic life to make use of non-labor factor markets—for instance, agriculture, or enterprises below a certain size—while excluding factor markets from the rest of industry. These can be regarded as NFM systems, if only because it is the feasibility or efficiency of the NFM sector of such a system which appears as problematical in the context of the Mises argument.

NFM socialism includes all forms of communism but has a wider scope. When some proposed socialist system is under discussion, it is best to ascertain whether it belongs to NFM socialism, whether it encompasses factor markets, or whether it is unclear on this point. The term 'market socialism' is often used, but is frequently ambiguous.[1] Many forms of socialism permit some role for the market, but exclude markets for all or most non-labor factors. Does the system under consideration involve the buying and selling of bricks, bolts, trucks, computers, land, factory and office buildings, machine tools, electricity, and so forth, among autonomous trading units (whether these units be called firms, enterprises, co-operatives, communes, collectives, production brigades, or whatnot)? In looking at the writings of socialist theorists with this question in mind, various problems may arise. A writer may not be commital on this question. Another writer may be commital on both sides of the question— describing some features of his system which presuppose factor markets and others which presuppose their absence. But it is always illuminating to pose the question, and if the answer is unclear, the discussion of the system in question must be conditional.

Despite such problems, it is fair to say that, during the period, say, from the death of Marx to the Second World War, NFM socialism, or some species thereof, simply *was* 'socialism' to most avowed socialists. A couple of examples will illustrate this.

Edward Bellamy's novel *Looking Backward*, published in 1888, quickly sold millions of copies in the U.S., and then throughout the world, and made many thousands of converts to socialism. (After *Uncle Tom's Cabin* and *Ben-Hur* it was the most popular book of the turn of the century. A sequel, *Equality*, also widely read, appeared in 1897.) *Looking Backward* describes a Bostonian who falls asleep in 1887 and wakes up in the Boston of 2000 CE, in a socialist United States. Bellamy repeatedly states that socialism has no trade and no money (Bellamy 1960, 70–78), yet every adult receives a spendable income denominated in dollars and cents; everyone has a "credit card", a term which Bellamy was the first to popularize; there is no cash. All persons' nominal credit-card incomes are equal (75). The prices and quantities of goods supplied to the consumers are determined by demand and cost (129–130). Costs are measured in labor-hours. Although the account of industrial administration is sketchy, it's clear that the whole of industry is organized as one great hierarchy (headed by the President of the United States), that there is no competition, no buying and selling among enterprises or departments, and no pursuit of profit. (William Morris, a thoroughly orthodox Marxist who also maintained a powerful esthetic preference for the medieval over the modern, disliked Bellamy's picture of socialism so much that it stung him into writing *News from Nowhere.*

Morris's socialism is bereft of any kind of price system, even of the credit-card type; its inhabitants simply cannot grasp the notion of payment.)

Writing in 1908, M.I. Tugan-Baranowsky expounds his views mainly by summarizing what others have said, with occasional criticisms and elaborations. He divides socialism into eight types (socialism and communism, each further divided into centralized, corporate, federal, and anarchical varieties). In his account, nearly all of these eight appear as at least probably NFM systems, and in the few cases where one might have doubts, he seems to think that they fall short of being truly socialist (for example, 149). He treats "centralized Socialism" (111) as "the reigning tendency of the socialistic movement of the present time", and expounds it by summarizing the Saint-Simonians, Pecqueur, Rodbertus, the Marxists, and Bellamy. He is most sympathetic to Pecqueur and Bellamy, whose systems are much the same. Tugan-Baranowsky's account of Pecqueur makes it clear that his is a form of NFM socialism (116–125; see also Pecqueur 1842). Money is used to distribute consumer goods and can never be converted into implements of production. Prices of consumer goods will be fixed by the labor expended on producing them, except where demand exceeds supply (!), in which case prices will be left to supply and demand (121).

— 3 —

THE ECONOMIC ORGANIZATION OF
POST-CAPITALIST SOCIETY

Socialism as a mass movement was, officially so to speak, a revolt against the employer, but in fact it was also a revolt against the dictatorship of the balance sheet. (Landauer 1959, 1657)

i. MARX ON COMMUNISM

Marx's *Capital* is devoted to an analysis of production under capitalist conditions and pays little explicit attention to communist society. Marx promises a "later analysis" of communist production (Capital II, 455), but he never got round to writing it. Yet in *Capital* there are asides about communist economic organization. Even where communism is not explicitly mentioned, Marx's tone and emphasis—for example, those aspects of capitalism which he views with contempt, implying that things could be otherwise—reveal his views about communism (Lavoie 1985, 29–30).

Apart from *Capital*'s dwelling on the degrading inhumanity of capitalism, the most striking theme of the work, in relation to the difference between capitalism and communism, is its repetitive harping on the fact that capitalism is unplanned and communism will be planned. Marx complains about the anarchic, spontaneous, or automatic character of capitalist production, contrasted with the rational, predetermined, and consciously governed character of communism (I, 336–37; II, 176, 318–19). The words "anarchy" and "anarchic" are employed very frequently to characterize the overall planlessness of the market (I, 337, 449, 457, 472; II, 473; III, 260, 881). So close is the identification of communism with planning that Marx sometimes employs an explicit reference to planning as an implicit but unmistakable reference to communism.[1] Yet Marx never dwells on the difficulties which might be encountered with society-wide planning, and gives almost no information about how the society-wide plan is to be drawn up or implemented. This may cause some readers to suppose that Marx cannot really be serious, despite his literal insistence on society-wide planning. But the fundamental reason for Marx's neglect of the serious difficulties of planning is that he does not foresee any. Such an attitude arises quite naturally, and has arisen independently with numerous writers, once the problem of economic calculation is substantially ignored.

Marx tells us that book-keeping, the "control and ideal synthesis" of production, will become "more necessary in collective production than in capitalist production"; he optimistically adds that "the costs of book-keeping drop as production becomes concentrated and book-keeping becomes social" (II, 137–38). There is no clue here as to what units are to be employed in book-keeping, though elsewhere (I, 83; III, 851) it's perhaps implied that labor-time-units will be used. Marx divides production into Departments I (production of capital goods) and II (production of consumer goods). He indicates in passing (II, 428–29) that these departments will continue to exist under communism, and that capital goods (in his language, "means of production") will continue to be distributed among the various branches of production. Marx holds that *all* "combined labour on a large scale" requires "a directing authority", just as an orchestra requires a conductor (I, 313), so managers are indispensable (III, 383). The capitalist owner is becoming superfluous in production; hired managers, members of the working class, take over all the capitalist's former functions (I, 314; III, 386–87). Part of what managers do is peculiar to capitalism, but part will remain necessary, Marx holds, under communism.

Referring to the capitalist's "fanatical insistence on economy in means of production", which "depends partly on the skill and intelligence of the labourers and partly on the discipline enforced by the capitalist", Marx adds that this discipline "will become superfluous under a social system in which the labourers work for their own account, as it has become practically superfluous in piece-work" (III, 83). Here Marx collapses the notion of an individual's working for his own account, with a perceptible improvement in his personal income if he works better, into that of each individual working for the account of everyone, with no perceptible change in the individual's well-being if he works well or badly. The remark confirms that communism would have to continue to economize on means of production, but there is no recognition that in order to economize, a comparative valuation of the costs per unit of all the various means of production is required. Marx contrasts the "over-production" of fixed capital under capitalism, which causes crises, with the systematic over-production of fixed capital under communism, as a safeguard against fluctuations (II, 473). He points out however (III, 847) that a form of insurance will be necessary under communism, as within capitalism.

There are other passages where Marx identifies ways in which communism will be substantially different from capitalism. He especially emphasizes that the laborers will be less hard-worked and less sharply disciplined. Although Marx is undoubtedly aware that the extent to which laborers can have an easier time is limited by output and therefore by productivity, he seems to assume that society is on the threshold of such abundance that great gains can be made in the laborer's job-satisfaction without any painful cut in output of goods other than job-satisfaction. Marx cites with indignation the remark of a capitalist named Ashworth, as reported by Senior. Mr Ashworth explained that, when a laborer laid down a spade, he rendered useless, for the period that the spade was unused, "a capital worth eighteen-pence", but when a laborer walked out of the factory, he rendered useless a capital which had cost £100,000. Marx comments sarcastically: "it is, in truth, monstrous that a single one of our people should ever leave the factory!" (I, 382). The hasty reader of *Capital*, or even its hasty writer, might gain the impression that the pressure to keep costly plant continuously in use is merely some kind of quirk of the market which would disappear with the establishment of "production for use", when in fact that pressure, like all pressures to reduce cost, though *transmitted* via the market, derives ultimately from the urgent desire of the mass of the people for a better life. (Since 'unused capacity' is a popular socialist indictment of capitalism, utilized by many Marxists, it's worth noting that Marx's indignation here implies that unused capacity doesn't matter, and there ought to be more of it.)

Marx asserts that "Machinery is put to a wrong use, with the object of transforming the workman, from his very childhood, into a part of a detail-machine" (I, 398). This suggests that machinery under communism would be designed to give more control to the human operator—that this is the 'right use'. Assuming that is preferable *caeteris paribus*, it does not follow that other goods—the products which the workers and machines are making—ought always to be sacrificed to that goal. No evidence is given that machinery in capitalism has the *object* of turning the worker into a certain kind of dependent creature, but only that this sometimes happens. The opposite also sometimes happens: new machinery gives the worker more control over the work. In a different context (I, 458) Marx celebrates an instance of this. To suggest that machines are introduced in order to subject the workers is to suggest either that capitalists will sacrifice profits for this objective or that pursuing this objective is profitable. If the first, it indicates a class-specific altruism that seems implausible and is not substantiated; it would tend to be eliminated by competition. If the suggestion is that machinery is introduced in order to make the workers dependent because this is profitable, then a great deal would have to be shown, which Marx does not bother to try to show, before we could conclude that this was a wrong use. Perhaps the idea is that workers made dependent by particular forms of technology will be easier to manipulate, will give less trouble. 'Easier to manipulate' would translate as 'easier to persuade to do what managers ask them to do in pursuit of profitability'. In this sense, on the face of it, everyone is better off, including those workers, if they are easier to manipulate, because their output is higher. The purpose of an industrial enterprise is to satisfy consumers' wants at least cost, and there is no particular reason why a truculent proclivity to obstruct this purpose should be considered praiseworthy.

However, the broad lines of industrial sociology since Marx seem to point in the opposite direction: 'human relations' management includes redesigning the work to give the workers more control over it, in some cases where this means foregoing some advantages of division of labor in order to reduce strikes, absenteeism, and sabotage, while Taylor's 'scientific management' (work-study) is utilized where the great advantages in output from dividing the work, generally in ways which give the worker less control over it, outweigh the fall-out in manifestations of worker discontent. If treating the worker as a mere cog in a machine tends to foster discontent and provoke recalcitrance, while giving the worker control over the technical process tends to make him more compliant with management's goals, then Marx would have the relationship the wrong way round.

To the extent that workers dislike working with certain kinds of machines more than they dislike the lack of the increased output which those kinds of machines would provide, workers will be ready to give up some money wages in order to work with more agreeable machines ('Giving up money wages' may take the form of fewer strikes, less absenteeism, less 'swinging the lead'—these are all ways of increasing the worker's payment of useful work to the capitalist in exchange for a given sum of money). But no form of society can offer any escape from the fundamental trade-off: designing machines to suit the worker's immediate gratification from using them, at the expense of producing most efficiently for external consumers, implies a reduction in output for those external consumers.

Marx's arguments have been developed by Braverman (1974) and applied to recent industrial developments. Braverman says that the trend is for most jobs to become less skilled, and that this is due to "capital" (in the Marxist sense) rather than to technology. Along with arguments by Bell (1973) and Levin (1987), Braverman's book has stimulated interest in the factual question of whether there is a 'deskilling' trend in modern industry. Some recent research suggests that the actual trend may have been in the opposite ('upskilling') direction (Bailey 1990), though the evidence is inconclusive.

If it were true that pursuit of increased productivity led to deskilling, then this would mean that there were a choice between, on the one hand, some combination of higher pay and shorter hours, and, on the other, more skilled work. Workers would have to decide whether they were prepared to sacrifice some pay or work longer hours to keep the work more skilled. Braverman's moral abhorrence of alleged deskilling therefore presumably commits him to at least one of these contentions: 1. There is not in fact a trade-off between skill and productivity; hence there is some special institutional reason why capitalism favors deskilling, unrelated to improved efficiency; or 2. Workers don't sufficiently appreciate the value of skills, and must be compelled to give up some pay or to work more hours, so that work can be made more skilled. Braverman describes all aspects of industrial evolution in tones of deep loathing, so that the specific grounds for his objections are difficult to identify, but he seems to favor 1. rather than 2. He assumes that capitalists benefit from depriving the majority of workers of "control" over production, and giving that control to technical specialists. Why or how such a policy would benefit the capitalists is nowhere explained— unless it be that it increases productivity, in which case some explanation is required of why this would be bad.[4]

An example which Braverman seems to view with particular disgust is Babbages's principle that if a task is divided so that its components can be done by several different people, then some of those components may be done by workers whose labor is cheaper (Braverman, 79–81). Braverman says that this principle "gives expression not to a technical aspect of the division of labor, but to its social aspect" (81), suggesting that the principle arises from capitalist institutions and would have no place under communism. But if one kind of labor is less costly than another kind, then it is wasteful to employ the latter on a task that can just as easily be done by the former. Having a surgeon sterilize her instruments or having a bricklayer carry his hod reduces output and therefore living standards, *unless* the sheer intrinsic desirability of having the same person do these different tasks is so great that it outweighs the loss of output elsewhere. A communist administration would have to observe Babbage's principle, if people continued to value higher incomes of other goods more than they valued a particular arrangement of workplace tasks.[5] (This point holds even though communism does not reward workers according to the value of their product. One kind of labor would not then be cheaper than another in the sense that the laborer would be paid less, yet it would continue to be cheaper in the eyes of the communist administration: the opportunity cost of employing some kinds of labor would be lower than the opportunity cost of employing other kinds of labor for the same task, so there would be a gain to society in substituting lower-cost for higher-cost labor in that task.)

ii. THE SUBSTITUTION OF MACHINERY FOR LABOR

Marx is largely heedless of intra-technique substitution, the substitution of a bit more of one factor for a bit less of another factor, within a given technique, but keenly aware of inter-technique substitution, switching to a different technique, with an abrupt shift to substantially different quantities and kinds of factors. Marx points out that variations in the level of wages, making "labor-power" less or more expensive to the capitalist, will determine whether various kinds of machines are introduced. High wages encourage the implementation of machinery, and some kinds of machinery will not be installed unless wages are above a certain level. Marx indignantly points out that machines invented in one country are sometimes introduced only in another country, where wages are higher (I, 370–72). Marx attributes variations in the level of wages among different regions to the fact that "the actual wage of the labourer at one time sinks below the value of his labour-power, at another rises above it" (I, 370).

If we consider a region where timber is sparse and good building stone plentiful, and another region where stone is sparse and timber plentiful, then, assuming significant transportation costs, we shouldn't be surprised to discover that house building in the first region typically used more stone in relation to timber than in the second region. In the market, this would be brought about by the ratio of stone price to timber price being lower in the first region than in the second region, but we should not therefore conclude that these differing ratios were mere artifacts of the market. The regional difference in construction materials ought to be aimed at by an efficient communist administration. In this sense the differing price ratios are, so to speak, rational or appropriate: they reflect real underlying conditions and something similar would have to be arrived at in any efficient system. A similar analysis can be made of the proportions of labor and machines employed. Without challenging Marx's theory of value, we can observe 1. that regional differences in the value of labor-power would have the same effect as unexplained divergences from that value; and 2. that even if we are dealing with departures of actual wages from value of labor-power, it has not been demonstrated that these departures are inefficient or would not require an analogue under communist planning.

Aside from such variations in the relative prices of machines and labor, Marx also argues that the market always tends to install too little machinery: that the price of 'labor-power' is always too low for efficiency. He holds that "in a communistic society there would be a very different scope for the employment of machinery than there can be in bourgeois society" (I, 371n). The reason is that bourgeois society considers price differences, whereas communist society would consider differences in quantities of labor-time. According to Marx's theory, 'profit' (interest) is produced entirely by labor, and not in the least by machinery or other equipment. Thus, the capitalist pays the full cost of a machine, but pays less than the full cost of labor. The capitalist sees the whole value of the machine as what he has to economize on, but only part of the value of labor[5] (that part laid out in wages) as what he has to economize on. It follows that the capitalist under-rates the cost of labor, and fails to introduce labor-saving machinery where it should be introduced. Many pages after discussing this matter in Volume I, Marx comes back to the same topic, and gives a detailed arithmetical example to make his position clear (III, 261–62). The example is one where a capitalist fails to introduce a new machine because it does not increase his profits, though in Marx's view its introduction would be an improvement.

Marx's efficiency ideal is communism, where workers would not get paid the full value of their labor, but where something analogous to this full value would be used in making allocative decisions such as when to substitute machinery for labor. Although, according to Marx, wages frequently rise above the value of labor-power, they don't often rise as high as the value of labor-power plus profit ($v + s$). But it is this total magnitude which in Marx's judgment represents the true cost of labor.

The underlying assumption of Marx's account is that *machinery ought to be substituted for labor whenever the labor-time required to make the machinery is less than the labor-time replaced by the machinery*. He condemns the market for departing from this standard, and he thinks that it departs the more from this standard the lower wages are. But if wages are as high as they can be ('wages' are for Marx exclusively a market phenomenon), there will still be under-installation of machinery.

According to Marx, labor-time is the only cost which should be taken into account, and a rate of interest should not be calculated on means of production. Notice that it is not the question of who gets the surplus-value which matters for this argument, but the fact that surplus-value (interest or 'rate of profit') enters into the picture at all. This objection of Marx's would apply even if surplus-value did not actually go to separate capitalists but was distributed among the workers (as in a market economy with all firms producer co-operatives) and it would also apply to any non-market society which, in its book-keeping, attributed any interest to capital-goods, or failed to attribute all the value added in production to living labor alone. Marx's argument implies that the communist administration would not calculate an interest-rate on means of production. Marx thinks that the abolition of interest on means of production will permit the substitution of machinery for labor to a greater extent than is possible in the market. But if we try to imagine this substitution at the moment of its implementation, we are struck by a difficulty. Society cannot instantly substitute machinery for labor if the additional machinery doesn't exist. Is there any appreciable quantity of unused machinery lying around in the market, which can be costlessly put to work under communism? It seems not.[7] Since the additional machines do not exist immediately, they will have to be produced. There will, then, be a delay before the "greater scope for the employment" of machinery can be realized. Where will the labor and machines come from to produce these additional machines? It will *not* do to reply that these factors will come from savings made by the superior efficiency of communism. The argument under consideration is one of the grounds for this superior efficiency, and the issue is whether this argument, considered on its own merits, is worth anything. Therefore, the additional factors cannot come from the abolition of useless occupations, or of planned obsolescence, or any of the other alleged sources of capitalist waste. Precisely what is in question is whether Marx has identified a distinctive source of capitalist inefficiency, independent of these other alleged sources.

There is a fallacy of composition in Marx's approach. It's easy to imagine a single capitalist buying more machinery, and thus 'substituting machines for labor'. However, for society as a whole, there can be no immediate substitution of machinery for labor unless there are stocks of unused machinery. There can be re-arrangement of the existing machinery and labor to produce more machinery, so that at a later date there will be more machinery per worker than there would have been without this re-arrangement. In that event, consumption in the near future is cut in order to increase the means to provide consumption in the distant future. If we imagine a society in which the rate of interest abruptly rises, say, from 2 to 5 percent, without any change in real conditions (such as population, skills, equipment, and materials), then there is no reason why there cannot be full employment of machines and labor both before and after the change: the difference after the change is that people's current spending on consumption has been increased; their saving and investment for the future reduced. The interest rate both controls the supply of new machines and rations out the existing machines among their possible uses.

Marx's "greater scope for the employment of machinery" is a physical impossibility. The scope for employing machines is immediately restricted by the stock of machines and in the longer term by people's unwillingness to tighten their present belts to make more future machines possible. We can have more investment in future machines by sacrificing current standards of consumption—but it is precisely this sacrifice of current workers' incomes to "the self-expansion of capital" which Marx rhetorically denounces in the most impassioned terms.[7]

We can now reconsider the proposition that *machinery ought to be substituted for labor whenever the labor-time required to make the machinery is less than the labor-time replaced by the machinery.* Machines are normally durable: a machine may continue to give its services (to replace labor-time) for decades to come. The labor-time required to make machinery is spent before the machinery goes into use, whereas the labor-time replaced by the machinery would have been spent later, and much of it years or decades later. If we count all that future labor-time saved as equivalent, hour for hour, with current labor-time used, then we will go to grotesque lengths to sacrifice the present to the future, since no matter how much of our current income we set aside for the future, there are always further opportunities to increase future output by greater current saving. In a fanciful scenario, we could all starve to death while working on fabulously sophisticated equipment designed to save a very large proportion of our great-grandchildren's labor. The solution to this problem of proportioning current and future outlays of labor and equipment is to *discount future returns* by a small but cumulative percentage. Thus, the labor-time saved in the future has to be discounted at a compound rate, reflecting the extent of our willingness to sacrifice benefits in the near future for the sake of larger benefits in the more remote future. This is accomplished through the market by means of the interest rate.

iii. THE MARXIST BACKGROUND TO MISES

a. Social Democrats on Economic Calculation

Marx's views on the replacement of commodity production by production for use were faithfully represented by his followers after his death. Plekhanov's *Second Draft Program* of 1887, an authoritative statement of orthodox Marxism, opens:

> The Russian Social-Democrats, like the Social-Democrats in other countries, aim at the complete emancipation of labour from the yoke of capital. This emancipation can be achieved by the transfer to social ownership of *all the means and objects* of production, a transfer which will entail:
> (a) the abolition of the present commodity production (i.e. the purchase and sale of products on the market) and
> (b) its replacement by a new system of social production according to a previously drawn-up plan with a view to satisfying the requirements both of society as a whole and of each one of its members within the limits permitted by the condition of the productive forces at the given time. (Plekhanov 1961, v1, 358)

August Bebel was the most conspicuous figure in the German socialist movement in the period after Lassalle. His *Woman and Socialism* was a phenomenally successful work. By Marxist standards, it devotes a lot of space to the way in which socialism will operate. Bebel states that all able-bodied persons will be compelled to work at the behest of the administration (1910, 370), but will be entirely free to choose their own work (374). Administration will be local, rather like contemporary municipalities, and "At the head of all local bodies there will be a central administration. This—let it be noted—will not be a government with ruling powers, but an executive board of managers" (371). This is the commonplace of traditional Marxism that the central administration under socialism will not be a government or state. There is broad and complete democracy, with recall of delegates. "Every individual chooses the branch of industry in which he wishes to be employed . . . If there is an excess of workers in one branch and a lack of workers in another, it will be the duty of the administration to . . . bring about an equalization" (374). There will be no "commodities" and no "trade" (371).

The administration will have to itemize all society's stocks of all factors of production and of consumer goods (372). Just as present-day states and municipalities decide their budgets, "this will in future be done for the entire social demand". Regulation using statistics is unfeasible in capitalism because of competition and clashing interests, which will be absent under socialism. Bebel sees all the difficulties of statistical calculation of production in capitalism as due to competition and conflicts of interest, and he sees competition as entirely useless. Under socialism,

> Everything is carried out according to plans, in an orderly way, and so it will be easy to determine the amounts required by the various demands. When some experience has been gained, everything will run smoothly. When the average demand for meat, bread, shoes, garments, etc., has been statistically determined, and when the output of the respective establishments of production is known, *the average daily amount of socially necessary labor can be established.* (374)

Before the First World War, Karl Kautsky was the acknowledged intellectual leader of Marxism (and therefore of Continental socialism), dubbed by opponents 'the Pope of Marxism'. Kautsky's writings show his evolution from a Marxian advocacy of completely moneyless 'production for use' to a less radical espousal of nationalization and other forms of socialization within a market economy. His *Erfurt Program* of 1892 states that socialism requires "substituting production for use for production for sale" (Kautsky 1910, 95). Since capitalism is hastening to its doom, and since this is obvious to everyone, there is little point in trying to describe how socialism will work (111). The necessity of socialism follows from the course of history and from trends within capitalism, so the treatment of socialism itself is cursory.

Socialism can come about only within boundaries at least as great as those of modern nation-states (101). In its early days the socialist regime will nationalize all the "large means of production" (129–131). Small property owners will not be expropriated, though it is suggested that they will gradually be recruited into the nationalized sector (131–32). "Since the tendency of socialist society is to substitute production for use for production for sale, it must be its endeavor to transform all social dues (taxes, interest upon mortgages on property that has been nationalized, etc., so far as these may have been not wholly abolished) from money payments into payments in products" (132). (This theme, of substituting, on principle, payments in kind for payments in money, has frequently been a prominent one in Marxist speculations about the transition from capitalism to socialism, but Kautsky himself was later to drop it. As recently as the 1970s it had considerable influence in China, Cuba, and elsewhere.) Distribution of consumption goods may for some time be essentially similar to the wage system. Equality of distribution is not intrinsic to socialism (141). There is no discussion of any problems of organizing socialist production. Kautsky assumes that there is a rapid, irreversible trend for larger units of production to displace smaller units and that this process has no limit short of one unit controlling the whole of society-wide industry.

The *Erfurt Program* went through many editions in many languages. The same is true of Kautsky's pair of lectures delivered in Holland in 1902 (Kautsky 1902). Stung by earlier remarks from Nikolaas Pierson, Kautsky was induced in the second lecture, 'The Day After the Revolution', to be more explicit about concrete measures. Kautsky observed that Pierson attended this lecture "where he made industrious notes and did not offer a word against me" (4). But Pierson's response was published shortly afterwards, and constituted the first clear explanation of the economic calculation problem (See below, 4.iii.).

In 'The Day After the Revolution' Kautsky emphasizes that socialism will not supplant capitalism at one stroke, and that the first tasks of the victorious proletarian regime will include such matters as relief of the unemployed and reform of the tax system. Many of the initial measures, as Kautsky stresses, are characteristically those of non-socialist, state-interventionist reformers. But, he argues, the implementation of these reforms will tend to push towards the replacement of capitalism by socialism. For example, Kautsky argues that comprehensive unemployment relief, by freeing workers from having to do the capitalists' bidding in order to survive, will tip the balance against the capitalists, so that the capitalists themselves will demand that their factories be taken over by the state, with compensation. Discussing the problem of incentives to work, Kautsky mentions pressure of habit, the workers' collective discipline (as shown under capitalism in strikes), and the potential for making work pleasurable. All this is in the traditional Marxian vein, but then Kautsky adds a further incentive: wages.

> What, it will be said, will there be wages in the new society? Shall we not have abolished wage-labor and money? How then can one speak of the wages of labor? These objections would be sound if the social revolution proposed to immediately abolish money. I maintain that this would be impossible. Money is the simplest means known up to the present time which makes it possible in as complicated a mechanism as the modern productive process, with its tremendous far-reaching division of labor, to secure the circulation of products and their distribution to the individual members of society. (129)

He adds that money will remain indispensable "until something better is discovered." Despite this important break with the Marxian view, Kautsky immediately goes on to insist that there will be no "value" in socialism, and that socialism will not be "production for exchange". Money will cease to be a measure of value, and wages will no longer be determined by supply and demand (133–34).

Exactly how Kautsky perceives the reconciliation between the market and production for use (formerly understood as non-market production) is unclear. He is vague about the relations among nationalized concerns, and the ambiguity is increased by his statement that already under capitalism, "production for the open market has disappeared" in the production of capital goods, since these are made to order (154). It is not clear whether, when one state enterprise receives means of production from another, the receiving enterprise is to pay a sum of money to the supplying enterprise, and if so, how the amounts of these sums are to be determined, and if not, how book-keeping of such a transaction is to be conducted, and in what units. If any degree of trading autonomy is to be permitted to the enterprises, then Kautsky's emphatic statements that all imbalance or overproduction will be eliminated by planning seems baseless. It does seem, though, that any money dealings between such enterprises, if they persist at all, are to be reduced to a subsidiary accounting function. The flavor of Kautsky's remarks is still that of production for use, with competition replaced by planning (148–158).

The problem of organizing all these enterprises throughout the German Empire is declared to be difficult, but its difficulties are reduced by: 1. the fact that socialism takes over an already operating system; 2. the fact that much production is concentrated in giant enterprises; 3. a further decrease in the number of plants, wrought by the socialist regime (Kautsky shows no awareness that plants or units of organization could conceivably be too big); and 4. the elimination of some of capitalism's sources of variations in demand.

In the years before the First World War, the Social Democratic Party, whose intellectual leader was Kautsky, made huge gains in German elections. From 1912 on, it was by far the strongest party in the Reichstag, and indeed, by far the largest and best-organized political party in the history of the world. Seeing the inevitability of military defeat in 1918, the German High Command handed over power to the Social Democrats. Although the precise timing of the sudden accession to power was unexpected, the Social Democrats had known that they would probably get the chance of forming a government before many years had passed, and it might have been expected that they would have worked out clear policies for converting industry to planned production for use. Instead, they found themselves in power and at a loss what to do. The German workers had already had much experience both of nationalization and of *Zwangswirtschaft* ('economy of compulsion', with industry nominally privately-owned but administratively controlled by the state). Both these measures, had been instituted under Bismarck, and had not proved popular with the workers. The Marxists had explained that such measures had nothing to do with socialism, but rather constituted the vilest forms of bourgeois oppression. But if nationalization and government regulation were each ruled out, what were the appropriate industrial policies of a socialist government? What was 'socialization'? (Mises 1969, 205; Ströbel 1922, 6ff).

The writings of the early Marxists display a rhetoric of transformation and a rhetoric of practicality. The rhetoric of transformation was at first justified by the abolition of the market. The more the Marxists backed away from the imminent abolition of the market, the more their proposals converged upon 'bourgeois' schemes for nationalization or state regulation. This process was obscured by the fact that various Marxists differed in the extent to which they treated such proposals as transitional, postponing more wondrous developments to an increasingly distant future. Still, they were reluctant to admit that even their transitional measures were fundamentally similar to some of the Bismarck policies, which they had got into the habit of excoriating as the antithesis of socialism. The rhetoric of transformation became a catless grin.[8] The Social Democrats held that socialization would be something very different from mere nationalization, or from nationalization as this had been experienced. They were thus able to regard as largely irrelevant any criticisms of historical examples of nationalization. Existing examples of state control were dismissed as 'not socialism', while the differentiating features of genuine socialism were sometimes left uncertain. Otto Bauer states, in a passage quoted with approval by Kautsky, that 'nobody manages industrial undertakings worse than the state. For this reason we have never advocated the nationalization of industry, but always its socialization' (Kautsky 1925, 207). Advocates of socialization draw attention to the many 'forms' it can take, but some of these—producers' co-operatives, consumers' co-operatives, ownership by trade unions, municipalization—are acknowledged to be limited in potential application and unsuitable for the biggest kinds of industry (which, Marxists mistakenly believed, presaged the future of all industry). Furthermore, the first three of these are possible voluntary forms of enterprise organization within a free market, and all four of them are concerned with internal enterprise administration, saying nothing about the administration of the whole of industry or the relations between enterprises.

For 'big industry', the 'forms' boil down to representation by various interest groups on the boards of nationalized industries. It is taken for granted that each 'industry' will be unified under a single management. Protestations that this is not nationalization but socialization do not seem to mean much. The Socialization Commission's 1919 report on the German mining industry proposed that the highest management be made up of 25% workers, 25% consumers, 25% state appointees, and 25% managers (Kautsky 1925, 209). Otto Bauer's proposal was for a board of directors consisting of one-third workers, one-third consumers, and one-third state appointees (207–08). Kautsky comments that numerous other proposals may be expected, but it is hard to see how any of them, any more than these two, can be anything other than different administrative schemes of nationalization. In both these schemes, for example, consumers are given special representation, but this can mean only consumer spokesmen, selected by some method determined by the state. Actual, living consumers will have lost the power they have in a free market, to refuse to buy one firm's products and patronize someone else, because the free-market arrangement, where anyone may open up a new business and any existing business may move into any new area of production, has been replaced by a coercive monopoly, where consumers are captive to the existing single firm, the 'industry'.

(Consumers in the free market could insist on buying only from those firms which had one-third or one-quarter consumer representation on their boards, but few consumers have shown any interest in this.)

There remained some outspoken proponents of the completely marketless society as an objective for the foreseeable future. The most conspicuous was Otto Neurath, who thought that the war economy had shown the practicality of a "natural economy" (Neurath 1919). Another example was the Austro-Marxist Otto Bauer (Bauer 1919). By contrast, the new 'market socialists', notably Heimann (1922), explicitly proposed that socialism incorporate factor markets.

Writing in 1922, Kautsky has retreated considerably from his own views of a few years earlier:[9] "All socialists who have been engaged upon the problems of socialization during recent years are agreed that it can only be effected gradually, and that for decades to come a considerable portion of our production will be conducted on capitalist lines" (Kautsky 1925, 132). He writes that "the creation of a socialistic organization" is "not so simple a process as we used to think" (143).

Much of Kautsky's discussion is given over to bitter criticisms of Bolshevism, the heretical Marxism which has taken power in Russia. Kautsky ridicules Lenin's contention that knowledge of simple arithmetic is sufficient for the armed workers to be able to replace the capitalists, but Kautsky seems unable to put his finger on precisely why the capitalists prove so difficult to replace. He mentions, for example, the capitalist's task of "accumulating capital, and constantly improving and extending his undertaking" (135), but does not explain why this cannot be, as Lenin claims, reduced to simple rule of thumb. Against Neurath's proposal for a moneyless economy, Kautsky argues that statistics would be too difficult to acquire, and this would rely too much on inefficient compulsion.

Kautsky raises the question whether socialist industry will be able to innovate, deprived of the possibility for entrepreneurs to gain profits from successful innovation. He replies that in each branch of industry, "nothing would be simpler or easier" than to set aside one business as an experimental testing ground. Kautsky's suggestion is that all proposed improvements be referred to the experimental business for testing (171). This shows that Kautsky is thinking merely of technical not economic efficiency. The key question is whether it would be possible to decide whether a proposed improvement were really an improvement or not. A 'test' has to determine whether the increase in output is greater or less than the increase in cost, or whether the reduced cost is greater or less than the rise in output. Furthermore, one enterprise cannot try out all the currently suggested improvements simultaneously, and even if it just tries out a few, it may be impossible to determine which, if any of them, is responsible for any rise or fall in productivity.

Kautsky proceeds to discuss speculation. Correctly anticipating price changes offers the capitalist profits, whereas failing to do so results in losses. "Here the resolute, but also cool and expert, initiative of the *entrepreneur* is not only a condition of progress, but a condition of life itself" (173). We see a tension between the old idea of production for use, which Kautsky is in process of tacitly abandoning, and his new kind of market socialism, which however is still presented as though it promised most of the perceived benefits of production for use. He states that speculation is inseparable from commodity production (174–76), which is both true and in harmony with traditional Marxism, but then implies that speculation will disappear with capitalism (176–77), even though commodity production will remain.

The Kautsky of 1922 wants what Marx had railed against as incoherent: commodity production without its anarchy. Kautsky wants to say that money and prices will continue to exist and be serviceable, but that production will be consciously planned. He asserts that there will be no trade cycle, because production will be planned as a whole. But if enterprises are permitted the independence of action necessary to a functioning market, then their interaction within the market will be largely unplanned. That being so, a trade cycle cannot be ruled out (assuming, as Kautsky does, that the trade cycle cannot be ruled out within capitalism). Alternatively, if enterprises are not to be allowed this independence, then Kautsky's concession to markets and money does not go far enough, for the spontaneous interaction of independent agents is required to make prices accurate as a guide to resource allocation. By 1922, if not before, the Marxist Kautsky has arrived back at the 'bourgeois socialism' rejected by Marx and Engels when they became communists in 1843. Yet Kautsky doesn't unequivocally embrace functioning factor markets under socialism.

b. Bolsheviks on Economic Calculation

Both the Russian Social Democratic Labor Party (Mensheviks) and the Russian Social Democratic Labor Party (Bolsheviks) accepted the traditional Marxist view that capitalism was a necessary preparation for socialism. Both Mensheviks and Bolsheviks therefore looked forward to a 'bourgeois revolution' which would establish a democratic republic.[10] Before 1917 Lenin repeatedly affirmed that the coming revolution could only be a bourgeois, and not a socialist revolution (LCW 9, 48–49). The Russian bourgeois revolution would be followed by a lengthy period of capitalist industrialization, unless perhaps a socialist revolution occurred first in the more advanced West. It was widely expected that working-class parties, headed by Marxists, would lead the bourgeois revolution. In Marxist theory the class nature of a revolution is not defined by the class background of the people who happen to lead or support it: a bourgeois revolution is one which clears the way for the development of bourgeois relations of production (commodity production).

Following the overthrow of the Tsar, the prevailing view among Marxists was that they should defend the new government, which would soon yield to a Constituent Assembly based on universal suffrage. When Lenin arrived in Russia, he astounded everyone by his new line that the revolutionary role of the bourgeoisie was finished, and that the Bolsheviks should intransigently oppose the government and the Mensheviks. This new analysis was embodied in the 'April Theses', to which he soon managed to persuade the rest of the Bolshevik leaders. The day the Bolsheviks seized power, Lenin made his famous declaration: "We shall now proceed to construct the socialist order!" (Reed 1977, 129).

Lenin's most widely-read work is *The State and Revolution*, written a couple of months before his seizure of power, and first published a few months after it. This work's twin claims to fame are that it expounds Marx's theory of the state and revolution, and that it sheds light on the Bolshevik regime. Yet its account of Marx's thinking is hopelessly inaccurate, and what happened after Lenin's *coup* was nothing like the scenario Lenin had foreseen. Most of this pamphlet is concerned with attacking Kautsky and other Marxists on questions relating to the exegesis of Marx and the strategy for revolutionaries, but it contains a chapter setting out Lenin's view of the economic transition from capitalism to communism.

Lenin proceeds by expounding Marx's *Critique of the Gotha Program*, where Marx distinguishes between two stages of marketless communism: an initial phase, with labor-vouchers, and a higher phase, with free access. Lenin adapts Marx's account in two ways, which have been passed off by most subsequent writers as Marx's ideas: 1. Lenin identifies the initial phase of communism with

Marx's pre-communist "revolutionary transformation" under the "dictatorship of the proletariat" (LCW, Volume 25, 473–74). 2. Lenin calls the first phase "socialism" and the second phase "communism" (475). As to 1., Lenin may misunderstand Marx, or may perhaps realize that he is innovating but may wish to avoid taking issue with the very text which he is using as his authority. As to 2., Lenin acknowledges that the socialism/communism terminology is not Marx's, but appeals to common usage, thereby obscuring to later readers the fact that his socialism/communism terminology is new to Marxism.

Lenin is urging a socialist revolution in Russia, against the traditional Marxists who argue that Russia is too backward for anything but a bourgeois revolution (475). Later commentators, including some quite unsympathetic to Lenin, are wont to present the traditional Marxists as dusty old dogmatists for taking the position that the Russian revolution can only be bourgeois, and Lenin by contrast as a refreshingly flexible thinker, not hidebound by doctrinal shibboleths. But these commentators' view of a socialist revolution is adjusted with hindsight to what actually occurred under Bolshevik rule. To Marxists in 1917, including Lenin, a socialist revolution still meant that capitalism had played out its historic function of building up a plentiful supply of the means of production, and that conditions were therefore ripe to commence the abolition of the market and the state. It was this kind of revolution which Lenin was claiming to be imminent in Russia, though he was also certain of its imminence in the West.

Lenin's identification of the first phase of communism with the "revolutionary transformation" means that the first phase now has a state, whereas in Marx there can be no state under communism. Lenin introduces the new idea, presenting it as Marx's, that the state can wither away only in the higher phase, or "complete communism" (LCW 25, 472–74).[11] The development of capitalism, says Lenin, creates the preconditions for all to take part in the administration of the state. "Some of these preconditions are: universal literacy, which has already been achieved in a number of the most advanced capitalist countries, then the "training and disciplining" of millions of workers by the huge, complex, socialised apparatus of the postal service, railways, big factories, large-scale commerce, banking, etc., etc." (477–78). Given these preconditions, it is possible, "immediately, overnight", to replace the capitalists in control of production and distribution (478).[12]

In socialism, all citizens become employees of a single nationwide syndicate. "The whole of society will have become a single office and a single factory, with equality of labour and pay" (479). The main requirement for the successful establishment of socialism is "accounting and control", a phrase which Lenin repeats numerous times here and in subsequent writings. All the necessary accounting and control "have been *simplified* by capitalism to the utmost and reduced to the extraordinarily simple operations—which any literate person can perform—of supervising and recording, knowledge of the four rules of arithmetic, and issuing appropriate receipts" (478).

Lenin's claim that little more is needed than knowledge of the four operations of arithmetic has frequently been cited with incredulity or with derision, but this kind of thinking is a routine feature of Marxism. What is odd is not Lenin's optimism about the administration of socialism, but his belief that the useful function now performed by capitalists is book-keeping. He states that "accounting and control should not be confused with the question of the scientifically trained staff of engineers, agronomists and so on" (478), who will remain specialists, working for the "armed workers" instead of for the capitalists, their wages reduced to the same level as everyone else's. It is strange that Lenin doesn't notice that book-keeping is one of the easiest tasks for the capitalist to delegate to workers—that even managers, whom Marx calls the NCOs of capital, delegate book-keeping to lowly clerks. Lenin could hardly fail to have known that book-keeping is generally not performed by capitalists at all. Yet he thinks that the "armed workers" need to learn book-keeping. Why can't they delegate this humdrum chore to specialists, as the capitalists do?

Before and after his seizure of power, Lenin harps almost obsessively on the need for "accounting and control", which he interprets as routine book-keeping and checking up on people. If the key role of the capitalist really were accounting and control, then the capitalist would indeed be easily dispensable. Lenin overlooks the functions of entrepreneurship and skilled management. Determining whether a factory will be kept open, whether it will expand, whether it will change its product line, whether an entirely different factory will be opened—such issues are given no attention. These tasks are for experts, or rather, for virtuosi—accomplished individuals, usually experts, who also happen to possess unusual talent and flair. These tasks cannot be settled by supervising, recording, and issuing receipts. There is every reason to suspect that the armed workers, as a group, must perform these tasks badly.

Another consequence of Lenin's collapsing Marx's two stages is that there evidently now has to be *another* stage or phase, immediately after the working-class seizure of power but before "socialism" has been established, that is, before all industry has been centralized in one organization, factor markets abolished, and equality of pay enforced. This stage also features the dictatorship of the proletariat, so in Lenin's account the dictatorship of the proletariat has a presocialist and a socialist stage. The presocialist stage of the dictatorship of the proletariat is not explicitly discussed in *State and Revolution*, which reads as if socialism arrives immediately the workers seize power, yet this presocialist stage is the subject of all of Lenin's other propagandizing at this time.

c. The War Communism Controversy

> In the sphere of distribution, the present task of Soviet power is to continue steadily replacing trade by the planned, organized, and nationwide distribution of goods . . . It is impossible to abolish money at one stroke in the first period of transition from capitalism to communism. . . . The R.C.P. will strive as speedily as possible to introduce the most radical measures to pave the way for the abolition of money, first and foremost to replace it by savings books, checks, short-term notes entitling the holders to receive goods from the public stores, and so forth . . . (LCW v29, 137–38)

From 1918 until 1921 the Bolshevik government pursued an economic policy which, after its abrupt abandonment, was posthumously baptised 'War Communism'. A proclaimed goal of this policy was to prepare for the permanent abolition of markets and money. Subsequent writing has interpreted the War Communism period in two opposing ways: either as a makeshift forced upon the Bolsheviks by circumstances or as a product of the Bolsheviks' Marxist ideas.

The 'makeshift' interpretation became the official account of the Soviet government, and therefore of the Communist Parties and their admirers in the West (Dobb 1948, 122; Webb and Webb 1935, 448–49; Carr 1980, 270–75), but it has also been endorsed by other Western scholars. In this view, which is reflected in the very name 'War Communism', the policies of War Communism did not constitute the attempt by a communist government to introduce communism. These policies were a pragmatic response to the emergency conditions of the time.

The makeshift hypothesis is now difficult to defend.[13] The Bolsheviks' proclaimed rationale for their seizure of power was that they were conducting a *socialist* revolution, going beyond the 'bourgeois-democratic' revolution, and Marxists viewed a socialist revolution as the abolition of commodity production. There are numerous state-ments by Bolshevik leaders during 1918–20 in which they unmistak-ably assert that they are abolishing commodity production and money, and that this is what socialist revolution means. It is sometimes implied that only extreme 'leftists' were responsible for such statements, but this is quite wrong.[14] *No* statements have been turned up in which any Bolshevik leader expressed reservations about the market-abolition scenario *at the time*.[15] At least some of the War Communism measures are extremely difficult to interpret as pragmatic responses to events. During War Communism, Lenin kept apologizing for the slowness of the movement towards socialism (LCW v27, 248, 253–255). When all fighting had ceased, the Bolsheviks stated that they could now move more rapidly with socialist measures, and it was at this point that the most extreme measures of 'War Communism' were implemented. When War Communism was abandoned, and a deliberate policy of permitting market forces some leeway was begun (the NEP), this was at first described as a defeat and a retreat for socialism, and the NEP was described as temporary, until the socialist advance could be re-sumed.[16]

In attenuated form, the makeshift hypothesis still has defenders (Nove 1969; Malle 1985). Although they accept that the Bolsheviks enthusiastically embraced the market-abolition measures, these writ-ers claim that such measures marked a departure from the more cautious policy pursued in the first few months of power. Nove claims that Lenin became emotionally caught up with the idea of immediate communism, against his better and earlier judgements. Malle emphasizes that the actual course of War Communism policies reflected the interplay of practical experience, differing opinions, and inter-group struggles. *Some* War Communism measures can be explained as responses to immediate circumstances. Lenin may have said and done things to placate extreme 'leftist' demands.

To put these arguments in perspective: It naturally took the Bolsheviks a few months to consolidate their power, so that they could seriously embark on the introduction of socialism. Lenin's writings in 1917 mainly reflect his 'April' measures (as advanced in *The Threatening Catastrophe and How to Combat it*)—'transitional' measures conceived as immediate steps towards socialism within a bourgeois-democratic framework. The 'April' measures were seen as well short of socialist revolution, and the Bolshevik regime was committed to socialist revolution. Some idea of what Lenin under-stood by a socialist revolution can be extracted from *State and*

Revolution. In some respects, War Communism never went as far as *State and Revolution* or Bolshevik intentions after taking power, which included universal equality of pay. No one claims that the actual detailed course of War Communism was charted out by Lenin in advance, though Malle makes a show of refuting this straw man. Any real-life attempt by Marxists to introduce communism would contain unexpected details. The Bolsheviks were firm believers in the theory that 'history' was driving them of necessity towards communism, so they were eager to find that 'circumstances' were 'compelling' them to introduce NFM socialism. As for Kollontai and others to the 'left' of Lenin, the mere fact that there was a vociferous tendency in the Communist Party which denounced the government for the tardiness and half-heartedness of War Communism is itself evidence of the grip that market-abolition ideas had on all the Bolsheviks.

An error running through much of this discussion is the habit of dividing human behavior into pragmatic actions determined by circumstances and ideologically-motivated actions determined by the actor's ideas. Every human action is determined by both circumstances and a guiding theory. If 'theory' is taken to include the actor's notions about circumstances and his values or objectives, then every intended action is always entirely determined by the actor's theory, though the action itself is determined by theory plus circumstances. When we say that an action was a response to circumstances, we mean that it was a response indicated by the theory held by the person responding—his theory of what the circumstances were and what his aims were. Circumstances by themselves never indicate any course of action.

A Muslim wants to undertake the *Haj* to Mecca, and decides to make part of the journey by plane. Due to a financial setback he has to revise his plans, and make that part of the journey by bus. Was this bus ride a 'makeshift', or was it motivated by 'religion'? Obviously both. Circumstances may make it impossible to go to Mecca at all this year, and our Muslim may try to compensate for this disappointment by more attention to study of the Koran. This is a different kind of makeshift. A Muslim may decide to go to Mecca for other than religious motives—say, because he thinks this will give him more respectability and hence more customers for his business. In this case, the journey is no longer (or not entirely) done for religious motives. But the other motives still arise from the person's 'theory', his beliefs and preferences.

When the word 'ideology' is used to characterize some ideas, this may be pejorative, or it may mean 'non-commonplace ideas'—often both. Thus, Nove (1969, 76–81) evidently assumes that, if the Bolsheviks were in their sober senses, they would take his own reasonable view of things. If they wanted to abolish the market, which he cannot deny that they said they did, and acted as if they did, extraordinary psychological stresses or 'ideological' factors in the sense of some crazily warped view of things requiring an exceptional explanation, must be brought in. The well-attested facts 1. that Marx saw socialism as a marketless society, and 2. that Lenin's rationale for his *coup* was the immediate commencement of the construction of Marxian socialism, are scarcely considered relevant. Supposing it to be true that the Bolsheviks in 1918 abandoned a more gradual strategy, then this phenomenon of rapid conversion from a slower to a quicker schedule for market abolition would still have to be explained chiefly in terms of the Bolsheviks' ideas prior to that conversion.

Malle states that "There are decisions that the Bolsheviks took at different moments, which may be explained without recourse to abstract principles. In some fields, decisions responded to long-standing aims, but were also conditioned by current circumstances" (Malle 1985, 23–24). No human action can be explained without recourse to the abstract principles in the minds of the actors. What Malle must mean is that some of the Bolsheviks' actions were determined by commonplace abstract principles, including aims we might expect most politicians to pursue, like staying in power and avoiding complete industrial collapse. This is undoubtedly true. But here we run into a complication. Like all Marxists the Bolsheviks held that their desire for socialism was not a good enough reason for introducing it. Socialism had to be implicit in the current stage of capitalism, and steps in the direction of socialism had to be demanded by 'practical' exigencies. The Bolsheviks' justification for their *coup* was socialist revolution. They took power eager to discover that urgent practical necessities would demand measures that constituted steps towards socialism, defined as production for use.[17]

— 4 —

THE DISCOVERY OF THE ECONOMIC CALCULATION PROBLEM

i. EARLY GLIMPSES OF THE PROBLEM

In 1776, Adam Smith argued that state planning of industrial life must be inefficient because the planners ("the sovereign") cannot respond knowledgeably to the local information available to market participants (Smith 1976; See below, 10.ii.b.). Smith, of course, was not confronted by demands for abolition of factor markets, and was not fully aware of the inter-relations of all markets via price-quantity relationships.

Hermann Heinrich Gossen wrote in 1854 that "Only under private property can the measure be found for placing a value on goods. Therefore the socialists would find that they had taken upon themselves a task to which they were not adequate" (Gossen 1983, 15). Gossen's work was overlooked by most economists for many years.

In the nineteenth and early twentieth centuries there were many anti-socialist writings, of varying quality. I do not allocate much space to most of these works because they miss the economic calculation argument, often relying heavily on arguments from motivation ("incentives") or from Malthus. Outstanding works in English are Mallock 1907 and Rae 1891.

The German economists of the 'young historical school' associated with the Verein für Sozialpolitik were dubbed "socialists of the chair" (*Kathedersozialisten*) by the liberal Heinrich Oppenheim, a potentially misleading characterization repeated by numerous subsequent liberals down through Mises, Hayek, and Rothbard. To understand the shock value of this term ('academic terrorists' captures more of the flavor in later usage), you have to be aware that no Social Democrat could expect to be allowed to hold an academic post, much less a chair, under the second Reich. The so-called

Kathedersozialisten were nearly all welfare-statists, opposed alike to socialism and to liberalism; that is, their political views were close to those of some Austrian economists, notably Wieser. Though the German writers shared common influences with Marxism and loathed the free market (the dreaded *Smithismus* and *Manchestertum*), they were mostly uncompromising in their view that socialism, as an alternative industrial system to capitalism, couldn't work. Hutchison says: "Their arguments were taken up in the 1920s by Mises and his followers", who "added a certain dogmatic extremism" (Hutchison 1981, 158). However, the earlier German writers do not clearly and explicitly isolate the economic calculation problem. They dwell heavily on incentives and general difficulties of administration, and attack the proposal to distribute income according to labor-hours[1] (See Schäffle 1881; 1892a; 1892b. On Brentano and Nasse, see Hutchison 1953, 293–98; Sheehan 1966).

ii. Wieser: The Two Services of Value

According to the economic calculation argument, any society which reaps the benefits of modern industry has to permit a functioning market in factors of production. This claim can be advanced in two stages, each evaluated separately: 1. Any modern industrial society has to organize its production so as to conform in certain respects to features which have been observed and classified in market societies; and 2. The only feasible way in which a society *could* conform to those features would be to rely on a functioning market.

We can make 1. more specific by saying, for instance, that such familiar market elements as rent, interest, and profit would have their analogues in any industrial society, or, if we suppose a hypothetical industrial society where the market is supplanted by society-wide planning, that the planners would have to employ book-keeping or computational categories analogous to rent, interest, and profit—leaving aside, in this stage of the argument, the issue of whether those categories would correspond to payments from one person or agency to another.

The early Marxists repudiated both 1. and 2. They acknowledged a few very broad similarities in the allocative pattern of communist and capitalist production, but did not accept any analogues of interest rates, rents, or wage differences under communism. (An internal Marxist dispute that flared up occasionally was whether economics as a science would cease to exist with capitalism—a view held by Luxemburg, Bukharin, and others, on the grounds that no scientific laws could hold where allocations were transparent and non-fetishistic). Marxism was born out of an intense conviction that these very fundamental market categories were just so much useless junk to be consigned to the scrap-heap, and that anyone who suggested otherwise was an imbecile or a rogue. Marxian socialism is characterized by what Landauer has aptly called "a revolt against the dictatorship of the balance sheet" (Landauer 1959, 1657), though Landauer misleadingly suggests that this revolt is identified only with rank-and-file socialist workers rather than socialist theoreticians. In recalling some of the precursors of Mises on economic calculation, we should therefore pay attention to some who argue for 1., without explicitly committing themselves to 2. The most striking of these is Friedrich von Wieser, in his *Natural Value* of 1889.

Natural Value is an outstanding work in the history of economic thought, a pioneering piece of economic theorizing whose subsequent reputation suffered because, around the same time, works were published by other economists (notably Clark and Wicksteed) which include most of its achievements, take its analysis further, and avoid its errors (see Stigler 1941). Wieser develops his argument throughout the book by criticizing socialist notions of 'value', in particular the ideas that socialist allocational principles could be radically different from capitalist ones and that labor-hours could be used as an accounting standard.

Wieser sets out to explain the returns to land, labor, and capital— that is, to all factors—in terms of the new marginal utility theory (Wieser originated the term *Grenznutzen*, 'border-use', which became Englished as 'marginal utility'). The value of consumer goods arises from consumers' subjective valuations, in relation to the stocks of goods available. The value of producer goods (factors) somehow derives from their anticipated contribution to future output of consumer goods. But where several factors co-operate, it seems impossible to split up the value of final output between the factors, since all are apparently necessary to the product. Some writers had actually declared it impossible to solve this riddle. Wieser, however, makes a bold attempt to solve it with his theory of 'imputation' (*Zurechnung*).

Wieser contends that behind the phenomena of price, including interest, profit, and rent, there lies a "natural value" which would have to govern allocation in any society. In the way Wieser develops

this concept, there is an unfortunate hangover from classical economics. He is concerned with a "value" which is not the same as
price nor clearly identified with, say, equilibrium price. It is something stable to which prices approximate. Thus, Wieser contends that
unstable, fluctuating prices do not represent value, and that such
features of the market as inequality of incomes cause prices to depart
from values (Wieser 1956, 61–62). The first of these could be
reconciled with the view of value as equilibrium or long-run price;
the second is arbitrary. Although Wieser's concept of 'value' is
untenable, his main point is correct: people's wants for goods, in
relation to their scarcity, impose principles which would have to
govern allocation in any society.

Wieser claims that no industrial society could operate by assuming
that only labor made a contribution to production: "Not for one day
could the economic state of the future be administered according to
any such reading of value; indeed the first preliminary arrangements
for its introduction would show its utter uselessness" (65). Rent,
interest, and profit would be necessary in socialism, claims Wieser,
but as he repeatedly points out, this does not mean that transfers of
resources, payments from some individuals to others, now called
'rent, interest, and profit' would necessarily have a place: "The
socialists continually overlook the fact—although, indeed, they only
follow in the footsteps of most of the economists—that value, in our
present condition of society, has two services to perform. The one is
to act as title to personal income. . . . The other . . . concerns the
economical balancing or weighing of goods against goods, and of
employment of goods against employment, without regard to distribution among persons, and simply with a view to reach the greatest
possible results" (162). It is this second function of 'value' with
which Wieser is exclusively concerned in *Natural Value*.

For instance, if a farmer has two fields, and works them equally
well with identical equipment, yet the one field proves consistently
more productive than the other, then it is clear that the additional
output from the more fruitful field should not be assigned to 'labor'
alone by the communist administration. Rather, the first kind of land
must be classified as making a bigger contribution to output than the
second kind, and because of that bigger contribution, the cost of
using the first land for non-agricultural purposes would be higher
than that of the second land (77ff). What is lost to society by using a
unit of the first land for non-agricultural purposes is greater than
what is lost by using a unit of the second land for non-agricultural

purposes. In the market, the first land would have a higher price (rent), which would constitute a payment of money to the owner. Yet supposing this payment abolished, communism would still have to attribute a 'rent' to the first land; it would have to be valued or costed higher than the second land.

Wieser argues that socialism will have to retain the second service of value (comparison and allocation) even though it dispenses with the first service. The later contention of Mises, Brutzkus, and Weber is that Wieser's second service cannot be performed without his first service, which NFM socialism excludes by definition. Wieser disavows any attempt to pronounce on the desirability or feasibility of socialism or communism: "The question whether such a community can or ever will exist is one which does not in the least concern us" (61n). Yet it is notable that he mentions this as a "question" at all. Wieser's argument doesn't imply that the two "services" of "value" *actually can* be separated, or that they cannot. Wieser foresees serious difficulties (34–36, 50, 213), but he leaves the question open. The inference that Wieser refuted Mises in advance (Heimann 1945, 93) is an extraordinary misunderstanding.

Wieser, a strong interventionist and welfare-statist, accords mathematical reasoning an important place in economic theory, though his own employment of mathematics is crude at best. Mises, whose political and methodological views are at odds with Wieser's, does not have a very high opinion of Wieser (Mises 1978, 35–36).

Wieser's general line of argument is advanced by several other writers more briefly, notably Böhm-Bawerk, Pareto, and Pareto's follower, Barone. Cassell (1903) and Fisher (1930) also claim that interest is indispensable in any industrial society.

The term 'imputation' has now dropped out of economic discussions, largely because economists take for granted that there are factor markets. Once that assumption is made, the distinction between 'imputation' and 'functional distribution' (the theory of how factor-owners are paid, or how their share in the value of output is determined) becomes unimportant. We can summarize the Mises argument as: No imputation without distribution, or more fully, No accurate imputation without distribution according to market prices, or yet again, No second service of value without the first service of value.

Whereas Wieser came close to a solution of the imputation problem, Wicksteed brilliantly solved it. Wicksteed always called himself a socialist, though the substance of his 'socialism' became thinner as his economic theory developed. Wicksteed refers to "the most difficult part of the collectivist problem": "If public bodies were the only employers, on what principle should remuneration of the different agents be fixed? Is it possible to conceive of any machinery by which the marginal significance of each should be determined without anything corresponding to the present system of free experimental combination and transference from group to group . . . ?" (1933, 682) Here Wicksteed comes close to stating the economic calculation problem, for if there's no way to determine the marginal significance of the various factors, then there's no way to select the least-cost combination, *leaving aside all question of remuneration.* Wicksteed seems to have been convinced that remuneration could not be severed from contribution; his 'socialism' came to consist of cautious piecemeal experiments with state-owned undertakings within a predominantly private market economy.

iii. PIERSON: VALUE AS AN INESCAPABLE PHENOMENON

Nikolaas G. Pierson was the most eminent Dutch economist of his day, and a sometime Prime Minister of Holland. His paper on 'The Problem of Value in the Socialist Community' was a direct reply to Kautsky's celebrated speech at Delft in 1902, which Pierson had attended. Pierson's paper, the first really clear exposition of the economic calculation problem, had very little influence until the 1920s, partly because it appeared in Dutch, and partly because its unassuming tone, its modest air of pointing out a few difficulties that would confront socialism, no doubt concealed from all the but the most attentive readers the possibility that these difficulties might be intractable. The true significance of the piece was probably further obscured by the fact that Pierson begins it (after a somewhat rambling introduction) by concentrating on the problem of how a socialist nation-state would conduct its foreign trade. There were still Marxists who denied that there could be such a thing as a socialist nation-state, or that there could be 'foreign trade' under socialism, but Pierson takes Kautsky's recent concessions as his point of departure. A further contribution to the piece's obscurity is that Pierson's textbook on economics (1912) briefly discusses socialism but makes no mention of the economic calculation problem.

Pierson states that he will not pronounce on "whether socialism can be carried into practice", but he challenges the socialist view that "value" will have no relevance in a socialist economy (Pierson 1935, 43). In order that trade between socialist nations will continue to be mutually beneficial, the national governments will have to find some way of valuing goods. Otherwise the movement of goods from one country to another will not be appropriately regulated according to the wants of the people in the various countries (55–67). Pierson suggests that under socialism trade between nations will have to be conducted on essentially the same principles as under capitalism: funds will still have to be borrowed, and interest paid on them; goods will be valued according to the services they render; and money and bills of exchange will still be employed.

He discusses national planning under socialism, assuming that "the division of income . . . is effected according to the most advanced method, that of communism" (70). A communist administration will have to distinguish gross income from net income. What Pierson means by this is that in order to ensure that there is net production—that more is yielded by the process of production than is destroyed therein, both in an individual project and in the totality of society's production—the administration will have to be able to measure outputs and inputs in common units. For, "we cannot subtract cotton, coal, and the depreciation of machines from yarn and textiles, we cannot subtract fodder from beast" (70). Yet if people consume more than they produce, "society has been impoverished" (70–71). The communist administration must be able to arrange things so that the amount produced equals or exceeds the amount consumed.

Now Pierson gets to the heart of the problem. Work can produce useful things and still be unproductive, wasteful, even destructive. Planting trees in an already richly-wooded area, or laying on a water supply where water is already abundant, "would not be production" (71). Pierson (not having witnessed Soviet 'industrialization', the Groundnuts Scheme, the Great Leap Forward, or the Ten Million Ton Sugar Harvest) concedes that such spectacular errors would not be committed. But less obvious, less easily discernable mistakes could be made, and work would not be production, but waste: "It is possible, for example, to miscalculate demand, to carry out works at too high a cost, to put up buildings in the wrong places and to design them in a manner inappropriate to their purpose" (71). There are examples in existing society where undertakings cost more than they realise in money. But these cases are exceptional; the money costs and money losses can be known (72–73).

What Pierson is driving at here is not the mere possibility that errors in production may occur. As he is aware, they are bound to occur in any society. His point is rather that in order to set up some system for avoiding or reducing such errors, it is imperative to be able to compare the "values" of many different kinds of goods. An administration which cannot make such comparisons cannot determine whether the resources used up amount to 'more' or 'less' than the goods produced, and if the administration cannot do that, it cannot determine whether a particular project is productive or wasteful.

Pierson supposes that individuals in communism will receive certificates, exchangeable at public stores. The communist administration (he says "State") will issue people with certificates, each certificate being a claim to a specific kind of product. Some individuals will find that they have certificates for goods they do not want, or that they want less than other goods. The "State warehouse" will therefore permit individuals to exchange some certificates for others. This involves fixing a "tariff" (an exchange-ratio between goods) as the basis for such exchanges. (It is not entirely clear whether Pierson means that the warehouse will itself conduct all the exchanges, or will permit the individuals to exchange among themselves, but most likely it is the former he has in mind. Although he doesn't say so, if the former were not permitted, the latter would certainly arise, whether 'permitted' or not. Neither does Pierson examine what would happen if all such "exchanges" were effectively prevented.

Not only will a "tariff" have to be determined; it will have to be changed repeatedly in response to changing conditions of supply and demand.

> Then price lists will be circulated which will tell us for how many cigar, tea, or coffee certificates we can buy other certificates. Thus the commercial principle, which such a society sought in vain to abolish, comes once more into the foreground. . . . The phenomenon of value can no more be suppressed than the force of gravity. What is scarce and useful *has value*. . . . to annihilate value is beyond the power of man. (75–76)

This passage is directed at the traditional Marxian view (Engels 1954, 430) that socialism will completely dispense with "value". Pierson also considers the proposal to pay workers in labor certificates, pricing consumer goods in labor-hours. Again, he argues that exchanges would have to occur. For example, some cabinets are better or worse than others, because produced by different cabinetmakers. A bad harvest of a particular crop would cause it to be in comparatively short supply. In numerous such cases, paying people equally in labor-hours would mean paying them unequally in fact, and in any case the goods which happened to fall into particular individuals' hands would sometimes be considered worth exchanging for others. Trade would emerge.

Pierson goes on to consider Kautsky's position, that wages under socialism will correspond to the productivity of labor. Kautsky had made this concession to the organizational principles of capitalism, but had failed to explain how, under socialism, the productivity of labor could be measured. In the absence of competitive markets, it is difficult to see how an assessment of the productivity of various forms of labor could be made.

It is possible that Pierson's argument here would have been easily misunderstood, for two reasons. 1. He refers to "manual labor", thus doing an injustice to the Marxists, who had always insisted that non-manual labor could be productive. 2. His readers may have assumed that he is concerned solely with the question of *rewarding* the different contributors to production, rather than with the problem of calculation. If we accept Kautsky's idea that workers will be rewarded in proportion to their productivity, this does not rule out the possibility that they will receive a part of what would in the market have gone to land- and capital-owners. Even were this so, it would be necessary to disentangle the contributions of land, labor, and capital factors, in order to gauge the productivity of various labor factors. Even if workers' incomes were not related to their productivity, it would still be necessary to know the productivities of different forms of work, in order to allocate labor factors. Pierson does not render this point sufficiently explicit. For instance, he supposes that 20 or 30 workers are producing in association, and a person joins them with knowledge they do not possess about technology and market conditions. Pierson asks: "is the work of this man not productive?" (82). However, a Social Democrat might have replied that this newcomer could just as easily be a state employee. The product of the knowledge he brings could be reflected in his wage, or partly treated as a 'social product' and spread around in higher wages for everyone. Leaving aside the question of whether that would be feasible, Pierson perhaps did not bring out strongly enough that, for allocative or planning purposes, this man's product, and the products of the 20 or 30 others, would have to be ascertained by the administration, whether or not it chose to follow Kautsky's proposal to make the productivity of different types of labor govern their wages.

iv. BARONE: PRODUCTION IS EXPERIMENTAL

An important precursor to Mises was Enrico Barone, who wrote on socialism in 1909. In a fatuous misreading, Barone's vigorous attack on socialism was for many years discussed as if Barone had attempted to demonstrate how socialism could work in practice.

Barone was a member of the 'Lausanne School' of Walras and Pareto. In 1874 Léon Walras (1954) showed how the general equilibrium of the market could be captured in a system of equations. All markets are inter-related. Thus, if the demand for steel rises, the price of steel will rise, and the quantity supplied of goods made with steel will fall. Thousands of remoter consequences will ensue, for example: other factors (plastic, wood, labor) will be substituted for steel in various applications, and the prices of goods made with these factors will rise, causing a reduction in the quantity demanded of goods made with these factors. In fact, there will be billions upon billions of adjustments of price and quantity consequent upon the rise in the demand for steel. Much of economics, especially in the tradition of Marshall, deliberately ignores most of these remote consequences most of the time. Thus, an increased demand for steel will lead to a higher price for steel, and a few other gross and obvious consequences—and the analysis normally stops there. The effects upon the markets for caviar or sheet music will not be examined, on the grounds that these are both difficult or impossible to trace and probably very slight. (Similarly, astronomy makes no attempt to analyze the gravitational effects of each asteroid or comet.) This 'partial equilibrium' analysis yields many results, some of them surprising and enlightening, which can be tested empirically (resulting in an impressive record of corroborations of price theory, at least equivalent to the empirical corroboration of any natural science). The Walrasian approach is to capture all the remoter effects as well, by means of a system of equations describing *all* markets and their inter-relations. It is out of the question to directly model any actual economy by this method, since the number of inter-relations among goods is too great, but it is hoped that certain general features of the whole economy may be established by manipulation of the equations in an illustrative fashion.

Just how informative the Walrasian approach may be remains controversial. In view of persistent misunderstandings, we should note that Walras never supposed that general equilibrium ever could be attained: innumerable new changes in the 'data' will always occur before adjustments have been completed. Walrasians recognize that all actual economies are characterized by continual disequilibrium, but they hope that analysis of the properties of general equilibrium may shed light on the direction of processes within actual markets. Pareto explicitly points out (1969, 171) that general equilbrium equations cannot be used to calculate actual prices. It is "absurd" to suppose that the information could be collected, and even a miniature economy of 100 individuals and 700 goods would require the solution of 70,699 equations. (More recently, Stigler [1987, 114] estimates the number at "easily 6×10^{13} equations for the American economy.") Pareto didn't bother to add that these would have to be solved afresh, with new data, every tiny fraction of a second, and that the results would still be of little practical use, since they wouldn't give the *path* to equilibrium.

Barone (1935) wants to show that any hypothetical socialist society could not avoid certain principles of allocation which operate within the market, and avoidance of which Barone takes to be a socialist objective. He first presents a series of equations for the equilibrium in a market economy, with given resources, and then argues that the same equilibrium would have to be reached in a socialist economy with the same resources, *if* the socialist administration both wants to maximize the satisfaction of people's wants, and is able to.

Barone employs the term "economic variability of the technical coefficients" to refer to the economic, rather than merely technical, aspect of efficiency. He contends that if the economic variability of the technical coefficients could be ignored, it would be "conceivable", though very costly in resources devoted to information-collection and computation, for the socialist administration to plan production by solving equations in advance. But it is "frankly *inconceivable*" (1935, 287) to take account of the economic variability of the technical coefficients in the same way, since the "determination of the coefficients economically most advantageous can only be done in an *experimental* way: and not on a *small scale*, as could be done in a laboratory; but with experiments on a *very large scale*" (288). The "creation of enterprises to be destroyed later" is therefore not peculiar to what the socialists call "anarchist" (market or capitalist) production (288). Barone here uses the term "*a priori*" to denote the organization of society-wide production by advance planning, an echo of Marx, who employed this term in just this sense (Capital I, 336).

Barone concludes that "all the economic categories of the old régime must re-appear, though maybe with other names: prices, salaries, interest, rent, profit, saving, etc." (289). Barone believes that he has shown "how fantastic those doctrines are which imagine that production in the collectivist regime would be ordered in a manner substantially different from that of 'anarchist' production" (289). He does not explicitly offer a judgment on whether socialism is at all possible, but he at least holds this open to doubt: "account must be taken of the necessary remuneration of the army of officials whose services would be devoted not to production but to the laborious and colossal centralization work of the Ministry (assuming the practical possibility of such a system)" (290).

v. Max Weber: Rational Calculation

The economic calculation argument was separately given a full and clear statement in 1920 by Max Weber, Boris Brutzkus, and Ludwig von Mises. It seems that none of the three knew beforehand of the similar argument of either of the other two, or of Pierson's and Barone's contributions. Weber, however, had already been impressed by Mises's earlier writings, and inserted a mention of Mises 1920, which appeared while Weber's own work was at the printer's (Weber 1978, 78, 107). In this case, the chief causes of the coincidence are clear: the growth of a powerful socialist movement in many countries, the accession to power of socialist parties in Russia, Hungary, Germany, and Austria, during 1917–1919, the attempt to introduce a communist economic order in Russia, which had to be openly abandoned in 1921 (and was already visibly in trouble by 1920), and the socialization debate in Germany and Austria, along with the manifest disorientation of the German Social Democrats and their accelerated retreat from Marxian notions of socialist revolution. Both Weber and Mises mention Neurath's arguments. In view of the voluminous debates anent both socialization and the Bolshevik policies, it is likely that Weber, Brutzkus, and Mises were each, rather than consciously propounding a new theory, restating what was already implicit in much previous discussion.

Weber's discussion is a small part of his major work *Economy and Society*, concerned with the definition and clarification of sociological concepts. The general framework of his remarks is dubious: he distinguishes economic from non-economic action in a way which has since been rendered obsolete by Robbins (Robbins 1935; and see Kirzner 1976). Weber is also concerned to distinguish "formal" from "substantive" rationality of economic action (1978, 85). The meaning of this distinction seems to be roughly this: formal rationality refers to the existence of accurate or competent calculations; substantive rationality refers to how well-adapted those calculations are to serving human purposes.

Like Mises, Weber was prompted to make his argument by Otto Neurath's writings. Weber agrees with Neurath's contention that a completely socialized, planned economy must be a natural (moneyless) economy. Technically or formally, says Weber, money is the most perfect means of economic calculation (86). Without money, calculation purely in physical units can be performed where wants "are strictly given" and "so long as the situation does not require a very precise estimate of the comparative utility to be gained from the allocation of the available resources to each of a large number of very heterogeneous modes of use" (87–88). Otherwise, scope for accurate calculation is limited, and even the simple, self-sufficient household faces problems, solved partly by tradition and partly by "very rough estimates".

The problems become more difficult with changes in wants and production conditions, with growing complexity, and with the decline of purely traditional standards. Given monetary calculation, costs can be assessed in money terms, but with moneyless calculation, all the different ways of using all means of production have to be taken into account. Weber suggests that the limitations of non-monetary calculation account for the fact that it has generally "remained strongly bound to tradition" (89), and that where such calculation has become large-scale, production surpluses have been used for "non-routine", especially artistic, purposes. Non-monetary economies have not been able very effectively to channel productive improvements into the greater satisfaction of "ordinary" wants, because this would require a major change in the allocation of resources, which these economies were unable to co-ordinate.

Weber then turns to a summary of capital accounting, noting that in the market, "every form of rational calculation, especially of capital accounting, is oriented to expectations of prices and their changes" (92). He observes that no economic system, even communism, "can directly translate subjective 'feelings of need' into effective demand, that is, into demand which needs to be taken account of and satisfied through the production of goods" (93), because there has to be a weighing of all the wants against other wants and against the different possible uses of means for satisfying them. Weber adds that "fictitious prices" and "mere tokens used as purely technical accounting units" will not suffice (93). His point here is that all capital accounting is related to anticipations of monetary income, and this income derives from the spending decisions of consumers.

Some calculations, even within the market, can be done in kind, but alternative production methods are compared "by making a calculation of comparative profitability in terms of money costs" (102). For "accounting in kind", says Weber, "there are formidable problems involved here which are incapable of objective solution." Even in cases where calculation in kind could apparently be employed, monetary calculation can do what calculation in kind cannot do, for example: estimating reserves for depreciation, in cases where the means of production requiring replacement might change. Monetary calculation makes it much easier to detect possibilities for improvements and cost-cutting. To do this by calculations in kind can be accomplished "only in very simple cases". This is not "a matter of circumstances which could be overcome by technical improvements in the methods of calculation". Exact acounting with calculation in kind is "impossible in principle" (102). Complete socialization leads to the disappearance of "effective prices" and therefore of accurate calculation. Science cannot pronounce on whether this loss would be worth it, for the sake of the ethical benefits of socialism, but:

> the possibility must be considered that the maintenance of a certain density of population within a given area may be possible only on the basis of accurate calculation. Insofar as this is true, a limit to the possible degree of socialization would be set by the necessity of maintaining a system of effective prices. (105)

Weber rejects the argument of Neurath that the German war economy has shown the possibility of efficient calculation in kind. In the war, everything was subordinated to a single goal: the postwar repercussions were sacrificed to the all-important attempt to win the war. Weber also refers to various departures from market pricing under the existing system. The complete absence of market prices would be more serious. The socialist idea that all the people working in financial calculations could transfer their energies to "a universal Statistical Office which would have the function of replacing the monetary business accounting of the present system with a statistical accounting in kind" confuses statistics with business accounting. These differ in both motive and function (107).

vi. BRUTZKUS: THE FAILURE OF BOLSHEVISM

Boris Brutzkus was an economist caught up in the Russian revolution, the subsequent Bolshevik *coup*, and the attempt by the Bolsheviks to usher in a communist order. In August 1920 the Bolsheviks were at their hour of greatest glory. They had defeated in the field all those prepared to resist them, including the token military forces sent to Russia by five foreign powers, and fastened their own unchallenged rule onto the Russian empire. The abolition of money was in progress. The national budget was calculated in labor-hours. The communist industrial structure was taking shape. Dislocations of production and mass starvation could still be blamed on the recent wars. At this moment, Brutzkus delivered a lecture to an academic audience in Petrograd, arguing that communism was "intrinsically unsound and must inevitably break down" (Brutkus 1935, xv).[2]

Any economic activity, argues Brutzkus, "must obey the principle that its results must correspond to the costs expended upon them" (9). In a small-scale natural economy this is fairly straightforward. In the capitalist system, the principle is followed by making sure that goods can be sold at a price which covers their costs of production. "This evaluation takes place by virtue of a spontaneous process, the results of which must be taken by the entrepreneur as data." Under socialism, economic calculation is of even greater importance:

> The capitalist entrepreneur may, if he likes, keep no books at all. So much the worse for him. . . . If he wastes the forces of production he will pay for his folly with his fortune and his social position. Not so in the socialist society. If a large-scale concern is conducted without the assistance of proper calculation, its manager may nevertheless lead an untroubled life, however great may be the waste of society's means of production . . . . It is true that milk is produced, bread is baked, rolling-stock is repaired, and coal is transported; but no one is able to say how much these processes cost us. This state of affairs necessarily led the economic system towards catastrophe, and the catastrophe has come about. (11–13)

The socialist administration would have to quantify everyone's needs and then specify the means for attaining them. Brutzkus argues that even to measure the population's requirements for foodstuffs would be extremely difficult, and to estimate all their needs would be beyond the capabilities of any administrative body

(37-44). But this is not the main problem. In the market, enterprises must pay their way or close down, but under socialism, "there exists no direct connection between the productivity of an undertaking and the supply of funds for its continuance" (45). Nor could there be, for under socialism there is no general measure of value (45-46).

Brutzkus presents a number of arguments aside from the economic calculation question. He points out that if the socialist authorities accept the need to keep material rewards for work in proportion to the productiveness of the work, they will be bound to introduce rent, interest, and profit. He argues that there are no grounds to expect any enhancement of personal freedom, much less the abolition of the state, from any attempt at socialist planning, and he questions the view that people will work more enthusiastically in a socialist society. Finally, Brutzkus claims that condititions in Russia, with its self-sufficient isolation and highly-concentrated industry, have been rather favorable to the institution of socialism. Consequently, its failure there is an especially conclusive refutation.

vii. Mises: The Market's Intellectual Division of Labor

In the 1920s, Mises enjoyed a considerable reputation among economists, mainly on the strength of his 1912 book on money.[3] That reputation was to be almost completely lost by the late 1930s, never to be recovered. Today Mises is of minor interest to historians of economic thought and has a comparatively small band of enthusiastic followers—his rating among mainstream economists is not much better than Marx's.

'Economic Calculation in the Socialist Commonwealth' first appeared in 1920, in the *Archiv für Sozialwissenschaft*, where so many ideas that were to shape twentieth-century thought were first mooted (see Factor 1988). Two years after its publication in the *Archiv*, Mises's piece was incorporated in his *Die Gemeinwirtschaft*, later translated as *Socialism: an Economic and Sociological Analysis*, which became an important source for European anti-socialism,[4] though it had little direct impact in the Anglo-Saxon world. 'Economic Calculation in the Socialist Commonwealth' appeared in English in 1935 and *Socialism* in 1936.

By the Second World War, the view that Lange had refuted Mises was becoming standard, and after the war, perceptions were much colored by the prevailing belief that Russia was both socialist and industrially successful. In the 1920s, European socialists took Mises's argument seriously, and he was able to reply to some of their objections in *Die Gemeinwirtschaft* and elsewhere. Later, Hayek and Robbins were viewed as the bearers of the Mises torch, and Mises's later writings on economic calculation—notably the second edition of *Die Gemeinwirtschaft* and his section on socialism in *Human Action*—were almost entirely ignored by his opponents. But in the 1920s it was Mises who delivered a palpable jolt to socialists. Oskar Lange (1938, 57) suggests that so great has been the stimulus Mises has given to socialist economics that a statue of him ought to occupy an honorable place in the great hall of the socialist society's Central Planning Board. The statue has not materialized, but neither has any Central Planning Board of the sort envisaged by Lange. The non-existence of Lange's great hall is more of a tribute to Mises than the erection of his statue within it might have been.

Mises's article is somewhat casually organized, and is dotted with the testy irony which so nettles his adversaries (socialists "invariably explain how, in the cloud-cuckoo lands of their fancy, roast pigeons will in some way fly into the mouths of the comrades, but they omit to show how this miracle is to take place"). Despite, or because of, these features, the argument is lucid and unambiguous, and it is remarkable that it should have been so frequently misread.

Mises explains at the outset that the administrative or political structure of socialist society is "of subsidiary importance" (1935, 89) and he makes clear that the way in which consumer goods are distributed is a secondary matter, though he provides some discussion of this (89–95). Like Pierson, he points out that once individuals in a socialist society have collected their "coupons", trade will emerge. But this trade will be confined to consumer goods. Production-goods (factors), because they will be owned by "the community", cannot be subject to commercial transactions:

> just because no production-good will ever become the object of exchange, it will be impossible to determine its monetary value. Money could never fill in a socialist state the rôle it fills in a competititve society in determining the value of production-goods. Calculation in terms of money will here be impossible. (92)

Under simple conditions, "a farmer in economic isolation" or Robinson Crusoe would not only value consumer goods but would also be able to impute value to production goods (96). Mises means here that if grain were valued, so would be a plow; if fish, a fishing-net; if wild boar, a spear; and so forth. Even at such a simple level, the producer would have to take account of "the intersubstitutability of goods" (97). Crusoe would have to make a rough-and-ready estimate of the importance of factors, but he would not be able to calculate costs of production in money prices. Neither would he have access to any units which could aid him in assessing whether a contemplated course of action (such as building a highly elaborate boar trap with materials that could be used for other purposes) were worth it. The isolated farmer can calculate his costs because

> the processes of production involved are relatively short and the expense and income entailed can be easily gauged. But it is quite a different matter when the choice lies between the utilization of a water-course for the manufacture of electricity or the extension of a coal-mine or the drawing up of plans for the better employment of the energies latent in raw coal. Here the roundabout processes of production are many and each is very lengthy . . . (96)

With the tremendous increase in complexity, vague estimates are no good. Exact calculation becomes necessary, and this requires units for the valuation of factors. But subjective utility (the satisfaction derived from consumer goods) does not offer any such units, since the utility of any good varies with the stock (96). In a society with complex technology, economic calculation is performed by reference to "the objective exchange-value of commodities": market prices expressed in money. The use of market prices, claims Mises, "entails a threefold advantage": calculation can be based upon the valuations of all participants in trade; monetary profitability gives an immediate indication of economical production; and values can be referred to a common unit. It is not enough to be able to value consumer goods, because

> No single man can ever master all the possibilities of production, innumerable as they are, as to be in a position to make straightway evident judgements of value without the aid of some system of computation. The distribution among a number of individuals of administrative control over economic goods . . . entails a kind of intellectual division of labour, which would not be possible without some system of calculating production and without economy. (102)

Second, there must be "a universally employed medium of exchange", money, used in the exchange of factors of production as well as consumer goods. Otherwise it would be impossible to reduce all the many exchanges to a common unit.

It is no use, says Mises, appealing to existing examples of "socialism", such as nationalized and municipalized enterprises, for these are only islands of state direction within an environment of commerce; they have access to information about what works and what doesn't work in private concerns. Furthermore, socialism cannot merely continue what was done previously within the market, for with changing conditions, the old methods of production will "become irrational" (105).

Because the socialist planners will be unable to reduce all the factors of production to a common denominator, they will be confined to hazarding "vague estimates". Under socialism, as in a modern market economy, most factories will be engaged in producing factors or unfinished consumer goods (106). Mises considers the building of a new railroad for freight traffic: "Should it be built at all, and if so, which out of a number of conceivable roads should be built?" (108) Within the market, this can be decided by comparing the reduction in transportation costs with the construction and maintenance of the railroad. It cannot be decided rationally without expressing both of these in common units, and that means, on the side of construction and maintenance, being able to express "hours of labour, iron, coal, all kinds of building material, machines", and numerous other things in a common unit. Mises claims that the possibility of exact calculation disappears along with the free market system: "Where there is no free market, there is no pricing mechanism; without a pricing mechanism, there is no economic calculation" (111). The reference here to a "free market" can be confusing, since a free market has rarely if ever existed, yet most of the time Mises is comparing socialism with the existing capitalist system.

Mises asserts that what he calls "the static state" (stationary equilibrium) "can dispense with economic calculation" (109). The static state is an imaginary construction employed by economic theoreticians, in which equilibrium has been reached and therefore all change ceases. It cannot exist in reality because "our economic data are for ever changing". But even if it were feasible to freeze all the data, the transition to socialism itself will "change all economic data in such a way that a connecting link with the final state of affairs in the previously existing competitive economy becomes impossible" (110). Here, at the outset of the economic calculation debate, Mises recognizes that socialism is logically and 'theoretically' possible under unrealistic conditions—for example, where there is no longer any need to adapt to change. It is change in what economists call the 'data' of the economic system (consumers' preferences, stocks of goods, and technology) which requires economic calculation, and therefore, according to Mises, requires market prices.

As a possible way out, Mises considers the division of industry into branches controlled by "syndicates" permitted to trade with each other. However, no factor prices could emerge except where the syndicates' autonomy was such that they held *de facto* property rights in their means of production: "This would not be socialization but workers' capitalism and syndicalism" (112). By "workers' capitalism", Mises means a market economy in which all firms are producers' co-operatives (see Chapter 14 below). A defining feature of socialism, for Mises, is the non-existence of factor markets because of the non-existence of private ownership of the means of production. 'Private ownership' evidently includes ownership by groups, as long as these groups have an autonomous right to dispose of their assets, so that they can engage in genuine trade.

Mises goes on to make some comments about "responsibility and initiative" in socialist enterprises (116–122). This passage is cast in terms of an incentives argument, even though it touches on an aspect of the economic calculation argument which Mises could have broached. Mises discusses the popular socialist idea that, just as directors work on behalf of the shareholders under capitalism, so under socialism they will work on behalf of society as a whole. Mises says that in smaller companies the directors generally are the shareholders, whereas in larger companies it is possible for the directors to run the concern in a way that opposes the shareholders' interests. However, the managers may still own some shares, or may hope to, and "are in a position to obtain profits by stock-exchange speculation in the company's shares" or by what is now called 'insider trading'. This discussion is unsatisfactory. The important thing for Mises to have emphasized here is surely that in the market the assets of the company have a capital value, the value of their expected future income. Mises could have argued that no socialist enterprise or department could be valued in the same way, since the assets of the enterprise are not freely traded. This market valuation of the company and of its assets is also the key to understanding the relation between managers and shareholders. The shareholders can always sell their shares. That they have not done so shows that they think their savings are in the place which will yield the best return. If the managers do not act for the shareholders by maintaining their expected future incomes, the values of the shares will decline. Presumably investors continue to patronize (buy shares in) corporations with a certain kind of structure (including a management with considerable independence from most shareholders) because that structure is advantageous to them in some way—maybe corporations with that structure out-produce corporations where the managers are more tightly reined in by the shareholders. Similar information about asset values could not be available for the socialist enterprise. Instead of developing some argument such as this, Mises lapses into an incentives argument.

After a brief review of the latest remarks of Otto Bauer and Lenin on the running of a socialist economy, Mises concludes by declaring that although "rational economic activity is impossible in a socialist commonwealth", this need not deter those socialists motivated by ascetic ideals, nor those prepared to abandon material affluence for the sake of an ethical goal. Mises doesn't dispute that a form of "socialism" may be possible at a low level of production and living standards, but he doesn't dwell on this, since the main thrust of socialist argument is that socialism will produce more than capitalism, not far less.

— 5 —

RE-READING MISES ON ECONOMIC CALCULATION

i. Misesian Apriorism

> In connection with the exaggerated claims that used to be made in economics for the power of deduction and *a priori* reasoning—by classical writers, by Carl Menger, by the 1932 Lionel Robbins . . . , by disciples of Frank Knight, by Ludwig von Mises—I tremble for the reputation of my subject. Fortunately we have left that behind us. (Samuelson 1964, 736)

Suppose that a busy commuter rail line is put out of action by an earthquake or a strike. It is natural to expect, or predict, that the roads close to the rail line will then experience heavier traffic than usual. This prediction is both obvious and fallible. Various possible circumstances can be listed which might falsify the prediction: strikers are picketing the roads; rumor of plague in the city causes commuters to stay at home; the habitual rail travellers are all members of a religious sect which forbids travel by car or bus. We know what would count as a circumstance falsifying the prediction. *We can thus formulate our prediction in such a way that it cannot be falsified.* A start in this direction would be: 'If certain individuals want to go to the city (or achieve any goal), and if the best means to execute this plan becomes unavailable, they will employ the next-best means'. More qualifications would be needed to make the formulation watertight: 'want' would have to be defined to exclude idle wants which individuals don't act upon; we would have to look at why road was second-best to rail, and exclude the possibility that whatever makes it only second-best were sufficient to cancel the desire to go to the city. And so forth. By careful definition, we could arrive at a statement of the form 'If conditions a, b, c . . . hold, then action p will be performed'. This new statement is neither obvious nor fallible. There is no question of testing this 'law' by empirical observations. The law follows from the assumptions, and any failure of the facts to confirm the law must be due to misidentification of the facts. Thus, such a law seems unlike a 'law of nature' in the usual sense, for such physical laws could be contradicted by statements describing factual observations. The law has more of the quality of a geometric theorem.

What gives our revised statement about the increase in road traffic its irresistible certainty? Mises and his followers think that such statements follow from apodictic truths about human nature, which they identify with Kant's "synthetic *a priori*". Mises proposes that there is a whole science of human action, called 'praxeology',[1] made up of such reasoning, founded on a few synthetic *a priori* propositions, and that this science includes the whole of economic theory. This has led Mises and his followers to take up positions which astonish other economists: most striking is the view that it is useless to test economic theory by prediction or observation; it can be tested only by scrutinizing the reasoning employed. Other singular Misesian positions include the claims that all human action is rational, and that mathematics is always out of place in economics (see Mises 1966, 11–41; 1960, 23–35; Rothbard 1957; 1962, 1ff; 1976).

The prevailing methodology among economists is unsympathetic to Misesian apriorism, and has become steadily less sympathetic since the 1930s. It is generally held that all economic theories are empirical laws which could be falsified by observations. Many economists subscribe to views akin to those of Friedman 1953, which seemingly constitute an extreme form of operationalism (but see Hirsch and de Marchi 1990). According to this popular neoclassical view, it does not matter whether the 'assumptions' of a theory are 'realistic' (that is whether the theory is true). All that matters is whether the theory yields predictions capable of being borne out by observations. Adherents of this view don't deny that they sometimes employ introspection and surmise in a quasi-praxeological manner, but they classify these mental operations along with intuition, in generating hypotheses without being able to arbitrate among them.

Yet Misesian and neoclassical approaches are more alike than might appear. In deciding where to apply a theory, the Misesian has to examine the facts to see which theory is applicable. There is thus an interaction between observation and application of the theory. Misesian praxeology is useless without a further body of theory identifying those aspects of reality to which various portions of praxeology can be applied. *This* theory (of the applicability of praxeology) is subject to empirical refutation. The Misesian claim achieves a more startling impression by the definitional fiat of excluding the applicability theory from economics. The Misesian consigns much of what the neoclassicists might call 'economics' to the categories 'history' and 'technology' (Dolan 1976, 14–15).

If we step back from the various schools of economic methodology, we see that virtually all economic theorizing consists of two components: 1. a 'story' of what happens under certain circumstances, and 2. an examination of 'the facts' to see how they fit the story. The alleged relationship between the story and the facts is what is controversial. The Misesian apriorist view appears as one in which, if we are careful about the story, even without checking against the facts, then the facts must conform to the story. Praxeology in 'history' (which includes all applied economics) is therefore seen as analogous with mathematics in physics: a system of postulates and deductive relationships which cannot be refuted by empirical findings, but is a useful tool for the interpretation of empirical findings.

The Misesian or praxeological view is sometimes called the 'Austrian' methodology, but no Austrian predecessor of Mises held any such view, nor has it been held by many recent Austrian-school economists, for instance Hayek, Lachmann, or Machlup. There is obviously a historical connection with the Austrian school's nineteenth-century struggle to vindicate the importance of pure theory, but the frequent attribution of the Misesian view to Carl Menger (for example by Selgin 1988) is mistaken. The Misesian conception is more akin to that of Cairnes or even Senior.

Praxeology is an important element in economic theory, for it emphasizes the importance of having a story, and of looking carefully at the story and at what follows from the story. The Misesian conception of all action as rational in a minimal sense is also sound and important. The rejection of this approach on the grounds that it is empty because compatible with any human behavior is no more persuasive than a similar rejection of Newton's laws of motion, on the grounds that they are vacuous since compatible with any observed behavior of particles.

However, the Misesian view that praxeology gives us the whole of economic theory as self-evidently true without any need for empirical test is misconceived. The theory of applicability of praxeology is an empirical theory, and without an applicability theory, praxeology is worthless. This fact has repercussions at all levels of analysis. Thus, although praxeology generates many interesting conclusions about 'money', it does not automatically settle arguments about just which credit instruments are to be regarded, in a modern economy, as money. And at the simplest level of an individual with a set of ends and means, establishing the identity and the stability of the ends and means can only be an empirical enterprise.

In Kirzner's discussion of an example from Tagliacozzo, a man gives in to the sudden impulse to throw his glass of wine at the bartender (Tagliacozzo 1945; Kirzner 1976, 169–172). This can be characterized as the switch from one rational means-ends framework (to sit quietly drinking at the bar) to another rational means-ends framework. The man does not, for example, wildly flail his limbs as in an epileptic fit but has a distinct purpose in view and rationally adjusts his actions to that (as it happens, arguably foolish and ill-conceived) end. Yet, if an individual were in the habit of switching to radically new ends, say, every half-second, it would be difficult to explain his actions by the application of praxeology. (Naturally, it may plausibly be claimed that many of the social regularities we witness would be unthinkable, or even that no social order could survive, if many individuals were so constituted, but this introduces quite a different form of argument for the applicability of praxeology; it is no longer claimed to be apodictically true of every instance of human action, but instead broadly and contingently true of human action in general.)

Furthermore, it is a stubborn empirical fact that individuals do *not* always conform even to the lean requirements of Misesian 'action'. There is a story about a man who, given the choice between cheesecake and chocolate cake, chose cheesecake. Then the waiter came back and said the restaurant did, after all, have a third option, carrot cake. The man replied: 'In that case, I'll have chocolate cake.' Although this is recognizably a joke, people can indeed be that muddled, and almost everyone is, once in a while. Observations show that individuals' preferences are not always consistent. (See the examples cited in Frank 1991, 226–246. Although Frank subscribes to a definition of rationality more restrictive than Mises's, some of these examples look like counter-instances to the Misesian definition too.) A determined praxeologist can account for every vagary (as Mises did: 1966, 103) by positing a different end-means scheme in each case, and in this way rescue the apodictic certainty of praxeology, but this would be at the cost of rendering it inapplicable because all too promiscuously applicable. Just as with Euclid's geometry, the praxeology that is apodictically true tells us nothing about empirical reality, whilst the praxeology that tells us something about reality is not apodictically true. Our revised statement about heavier road traffic is indubitably true in the sense that it follows inexorably from the axioms. As a prediction about reality, it may be false.

The frequent references by Misesians to the analogy between praxeology and geometry (such as Mises 1966, 38) can be taken seriously. There are infinitely many possible geometries, Euclid's being one that has been extremely useful. Within Euclidean geometry, such propositions as Pythogoras's Theorem are necessarily true because analytic: they follow from the axioms. When converted into empirical claims, such theorems become open to falsification, and indeed now seem to be false (though close approximations to the truth). Different axioms will give us different geometries.

Praxeology has a similar status, and can claim no more. Praxeologists are not entitled to wax 'more realistic than thou' anent the 'assumptions' of neoclassical economists. Misesians often denounce indifference curves for their unrealism, but the Misesian conception of an individual with a consistent, stable ordering of preferences is, also, literally false if taken as a claim about every individual at all times.

The pure Misesian analysis of action (or 'logic of choice') has to be informed by the awareness that certain of the axioms (such as transitivity of preferences) are not necessarily true and none of the axioms can be applied to observable reality except with the aid of auxiliary assumptions (such as the scrutability and stability of preferences). Once this fact is faced, the praxeologist can legitimately derive support from the observation that many of the particular counter-instances to the axioms, or to their application, are unusual, and that therefore the theory is more likely to be true where large numbers of people are involved than in the case of any particular individual at a particular time and place.

The application of a praxeological theorem turns it into an empirical theory. The axioms may not hold in particular cases, or may be wrongly identified. It follows that there is no sharp distinction between the axioms and any chosen axioms which appear to be useful. For example, it is a well-known fact that people with higher incomes generally save a higher proportion of their incomes than do people with lower incomes. Mises comments that there is "a grain of truth in such observations. However, they are statements about psychological facts and as such lack the universal validity and necessity inherent in praxeological statements" (1966, 533). Mises goes on to assert that nineteenth-century French peasants were "widely known for their parsimonious habits" while the rich "were no less renowned for their profligacy", so that the generalization about the relation of saving to income is not universally true. Leaving aside the cavalier technique of refutation by appeal to folklore, there is nothing to forbid the development of a theory which applies only to those circumstances where the rate of saving increases with income. The possibility may have to be investigated that in some particular instance this condition does not hold, but this is not really so very different from the case of 'praxeological statements'. In either case, we have a set of axioms, whose applicability to any observable is always tentative and fallible, from which certain theorems can be deduced. There is no requirement that the axioms all have to be implicit in the definition of action. We can add any axioms we like, based on pure surmise, and drop them only when they fail to test out well. (It would be progress if we could establish the more fundamental conditions which determine whether the saving rate rises with income, especially if we could associate these conditions with observables, and thus predict when the rule will hold and when not.)

Does this lead us to embrace the extremely anti-Misesian contention that 'the realism of the assumptions doesn't matter'? 'Unrealistic assumptions' is a euphemism for false assumptions. If 'the assumptions' are part of the theory, then false assumptions mean that the theory is false. The claim, then, is that it doesn't matter whether the theory is false. The claim is usually followed up with the assertion that 'what really matters is whether the theory predicts well'. But if the assumptions are part of the theory, then the theory predicts its own assumptions, and is immediately refuted if one of its assumptions is shown to be false. There can be no worse predictive performance for any theory than for it to be found to require a false assumption: the theory is immediately a failure, as far as prediction goes. We can instead say that 'the assumptions' are not part of the theory, but then it is not clear that the theory needs the 'assumptions'. If the assumptions are expository mnemonics not implied by the theory, or metaphysical views that people who hold the theory find congenial, then there is no reason why they need to be true.

What seems to lie behind this fashionable doctrine is the commonly encountered situation where markets appear to work more efficiently than they ought, on grounds of commonsense conjecture, to do. For example, in the 1960s customers at various neighbouring gas stations were interviewed about gas prices at those stations, and it was found that they were largely ignorant of these. But when the behavior of the customers was studied, the competitive process worked as if they were very well informed about alternative prices. The assumption that entrepreneurs make decisions to maximize profits is a good predictor of business behavior, but it seems obvious that not all entrepreneurs, all the time, are uninfluenced by any other consideration. Again, analysis in terms of marginal concepts explains business behavior quite well, but investigation shows that many business decision-makers are largely ignorant of marginal concepts and never consciously employ them. From such examples, many economists draw the correct conclusion that inaccurate assumptions about people's behavior may be useful. But this conclusion doesn't mean that the truth of assumptions may be ignored, nor does it mean that we can simply brush aside questions of the kind 'Given what we think we know about human motivation, how could that possibly be the case?'

An example may be taken from evolutionary biology, which sees organisms conducting 'strategies' in order to maximize reproductive profitability. (Such analyses now routinely employ cost and revenue curves, which illustrates the falsity of the claim often implied by Misesians that there is an unbreachable link between such concepts and subjective conscious purposes.) No biologist imagines that all organisms consciously formulate 'strategies', but the strategies remain excellent tools of analysis. This certainly does not mean that 'the assumptions don't matter' or that the biologists' theory commits them to holding false theories. Rather, the biologists hold that there exists a true explanation (known or not) for the predictive power of the 'strategy' model. It is a reasonable and permissibile question just how it can be that the organism behaves in conformity with a postulated 'strategy', though sometimes it may be fruitful to concentrate on the strategies and treat the precise mechanisms as an unexplained 'black box'. The knowledge that the strategies are the outcome of minute differences in little bits of DNA, selected by many generations of differential reproductive success, provides general guidance to the kind of explanation that may be acceptable (for example, some strategy that could not have developed by minute increments, or some strategy that involves looking ahead to remote consequences for the population as a whole, is ruled out).

All this has its analogue in the case of economics. It is unexceptionable to explain human behavior by a model that cannot be true, provided it is recognized that there does have to be some explanation —whether we know it or not—of why reality corresponds with the predictions of the model, if it does. The theorist is not committed to evident falsehoods, because the theorist is aware of a more complete statement of the theory, which we hope may be true, or a good approximation to the truth. Thus, the theorist can say that profit maximization is a good model without asserting that entrepreneurs always maximize profits. The theorist can reasonably be asked how it can be that the outcome of people acting without maximizing profits can be so close to the outcome we might expect if they did always maximize profits (and such theories as the 'survivor principle' can be offered as answers). Part of an explanation for why gas station customers in the aggregate behave as if they were more knowledgeable than they seem to be could be that a few individuals are alert to prices and others follow their advice.

Misperceptions of Mises's economic calculation argument may have arisen because of the conviction that he was offering an aprioristic proof that NFM socialism was unworkable. Although Mises may have thought he was doing this, he in fact offered no such proof. For example, Mises's key claim that "the bewildering mass of intermediate products and potentialities of production" is too complicated for the human mind to grasp without prices is a 'factual' premiss, not a proposition deduced from the very notion of human action. Indeed, it seems that almost any general appraisal of institutions cannot be demonstrated on entirely aprioristic grounds. In the market there is a lot of tacking about, and the opinion often held by socialists that the aggregate outcome of all this tacking about is less efficient than collective pursuit of a goal, cannot be refuted by praxeology alone (it may possibly be refuted by a combination of praxeology with observations).

Mises doesn't offer any 'proof' that NFM socialism cannot work.[2] The Mises argument is best seen as a bold claim, challenging refutation by a possible counter-instance, coupled with a story or set of stories about certain kinds of human interactions which illustrates how the bold claim might be true. The bold claim is that no account can be given of any method by which NFM socialism could come close to being as efficient as the market. After 70 years of criticism, this claim has not been toppled.

Mises sometimes seems to phrase his argument as though all the activities of the NFM socialist administration must be utterly senseless or totally lacking in rationale. He never tries to argue for this proposition, which is more ambitious than anything he needs to support his argument. The grossly inadequate is distinguishable from the totally lacking in rationale. If I jump as high as I can, in an endeavor to reach the Moon, this is not totally lacking in rationale. The NFM socialist administration need not be totally lacking in rationale. For example, if an epidemic suddenly wiped out most of the world's cotton crop, the socialist administration might infer that the cost index of cotton and its close substitutes should be immediately raised. Though they couldn't know the precise amount of these increases, it is reasonable to suppose that 50 percent increases would probably be better than 90 percent decreases.

ii. The Misesian Typology of Economic Systems

a. Mises's Analysis of Interventionism

Mises employs the mutually exclusive terms 'socialism', 'capitalism', 'syndicalism', and 'interventionism' in conformity with his distinctive taxonomy of economic systems. Although Mises makes criticisms of syndicalism and interventionism, he considers that his arguments specifically against socialism have succeeded if, in response, socialists propose modified 'socialist' systems which he classifies as syndicalist or interventionist.

Taken together, Mises's broad judgments on these four systems appear to lead to an arresting conclusion. In his comments on syndicalism and interventionism, Mises argues that these are not coherent systems—they are not genuine alternatives. Thus, we are left with the choice between socialism and capitalism, and according to Mises, socialism is not a feasible system. If syndicalism, interventionism, and socialism are all incapable of existing, and if there is no further alternative system, then only capitalism can exist. It immediately follows that it is pointless to argue for or against capitalism. Mises doesnt accept this conclusion because his discussion applies only to "systems of social co-operation". The alternative to capitalism, then, is industrial collapse, the disappearance of large-scale organized society, the relapse into primitive barbarism (from which, one presumes, the market and eventually capitalism would once more painfully evolve). Yet it is open to question whether there has at any time existed a pure free-market system, which Mises often seems to equate with capitalism. If *some* interventions are to be admitted into 'capitalism', then it's unclear where the line is to be drawn between capitalism and interventionism.

Mises could be saying that interventionism cannot last. He does indeed say: "The interventionist interlude must come to an end because interventionism cannot lead to a permanent system of social organization" (Mises 1966, 858). Some Misesians think that the present heavily-regulated welfare states must disappear, either by the revival of free-market capitalism or by moving in the direction of socialism, and hence, the breakdown of the great society and a relapse into unco-ordinated bands of subsistence farmers and brigands. While neither of these possibilities can be ruled out, there is nothing in the nature of intervention which must lead to one or the other. There is no fundamental reason why capitalism modified by a considerable degree of interventionism could not survive indefinitely (just as there is no fundamental reason why a free market, without any interventions, could not survive indefinitely). Mises offers three arguments which might be construed as arguments against the possibility of a stable or indefinitely existing regulated market.

1. "Restrictive measures always restrict output and the amount of goods available for consumption. Whatever arguments may be advanced in favor of definite restrictions and prohibitions, such measures in themselves can never constitute a system of social production" (1966, 858). It's true and important that interventionist measures alone cannot constitute an economic system, but this says nothing against a market system modified by numerous interventions. Human bodies cannot function by medicine alone; medicine intervenes in a system which functions largely independently of medicine. But this doesn't rule out a body, or a population of bodies, indefinitely subject to considerable medical modification.

2. "Interventionism aims at confiscating the 'surplus' of one part of the population and giving it to the other part. Once this surplus is exhausted by total confiscation, a further continuation of this policy is impossible" (1966, 858). This argument is empty for three reasons. First, even if an accumulation of transfers makes the *extension* of those transfers (the addition of new transfers) impossible, it does not make the continuation of the existing level of transfers impossible. Second, not all interventions are primarily transfers. Third, there is no surplus, though some have assets that others would like to get their hands on.

3. Interventions lead to undesired consequences, which call for further interventions, which call for yet further ones in an indefinite succession. The intervening government finds itself drawn into ever more extensive and numerous interventions. The government embarks upon the complete replacement of the market by degrees. But this is tantamount to socialism, which, because of the impossibility of economic calculation, can only collapse into chaos. This is the argument that Mises relies upon most conspicuously (1966, 858; 1969, 61–66).

Among his illustrations is a government which decrees a price for milk lower than the market price. This leads to an unwelcome fall in the quantity of milk supplied. The government then has to choose between abandoning the controls or imposing lower prices for the factors of production used to produce milk. The latter course leads to a fall in the quantity of these factors supplied, and if the government chooses to proceed with its interventionist approach, lower-than-market prices will be decreed for the factors required to make those factors. The government pursues this process until it fixes all prices throughout the economy, leading to what Mises calls "the German pattern of socialist planning" (1969, 62–63), meaning effective abolition of factor markets along with nominally private ownership of factors.

That scenario applies only to government attempts to fix prices. Mises mentions that the government could instead use taxes to buy milk and resell it at a lower price, without the cumulative consequences of price controls (62). But this too is a form of intervention. There are also numerous cases of intervention where the cumulative consequences are not so easy to predict: government regulations forcing people to do things (send their children to school), or prohibiting sale of certain commodities (heroin, cars without seat belts). Thus, there is plenty of scope for intervention which doesn't have the consequences predicted by Mises. Mises seems to view some of these as not cases of intervention, which as Lavoie (1982) points out, leaves a hole in Mises's argument against all systems other than the free market.

Yet even in cases of price control, the conclusion drawn by Mises doesn't follow. The government might impose a below-market price for milk and then do nothing about the resulting milk shortage. Mises tacitly assumes that the government is singleminded and consistent and will always negatively value the disorganization and loss of output caused by each intervention more highly than it positively values the desirable results of the intervention. But government policy emerges from the trading of various interest groups. One interest group might be paid off with the below-market price for milk, while another group resists the further interventions suggested. For this very reason, the goals of the below-average milk price may well be pursued by other means. In the U.S. today, the government both subsidizes milk prices and distributes food stamps, encouraging food producers to apply price discrimination. Additional programs provide 'good' food to mothers and their children at zero price to the consumers, but with full compensation for the producers.

Among cases where price control is now widely employed are rent control (below-market price for rented accommodation) and the minimum wage (above-market price for labor). Rent control produces a housing shortage and the minimum wage produces unemployment. Yet we find these measures persisting, in some cases for many decades, without being abandoned, and without the chain reaction of ever-widening interventions envisaged by Mises. Purely on grounds of economic and political analysis, there is no reason why these measures could not persist for centuries. (For a different analysis of coercive intervention, which depicts an equilibrium being determined by the demands of interest groups and the resistance of taxpayers, see Demsetz 1989, 295–307. See also the two classic articles on regulation, Stigler 1971; Peltzman 1976.)

Mises fails to show what he seemingly sets out to show. His arguments could be re-interpreted, as applying only to price controls, or as being directed against a proposed method for attaining specific goals. Against a program of price controls, it is relevant to point out that the market cannot operate if all prices are fixed by the government, and that interventionism has no meaning as a pure system: it has to be limited to piecemeal and costly modifications of the market. Mises's views were developed in response to price control policies prevalent in Central Europe, especially after 1914. Mises combatted the view that the market could be modified by price controls without major deleterious consequences, the position that price controls could be a workable transitional stage to workable socialism, and the standpoint that interventionism constituted a third system, neither capitalism nor socialism. Mises never dealt explicitly with a fourth approach, and one that has now become the most serious rival to free-market liberalism: this fourth position may be called 'welfare-state capitalism'. Its principles are: a. The great mass of assets are to remain privately owned and, within broad limits, freely traded; b. Private property and the market are to be recognized as indispensible preconditions of affluence, and their preservation therefore to be a goal of government policy (curtailing the pursuit of other goals); c. Price controls are to be rarely if ever employed; d. Limited objectives are to be pursued by combinations of measures including discriminatory taxation, licensing, quality controls, prohibitions, and compulsory requirements. Although Mises, as a liberal, was opposed to welfare-state capitalism, his arguments don't directly confront it. Mises often writes of "capitalism" as though it were equivalent to *laissez faire*, but most of his arguments for capitalism omit to address this fourth variant of interventionism.[3]

For most of Mises's lifetime fashionable ideas included the view that factor markets and financial markets could be replaced by 'conscious' planning and the view that interventions could be made at will in the market, for example, by fixing any and all prices at any level the government chose. Mises's critique of these two conceptions, and his analysis of the relations between them, are of enduring importance, and helped to defeat these ideas. Henceforth, in part due to Mises's efforts, it may be accepted as truistical that private property in the means of production, a functioning market in factors, substantially free financial markets, and a diversity of levels of income and wealth, have to be preserved, as institutional equivalents of a clean water supply and proper sanitation. Yet these fundamental presuppositions of a great and affluent society still leave open an enormous range of feasible government interventions. Many serious arguments may be brought against these interventions, but the contention that they necessarily menace the continued existence of a functioning market is not supported by the arguments Mises presents.

b. Mises's Conception of 'Socialism'

Many actual and hypothetical systems have been called 'socialist' to which Mises's argument does not apply. For example, it clearly does not apply to present-day Sweden, and a detailed discussion might be necessary to determine its applicability to pre-1991 Yugoslavia. These broader uses of the term 'socialism' seem to have been more common in the Anglophone than in the Germanophone world at the time when Mises first advanced his argument, and to have become more common still since that time—in part because socialists, under the impact of Mises's writings, abandoned unambiguous NFM socialism in favor of systems which encompassed factor markets or were equivocal on that score.

The conception of socialism as ruling out factor markets corresponded to that of the overwhelming majority of avowed socialists in the German-speaking world in the 1920s. One measure of this wide acceptance is that all the major critics of socialism (including Pierson, Brutzkus, Weber, and Mises) each independently took it for granted. Another is that early respondents to Mises nearly all omitted to challenge this conception, the major exception being Eduard Heimann. Mises clearly lays down that it is crucial to his argument that there can be no factor markets under socialism. Nothing would have been simpler than for socialists to have repudiated this point, thus easily disposing of the first step in Mises's argument. In the main, they did not do so, because here they agreed with Mises.

c. Mises's Modification of his Argument

Although Mises's definition of socialism appears straightforward, there is one aspect which both his critics and defenders have largely overlooked. In the 1920s, Mises introduces a new argument, incorporated into the second edition of *Die Gemeinwirtschaft* in 1932. Here Mises declares that "Some of the younger socialists believe that the socialist community could solve the problem of economic calculation by the creation of an artificial market" (Mises 1981, 119). According to Mises, these socialists hold that, just as managers of joint stock companies work not for themselves but for the shareholders, so under socialism they can work for the community. Otherwise, they can operate in the same way, buying and selling and aiming at a profit. Mises responds that:

> it is a complete fallacy to suppose that the problem of economic calculation in a socialist community relates solely to matters which fall into the sphere of the daily business routine of managers of joint stock companies . . . it is above all necessary that capital should be withdrawn from particular lines of production, from particular undertakings and concerns, and should be applied in other lines of production, in other undertakings and concerns. This is not a matter for the managers of joint stock companies; it is essentially a matter for the capitalists—the capitalists who buy and sell stocks and shares, who make loans and recover them, who make deposits in the banks and draw them out of the banks again, who speculate in all kinds of commodities. It is these operations of speculative capitalists which create those conditions of the money market, the stock exchanges, and the wholesale markets which have to be taken for granted by the manager of the joint stock company. (1981, 120–21).

Here Mises rests his case on the indispensability of financial markets (capital, money, and commodities markets). Mises implicitly abandons his earlier claim that the the means of production under socialism are necessarily *res extra commercium*, that common ownership excludes factor markets by definition. In 1920 Mises assumes that FM socialism is a contradiction in terms. In 1924 he maintains that FM socialism is not enough. When the debate moved to the Anglophone world, no one was to pay any attention to this important development of Mises's argument. Mises himself did not fully appreciate what had happened: the 1932 edition of *Die Gemeinschaft* retains both the passage where the means of production are declared to be necessarily *res extra commercium* and the above passage where they are acknowledged to be not necessarily so. A whiff of Mises's earlier position lingers in his use of the term "artificial market", and his statement that the market "cannot be artificially imitated under socialism". Exactly what this means is unclear. Organs of government can trade with one another, and the markets thus formed are genuine markets (see below, Chapter 11), though the outcomes of their trading will be different from the outcomes of trading among private companies.

iii. MISREADINGS OF MISES ON ECONOMIC CALCULATION

a. Is NFM Socialism Impossible in Theory or Merely Impossible in Practice?

In the popular account by Lange, Mises's argument was easily refuted, whereupon Mises's London-based defenders in the 1930s, Hayek and Robbins, retreated from the Mises position. While Mises denies the "theoretical" possibility of rational allocation, Hayek and Robbins concede the theoretical possibility and question only "the possibility of a satisfactory *practical* solution" (Lange 1938, 62; Landauer 1959, 1640).

In Mises's writings, his claim that socialism is "impossible" is always clearly intended to mean that NFM socialism is not practically feasible, and nothing more. For example, the chapter concluding the discussion of economic calculation in Mises 1922 is headed "The Impracticability [*Undurchführbarkeit*] of Calculation in Socialism". Throughout the discussion of economic calculation from 1920 on, Mises alternates freely between the terms "impracticability" and "impossibility" in a way that clearly indicates he is using them as equivalent expressions. Mises never states, hints, or insinuates that socialism is impossible 'in theory', or 'logically' impossible.

Furthermore, neither Hayek nor Robbins states that socialism is possible 'theoretically' or 'in principle'. Hayek and Robbins argue that socialism cannot work in practice, and they seem to feel no need to distinguish the 'practical' from the 'theoretical' (except insofar as this distinction is raised by their opponents). In his summary of the debate, Hayek states that defenders of "central direction of all economic activity" merely attempt to "prove that 'in principle' a solution is conceivable. Little or no claim is made that such a solution is practicable" (Hayek 1935, 202).

What could be meant by the statement that 'socialism' (under-stood as NFM socialism) is impossible, not merely in practice, but also in theory? This could be taken to mean that socialism is impossible, not merely under actual conditions, but also under conditions not encountered in reality, described in various theoreti-cal models. But Mises asserts that, if we assume stationary equilibri-um ("the static state"), "we might at all events conceive of a socialist production system which is rationally controlled from an economic point of view." He dismisses this with the comment: "But this is only conceptually possible" (1935, 109), followed by his reasons for its impossibility in practice.

A true theory cannot conflict with any "facts" (actual states of affairs) and in this sense must correspond with "practice". If something is impossible in practice and our theory says that it is possible, then our theory is false. References to a divergence between theory and practice may arise because many theories, or theoretical models, apply to conditions which are rarely or never encountered in reality. Such a theory may be useful, if conclusions can be drawn from it in conjunction with information about the difference be-tween the conditions for which the theory would hypothetically hold and actual conditions. In some cases the actual outcome may be an approximation to the theoretical prediction. In other cases the outcome may not be an approximation, but may still be related, in a determinable way, to the outcome predicted by the theory. But in either case, the way in which the prediction of the 'theory' is adjusted to real conditions is also a matter of theory (see Kant 1983, 61–62). In such cases we may loosely say: 'The theory says such-and-so but in practice the result will be different'. But this statement is itself theoretical; it is merely a way of saying that one part of our theory says such-and-so, but the complete theory says something different. We are dealing with two or more theories, not with theory and practice. All discussion of practice is theoretical. A divergence between theory and practice means that the theory is false, though it may be false because incomplete, and the false theory may remain useful as part of a fuller theory.

b. Economic Theory and Institutions

There is an interpretation of the theory-practice distinction which is helpful in understanding the historical course of the calculation debate. In this interpretation, 'in theory' means 'according to the corpus of economic theory' and 'in practice' means 'for reasons about which economists *qua* economists can say nothing'. Economists taking this view often maintain that economics can say nothing about the comparative merits of different institutions. Such a view is taken by Durbin, who attributes to unnamed critics of socialism the judgment that the socialist administration can know what should be done but will refuse to do it or will find other individuals reluctant to do it. Durbin comments that these "are not problems that the professor of economic theory is competent to discuss . . . economists may not dogmatize on such practical questions as these" (Durbin 1949, 143). Durbin holds that predictions of people's actual motives and behavior belong to sociology and psychology.

Durbin's remarks (140–43) are ambivalent on the relationship between economic theory and institutions. He seems at times to maintain the view that the same information is available to individuals under any possible institutions, and that differences in behavior in different institutional environments can reflect only the impact of these environments upon motivations. Alongside these remarks are others where Durbin has no hesitation in making categorical statements as to the necessity or desirability of certain institutions, on grounds that he doesn't seem to exclude from economic theory. Ambivalence amounts to clear contradiction when Durbin, for example, says: "If there is to be no wastage of resources, the costs of one commodity must be assessed in quantities of sacrificed alternative goods; there must . . . be a free market for the factors of production" (141), and then two pages later: "The ability to discover marginal products is not dependent upon the existence of any particular set of social institutions—certainly not on those of *laissez-faire*" (143). We have to assume that Durbin distinguishes between a free market and *laissez faire*; perhaps he thinks of a free market as state-owned industry in which enterprise managers make many price and quantity decisions without these being imposed by a central office. Even so, a free market in factors is not compatible with any and all institutions. If a free market be necessary to avoid wastage of resources, then not all institutions are alike in being able to avoid wastage of resources.

One rejoinder to Mises is that economic theory shows that the same allocative principles apply to all forms of society. Hence, they apply to socialism, and hence, socialism cannot be unfeasible. Alternatively, socialism cannot be unfeasible on theoretical grounds —it could only be unfeasible for 'practical' reasons, meaning: reasons about which economic theory can say nothing. This extraordinary argument used to be fairly popular. Lange, perhaps tongue-in-cheek, accuses Mises of "institutionalism" for denying the possibility of rational allocation under socialism (Lange 1938, 62; 'institutionalism' is a theory which holds that there are no general economic laws applying to all cultures). Lange and Schumpeter popularized the story that Mises was answered in advance by Barone, who argued that allocative principles in socialism must be the same as those of capitalism. "At a logical level," contends Little, Mises was answered by the demonstration that "the welfare skeleton of pure competition" was "not logically incompatible with socialist institutions" (Little 1950, 253). Heimann (1939, 93) thinks that Wieser showed the feasibility of socialism in 1889.

Consider a proposed society in which all industrial decisions are made by a single monk, consulting the *I Ching*. This monk wears a saffron robe and subsists on a macrobiotic diet. Is such an industrial order feasible and efficient? According to the argument, it must be so, or, if it is unfeasible or inefficient, this must be for non-theoretical or 'practical' reasons about which economists cannot pronounce. The economic theory of production applies to all societies, no matter how they are structured, so it applies to our monk-governed society. Therefore, economics allows us to say nothing about any possible difficulties that might ensue from entrusting the allocation of all resources to our enlightened monk.

It ought to have been obvious that the economic theory of production describes properties of the optimal allocation of resources, and gives some pointers to conditions that have to be fulfilled for that allocation to be attained. The fact that it is true of any society that if it is to achieve efficiency it must conform to these properties and conditions doesn't imply that all forms of society are equally successful at approximating the optimal allocation. The question is not whether the same allocational principles that economics has uncovered in analyzing the market would also have to apply to any NFM system—just this is maintained by Mises. The question is whether these principles *can* be applied to any NFM system—just this is denied by Mises.

Heimann misses the point when he suggests that by not acknowledging a contradiction between his own argument and Wieser's remarks about socialism, Mises "may have preferred to cover with silence what must have appeared to him a formidable blunder on the part of an otherwise estimable man" (1939, 93). Aside from the fact that Mises did not consider Wieser an estimable theoretician, Wieser's analysis does not, and was never intended to, offer any support for the feasibility of NFM socialism. There is no attempt in

Wieser to argue that, as Heimann has it, there exist "objective standards of rational orientation for a socialist economy" (ibid.), and it's likely that Wieser would have disputed any such claim.

c. Barone and Mises

It's often claimed that Mises was answered in advance by Enrico Barone's paper written in 1908 (Lange 1938, 59, 64; Schumpeter 1950, 173; Mandel 1970, 634). Yet it was far from Barone's intention to show how socialism might work; he tried to show the impossibility of socialism as it was conceived by most socialists at the time. If one wanted to argue that socialism was unfeasible, one could approach this in either of two ways. One could declare socialism to be unfeasible, and give one's reasons. Or one could discuss necessary requirements, in order to show that these requirements contradict defining features of socialism. The latter was essentially the approach of Barone. If it were proposed that human beings should live in the center of the Sun, and various hints were thrown out about the way of life of these solar inhabitants, a skeptic would proceed by asserting that they would have to solve various problems, and then examining the difficulties they would face. The fact that some skeptics explicitly stated 'It's impossible to live in the center of the Sun' while others didn't would not necessarily mean that these two groups were taking up mutually opposed positions, still less that the latter group were 'showing how, in principle, humans could live inside the Sun'.

The idea that Barone attempted to demonstrate the possibility of socialism has even been accepted by Mises's defenders, notably Hayek (1935, 29). The most remarkable case is that of Henry Hazlitt, a Misesian whose works are aimed mainly at popularizing Misesian economics to non-scholars. Hazlitt's *The Great Idea* is a novelized presentation of the economic calculation argument, in which the well-intentioned dictator of a socialist world gradually rediscovers and re-introduces the market. Hazlitt has Barone as one of the characters who come forward offering a non-market system of planning by solving equations (Hazlitt 1951, 138–42).

The real Barone advances an argument more similar to Hazlitt's. Barone begins his paper by declaring that it is fruitless to expose "the errors and absurdities" in socialism, since socialist theory can be amended to remove these faults (presumably he has in mind doctrines like surplus-value or historical materialism). Absent these faults, "one can very well imagine an economic system which would realize the spirit of the Marxist system" (Barone 1935, 245). Barone proceeds to argue that one feature after another of the market economy will turn out to be essential under socialism, in much the same way that Hazlitt's dictator gradually re-introduces the market. The irony is all the more striking because Barone wrote a further contribution, which has apparently not come to light (246n), in the fictional form of a speech by the socialist Minister of Production to his colleagues. From the indications in Barone 1935, it appears virtually certain that in this lost work the Minister apologetically explains why socialism has to be run just like capitalism in order to avoid industrial collapse. Barone, it seems, was the author of an earlier version of *The Great Idea*.

Mises is not generous in his reference to Barone. Mises lists Barone (1966, 701) as one of those who, unlike Pierson, "did not penetrate to the core of the problem". Mises dislikes the mathematical economics of the Lausanne School and prefers the verbal arguments of Marshallians such as Pierson. Like Pierson, however, Barone sees the key difficulty with NFM socialism, the valuation of factors in the absence of a market.

d. Explicability Doesn't Imply Reproducability

A common assumption in the 1930s and later is that if we have a correct theory of the market economy, identifying optimal relationships among prices and costs, it must be possible to duplicate these relationships in a non-market economy. What we can explain, we must be able to reproduce. This assumption is very strong in Hall 1937, but seems to influence all the writings of the period which argue for socialism without rejecting neoclassical economic theory. Lavoie (1985, 122) reverses the argument: since it's not possible to duplicate the optimal relationships, the neoclassical theory must be incorrect. However, there is no reason to suppose that a theory must enable us to reproduce the detailed events the theory explains. No theory says everything about the entities it describes. The fact that there is not, and doubtless never will be, a perfectly precise solution to the *n*-body problem doesn't cast doubt on the theory of gravitation. There is a theory, which seems to be true, that many animals adjust their output of offspring to the availability of food. This theory may be true, adequate for our purposes, and illuminating, yet we may not know what environmental clues inform the animals of food availability, and even if we establish this, we may not be able to duplicate the animals' achievement in perceiving all the clues on which the adjustment of fertility depends. (It is interesting, but irrelevant here, that the reverse is also true: we may be able to duplicate or simulate something without being able to explain it.)

The theory that explains the effectiveness of markets by reference to a perfectly competitive model in which prices equal marginal costs does not imply that anyone can know what particular marginal costs are, much less that anyone can bring about the equation in the absence of a market. (This holds independently of the fact that much of neoclassical theory is not supposed to apply directly to the real world, but is a kind of idealized picture, like the theoretical description of a perfectly efficient machine.) In price theory there is a special additional reason for the gap between explicability and full knowledge: price theory specifies the *direction* of change without specifying its magnitude. To specify magnitudes would require knowing all the relevant elasticities (the degrees of responsiveness to change, for example: how much the quantity purchased of milk would fall in response to a 13 percent increase in its price). Although past observations may give us some basis for the approximate estimation of elasticities, such estimates are limited and fallible.

e. Landauer on Mises and Utility

Carl Landauer gives a special twist to the view that Mises argued for something other than practical unfeasibility (a similar interpretation of Mises's argument is given in Williams 1950). Landauer agrees that Mises is correct in claiming that "there can be no highly developed economy without value units" (Landauer 1959, 1637) and therefore acknowledges that Mises's argument shows the unfeasibility of any advanced economy in which factors are measured only in kind. But according to Landauer, Mises's key point is that subjective utility (the gratification consumers derive from consumer goods) is in principle not measurable.

Mises does state that "there can be no unit of the subjective use value of commodities. Marginal utility provides no unit of value . . . The subjective valuation of one individual is not directly comparable with the subjective valuation of others" (Mises 1935, 98–99). According to Landauer's reading, Mises simply deduces from this that, since the value of factors is derived from the value of final products (consumer goods), no value can be ascribed to factors. Landauer claims that subjective utility is measurable, and that therefore "in principle" it is possible to value consumer goods in units of utility, and then work out the values of factors.

In Mises's view, it is not possible to compare different individuals' subjective utilities because 1. it is inadmissible to compare different individuals' utility scales, and 2. even with a single individual, we cannot measure that person's utility in units. Utility is a matter of scales and grades, like the measure of the hardness of materials, which cannot be expressed in arithmetic units (in technical language, utility is ordinal, not cardinal). In both respects, Mises is in agreement with most modern economists, and Landauer's is a minority view, but still, Mises could be wrong and Landauer right. Yet these arguments have little to do with the economic calculation argument. Landauer and Williams have each misread Mises in attributing a crucial role to the non-measurability of utility.

Landauer contends that the measurement of subjective utility is feasible, but he does not explain how it might be accomplished. Landauer's sole purpose in raising the issue of measurability of utility is to dismiss Mises's argument by saying that utility is measurable "in principle". Having made this point, he forgets all about measurability of utility, as though it were irrelevant to the discussion of socialism, as indeed he acknowledges it to be (1639–640). Like many writers from 1935 to 1985, Landauer holds that Mises claims that socialism is 'impossible' in some sense so severe that even the claim that factor prices could be arrived at by some admittedly impracticable method constitutes a refutation.

Mises's remarks about the unmeasurability of utility fall quite naturally into the context of his argument that socialism is not practically feasible. Mises asserts that factors have to be valued in units, and that this cannot be done accurately without market exchange of factors, which is incompatible with 'socialism'. Most of his remarks in support of this concern the complexity of the society-wide structure of inter-related factors and the market's "intellectual division of labor" which splits up the work of processing information about costs. In this context, Mises briefly observes that it is not possible to measure utility directly and impute this measurement to factors (1935, 96).

Landauer believes that the economists' treatment of the individual's "marginal rate of substitution" reveals "a hidden assumption of measurable utility" (1959, 1639). (A marginal rate of substitution is the rate at which a person would exchange one good for another, given his stocks of those goods. Thus, if a person has ten bananas and six peaches, he might be prepared to give up three bananas for one more peach, but if he has ten bananas and nine peaches, he might be prepared to give up three bananas only if he could get at least two more peaches for them. Some economists like talking about marginal rates of substitution because it enables them to avoid talking about the unobservable entity 'utility'.) Landauer makes no attempt to show how that measurable utility would be identified, and it is difficult to see how this could be attempted, except by deduction from observed consumer behavior. Landauer says that "Walras had already shown in principle how to derive the prices of capital goods from known prices of consumer goods" (1639). But factor prices cannot be deduced from consumer goods prices alone: the available stocks of various resources and the possibilities of combining them also have to be taken into account, and precisely Mises's point is that this cannot be done without drawing upon the dispersed, uncentralized knowledge of numerous market participants. In any case, for anyone who thinks that factor prices can be deduced directly from consumer goods prices, there is no need to bring in the question of the measurability of utility.

f. The Administration's Valuation and Choice of Consumer Goods

Mises says that it will be "evident" in a socialist society "that 1,000 hectolitres of wine are better than 800, and it is not difficult to decide whether [society] desires 1,000 hectolitres of wine rather than 500 of oil". Such facts can be established without calculation, but "once this decision has been taken, the real task of economic calculation only commences" (1935, 103).

Landauer (1959, 1638) asserts that Mises is making too big a concession here. Certainly, if Mises is claiming that a socialist administration could draw up an accurate list of what could realistically be produced, this falls foul of his own argument. Landauer points out that some consumer goods like cars and houses would require comparison of their costs with the services they would yield throughout their lifetimes. But if we abstractly eliminate this by supposing that all durable consumer goods are rented, then a more fundamental problem arises. Consumers cannot compare different consumer goods until they know their prices, and their prices cannot reflect their costs of production until values have been assigned to factors. Prices of factors and of final goods have to be determined mutually and simultaneously.

This problem tends to be hard to visualize because we think of the socialist administration making a judgment, based on recent history, of the sort: 'Every household requires a refrigerator'. This sounds straightforward, but there is an infinity of different designs of refrigerators, as well as an infinity of ways of making each design. Suppose that because of changing availability of some factors, the design favored heretofore becomes more costly, and opportunities arise to change the design to one that will now be cheaper. In the market, the consumers can be given the opportunity of choosing between the two designs, at their appropriate prices. In the absence of a sufficient price difference, the consumers might insist upon the old design. Taken in isolation, this may not sound very serious. But it is only because such adjustments can be made simultaneously in all lines of production that we can be in a position to make the confident judgment that 'society is able to give every household a refrigerator'. An accumulation of uncorrected inaccuracies in all lines of production will produce considerable impoverishment, as well as indeterminacy in consumer goods prices.

If we take Mises's point as being simply to separate choice of consumer goods from organization of production, we could interpret him as saying that *if* economic calculation in production were possible without factor prices, then it would provide information about costs which could be used to help assign prices to consumer goods. The reference to a choice between 1,000 hectolitres of wine and 500 hectolitres of oil can then be taken to imply that the administration knows it has a choice betwen these two alternatives, and that these two alternative increments are equal in cost. This reading is borne out by a passing remark a few pages later: the administration "will know, or think it knows, the ends to be achieved . . . " (106). Be that as it may, Mises later wrote: "In any social order, even under Socialism, it can very easily be decided which kind and what number of consumption goods should be produced. No one has ever denied that" (1981, 123). Well, I deny it. A society that cannot value factors *ipso facto* cannot value final goods—therefore a society that can value final goods can value factors, so Mises's unwarranted concession about consumer goods contradicts his economic calculation argument. Without knowing what consumer goods cost to produce, the administration is in no position to select the kind and number of consumer goods.

My explanation for this apparent lapse is that some members of the Austrian school have never freed themselves from the notion that *first* consumer goods prices are determined by consumer demand, *then* factor prices are determined by derived demand or imputation. This mistake derives historically from the Austrian school's battle to insist that 'prices determine costs' against the old notion that 'costs determine prices'. The Austrians were right, in the sense that the costs of production of a consumer good derive from the competing demand for factors stemming from the demand for other consumer goods. But since the price of a good is partly determined by the available stock, it follows that consumer goods prices are not determined independently of the prices of factors. If we suppose, as a mental experiment, that there is some change in the supply of a factor, say a great increase or decrease in the availability of petroleum, then clearly this will change all prices, of factors and of final goods.[4]

If factor prices cannot be determined under socialism, then consumer goods prices cannot be determined either, except in the trivial sense that prices may be reached which will clear the stocks of consumer goods which happen to become available. These prices will not reflect production conditions, any more than, for example, the prices which emerge inside a prison camp for the contents of Red Cross parcels. (The contents of these parcels and their proportions are decided taking factor costs, in the wider market outside the camp, into account. In that sense, the socialist scenario envisioned would be much worse. But still, prices emerging inside the camp reflecting inmates' demand schedules for the various contents, are not fed back into the planning of production of those contents. Under NFM socialism, all consumers would be effectively inside such a camp. A market would prevail for consumer goods, but information from that market could not properly govern the administration's perceived costs of production.)

g. Mises and his Defenders

In the 1920s, debate over the Mises argument occurred mainly in the German-speaking world. With the rise of National Socialism, many participants in the debate moved to the English-speaking world. Mises went to the United States and Hayek to the London School of Economics. For a few years Hayek's theories, especially his approach to the trade cycle (Hayek 1931; see Hicks 1967) were in vogue among English-speaking economists, until they were, abruptly and thoroughly, overwhelmed by the 'Keynesian Revolution'. A number of economists who later made a name as Keynesians (notably Gottfried Harberler, Lionel Robbins, and Alvin Hansen) were for a while closer to Hayek and even to Mises. The collection *Collectivist Economic Planning*, edited by Hayek when he was at the height of his influence, made the Mises argument very well-known in the Anglophone world at a time when explicit 'socialism' was perhaps more popular than ever before or since. Socialist writers often contend that Hayek and Robbins retreated in the 1930s from the position advanced by Mises in the 1920s, but accounts differ as to the nature of the retreat—the position taken up first, and the position retreated to. Lavoie (1985) has given a detailed defense of the view that Hayek and Robbins essentially defended Mises's original position. The appearance of a 'retreat' is superficial. Mises had a more belligerent prose style than Hayek or Robbins, and the critics of socialism had to develop more subtle and qualified arguments to keep up with the retreating socialists, who conceded ground and incorporated elements of hated 'capitalism' into 'socialism'. Also (Kirzner 1988), the proponents of the Mises case developed a new understanding of the market economy in the course of the debate.

Some writers assert that Hayek and Robbins rest their case on the prodigious computational task of solving millions of simultaneous equations, with the implication that this is a purely 'practical' difficulty, and therefore a departure from Mises (Mandel 1970, 634). The proposal to solve millions of simultaneous equations had not originally faced Mises; it was advanced as a reply to Mises (Tisch 1932; Dickinson 1933), but soon abandoned as impracticable. Mises, Hayek, and Robbins all respond to such proposal by pointing out that 1. there would be too many equations to solve in a short enough time (Mises 1966, 714–15); 2. it would be impracticable to gather all the information ('data') required to write out the equations; and 3. the equations describe equilibrium, and do not indicate the best path to equilibrium (Mises 1966, 710–11).

Another common version of the gulf between Mises and his defenders is the claim that Mises denies the possibility of existence of factor prices under socialism, whereas Mises's defenders discuss the adequacy of such prices (Durbin 1968, 47n; Hall 1937, 68–73). This is a misunderstanding of terminology. Mises confines the term 'price' to actual market exchange-ratios, and points out that it follows from the absence of market trading under NFM socialism that there can be no factor prices. Some writers use 'price' for any attribution of value or cost to factors, no matter how achieved. It is trivially obvious, for example from Mises's discussion of the labor-hours proposal, that Mises does not dispute that the administration can attribute numbers to factors. He questions whether such numbers can be a basis for efficient allocation: whether they can be revised to accurately reflect changing valuations and discoveries.

Hayek does attribute to Mises "the somewhat loose statement that socialism was 'impossible' when what he meant was that socialism made rational calculation impossible" (Hayek 1948, 145–46). Hayek immediately goes on to defend what he says Mises meant. However, even this difference between Mises and Hayek is one of terminology. Mises defines 'socialism' to *include* the result the socialists expect from it: output at least as high as that of capitalism. Hayek defines socialism purely in terms of the means adopted (130–31).

There may be a difference between Mises and Hayek on the scale of the drop in output. The tone of Mises's remarks suggests that when an attempt is made to implement world-wide socialism, the collapse will be so great that the prerequisites of large-scale society will be unsustainable, and society will fragment into unco-ordinated bands. (This reading, however, contradicts Mises's disclaimer at the end of his 1935, to the effect that the ascetic socialist will be untroubled by the economic calculation problem.) Hayek seems to concede that output under socialism, though lower than under capitalism, could eventually rise to overtake the capitalist output of the past and could then perhaps grow indefinitely (1948, 150).

Another accusation of 'retreat' arises from the publication of Hayek's *The Road to Serfdom*. It is certainly contradictory to maintain, first, that socialism is unfeasible, and second, that it is (irrespective of the wishes of its proponents) bound to be a horrendous dictatorship. The inconsistency can be removed in two ways: 1. by accepting the possibility of socialism existing as an enclave in a capitalist world, able to make use of world prices, and 2. by attributing the horrendous dictatorship to any serious *attempts* to introduce socialism, while still maintaining that this will ultimately not be feasible.

More recently, a subschool of uncompromising Misesians has claimed that Hayek misrepresents Mises and that Hayek's version of economic calculation is inferior to Mises's. Salerno (1991) and Rothbard (1991) deny that Mises's argument is based on 'information'. Their position is elusive. Salerno, for instance, doesn't argue that socialism is unfeasible for merely praxeological reasons, since he adduces the wide variety of intersubstitutable resources (52–53). He contends that a mind simultaneously aware of all resources, techniques, and consumer preferences would still be unable to arrive at an optimal plan (or one that was not disastrously suboptimal). Since he doesn't dispute the truism that given resources, knowledge, and preferences strictly imply an optimal allocation, the reason for the impossibility can only be that the computational task would be too great. But the rest of his piece doesn't encourage me to think that he would be happy with what Lavoie (1985, 80) calls the "computation argument", especially as this argument is popularly associated with Hayek and Robbins. Salerno frequently adverts to Mises's own language just where we need elucidation as to Salerno's distinctive interpretation of that language.

— 6 —

USING LABOR-HOURS TO PLAN PRODUCTION

Economy of time, to this all economy ultimately reduces itself. (Marx 1973, 173)

i. CALCULATION IN KIND

Marx anticipates a society without money in which book-keeping will be even "more necessary" than it is within capitalism. In what units will book entries be made? Only two clear answers are common in the Marxist literature, and all the nebulous answers float somewhere between these two: calculation in kind and the use of labor-time as a measure of cost. Despite some vagueness, Marx, Engels, and other early Marxists like Bebel seem to favor the labor-time approach.[1] Non-communist NFM socialists may entertain the idea that factor valuations can be imputed from consumer goods prices by the central authority, but this idea is excluded for strict communism, where there is no market even for consumer goods.

Advocates of calculation in kind (*in natura*) claim that there is no need for any general unit of economic calculation. There are simply physical quantities of all the various kinds of factors, and there is no need for a single unit which can be applied to all factors to measure their value or cost. All the writers who advocate such an approach skip very lightly over the specifics and fail to address the fundamental question of how to compare the costs of alternative aggregates of factors.

Two themes recur in these writings: 1. that calculation in kind is already widely used in industry; 2. that recourse to a common unit of cost is necessary only where there is commodity exchange. By analogy with 1., we could just as easily say that, since many measurements carried out today are not measurements of weight, therefore nothing would be lost by abandoning all measurements of weight. As for 2., abolition of the market does not eliminate the need to compare the total costs of alternative production methods, where each method requires the use of different combinations of factors, and where each method uses less of some resources and more of other resources than the alternative methods (see 1.iii–1.iv above).

In the early years of the Bolshevik regime, calculation in kind was for a while espoused by Bukharin, whose references to it remained brief and nebulous (Bukharin 1971). The idea was worked out in greater detail by Tschayanoff (1923; see Hoff 1981, 70–75), who tried to establish 'marginal norms' for the quantities employed of various broad categories of factors (such as land, labor, buildings, materials). The averaging involved in arriving at these norms must either be arbitrary or must tacitly refer to some common measure of value. But even when the norms have been calculated, they do not afford a way to compare the costs of different aggregates of factors. Tschayanoff's scheme was criticized by the Bolsheviks Strumilin and Varga who both concluded that labor-time would be socialism's measure of cost (Brutzkus 1935, 14–15).

The most celebrated socialist to advocate calculation in kind is Otto Neurath,[2] who draws from the German war economy the lesson that monetary calculation, or any other use of a common measure of cost, is unnecessary. His best-known collection of essays on economics is entitled *Through the War Economy to the Natural Economy* (1919). The term 'natural economy' is a technical term for a moneyless economy, and doesn't imply that the institutions of the natural economy are any less artificial than those of a money economy. Neurath states that "in the last analysis, every completely administered economy is a natural economy" and that "to socialize means to extend the natural economy" (1919, 216–18). It is likely that this very passage made a strong impression on both Mises and Max Weber, provoking the thought that 'full' socialization would lead to the breakdown of calculation. Although this thought of Neurath's perfectly sums up a pervasive assumption in Marx, by the time Neurath wrote most Marxists had backed away considerably from the Marxian espousal of a natural economy. Neurath, who was hardly a Marxist, was in the position of pointing out to the Marxists that the 'socialization' they endlessly talked about logically implied a natural economy. His views were not so *outré* as to prevent his being appointed Commissioner for Socialization in Saxony and then president of the socialization agency in Bavaria.

Neurath foresees a single supreme body directing the economy, a *Naturalrechnungzentrale* or 'natural calculation headquarters'. He is most emphatic that this democratically-chosen body will have no use for general units of any kind, not even labor-hours, just as commanders on the battlefield do not employ 'war units', and hospitals and schools are not planned by adding up 'health or instruction units' (217). Similarly, all productive projects are to be evaluated "through direct observation", solely according to their "economic desirability". The headquarters will draft several plans, on different assumptions, the plans will be compared, and the most desirable outcome selected. Neurath's examples include a choice between a. a power dam and agricultural improvements and b. a canal and a steel mill. He seems unaware that for the whole economy there would be billions of combinations of millions of projects, not to mention an infinity of different precisely defined ways in which each project could be executed. He also seems to assume that the headquarters will be able to pick among combinations of feasible projects which use available resources to the full. But either this requires an exhaustive inventory of all available resources and a perfect knowledge of all their potential uses, all centralized in one office, or it requires projects to be compared for cost as well as desirability, which necessitates the very units Neurath hopes to dispense with.

Calculation in kind is favored by Amadeo Bordiga (see Buick 1987, 140–43). A more recent advocacy is Buick and Crump 1986, 134–142. They explicitly exclude the existence of money or any other general unit of calculation. Although Buick and Crump refer to Pierson and Mises, their response is merely to declare that the need for economic calculation arises exclusively from the existence of the market. They briefly suggest that cost-benefit analysis could be used, without prices, and that "points systems" (139) could be employed, to add up the advantages and disadvantages relevant to particular decisions—though they add that the "advantages/disadvantages and even the points attributed to them can, and normally would, differ from case to case". They also countenance the use of input-output tables (141).

Buick and Crump seem to envision that their proposed socialist administration would *not* be able to say, for example, that 'copper is more costly than aluminum and therefore should be reserved for more urgent applications', or 'Method of production x has some advantages over method of production y, but uses up too great a quantity of valuable resources, so we are better off plumping for y'. Such comparative judgments require the ability to assess the costs of copper, aluminum, and all other resources, in the same units, and in units which do not differ from case to case. Since Buick's and Crump's socialism permits no mechanism that would enable the administration to make such judgments, it is not clear what sense we can make of the authors' assertion that "socialist society still has to be concerned with using resources efficiently and rationally" (137).

The term 'calculation in kind' is normally reserved for attempts to dispense with any general unit of calculation. It is usually not taken to include cases where a general unit of calculation is arrived at without reference to money or markets. Thus, it is not applied to Taylor-Lange accounting prices (see Chapter 7 below), nor to the notional 'prices' ascribed to all commodities in an attempt to replace the market by solving a large number of simultaneous equations (Tisch 1932), nor to the use of labor-time as a measure of cost. Advocates of labor-hours for socialist planning accept the need for some general unit of economic calculation, yet there is a similarity between their position and that of 'calculation in kind': the administration starts, so to speak, from a vast array of unpriced goods, and endeavors to ascribe a valuation to all of them; this contrasts with production in the market, where a spontaneous social process yields actual prices for all goods. Calculation in kind and the labor-time proposal both allow the administration to be viewed strictly analogously with an isolated Crusoe, whereas the use of market prices introduces a form of information which can be generated only by inter-individual interactions.

Much of what I have to say about the labor-time proposal could be extended to any other proposal for a planning administration to determine some valuation of all factors in terms of a single factor (or average of a single class of factors). In practice the only such proposal to have attracted much of a following is the use of 'energy-units'; its most conspicuous proponents are members of the political movement known as Technocracy. Technocracy was a force to be reckoned with in American intellectual life in the 1920s and 1930s, influencing Veblen and Lewis Mumford, and even foreigners like H.G. Wells (for historical accounts see Elsner 1967 and Akin 1977; for standard criticisms see Dickinson 1939, 71–72).

Technocracy still exists as an organization publishing journals and pamphlets. Its members continue to denounce 'the price system' and to propose as replacement a system of 'energy accounting', but this sketchy proposal is merely reiterated without fresh elaboration or critical scrutiny (see any issue of the *Northwest Technocrat*, Seattle). No explanation is given of how it might be possible to arrive at true economic cost, or opportunity cost, from embodied energy-units. Like labor-hours, energy-units cannot accurately measure the cost of nature-given materials or of produced factors. Furthermore different forms of energy employed under different circumstances ought not to be treated as equivalent in cost merely because their physical measurements (foot-pounds or whatnot) are the same.

ii. The Labor Theory of Value and the Labor-Time Planning Proposal

"Take this pipe"—he pulled it from his mouth and I surveyed the hateful object with disgust—"Then this pouch." I looked with similar loathing at that. "And then this lamp-post"—he pointed with the stem of his pipe at the post in question. "Now what I want to do is explain to the ordinary man the relation between the amounts of labour power in these three objects". (Fox 1938, 41–42)

Numerous Marxist writers, from Marx and Engels down to Charles Bettelheim, have favored employing units of labor-time for planning production under socialism. This proposal is often referred to as an application of the labor theory of value, though that usage is not in conformity with Marx's. The Marxian labor theory of value (LTV) is intended to explain the determination of prices under commodity production (this is occasionally denied, but see Steele 1986). In Marxian terminology, there can be no 'value' in post-capitalist society. Both the LTV and communist planning conceive of resource allocation being guided by quantities of labor-time. Yet the LTV as an explanation of market prices and the labor-time planning proposal are two distinct theories, which may stand or fall independently. If the LTV were the correct explanation of market prices, this in itself would not show that units of labor-time could be of any practical use in the administration of communist industry. And if units of labor-time could effectively be employed for communist planning, this would not require that the LTV be the correct explanation of market prices. We shall see below that Marx's exposition of his LTV actually goes against the labor-time planning proposal, suggesting that it is unfeasible. Nonetheless, many Marxists have supposed that the LTV were true, and that it lent support to the labor-time planning proposal. Furthermore, some of the standard objections to the LTV arise in strikingly parallel terms as objections to the use of labor-time units for planning production under communism.

According to Marx's theory, actual prices will virtually always diverge from 'values' defined as units of labor-time. In Marx's thinking, after 1860, the relationship between 'value' and observed market prices is somewhat analogous to the relationship between 'mass' and heaviness, or between 'heat' and everyday awareness of temperature. Marx's 'value' is purportedly necessary to explain price, but it does not correspond to price or equilibrium price (often not even roughly) and therefore obvious disparities between value and price are not seen by Marx as refutations of his theory, though they are seen as contradicting the simple models employed in the early stages of expounding his theory in Volumes I and II of *Capital.*

Marx's analysis explains 'exchange-value' by means of the concept 'value'. (Common errors of Marx-interpretors are to identify these two distinct and mutually exclusive concepts or to treat the former as a species of the latter[3]). Marx appears to use the term 'exchange-value' sometimes to mean the proportion in which one commodity exchanges with other commodities and sometimes to mean the quality of being exchangeable with other commodities. Value is defined as the quantity of socially-necessary labor-time 'congealed' or embodied in a commodity.[4] Marx maintains that 'value' is necessary to determine exchange-value, and hence price. He reserves the term 'price' for money price.

Marx believes that behind the fluctuations of prices, there has to be some definite, law-governed magnitude which makes sense of the fluctuations. He sometimes refers to this magnitude as "average price" and sometimes as 'market-value' (III, 178–194). Marx is very insistent that market-value "explains the fluctuations of supply and demand" and not *vice versa* (III, 192). One argument repeatedly given by Marx for his view that market-value lies behind and 'explains' actual prices is that we cannot explain prices by supply and demand, since when supply and demand "balance" or "equal" one another (III, 189–190) they cancel each other out. Therefore, when they cancel each other out, something else has to be determining what the price is at that point. This reasoning is a simple error understandable in a writer whose thinking was shaped in the early nineteenth century and who lacked mathematical expertise. The notion that supply and demand can "balance one another" arises from viewing supply and demand as magnitudes or numbers. If instead supply and demand are viewed as schedules or functions, an argument like that advanced by Marx cannot be framed. 'Supply' and 'demand' each refer to an array of counterfactuals: quantities which would be supplied at different prices. Generally, these quantities are the same for both supply and demand at only one price. Thus, when supply and demand are "in balance", they do not really cancel out or cease to act; rather, they coincide, in the sense that at that price and only at that price, the quantity supplied is the same as the quantity demanded. The price is completely determined (proximately) by supply and demand. Suppose that I want to take a flight from Chicago to Los Angeles. There are various imaginable departure times having varying degrees of convenience to me, and various departure times offered by several airlines. The actual time of my flight is going to be one of the times convenient to me, where this corresponds with a time offered by an airline. No one would claim that since this particular time results from both the airline timetables and my 'convenient departure-time schedules', the airline's offered times and my convenient times 'balance' and therefore 'cease to act', so that neither the airlines' offered times nor my convenience plays any part in explaining the actual time of departure (see Böhm-Bawerk 1962, 282–84). The purpose of my criticism here is not to denigrate the search for a magnitude lying behind observed price, but to point out that the determination of that magnitude would have to take into account the forces which actually fix observed prices. Marx was led into error by his supposition that prices were immediately influenced by superficial forces susceptible to merely 'vulgar' analysis while values, lying behind prices, were determined by quite different forces. His theory suffers from a failure to properly integrate the 'vulgar' and the 'profound' parts of his analysis. Instead of striving at every step to 'save the phenomena', he permits himself to make arbitrary links between the profound and the superficial—arbitrary in the sense that their only function is to reconcile the profound and the superficial.

In Volumes I–II of *Capital,* Marx treats the value of a commodity as its average price, while revealing by occasional hints that this is in conflict with facts. (Like most nineteenth-century economists, Marx fails to draw a clear distinction between average and equilibrium price.) In Volume III, Marx explains that a commodity's average price (or market-value) is not its value, but its modified price of production. He justifies his frequent references to exchange-value as the form of 'value' (labor-time) by claiming that modified prices of production are 'transformed' values. Marx defines the 'value' of a commodity as the average socially-necessary labor-time required to produce it. The qualification 'socially-necessary' refers, first, to the amount of time required under average conditions; thus, typically, at any given time, a commodity will be produced in some factories at greater than socially-necessary labor-time (these factories will make below-average profits) and in some factories at less than the time socially necessary (these factories will make above-average profits). Second, 'socially-necessary' means that the relevant amount of labor-time is that required under present conditions—not in the past, when, perhaps, the commodity in question was actually made.

In explaining the divergences of actual prices from average prices, Marx is concerned with transitory fluctuations in relation to an equilibrium or average price. In explaining the divergencies of average prices from values, however, Marx is concerned with a shifting of the equilibrium or average point itself. In Marx's theory, it is average prices and not values towards which prices regularly and permanently tend. But it is value which, according to Marx, explains average price: in Marx's theory, the average price of a commodity is *entirely* determined by values—partly, that is, by the value of that commodity, and partly, in specified ways, by the values of other commodities. In explaining all the adjustments necessary to get from value to average price, Marx is dealing only with quantities of socially-necessary labor-time. Thus despite all the elaborate adjustments which Marx makes, he has a price theory in which average prices are strictly determined by quantities of socially-necessary labor-time and by nothing else.[5]

iii. Measurable Labor-Time and Appropriate Prices

Suppose that Marx's labor theory of value were an accurate explanation of market-oriented production. The question would then arise what help this theory might be to the administration of a non-market economy, in which there would be no prices, exchange-values, or 'values'. If quantities of socially-necessary labor-time explain prices, but actual labor-values depart from actual prices, then it could still be that the administration ought to use socialist analogues of prices rather than socialist analogues of values. In that case, the question would arise whether first finding analogues of values would be a necessary, or a possible, way to find analogues of prices.

I will show: 1. that at least many of the market's departures of actual prices from labor-values are desirable; 2. that the socialist administration ought to make allocative decisions by analogues of market prices rather than analogues of values; 3. that the socialist administration would be unable to determine socialist analogues of values (quantities of socially-necessary labor-time); 4. that even if the administration could determine analogues of values, it would be unable to use these to calculate analogues of prices; and 5. that, if the administration could calculate analogues of prices, the information the administration would require would mean that they would have no need to refer to analogues of values. All five points hold independently of a. whether the labor theory of value is a correct theory of market prices; or b. whether there exists some way for the administration to compute non-market analogues of prices.

Would the administration know how much labor-time to attribute to each product? At first glance this seems simple: the time taken to produce something can be recorded, then multiplied by the number of workers. Yet recording the labor-time expended on a product is perhaps more complicated than some adherents of labor-time accounting units have considered. It is not enough merely to measure the amount of time taken by the workers; an amount has to be added for raw materials, fuel, wear and tear of machines, and so forth. According to Marx this amount represents past labor embodied in these items and transferred to the product. A system of measuring and adding on quantities of labor-time would require an apparatus of book-keeping almost as extensive as that used for financial purposes in the market. An alternative approach might be to say that only 'average' inputs of labor were to be considered. But finding a useful average requires a fairly large number of instances of precisely the same task, which would not be possible in many cases. Nonetheless, using an average, in a few suitable cases even an average based on sampling rather than a complete report, might make the task of costing somewhat easier, though less accurate. Unfortunately, as we shall see, the estimation of actually-expended labor-hours, whether or not this is facilitated by recourse to averages, would be useless for purposes of economic calculation, or indeed, for any purpose.

a. Fluctuations in Supply and Demand

In a fishing port, there will be periods when the trawlers land large catches, and periods when no catches are landed. The price of fresh fish in the surrounding markets will rise when no catches have been landed for a while, and will fall when catches are landed. Let's suppose that this goes on for many years without any change in the underlying conditions, so that the average price of fish over a year or so remains the same. The labor-value of fish then remains unchanged.

If we were to even out these fluctuations, sticking to the average price at all times, there would be surplus unsold fish in periods of plentiful fish, and rationing by 'first come, first served', or costly queuing, or bureaucratic whim, or some other inefficient mechanism, in periods of reduced supply of fish. In both situations—that is, almost all the time—sticking to the average price would cause inefficiency: it would reduce the satisfaction of people's wants. Again, without challenging the labor theory of value, we see that at least some divergences from value (or from average price or market-value) are by no means regrettable. The socialist administration would have to recognize the need for departing from the measure of cost implied by socially-necessary labor-time.

This point stands whether or not there are *some* cases where it would be better for price fluctuations to be ironed out (though that is dubious: it has never been shown that there is any such thing as a price fluctuation which is nothing but meaningless noise). Some fluctuations are due to successive guesses as to the equilibrium price, rather than to rapid changes in the objective determinants of the equilibrium price, as in the fish example. Inasmuch as fluctuations represent groping towards the equilibrium price, it would be better if we went straight to the equilibrium price without any tacking about. But this statement is unhelpful in that it assumes that someone knows something that we have every reason to suppose no one does or can know. It is analogous to saying that if we have lost a ball in a field, the best search technique is to walk straight to where the ball lies.

b. Different Kinds of Labor

One of the classic objections to the Marxian labor theory of value is the 'reduction problem' (Böhm-Bawerk 1962, 269–274; see Blaug 1986). Marx states that value is defined in terms of hours of labor, but he readily acknowledges that the labor of a highly skilled worker will normally be more productive of value, hour for hour, than the labor of a less skilled worker. Against Marx, Böhm-Bawerk argues that this reliance on the reduction accomplished by the market is circular. Suppose we observe that the price of an hour's output of a skilled engineer is five times that of the price of an hour's output of an unskilled laborer. Marx asserts that an hour of the skilled engineer's work 'counts as' five hours' work by the unskilled laborer. But the only way we can tell that the engineer's work is more productive of value than the laborer's is by looking at the price of the output, and the only way we can tell *how much* more—not twice as much, not 50 times as much, but five times as much—is by looking at the price of the output. Something irreducible and unexplained is being called upon to account for the difference, and furthermore that irreducible, unexplained element—observed differences in market prices—is precisely what the labor theory of value is designed to explain.

The market is supposed to perform the task of 'reducing' all the various kinds of skilled labor to a common measure, but with the market abolished, how will the administration perform this task? Even if it were true that differences in labor quality could, in the market, be entirely accounted for by past inputs of training labor, this would not help the administration, because training labor is itself allocated, in the market, where it will yield the highest return: it would be easy to squander training labor on giving workers skills which were not the most urgently required. Particular skills become comparatively devalued by changing conditions. It is necessary to make a prior judgement that labor of a certain kind will be more productive, before deciding to allocate training labor to producing that labor. And while training labor is being invested to increase the supply of a particular kind of skilled labor, that skilled labor must immediately be costed more highly.

We should not be misled by casual talk of 'skill' as though it were a homogeneous quality that inhered in different kinds of labor in different concentrations. If we take two 'skilled' workers, say a dentist and a computer programmer, we cannot really say that one job is 'more skilled' than the other. (Perhaps there may be some physiological sense in which we could, but if so, that would not govern prices.) Strictly speaking, of course, all work is skilled, and when we refer to unskilled work, we usually think of work that many people can quickly learn to do—but this introduces an element other than 'skill', to wit, relative scarcity of the particular type of skill, or of the aptitude to learn that particular type of skill. There is no independent measure of 'skill' which can tell us what the value of the products will be, and indeed, there may well be two 'skills', A and B, A being more productive of value than B at one time, and B more productive than A at a subsequent time.

The administration must rate some kinds of labor as more valuable, or more costly, than others. The administration must have a practical method for deciding whether, for planning and book-keeping purposes, an hour's typesetting is to be rated as more or less than an hour's airplane piloting, and exactly what the ratio of the two costs is to be. It is no help to the administration to hold the view that treating different kinds of labor as containing the same essential substance in different amounts is a useful explanatory device for illuminating what happens in a market economy, even if that view be correct. Observable, measurable, or 'concrete' labor-time is not homogeneous socially-necessary labor-time, and any utilization of homogeneous socially-necessary labor-time must presuppose a method of finding how much homogeneous socially-necessary labor-time is contained in each and every hour of observable labor-time. The administration has to find the appropriate ratios, the correct 'weighting' of different kinds of labor, and if they could do this, they would have no need to refer to homogeneous socially-necessary labor-time. (Under communism, this would be independent of the incomes of the laborers. All individuals may be supposed to get the same incomes, or the same labor-voucher rate per hour, or different incomes according to non-work-related criteria. This does not affect the problem.)

The idea might occur to some to ignore the differences in labor quality and treat all concrete labors as the same. The fundamental reason why labor a. must be valued more highly than labor b. is that a. makes a greater contribution to consumers' satisfaction in alternative uses. The effect of the administration's treating all labor as the same would be somewhat analogous to the effect (within the market) of a law mandating equal wages for all kinds of work. In either case, for instance, there would be no way to signal that a particular type of labor was exceptionally valuable and therefore had to be rationed to a small number of most-urgent uses. Not only would the administration's information show them nothing wrong with allocating a brilliant computer programmer to a nurse's job, but their information would fail to alert them to the fact that there were only, say, six such high-quality programmers in the whole society. Even if they had this fact as an independent piece of information, they would be confronted with, say, 50,000 enterprises requesting the use of such a high-quality programmer. The market would tend to ensure that those six programmers went to those of the 50,000 who would pay enough to bid the programmers away from the other 49,994, and thus the programmers would tend to go to where their contribution to society's output was highest. In the market, no outside observer can know or needs to know what the ultimate allocation of these six programmers will be. The situation is further complicated because all workers can do many jobs, with varying degrees of competence, and the workers' own preferences have to be taken into account. One of those high-grade programmers might decide to give up programming and live a quiet life on a small farm, subsidized out of his savings. The benefits of this choice outweigh the high wages he would get by continuing programming. The external consumers' loss ('society's loss') is outweighed by the gain of this individual. Such an outcome is efficient: forcing this programmer to work for external consumers would be inefficient.

Aside from the direct allocation of labor, all the products of those six programmers would be undervalued in a system where all labor-hours were treated as equal. This would show some produced factors as more costly, others as less, than they really were in terms of opportunity cost. Such a system would quickly break down into chaos, because, for example, the administration would treat various industrial appliances which happened to be produced by highly-skilled labor as being much less costly, and therefore much more plentifully available, than they in fact were. The result would be that many of the enterprises requesting supplies of such appliances would be disappointed.

A way around the difficulty could be found if observable labor-time (concrete labor) came to correspond closely to socially-necessary labor-time (abstract labor). This could occur if all workers were becoming equal in abilities, and thus interchangeable. Just this notion does seem to have been entertained by Marx, who thought that workers were becoming increasingly interchangeable, except for a few broad divisions based on age and sex. Marx was struck by the disappearance of old craft distinctions, and failed to pay attention to the growth of new skills. Aside from genetic differences in individuals' capacities, their skills are also differentiated by their experiences to date, so it doesn't seem likely that universal interchangeability will ever be approached.

c. The Cost of Unproduced Resources

Suppose that, to make a certain commodity, which we will call a grimp, requires two ounces of a raw material, kryptonite, and one hour of manufacturing labor. Does the Marxian LTV fully account for the contribution of the two ounces of kryptonite? Yes, says the Marxist. In the Marxian theory, we add to the one hour of manufacturing labor the value of the two ounces of kryptonite. The value of these two ounces of kryptonite is the socially necessary labor-time required to produce (locate, extract, and transport to the grimp factory) these two ounces. This total, the value of the two ounces of kryptonite *and* the one hour of labor-time required to turn them into a grimp, gives us the full value of a grimp. It may indeed seem to a superficial glance that the Marxian approach fully acknowledges the contribution of the two ounces of kryptonite.[6]

Suppose that the socially necessary labor-time required to locate, extract, and transport an ounce of kryptonite is one hour. Call this labor 'extractive labor'. Suppose for simplicity that one hour of extractive labor is equivalent in quality to one hour of manufacturing labor, and that they are each equivalent to one hour of average socially-necessary labor-time. The value of a grimp, then, is three hours' labor-time:

value 1 grimp = 2 hrs extractive labor + 1 hr mfr. labor = 3 hrs

Now suppose that there is another commodity, called a klonch. To make one klonch requires one ounce of kryptonite and two hours of manufacturing labor. Thus, according to Marx's theory, the value of a klonch, like that of a grimp, is exactly three hours:

value 1 klonch = 1 hr extractive labor + 2 hrs mfr. labor = 3 hrs

But upon reflection this is seen to be a simple blunder. By *any* relevant considerations, the value of one grimp is *greater* than one klonch, though each has congealed in it three hours of socially-necessary labor-time, no more and no less. Within the market, a grimp will sell for a higher price than a klonch. And within an efficiently-functioning communist system, the cost of a grimp will be rated by the planners as greater than the cost of a klonch. Of course, one can simply say 'by definition, the value of a grimp is equal to that of a klonch'. But this definition has no explanatory or normative application. It doesn't help to explain market prices; in fact it is seriously misleading in the explanation of market prices. It doesn't assist in the efficient allocation of resources; it would be seriously misleading here too, and for parallel reasons.

Both a grimp and a klonch need three hours' labor, but a klonch additionally needs one ounce of kryptonite and a grimp additionally needs two ounces of kryptonite. The grimp requires one ounce more kryptonite (one ounce more of 'natural resources') than the klonch, over and above *all* the labor required. This would be immediately clear if there were a fixed, known amount of kryptonite 'in the ground', untouched and waiting to be mined. Society would have to economize on its stock of kryptonite, *in addition to economizing on labor-time.* (Even if *all* kryptonite employed could be recycled, the total stock might still have to be allocated to a fraction of the possible current uses.) Each use of an ounce of kryptonite would be a deduction from alternative uses, even though some of these alternative uses might be in the distant future. In reality, mineral reserves are not like that; instead, there are deposits of mineral ores which vary considerably in quality. Thus, at any time, there are reserves of gold or iron which are not worth mining at current prices, but would become worth mining at higher prices, and there are reserves currently worth mining, which would stop being mined if the expected price fell.

If there are two natural resources, kryptonite and vulcanite, and kryptonite is twice as easy to mine as vulcanite (it takes half the socially-necessary labor-time to produce one ounce of kryptonite as to produce one ounce of vulcanite) but the reserves of vulcanite in the ground are generally believed to be, say, 20 times as abundant as those of kryptonite, then the price of an ounce of kryptonite may well be higher than that of an ounce of vulcanite. The price of a natural resource to industry will reflect reserves and expected future demand.

d. Differences in Organic Composition of Capital

Commentators on Marx sometimes interpret his notion of exploitation as follows. From Marx's standpoint, it doesn't matter whether machines produce value; what matters is that earlier laborers produced the machines; therefore the product of the machines is labor's product, not the capitalist's (Sowell 1976). Such an interpretation betrays the most spectacular misunderstanding of Marx's theory. In Marx's view, if a worker saves out of her wages, uses the wages to buy machines, thus becoming a capitalist, and then employs workers to make a 'profit' (interest return), every bit of that 'profit' is entirely due to the workers currently employed and not in the least to those machines.[7] Only 'living labor' can create value. Capital equipment or 'dead labor' can never create new value, and therefore cannot create 'surplus-value' or the interest return on capital. This is the distinctive doctrine of Marxian economics, from which all its peculiar claims and difficulties flow.

Marx's view that surplus-value is created by living labor alone implies that the interest return on capital (the 'rate of profit') will be proportionate to wages alone, and will not be affected by other production costs. It follows that, if capitalists measure their profit against their total outlay, they will make lower profits, as a percentage of that outlay, if they use more capital equipment. Capital-intensive firms or industries (in Marx's language, those with high 'organic compositions of capital') will have lower rates of return than labor-intensive firms or industries (those with lower 'organic compositions of capital'). "This law," says Marx, "clearly contradicts all experience based on appearance" (I, 290). In the real world there is a powerful tendency for all industries to show the same rate of return, and no observable tendency for capital-intensive firms or industries to be less profitable than labor-intensive firms or industries. In *Capital*, Volume I, Marx promises that the seeming contradiction will be resolved by the later development of the theory.

Marx died before Volume II appeared, in 1885, with no solution of the contradiction, but with a preface by Engels promising a solution in Volume III. Engels threw out a challenge to all comers to anticipate Marx's solution before it appeared, and several attempts were made. Eugen von Böhm-Bawerk pronounced that a satisfactory solution was impossible: either goods do sell at prices in direct proportion to labor-values, in which case "rates of profit" will permanently differ between labor-intensive and capital-intensive industries, or rates of profit are equalized by competition, in which case the selling prices of goods permanently diverge from labor-values (Böhm-Bawerk 1959, v1, 281–302). When Volume III appeared in 1894, it turned out that Marx, in effect, had accepted in advance this judgment of Böhm-Bawerk's. Marx agreed that rates of return on different capitals tended to be equal, and that it therefore followed, exactly as Marx's opponents had insisted, that products manifest *no* tendency, in the real world, to sell at their labor-values. The actual 'market-value' or 'average price' is made up of labor and capital costs (the sum of living and dead labor), plus the standard rate of return or interest. Marx calls this price, at which a commodity will actually tend to sell, its "price of production" (III, 157–168).[8]

It is entirely acceptable for the simplified model used in the early stages of an economic theory to be contradicted when the more realistic complications are added at a later stage. However, the 'contradiction' is a weakness in Marx's theory in three ways: 1. Marx gives only one clear argument for his labor theory of value, the argument that when two things are exchanged they must have some common 'something', in equivalent quantities, and that something can be nothing but labor.[9] This argument is undermined by the acknowledged fact that, when two things are exchanged, they do not necessarily possess equal quantities of labor—and almost never can possess equal quantities of labor, even as an equilibrium tendency. 2. Marx appears to have moved, by way of labor-values, to a traditional 'cost of production theory of value', in which the value of a product is determined by adding up costs and then adding interest. This suggests that the use of labor-values may have been a redundant detour.[10] 3. Simply as a mathematical operation, the move from Volumes I–II to Volume III, the transformation of values into prices of production, seems to be either unsound or not capable of preserving the assumptions Marx needs for his key conclusions.

Marx maintains that his 'prices of production' are derived from values, and that therefore values ultimately determine prices. Values are 'transformed' by market competition into prices, and Marx's simpler model shows how the amount of surplus-value is determined. There has been much discussion of whether it is possible to transform values into prices, that is, whether it can be done mathematically without absurd results (see Böhm-Bawerk 1962, 201–302; Sweezy 1968, Chapter 7; Steedman 1977). A possible mathematical solution of the transformation problem is a necessary but not sufficient condition for the validity of Marx's theory. A successful solution would not prove the theory correct. This can easily be seen from the fact that *any* input could be chosen as creator of value, and then the resulting 'values' could be 'transformed' into prices of production. Thus, a 'paper theory of value' would hold that prices were ultimately determined by values, defined as quantities of 'socially necessary paper' (measured in pounds weight). The organic composition of capital would be the ratio of non-paper means of production to paper, and it would be asserted that only paper created new value, and therefore surplus-value. The whole of *Capital* could be rewritten, substituting 'paper' for 'labor'. Exploitation of paper-owners would occur because paper-owners do not really sell their paper, but rather their 'paper-power'. Goods requiring no paper inputs would be regarded as having 'imaginary prices', just as Marx regards salable goods which require no labor inputs. The same thing, of course, could be done with 'electricity', 'liquid', 'metal', or 'machines', or it could be done with 'capital' (constant capital, which would then have to be renamed variable capital), thus showing that the capitalist class produces all wealth and is exploited by other classes, especially the wholly unproductive working class, which contributes no capital and therefore no value. To provide support for Marx's theory, it is necessary to show *both* that prices can be mathematically derived from labor-values (the transformation problem) *and* to present a good argument why we would wish to do this—why the class of inputs known as 'labor' should be given this privileged position in the determination of prices.

Now we turn to the administration of communist industry, and the question arises: granted that neither 'values' nor 'prices of production' in the Marxian sense would any longer exist, should the administration use analogues of values or of prices of production? Marx contends that communism will use analogues of values. In *this* restricted sense, there is truth in the statement that Marx thinks the law of value will come into its own under communism (Robinson 1966, 23). Marx holds it to be a failing of capitalism that it converts values into prices of production by arriving at a uniform rate of profit on outlay (constant-plus-variable capital).

In the market, capitalists receive the same rate of return on their invested funds, regardless of the composition of the assets on which those funds are spent. The return on labor-intensive investments is the same as that on capital-intensive investments. Taking the extremes, an industry employing labor only would get the standard rate of return, as would a fully automated industry employing capital only. Marx claims that what is really going on, under the surface, is that the entire rate of return is being generated by living labor and is then being spread out among all industries in proportion to invested capital. Marx further says that in communism such spreading out will cease, and the entire return will be attributed to labor, making labor more costly and capital less costly. I've already pointed out (above, 3.ii.) that this is an illusion, and that communism cannot make machines any less costly.

Any investment can be seen as analogous to a loan. Take the pure, fictitious case where a capitalist has no expenses except wages. Here the employer advances money as wages. Essentially, the employer loans the workers money, and later collects the interest on the loan. This would be clearer if the workers sold the products, then reimbursed the capitalist for her outlay. Instead, usually the capitalist sells the products (they are her property before sale) and pays the workers somewhat less than the total proceeds of the sale. The difference is still the capitalist's interest return, and is the same quantity as it would be under the other arrangement. Next, consider the case of a capitalist who owns machines which she leases to other enterprises. This is somewhat as though she loaned the enterprises the money to buy those machines. Again, she advances a certain sum, or certain sums, and her return is the going rate of interest. It is easy to see that the same rule applies to mixed investments of wage-labor and machines: no matter what the mixture, the rate of return will be the same, and will be equivalent to the going rate of interest.

Interest is paid because there prevails a positive rate of time preference. No one regards $1,000 paid in 10 years' time as equivalent to $1,000 paid today. If someone gave you a certificate entitling you to $1,000 in 10 years time, you would be an idiot not to take $900 today in exchange for that certificate. (Assuming no inflation and an interest rate of four percent, the present value of that certificate, if its honoring is certain, is about $820.)

Now let's consider the situation under communism. There are, of course, no prices (defined as exchange-ratios), no money, and no ownership-linked returns to specific individuals. But certain elements of capitalism abide under communism. There is an administration, which may be loosely compared with the entire capitalist class in the market, since this administration controls the allocation of everyone's savings. The administration does not seek a monetary return for 'loans', but it does have to make decisions about investing each portion of society's stock of resources in different projects. A positive rate of time preference still prevails: whatever the units for measuring the value and cost of resources, these will be discounted over time, so that a given quantity of resources years from now will be valued less than an otherwise identical quantity of resources within the next six months. The administration has to consider the most productive yields for its many and varied investments. On a very abstract level, this consideration has many similarities to the making of loans. There has to be some way of measuring the return, and moving resources from projects which are not turning out well to projects which are yielding a high return. All resources, equipment as well as labor, have to be moved from low-yielding to high-yielding projects. Equipment which remained in a low-yielding project would represent a loss to society, even though that equipment might replace the labor and other resources that produced it.

e. How Marginal Productivity Eliminates Surplus-Value

It is open to anyone to examine or to dispute the ethical or social claim of any factor of production to a share, in accordance with its marginal significance, or to argue that there is no industrial necessity to allow such a claim; but it is not open to anyone who understands the facts to argue that when, by a marginal distribution, every factor . . . has been satisfied, there remains any residuum or surplus whatever to be divided or appropriated. The vague and fervid visions of this unappropriated reserve . . . must be banished for ever to the limbo of ghostly fancies. (Wicksteed 1933, 573)

The marginal productivity theory of distribution was developed by a number of writers around the end of the nineteenth century, notably Wicksteed and Clark. This beautiful theory is empirically well-corroborated as at least a good approximation to the truth in most instances, and definitively solves a swarm of theoretical niggles that beset earlier economists. The theory completely undermines the concerns that led Marx to develop his theory of surplus-value. Marginal productivity is explained fairly rigorously in any textbook of price theory. Here I merely want to capture the gist of the theory, and indicate its relevance.

Suppose that a food crop is produced by combinining two factors: labor and land. Labor is applied to a field of fixed area at the rate of, say, 20 worker-hours per day. Can we say how much of the output of crop is attributable to the labor and how much to the land? Suppose that the 20 worker-hours were to be increased or decreased by a small amount—say, five worker-minutes per day. A small increase or decrease in the labor will cause a small increase or decrease in output of the crop. If we take the amount of the increase or decrease in the product associated with an increase or decrease of five minutes of working time, and multiply this by the number of five-minute periods in the total working time, that is by 240, we will have a figure which will be some fraction of the total output less than 1. (The reason it will be less than 1 is that we are operating with "diminishing marginal returns': for example, the addition to output from using 20 rather than 19 worker hours per day is slightly less than the addition to output from using 19 rather than 18, if the area of land worked remains unchanged.) Call this fraction labor's contribution to total output. We can also perform exactly the same operation in reverse. We hold the number of worker-hours fixed, at 20 per day, and vary the area of the field by a small amount, say by one square yard, find out the difference this makes to the total output, and multiply by the number of square yards in the field. This will also give us a fraction of total output. This fraction and the earlier fraction we found for labor will add up to 1 (the whole of the output[11]). And this will work for any number of factors. If we add fertilizer, a tractor, and three kinds of tractor-pulled machines, we now have seven factors, and the same operation will still 'exhaust the product': we will get seven fractions whose sum is 1.

This analysis (and its further development, which can be found in a good textbook) has the following two related consequences: 1. This method of attributing contributions to the different co-operating inputs would have to be followed, as the way to ascribe costs, by any administration pursuing efficiency, for example, the administration of a hypothetical socialist society;[12] 2. This method, as a matter of fact, explains the incomes people are paid in the market: the owner of each input gets its marginal product.

One of many fateful consequences of marginal productivity is that it sweeps away such theories as Marx's which see interest as consisting of 'unpaid labor'. Under competitive market conditions, a worker tends to be paid what his labor contributes to output, no more and no less.[13] The same goes for the owner of a machine or a piece of real estate. The analysis demonstrates the symmetry of all types of inputs: there is as much sense in saying that capital exploits labor as in saying that labor exploits capital, or that electricity exploits roofing tiles. Of course, this does not touch the ethical arguments of socialists who acknowledge that non-labor factors make a determinate contribution to output, analytically separable from labor's contribution, yet still contend that it is illegitimate for anyone to own capital or land and reap the payment for their services. But that is not the position of Marx, nor of many other socialists. They specifically contend that, given a resource-owner's right to the product of the resource he contributes to production, positive net incomes to non-labor resource-owners are entirely created by owners of labor resources. It certainly clarifies the discussion to recognize that *this* position is untenable.[14]

Prior to the formulation of marginal productivity, confusion reigned over the contribution of the different inputs. It was sometimes argued that no such attribution could be made, since all the inputs are necessary to the product, and cannot be disentangled. (One can imagine cases where all inputs would not be necessary, for example, wild fruit trees might produce fruit by themselves: the whole product would be due to land. One could then introduce labor in the form of tending the trees. If a large amount of labor were employed, land's contribution to output would not be the amount of output without any labor, but considerably larger. Reflection shows that this superficially puzzling fact is actually quite satisfactory. After all, when laborers use a lot of sophisticated equipment to turn out some product, few would claim that labor's contribution is confined to the amount of that product the laborers could produce without any equipment—in many cases nothing.[15]) Another result of the confusion was that there was a tendency to look for one factor which would be the 'residual', getting the remaining 'share' after all the other factors had been satisfied. This kind of thinking can be seen as the background to theories like Marx's. But Marx's theory can also be seen as an expression of exasperation with the untidy nature of such thinking, as a scientifically-motivated attempt to bring all the factor returns under a common explanation. Unfortunately Marx took a wrong turn by trying to conceive all returns as due to labor, instead of seeing returns to all inputs as determined in the same way.

The marginal productivity theory demonstrates that in a competitive market all individuals receive what they produce—what is produced by the resources they own. It's true that in establishing this conclusion the concept of 'what they produce' has been redefined, but the new definition captures much of the commonsense usage, and it can be seen that any other definition is fallacious, incoherent, or inapplicable. The theory does not apply with strict literalness to any real economy (there must be constant returns to scale, no indivisibilities, and no uncertainty), but this kind of limitation applies to any alternative theory, notably to Marx's. In the real world, marginal productivity applies as an excellent approximation in most cases. Uncertainty introduces entrepreneurs' profits and losses. However it is not entrepreneurial profit to which Marx and other socialists primarily object, but interest.

Let us now step back from the above four paragraphs. I have tried to indicate the revolutionary power of marginal productivity theory, but what I have said here is stronger than is necessary to show the importance of marginal productivity and the irrelevance of Marxian labor-values for the socialist administration. As a matter of the practical pursuit of efficiency, there simply is no alternative to marginal productivity. This is because the theory focusses on what is lost in one line of production and what is gained in another, by moving one or a few units of a factor from the former to the latter. And there can be no dispute that this is of enormous practical urgency. No matter what the contortions to which we may resort to save the formula that the whole output is produced by labor alone, as a practical matter, non-labor factors have to be economized too: they have to be moved from applications where their contribution to future output is lower, to applications where their contribution to future output is higher.

iv. Social Necessity: Bygones are Bygones

Any intuitive plausibility the LTV may possess derives from the commonsense theory that product prices are determined by adding up the costs of production, together with the less commonsensical notion that all costs may somehow be reduced to labor. But there is a fundamental flaw in all attempts to plan production on the basis of costs, in the sense of resources expended in the past. Measured labor-time can only relate to the past and is therefore always obsolete. What we would need to know is not how much labor-time was allocated in the past, but how much 'should' be allocated in the future.

In Marx's conception of socially-necessary labor-time, neither the labor actually employed to produce a commodity nor the labor required (at the time production takes place) to produce the commodity has any influence upon that commodity's "value". The only labor that confers value is 'socially-necessary' labor,[16] and this is determined by conditions subsequent to production, at the time of sale, though the amount of labor-time actually allocated to a particular commodity will be adjusted towards the socially-necessary amount, as an indirect result of capitalists endeavoring to maximize profits (Capital I, 203). According to Marx, each commodity of a particular sort may have the socially-necessary amount of labor spent on it, but if 'too many' or 'too few' specimens of that commodity have been produced, then it will be as if the amount of socially-necessary labor spent on each specimen were lower or higher than the amount spent. This is revealed by how many of these commodities the market can "stomach", or by how many commodities can be sold at a price which covers costs plus interest (I, 108–09). By Marx's account, even where the exact socially-necessary amount has been spent on each of a particular kind of commodity, the market determines whether 'too much' or 'too little' of society's resources have been allocated to that kind of commodity.

Here Marx partly anticipates the modern conception of 'opportunity cost', the view that past costs expended, or historical costs, have no influence upon product prices. There is no rationale for charging more for a product because it cost (past tense) more to produce, or less because it cost less, and market agents do not, as a matter of fact, generally do so. Cost consists of the opportunities foregone at the time of decision.[17] The observed tendency for products to sell at costs plus interest arises because entrepreneurs move factors from unprofitable lines into profitable lines (thereby reducing the 'profit' in the profitable lines to the rate of interest).

G.A. Cohen (1988, Chapter 11) points out that Marx's definition of socially-necessary labor provides a simple refutation of his theory of exploitation: it is not the amount of labor actually expended by the worker that endows his product with value, but the amount that later turns out to be socially-necessary. However, a modest reformulation suffices to save Marx's theory from this particular refutation, since surplus-value can still be calculated by subtracting wages plus constant capital from total output; the working class as a whole would remain exploited (except at the beginning of a major slump).

Socially-necessary labor-time corresponds to actually-expended labor-time only in equilibrium, which never occurs. This may be defended as a theoretical model for the explanation of price determination, but it means that 'value' cannot govern prices and production except insofar as value manifests itself through market demand. In the absence of the market, the communist administration cannot directly observe quantities of socially-necessary labor (nor can these be observed in the market either, but they are supposed to govern prices and production without having to be observed). If units of socially-necessary labor-time are to be employed by the administration, then, at the very least, some highly complex system of computations will be needed, though it's far from clear how the adminstration would even begin.

Instead of supporting labor-time planning, Marx's theory of value tends to cast doubt upon its feasibility. Marx clearly understands that, under capitalism, the amounts of labor actually expended upon commodities in the past have no effect whatsoever upon their values or their prices, and, of course (though Marx does not say this) nothing is to be gained under communism by taking any notice of amounts of labor expended in the past (except only insofar as these may provide some point of departure for calculating the direction investment of labor ought to take in the future). It might conceivably be useful to the communist administration to know the amounts of socially-necessary labor associated with all kinds of goods, but an amount of socially-necessary labor is always an amount of labor that 'should' be devoted to producing some article, not an amount of labor that *was* devoted to it. (From one day to the next, these will normally correspond quite closely, but it is the market which brings them into approximate correspondence, and it is the continuous correction of discrepancies which is vital for economic calculation.) Charles Bettelheim is a Marxist-Leninist who has understood this point. He criticizes Marxists who believe that "empirically-recorded labour-time" can be used as a basis for fixing prices in "socialist" countries like Russia and China. Calculations with such quantities "can never tell what it is desired they should tell": in what proportions to allocate labor and other resources to the various branches of production. Socialist planners need to develop theories accounting for the divergences of prices from values (1975, 219). But Bettelheim holds that labor-time calculations must eventually be used in socialist planning. He seems to overlook the fact that it would be of little help to acquire a detailed knowledge of the way in which prices diverge from values. If the planners could know, in the absence of prices, what prices would have been, then they would not need to know quantities of socially-necessary labor, and there is no reason to suppose that finding quantities of socially-necessary labor would be any easier than finding what prices would have been.

The administration might decide to ignore measured labor-time and arrive at an estimate of how much labor-time is required currently for all kinds of tasks. But immediately this approach is taken, the problem arises of defining each task. And any specific product can be produced by a great variety of alternative methods, each one technically efficient and each one entailing a different expenditure of labor-time and non-labor resources. The illusion that labor-time offers a method of economic calculation is effective only because of the notion that the administration can look and see what labor-time quantities are appropriate to each product. But in fact (dismissing *ex hypothesi* a whole lot of other difficulties with labor-time units), no one can simply look and see the appropriate quantities of socially-necessary labor-time. Gauging such quantities is a task which bristles with as many difficulties as gauging what market prices would have been, in the absence of a market.

The key to understanding the Marxian conception of capitalist and post-capitalist societies is that under commodity production, the producers, in their production decisions, are separate and seem to be mutually independent. Their mutual dependence is manifested in the market, through the trading of their products (Capital I, 109–110). To Marx, it seems that this is the wrong way about: people are rational and social creatures who should collectively decide what to do and then do it. It's self-evidently demeaning and inefficient that they should 'blindly' try out what to do, and then have to be vetoed or approved by an impersonal process they can't control. Since Marx believes that all allocation is allocation of labor-time, he sees this mutual dependence of the producers as being mediated through 'value', a measure of a portion of society's aggregate labor-time which is arrived at by an automatic process. The obvious corollary is that under communism labor-time will continue to be the basis of social allocation, but will be consciously and deliberately measured and applied by the democratically-organized producers (III, 187).

Pursuing this line of thought, Engels argues that the separation of the producers under commodity production leads to the appearance of value as a "roundabout" expression of quantities of social labor. Under socialism the labor of each individual becomes "directly social labour". The quantity of social labor contained in a product "need not then be established in a roundabout way; daily experience shows in a direct way how much of it is required on the average" (Engels 1954, 426–29).

Even in Marx's theory the money price does not show the amounts of concrete labor-time 'contained' in any product, and it is this actual labor-time, at best, which is shown by daily experience. Furthermore, what is represented in the price is, on Marx's theory, not even the socially-necessary labor-time, but some adjustment of this, to take account of organic compositions of capital, turnover times, rent, temporary disequilibria, and so forth. This adjusted magnitude is the correct guide (or at least, a more correct guide) to efficient allocation, not the unadjusted 'value'. And it is not practically feasible to calculate the value from the adjusted magnitude or *vice versa*. So on the basis of Engels's own theory, his claim is mistaken. The "roundabout" method produces a magnitude which is different from that shown by daily experience, and more useful, and which we do not know any other, more direct, way to discover.[18]

V. MARX ON THE DIRECT MEASUREMENT OF SOCIALLY-NECESSARY LABOR TIME

Marx is full of scorn for the proposal, advanced by some socialists during his lifetime, to arrange things so that commodities would *actually* exchange in proportion to the labor-time embodied in them. In the course of his arguments on this topic, Marx contends that the proposal is impracticable because the amounts of socially-necessary labor-time embodied in commodities *cannot be known* except by inference from observing the market process, and therefore only approximately and only after the fact. Marx returns to this point repeatedly, in somewhat different terms on different occasions.

In 1847, Marx argues both that the value-ratios of different kinds of labor are found by competition (MECW v6, 126) and that the market apportions capital according to demand, informing the producers how much labor they should allocate to particular lines of production (132–37). In 1858 he argues that finding the labor-time embodied in commodities requires comparing all commodities with a standard commodity (money), not labor-time directly (Marx 1973,

157–173). In 1859 he uses a somewhat similar argument, with more attention to the contrast between abstract and concrete labor (1970, 83ff), to criticize John Gray. These are all versions of the same argument. Marx is saying that there is no way to observe or measure "value" directly: we can only deduce its existence from a welter of competitive phenomena. (It is perhaps inevitable that some readers should have inferred that Marx is arguing for the retention of the price system. Sowell [1980, 218–19] concludes from these passages that Marx is a market socialist opposed to central planning.)

If communism dispenses with the market, and if only indirectly through observing the market can we know what the appropriate quantities of labor-time are, and if (as Marx repeatedly indicates) all allocation is based on allocation of labor-time, then how can communism work? This line has been taken up by Moore, a market-socialist critic of Marx, who claims that Marx's argument against Proudhon's socialism boomerangs against Marxian communism. Moore states: "If in every complex economy a labor market is required for translating concrete into abstract labor, the communist economy that Marx predicts is not simply remote but unattainable" (1980, 75).

Moore has a strong point, but he skips an important step in presenting it. Marx does not concede that the communist administration will have the slightest difficulty in calculating quantities of socially-necessary labor-time. Marx's statements about the impossibility of so doing apply solely to *commodity production*, where the producers are separate and mutually independent in their production decisions. Marx holds that bourgeois socialists want the market without the market's necessary consequences. If, argues Marx, socialists really want 'directly associated labor' (all the producers getting together and administering production according to a society-wide plan) then they must give up commodity exchange, and therefore prices and money, but it is illogical for them to want to keep commodity exchange yet try to reform it as if directly associated labor prevailed. It is in this context that Marx points out that, as there can be no directly associated labor under commodity production, the producers are mutually independent ('private', though not necessarily in the simple legal sense), and therefore socially-necessary labor-time can only take the form of 'value', an entity inferred from the equilibrating tendency of the forces of competition. Everything Marx says is entirely consistent with the view that the communist administration will have no trouble planning everything in labor-time-units. The difficulty Marx sees for Proudhon's socialism arises from the separation of the producers, which will be overcome under communism.

For Marx, anarchy of production is *not* an emergent quality of markets, visible in the trade cycle and other palpable maladjustments. The market does not cause anarchy of production. Anarchy of production causes the market. Since numerous producing units are mutually independent, the market is necessary. As soon as they conform to a common plan, but not before, the market becomes redundant and its survival inconceivable. Marx's argument is that wherever there is money, there is commodity production; wherever there is commodity production, there is mutual independence of the producers; wherever there is mutual independence of the producers, there is no hope of being able to measure 'social labor' directly, and therefore the demand for labor to become money, or for prices to conform to labor-times, is a muddled and foredoomed attempt to combine elements of the market with elements of communism.

Yet it is reasonable to acknowledge that such is Marx's position, and still raise the question of how the administration can ascertain socially-necessary labor-time. Some 'conscious' process must replace the market's spontaneous social process. Perhaps some kinds of information can be elicited only by spontaneous social processes, and not by 'conscious' deliberation. Furthermore the task facing the administration would be immensely more complicated than Marx or even Moore seem to have realized, since, as we have seen, many ways in which prices diverge from values would have to be somehow captured by the administration's computations.

Marx supposes that since the separation of the producers would be overcome under communism, the administration would have no difficulty in determining quantities of socially-necessary labor. This is one variant of a persistent theme in socialist thought: that the absence of an omniscient view of the production process is purely a *result* of private property and the market. Only get rid of the market, with its distracting price adjustments, and everything will be clear. Now we see through a glass, darkly, but then—face to face.

7

FROM MARKET SIMULATION BACK TO MARKET SOCIALISM

i. Market and Non-Market Socialism

Marxism, with its ultimate goal of production for use, achieved intellectual dominance over continental socialist theory by the end of the nineteenth century. Yet versions of socialism which did not unambiguously reject the market never died out, and may have been growing among German Social Democrats before 1920. Early respondents to the Mises challenge were the 'market socialists' Eduard Heimann and Karl Polanyi. It was in the early 1920s that the expression 'market socialism' (*Marktsozialismus*) became commonplace. A special term was considered necessary to distinguish those socialists prepared to accept some role for factor markets from the now mainstream socialists who were not.

The two major points in Mises's reply (1924; 1928; 1932) to the market socialists were: 1. that they were unclear about whether their proposals were really syndicalist or socialist (whether the separate 'industries' or 'society' would in fact own, or have final authority over the disposal of, the means of production); and 2. that the efficient dissemination of information requires, not merely factor markets, but also financial markets. With the rise of National Socialism, the debate moved from the Germanophone world to the Anglophone. The English-language socialist writers of the late 1930s paid little attention to earlier discussions of 'market socialism'; though many of them gave potted histories of the dispute, they almost never referred to the market socialists of the 1920s or to Mises's replies.[1]

ii. LANGE'S SYSTEM

a. An Outline of Taylor's and Lange's Proposals

In 1928 the American professor Fred M. Taylor gave a brief talk outlining a system of socialist planning (Taylor 1929). His suggestion did not immediately arouse much attention, but in 1936 it was incorporated into Lange's proposal. Taylor's talk was reprinted along with Lange's proposal (Lippincott 1938), and this volume rapidly became by far the best-known work on the economics of a socialist society; 50 years later it seemed to be perpetually in print. Anywhere in the West, if a student read only one book on the economics of a socialist society, it would with overwhelming likelihood be this work, which contains its own sketch of the Mises debate, and is thus, for most people who have ever heard of that debate, the main, and probably the only, source of their knowledge. Schumpeter 1950 [1942] faithfully echoes Lange.

In Taylor's socialism, the state is the sole owner of industry and the sole employer. It "maintains exchange relations with its citizens, buying their productive services with money and selling to them the commodity which it produces" (Lippincott 1938, 43). The central planning authority periodically compiles "factor-valuation tables", containing numerical "valuations" of factors of production. Taylor holds that only land and labor factors ("the primary factors") would be included in these tables (45–46), apparently supposing that the administration could simply add up the primary factors used to make capital goods in order to find their valuation. Consumer goods prices are set "at a point which fully covered the cost of producing" them (45), as indicated by the factor-valuations, which thus replace market prices for factors. Like so many writers before the Second World War, Taylor just takes it as self-evident that since the state owns all factors except labor, these factors do not change hands on the market, and therefore cannot have market prices. From time to time the state planning authority revises the tables in the light of experience. On what basis could the authority revise the tables? Taylor contends that they can do this by observing surpluses and deficits in stocks of factors:

> a too-high valuation of any factor would cause the stock of that factor to show a surplus at the end of the production period . . . . a too-low valuation of any factor in the tables would be certain to cause a deficit in

the stock of that factor. Surplus or deficit—one or the other would result from every wrong valuation of a factor. (53)

A surplus is followed by a raising of the factor-valuation and a deficit by a reduction of the factor-valuation for that particular factor.

Lange incorporates the basic idea of Taylor's scheme into his own proposal, with changes of terminology. In Lange's terms, the planning authority becomes "the Central Planning Board" and the factor-valuation tables become "accounting prices". Just as in Taylor's scheme, these "accounting prices" are revised by observing changes in the stocks of factors.

Lange further specifies two rules. 1. Managers of enterprises are to choose the combination of factors which minimizes average cost of production. 2. Managers of entire "industries" are to fix the scale of output so that marginal cost equals the price of the product (Lange 1938, 75–78). These rules are taken from the standard textbook account of a competitive market.[2]

b. The Puzzling Reputation of Lange's Scheme

From the late 1930s until the 1980s, Lange's was widely viewed as the standard work on the economics of socialism, yet it is doubtful if Lange's proposal ever had a single committed advocate. Lange's scheme became something that socialists could point to as a theoretical demonstration that socialism was in principle economically feasible, and then ignore. Lange is widely thought to have made a decisive contribution to the debate, yet it is difficult to find anyone who will specify what that contribution is.

Lange contends that his system is a 'practical' response to Mises, who has already been refuted 'theoretically', but later admirers of Lange generally present his system as a 'theoretical' refutation of Mises, or a refutation 'in principle', lacking 'practical' application. Lange's scheme is not a model of 'socialism' in Soviet Russia or other purportedly socialist countries. Amid all the increasingly urgent calls, from 1953 until 1990, for reform of Soviet-bloc economies, no one—including Lange—seems to have thought that Lange was of any relevance. Finally, there is the curious circumstance that Lange's system is widely hailed as a pioneering effort in the theory of market socialism, when it is demonstrably no such thing: even the name 'market socialism' predates Lange, and Lange's system is explicitly a proposal to replace the market with a non-market system.

The view that Lange's proposal gives the quietus to Mises is often voiced with great confidence during the period 1938–1985 (Heilbroner 1970, 88; Mandel 1968, 634; Harrington 1982, 245). Despite this seeming consensus, dismissive judgements are made from time to time. Little states that "Probably the great majority of socialist economists are already convinced that the marginal-cost scheme is absurd. Most practical socialists dismissed it from the first" (Little 1957, 265). Drewnowski dismisses Lange's system as "utopian" and unrelated to Soviet practice (1961, 341–42). Steindl, a socialist economist whose evident sympathy for Lange could hardly be greater, praises Lange's article as an "inspiration", but concludes: "Looking back now, with a sober mind, on the vast imposing scheme, we realise how impossible it would have been to carry it out" (Steindl 1965, 553).

c. The Market and Lange's System

Lange's proposal of the 1930s is commonly described as a species of 'market socialism' (Bergson 1967, 656; Grossman 1967, 98–99; Lavoie 1985, 118; Maksimović 1965, 349; Nove and Nuti 1972, 12). But this is what Lange says:

> As, in consequence of public ownership of the means of production, there is in a socialist economy no market on which capital goods are actually exchanged, there are obviously no prices of capital goods in the sense of exchange ratios on a market. (Lange 1938, 61)

All the peculiarities of Lange's scheme arise precisely because he is endeavoring to offer an alternative to factor markets, which, he states, cannot by definition prevail under socialism (except possibly for labor factors). Lange states that in his socialism "there is no market for capital goods and productive resources outside of labour" (73). He contrasts "a socialist economy" with "a competitive market", always treating these as mutually exclusive (65, 80). He asserts that under socialism a "Central Planning Board performs the functions of the market" (82–83). In Lange's account, capital goods have no market prices but only "accounting prices", the state enterprises do not make or receive monetary payments, they do not (and cannot) make any effort to be profitable or to cover their costs, and they do not (and cannot) compete.

Part of the explanation for the confusion is that Lange allows some supplementary market features, and in doing so, he considers *two* alternative socialist systems.[3] The second of these systems, which he does not recommend but which he holds to be feasible, dispenses with *all* markets, even for consumers" goods (90–98). In Lange's first system, the system he is actually advocating (72–90), there is a market for consumer goods, a market for labor (73), and some private trading (120). Lange holds that these concessions are optional; he does not believe that his system requires them (95). None of these concessions to the market is new, and they are not the distinctive elements of his proposal. Lange prefers the market for consumer goods and labor, not on grounds of practicability or efficiency, but on humanitarian grounds. He holds that his system could, if it were thought desirable, obviate the need for any markets whatsoever. His preferred system permits a market only where it abandons his distinctive proposal, which supplants the market wherever it prevails.

It is all the more remarkable that *Lange himself*, nearly 30 years later, looks back on his proposal as one which has "refuted the Hayek-Robbins argument by showing how a market mechanism could be established in a socialist economy" (Lange 1967, 159). In saying this, Lange falls into line with the common view of his work, but that view is inconsistent with his own statements in 1938. Of course, theorists may misdescribe what they are doing, but the 1938 Lange did not. Even if Lange had explicitly said that his proposal was market socialism, a look at that proposal could have shown this to be untrue. Following Lange's 1938 article, 'market socialism' made great strides politically, especially after 1953. But the 'socialist' markets permitted in Eastern Europe and elsewhere were markets in which enterprises pursued profits, and in which legal title to capital goods was exchanged for legal title to sums of money. In the Soviet Union observers believed that the official prices of capital goods were artificially fixed with little or no direct influence from market forces, but no one claims that these prices were revised in the manner of Lange's 'accounting prices'.

In the 1930s it would have been a great concession for an ostensibly Marxist theoretician, aligned with the Comintern, to acknowledge the need for factor markets in socialism. Lange was a Comintern sympathizer who rejected Marxist economic theory. His proposal avoided the need for a market, and yet appeared to draw upon some of the characteristics of the market, notably the uncentralized nature of decision-making. By the 1960s, Soviet-bloc ideological spokesmen no longer emphasized the incompatibility of socialism and market prices for capital goods, nor did they wish to draw attention to the fact that their position had shifted. Today, if there are any students who actually read Lange's article with their own eyes, instead of reading into it the 'market socialism' their professors tell them is in it, they may be quite puzzled at the pains Lange takes to avoid admitting factor markets (other than labor markets) into socialism.

Lange's article has an appendix on "The Allocation of Resources under Socialism in Marxist Literature". Here Lange uses misleadingly selective quotations to support the claim that leading Marxist theoreticians have always appreciated the need for money and prices in post-capitalist society.[4] It is possible that Lange was attempting to use his role as defender of Marxism in order to educate Marxists. If so, this doesn't seem to have worked. More orthodox Stalinists responded to Lange's article by briefly citing it as a demonstration that socialism was feasible, yet rejecting Lange's system as unplanned, and in this respect, too reminiscent of capitalism (Dobb 1940, 276; Sweezy 1949, 233).

I contend that the Lange of 1936–38 perceives his proposal as a form of NFM socialism, and indeed that he agrees with Marx and Mises in defining socialism as NFM socialism. This reading might be contested. Lange's equivocation on "prices" in his appendix and his retrospective description of his proposal as employing the market might be given a lot of weight. Proposals for incorporating aspects of the market into socialism were in the air in the 1920s and 1930s. The new proposals were being developed by many individuals, and rumors of their ideas were topics of interest before the proposals appeared in printed form. The fact that Lange's proposal was received as a 'competitive' system may arise from oral reports of this system prior to its appearance in print, and these oral reports might capture something in Lange's thinking (and see Nove 1991, 129). If so, some readers might still hold that Lange assumes that his state enterprises will have their own bank balances and that the managers will strive to maximize profits or avoid losses (despite the fact that this is contradicted by Lange's actual proposals). In that case, Lange's system would be transformed, and much of what I say in the next two sections would not apply. An enterprise which has to pay its bills and strives to avoid losses is *ipso facto* following a 'rule' more sweeping and decisive than Lange's two rules, a 'rule' which would automatically mean that the two rules would be little more than frills, if they could be enforced at all. However, some of my comments below (7.iii.) on theorists other than Lange would then be applicable to Lange too. And my discussion of Lange's scheme as a particular kind of *simulated* market would still help to clarify the discussion by isolating and appraising one component of the Lange package.

d. Lange: Last-Ditch Defender of Non-Market Socialism

Lange proposes to abolish the market and pursuit of profit in arriving at general units of calculation for productive assets. His pure system has no market prices, and no profits, either in the "accounting" sense (which is not, of course, the accounting sense) or the tangible monetary sense. Managers of enterprises and industries do not pay any attention to profitability (it would be pointless for them even to keep accounts in the form of financial statements, since profitability cannot affect their behavior, if they behave as described). The managers follow the rules, using only "accounting prices", and the accounting prices are adjusted according to physical surpluses or deficits of stocks.

This is decidedly not a market system. The managers are not exchanging the factors thus valued. There is no bargaining and no rivalry. Prices are changed only by the central planning board; two state enterprises cannot agree upon a price of their own. Unfortunately, Hayek, in the best-known criticism of Lange's system, classes it as a species of "competitive" socialism, thus helping to perpetuate the confusion about the nature of Lange's system (Hayek 1940). In the sense of rivalry between enterprises, or of enterprises (for instance) seeking to increase their sales by lowering their costs and thus the prices of their products, there is no possibility of competition in Lange's system.

Equally, Lange's is not a system of society-wide planning. There is no room for any overall planning, any more than there is in a free market. Although Lange's system features a "Central Planning Board", the board has no discretion; like the managers, it mechanically follows rules. Lange's Board cannot do precisely what, in traditional Marxist doctrine, the socialist administration is supposed to do: 'consciously' determine the composition of output. This function is as automatic or anarchic in Lange's system as it is in the market.

As Roberts points out, Lange's Board is virtually redundant, since its tasks too could be given to the managers (Roberts 1971a, 94). Roberts concludes from this "polycentric" quality that the Lange system is tantamount to a market system. But characteristics other than polycentricity are entailed by a market. The essence of a market is trade. There is no trade in Lange's system, or at least, to the extent that everyone follows the rules and the system works as described, the logic and rationale of the system do not derive from trade. (Here as elsewhere, I refer to Lange's system in its pure form. Lange admits trade into his preferred form of socialism, but only as an option, and only where the distinctive features of his proposal are not implemented.)

Many subsequent writers have ignored the peculiar nature of Lange's system. They have readily collapsed it into schemes for marginal-cost pricing or, even more carelessly, into straightforward market socialism, where state enterprises buy and sell factors, and pursue profits in the conventional way. Marginal-cost pricing, as a rule for nationalized industries, means that, in determining the prices of their products, the industries should make them equal to marginal costs. In this proposal, there are no 'accounting prices', but only genuine money prices.[5] Each industry operates within a market environment, in which inputs have to be paid for and products have to be sold.

The idea behind marginal-cost pricing is that, since nationalized industries are monopolies, and since it is believed that monopolies, endeavoring to maximize profits, will raise prices and reduce output below the optimum which would emerge in perfect competition, the industries should be instructed not to maximize profits, but to make their product prices equal to their marginal costs. This has superficial similarities with Lange's scheme, but it is fundamentally different because there is a functioning market. In marginal-cost pricing, the industries buy factors for money and sell their products for money. There is thus an automatic pressure for industries to attempt to cover their costs, unless some specific subsidy is arranged, in which case they are still impelled to cover their costs from sales plus subsidy. This pressure to cover costs does not exist in Lange's system and cannot be introduced into Lange's system without transforming it.

Various reasons have been advanced why Lange's system might not work. I rehearse a few of them below. There are, however, two categories of objections to Lange's proposal which I will mention here in passing. First, there is the possibility that the managers might not be properly motivated, might not have adequate incentives, to make the correct decisions. By 'incentives' I mean inducements to do what is supposed to be done, rewards which stimulate a sufficiently strong desire among the managers to follow the rules (see Chapter 11 below). Second, there has been discussion of whether the two rules chosen by Lange would be the best rules that might be proposed. Various modifications to the rules have been suggested. A similar discussion of the best rules has gone on among economists discussing the marginal-cost pricing proposal for nationalized industries operating within a market system. I will generally ignore this aspect, and confine myself to difficulties which would arise no matter how the Langian rules might be modified.

But there is one conceivable alternative to Lange's rules which is worth pondering: why not have the managers maximize 'accounting' profits? It may seem strange that such a system has never, to my knowledge, been proposed. Many there have been who have concluded that Lange's scheme is unfeasible and that profits are the only practicable general objectives for enterprises. But in all such cases, it is simply assumed that the alternative to the marginal cost rule is pursuit of profits in the conventional sense, profits derived from market trading and measured by reference to market prices expressed in money. No one has proposed to replace the marginal cost rule with the pursuit of 'accounting profits'—profits measured in 'accounting prices' determined by responding to surpluses and deficits in stocks.

We could imagine going one step further. Enterprises would pursue profits, and prices would be formed in the normal way, or strictly analogously with the normal way, by agreement between the transactors. There would then be no accounting prices and no system of watching surpluses and deficits in stocks. This would be a pure simulated market. Does such a conception have a clear meaning? If a system simulates the market closely enough, in what precise sense is it not actually a functioning market? The pure simulated market was not discussed in the 1930s. For a serious exposition, we had to wait for Carens (1981), whose fascinating suggestion I examine below (11.ii.).

Lange presents three ideas simultaneously: 1. market trading will be replaced by a simulation, achieved by enterprise managers conscientiously following rules; 2. the 'marginal cost rule' (actually the two rules) will replace pursuit of profits as the 'rule' to be followed by managers of enterprises; and 3. changes in prices will be made by observing surpluses and shortages in stocks. These three ideas are in principle distinct, but the impact made by Lange's proposal seems to have derived from presenting them simultaneously, as an integral scheme. The general muddle about what Lange was proposing, whether it was market socialism or not, meant that it was a long time before these elements were disentangled. This muddle was encouraged by the propensity of mainstream economists of the 1930s to suppose that economic theory had nothing to say about comparative institutions; the distinction between functioning and simulated markets seemed inconsequential.

If the discussion had proceeded in logical stages, Lange's scheme might have been criticized and modified, until we were left with a pure simulated market, something like Carens's system. Instead Lange's proposal was confused with other systems—some of them clearly FM systems, others ambiguous. After the Second World War, academic socialists weren't interested in Lange's efforts to avoid FM socialism, and Carens published his proposal in 1981, without mentioning Lange. Economists with socialist sympathies or socialists with some knowledge of economics came to accept the FM-socialist ideas of the early 1920s, even down to the very name 'market socialism', but instead of recognizing this as an abandonment of Lange's last-ditch efforts to save non-market socialism, in favor of the earlier ideas which had been criticized by Mises and rejected by socialists before Lange wrote about socialism, these socialists innocently hailed Lange as a pioneer of the theory of market socialism, to which Lange in fact contributed nothing.

e. The Feasibility of Lange's System[7]

1. Limitations of the Perfect Competition Analogy

Lange's scheme draws upon the illustrative fiction of perfect competition,[8] re-arranging its elements. Mises had no time for perfect competition, and Misesian critics of Lange often dispute the legitimacy of this model. Yet the most ardent proponent of perfect competition never claims that it is an accurate depiction of the operation of any actual market (though it often yields approximately the same outcome). In perfect competition, certain features of real markets are ignored and others are drastically simplified for analytic purposes. There is no role for arbitrage or other forms of speculation, since any departure from the single ruling price for each class of commodity is impossible, and product innovation is difficult to handle, since the first producer of a new product cannot be a price-taker. Whether or not we have reservations about the fruitfulness of the perfect competition model, it doesn't impugn that model to suggest that it cannot serve as a basis for market simulation.

There may be a temptation to suppose that it doesn't matter that Lange's scheme leaves out certain aspects of reality ignored by perfect competition, because perfect competition is a welfare ideal. By decreeing a single price for all goods of a certain type, we therefore copy the ideal. If this departs from the market's reality, so much the better. But there are two mistakes in this supposition. First, perfect competition is a welfare ideal only in the sense that *some* departures from it are inefficient. Other departures are improvements. Second, if perfect competition embodies in extreme form a tendency found in actual markets, we cannot rely upon being able to simulate that tendency after paralyzing the mechanism by which it emerges. In an 'efficient market' we observe that all information is swiftly incorporated into prices. We may say, as a simplifying assumption, that this happens instantly, but in fact it happens by thousands of unknown individuals being continuously alert to possible discrepancies. (The stock market, the paradigm of an efficient market, is unusual in that there is normally very little uncertainty about which classes of securities are perfect substitutes. For most goods, the characteristic situation is that there are numerous varieties which are somewhat imperfect substitutes. The closeness of substitutability is itself something hazy, shifting, and uncertain, something about which information is costly. We often lack information as to whether or not a particular price difference would be removed by further information: in other words, empirically there is no clear distinction between the same goods having different prices and superficially similar goods being in fact different goods.) The observable tendency for all goods of a certain type to have the same price, and that the 'correct' price, is taken to its extreme in perfect competition, where there is general omniscience. But in the real world price discrepancies are themselves important communicators of information, and speculation is a vital equilibrating force. Much of the observable tendency for prices to converge arises out of the rippling of information from many centers. The decreeing of a single price from a single center cannot but lead to a 'wrong' price, both because it will treat goods that are not perfect substitutes as perfect substitutes and *vice versa*, and because it cannot quickly incorporate the initiatives of individual speculators.

There is a speculative element inherent in production: a producer combines factors in the expectation that the output can be sold to cover the cost of the factors. If a producer hits upon a new way of combining factors, which she thinks will enable the product to sell at a lower-than-prevailing price and still cover costs, she is able to try this method out. If she succeeds, she takes away customers from other producers, who are under pressure to reduce prices. Such a producer (or her counterpart as manager of a state enterprise) under Lange's system would not be able to offer her products at a lower price, since the price of that class of commodity has to be fixed by the center watching total stocks. This kind of difficulty becomes magnified in the case of product innovation.

One of the advantages of the market is that various voluntary arrangements (such as futures contracts) can be made to transfer risk from one person or organization to another. This leads to a form of specialization whereby the risk inherent in change tends to move to those most willing to bear it, and these people become specialists in gathering information relevant to those forms of risk. It's difficult to imagine any counterpart of these arrangements under Lange's system. This is a malaise that seems to afflict Lange in all those cases where, within the market, someone uses her intelligence to discriminate among market signals. For example, the entrepreneur does not react mechanically to a rise or fall in demand for his product, but tries to disentangle the fleeting from the more lasting components. Such discernment is of the essence of astute business judgment, and it greatly benefits the population if the aptitude for it can be encouraged and trained. But it's not easy to see how this can occur under Lange, which follows a simplified picture of the market wherein entrepreneurs react mechanically to price data without trying to understand them.

2. The Allocation of Capital to Enterprises

Lange's system has no provision for a large category of everyday market developments: those that relate to the closing of existing enterprises and the opening of new ones, the shrinking of some enterprises and the expansion of others, the allocation of society's stock of savings to firms by lowering the boom on some and providing generous support to others, the decision of an enterprise to stop making a product, or to start making a new product—one it has not made before, or one that no one has made before. There is nothing to take the place of the capital and money markets, through which investors bring about the rise and fall of different enterprises (Mises 1966, 706–09).

An enterprise producing a particular capital good might find that no one was using this article. In the market, the enterprise might notice that an opportunity existed to switch to the production of a different kind of capital good which, in the judgment of that enterprise's management, might be more marketable. But in the

Lange system there is no such category as 'marketable', as applied to a capital good. Lange's rules do not permit the enterprise manager to make such a commitment, based upon his judgment of the situation, and in any case, he doesn't have the information to make such a judgment, since he doesn't know what lines are profitable and what lines are not. We have to suppose, therefore, that the observable stocks of this capital good start to pile up, and the price of that good is progressively reduced. There is no provision for discontinuing production of that capital good as soon as its accounting price falls below its production cost—nor should there be, for it is possible that further price changes would demonstrate such a decision to have been mistaken. We can suppose that someone at the head of the industry decides to discontinue production of that good whenever certain conditions are fulfilled: when its price has been below its production cost ('prices' always meaning accounting prices in the state's published tables) for a certain period of time. It might also be a warning sign if the price of a newly manufactured article fell to zero, or below zero, or was demanded by enterprises to be used as scrap. Again, one can imagine criteria by which industry heads could close or open, or shrink or expand, various enterprises. These criteria might not be totally bereft of all rationality, but still, they would be bound to be inefficient. This must be so because the enterprises do not recognize profit and loss, and there is no general measure, such as an enterprise's net present value, to help monitor the performance of an enterprise.[8]

3. The Method of Physical Surpluses and Deficits

Lange's system adjusts accounting prices by observation of physical surpluses and shortages. Lange introduces this method by stating that "*Any price different from the equilibrium price would show at the end of the accounting period a surplus or a shortage of the commodity in question*" (82). He later asserts that equilibrium can be "determined by a method of *trial and error* similar to that in a competitive market" (86). A little later he actually says it is "the same process of trial and error" as the market (87).

Lange refers to Taylor's account, but as far as we can judge from Taylor's sketchy description, Taylor sees socialist industry as a single organizational unit, whereas Lange sees it as divided into numerous enterprises, each with somewhat independent managers and bookkeeping. Lange refers to "the quantity demanded and supplied of each commodity" (86), which only makes sense where there are separate agencies demanding and supplying. Taylor confines his method to "primary" land and labor factors, while Lange extends it to all factors (87). Taylor apparently thinks that if the "primary" factors are valued, the remaining factors, intermediate goods or capital goods in the broadest sense, can be valued on the basis of the primary factors. But consider a type of machine (say, a type of printing press) which is still in widespread use but no longer being manufactured. Such a machine would have to be valued independently of the past or present valuations of primary factors. And quite apart from such special (though common) cases, there must be mutual determination of all prices in an equilibrating system: prices of primary factors cannot be determined without prices of consumer goods, capital goods, and intermediate goods also being determined.

What is meant by a surplus or a shortage in stocks of goods? Any simple meaning we care to give this phrase seems obviously inadequate for the practical task of price adjustment. At the very least, we have to decide 1. what counts as the total stock, and 2. what is the level above and below which a surplus or shortage is calculated.

Since Lange talks in terms of supply and demand, and emphasizes the similarity of his method to the market, we should consider the part played by quantities of goods in forming market prices. There is one price which equates the quantity of a good offered for sale with the quantity which people are prepared to buy. Only one price will clear the market: at a higher price, some goods will be unsold (which the prospective sellers would like to have sold at that price), at a lower price, some willing buyers will be unsatisfied. In this familiar story of how prices are determined on the market, no one needs to know (and in fact no one generally does know) what the quantity sold at the equilibrium price will be. Specific quantities are associated with specific prices, but these quantities are the quantities which would change hands. Now moving to the Lange proposal, we presumably have to simplify by equating 'changing hands' with transfer from one productive stage to another. But where now is the physical stock of goods which should be watched in order to adjust the accounting price? If we simplify the problem by supposing that a particular kind of good will always be produced by a certain known kind of enterprise and then used by another kind of enterprise, without middlemen, then we have a. the sum of the stocks held by all the producing enterprises; b. the sum of the stocks held by all the using enterprises; and c. the sum of a. and b. Let us assume that c. is meant, because there is no particular rationale for looking at a. or b. in isolation. How could it be decided whether there was a surplus or a deficit? In the market, inventories (stocks of goods measured in physical units) tend towards a level determined by profitability. From a private or social point of view, inventories can be too low or too high. Both divergences from the optimum constitute inefficiencies—they constitute a waste of real resources. If inventories are too high, resources are 'locked up' in inventory which could be more productive elsewhere. If inventories are too low, the even flow of production is disrupted in ways that are more costly than the best alternative use of the resources which could be employed to build inventory. In some cases the optimum inventory held by a particular enterprise is zero; in other cases it is counted in thousands.

It does not seem easy for the Langian administration to determine the optimum level of inventory. The obvious idea would be to use the accounting prices to enable managers to apply a formula for optimal inventory of the sort used by managers in the market. The total stock would then be the aggregate of all the managers applying the formula. Still, it's not clear how this would work. If a good becomes under-priced, then the using enterprises will overdemand it. The immediate effect is to increase the stocks of the using enterprises and deplete the stocks of the producing enterprises. At that point, the total stock has not changed, yet the producing enterprises should increase output, or the price should be raised, or both. The market practice of leaving it to the producing enterprises to determine to what extent to increase output and to what extent to raise prices is not available, since it depends upon estimates of profitability. If the depletion of stocks of the producing enterprises is permitted to become a real 'shortage', then inefficiencies will be generated, with the total supply allocated among users by inferior non-price methods.

There are also many unique goods: unique natural features, such as a harbor; produced goods that were made one-of-a-kind, or goods that, because of their history and state of repair, are now one-of-a-kind. Such unique goods, not part of any homogeneous stock, have to be allocated to their best uses, just like other goods. In the Lange system, their accounting prices are apparently indeterminate, since there cannot be surpluses or deficits in their stocks.

Supposing that the equation of prices with marginal costs (or some other rule) is correct, it is not enough that we move towards the equation of prices with marginal costs. The route by which we move is important. As one determinant of this route, the comparative urgency with which different divergences from the equation are viewed is important. It seems intuitively appealing that these determinants of the best route are approximated in the more fundamental 'rule' of the market, that entities cover their costs or 'stand on their own bottoms'. Though I don't know how to attempt to prove this, it is at least clear that, out of the infinity of possible routes to equilibrium, the more basic market 'rule' eliminates from consideration a great many which would in practice be grossly inferior. (Thus a firm faced with large and continuing losses will not view this as one more divergence of prices from marginal costs, just like modest profits, but as a crisis calling for drastic emergency measures.) Similarly, in real life where the data are continually changing, it is desirable to adjust to some maladjustments (like temporary local shortages), and not to the imaginary situation which will emerge when all adjustments are complete. A related puzzle is *by how much* to adjust prices. Some discussions assume infinitesimal adjustments, but in a dynamic world where delay is costly, estimating the magnitude of optimal price and quantity adjustments is a useful knack that ought to be encouraged and cultivated.

Problems of this sort arise because Lange's is a purely 'static' system. His essay is heavily influenced by the brilliant static analysis of Walras. In economics, 'statics' refers to imaginary scenarios in which 'the data' (preferences, knowledge, resources) do not change. Thus, statics is illustrative and not intended to be necessarily true to life. Statics also generally implies that delay is costless: as long as equilibrium is reached, it doesn't matter how long it takes. This goes along with the freezing of the data. When 'dynamics' is introduced, we confront the fact that equilibrium is constantly moving and the path to equilibrium affects future equilibria. Statics is a worthy and useful attempt to simplify the analysis by abstracting from this problem.[9] But turning to dynamics, it is immediately obvious that rapid movement towards approximate equilibrium is vital, whereas ultimate arrival at precise equilibrium is of no importance. Furthermore, the movement must be feasible: if an enterprise is to move goods by road, it must actually have the trucks, drivers, and gasoline. If these are not available right now, then something else must be done, even if the eventual equilibrium 'solution' indicates road transportation. A tolerably efficient economy must be able to adapt to its own actual inadequacies.

In 1940 Lange wrote a letter to Hayek, responding to Hayek's criticisms. Lange states that Hayek has moved "the weight of the argument from pure static aspects to the dynamic ones", concedes that Hayek has raised problems yet to be solved, and asserts that Lange will write a reply to Hayek's paper "some time in the fall" (quoted from the collected works of Lange in Polish, in Brus and

Laski, 160, n15). Lange's reply never appeared, though he lived until 1965. As we have seen, Mises had always insisted on the dynamic nature of the economic calculation problem, and Lange had claimed to provide a *practically workable technique* for administering NFM socialism.

4. The Subjectivity and Objectivity of Costs

In the market, entrepreneurs anticipate, speculate, agonize, guess, and take risks. They also frequently perform elaborate calculations, aware that the results of such calculations are only as good as their assumptions. Always enveloped in a cloud of ignorance, market decision-makers strain to discern the indefinite contours of the changing shapes that loom ambiguously out of the fog. They combine exact computation with honed intuition, in varying proportions.

In Lange's system, all the managers have to do is to follow a couple of simple rules. Something appears to be missing. At this point the discussion can go in either of two directions. We could say that the rules are sufficient, that they dispense with the need for judgment, or alternatively that all the judgment, all the arduous effort to maximize profits, will have its counterpart in similar judgement, and similar arduous effort, in pursuit of following the rules. Let us consider each of these in turn.

Consider two entrepreneurs in the market. They each, in different contexts, believe that a new variety of a product can be made by a new, untried process, which will result in sufficient sales, at a price that will cover costs, to pay for the investment in the process. They may believe that some consumers will prefer the new variety to existing varieties, and that some will shift from the existing varieties because of the lower price of the product. Their judgment about the cheapness of the new method may involve a judgment about the ability of engineers to iron out certain wrinkles in the process during the first couple of years' production. Both of these entrepreneurs manage to persuade investors to back them. One of these entrepreneurs succeeds, because he judged correctly. The other fails because he judged incorrectly. In the first instance, production of the new product is expanded, and other producers begin to imitate the entrepreneur, who finds himself now with more control over the disposition of resources. In the second case, production of the new product is stopped, perhaps abruptly and to many people's annoyance. The factors formerly tied up in that line of production are swiftly shifted to other lines of production which have not yet been vetoed by losses. That entrepreneur's control over the disposition of resources is curtailed.

There are several features of this story which must be reproduced in any non-market system if it is to simulate the market. Most conspicuously, it must be possible for someone to undertake a project which has no guarantee of success, without persuading the authorities or experts that he is right, and for the results of that project to demonstrate, in due course, whether he was right or wrong. As a result of the sequence of events in the above story, there is additional information, which helps to guide production. If the Lange system is to simulate the market, it too must generate this new information, in corresponding circumstances, and use it to guide production.

Following the two rules does not enable the Lange system to reproduce these features of the market. In order for comparable results to emerge from following the Langian rules, it would be necessary for individuals to do better or worse at following the rules, and for the better choices to be somehow favored by a selection process over the worse choices. Mechanical following of rules, without the use of judgement, cannot give this result. If the two market entrepreneurs in our story were transported to the Lange system, they would each follow the rules as they saw fit, and presumably they would both keep their jobs, along with control over the same amounts of resources. As far as we can tell, they would either both be unable to proceed with their new ideas, or both would proceed and both projects would be continued indefinitely.

We therefore turn to the alternative, that Langian managers can use their judgement in striving to apply the rules, rather as entrepreneurs use theirs to maximize profits. But this presupposes that the rules can be followed well or badly, and that there is some way to test the results.

Thus, whether we interpret the Lange rules as being applied mechanically (if conscientiously), or whether we interpret following the rules as requiring judgement, we have to conclude that the rules cannot perform the function required of them. That such a fundamental point could be so often missed seems to have arisen because most discussants of Lange's proposal have not taken its distinctive features seriously—they have instead tacitly supposed that there is some kind of ghostly market in existence, providing the Langian managers with information.

The proposal to replace the market with Langian rules may be illustrated by applying a similar approach to chess. Chessplayers try to win, and failing that, to avoid loss. They make complex evaluations of positions, revising these evaluations in the light of new developments and new insights. We might propose to replace all these exhausting evaluations and calculations with a simple rule: always make the best move. This rule is proposed to replace any striving for checkmate, or avoidance of being checkmated. But the rule cannot function as a substitute for preoccupation with checkmate. The concrete significance of the rule in any particular case can only be found by reference to checkmate possibilities, and the rule is merely a generalization of many complex considerations viewed in the light of checkmate possibilities. This might be unclear with such an evidently vacuous rule, but we can translate it into more concrete-sounding terms, say: 'Maintain the optimum balance between force and space.' Similarly, concepts like marginal cost are merely helpful generalizations of what people may do when preoccupied with profitability. Since costs are foregone opportunities, any reference to costs is a tacit reference to hypothetical future income.

Lange sometimes argues as if the way in which accounting is done determines business decisions. But this is like saying that the counting of pieces on the board determines chess moves. Accounting is a useful tool of business, but it can never replace entrepreneurial or managerial decision-making. Since most accounting magnitudes embody estimates of uncertain future events, the best accounting procedures can easily show a loss where there is a profit or a profit where there is a loss.[10] But even if we grant that financial statements give an accurate picture of the situation, they are inherently incapable of telling us what to do about it. A consummate accountant may be a hopeless entrepreneur, while an entrepreneur of genius may know very little accountancy.

Lange's scheme has often been criticized by Austrian-school economists on the grounds that 'costs are subjective'. This formulation can easily give rise to misunderstanding. If costs were purely subjective, in the sense of expressing decision-makers' tastes, then it would hardly matter that Langian managers could not simulate the decisions of market managers and entrepreneurs: this matters only if decisions (and therefore costs) can be evaluated by objective standards. Costs are subjective in the sense that they reflect consumers' judgments, but in evaluating enterprises under different institutions, consumers' preferences have to be taken as given, hence as objective data. The optimal disposition of factors to serve consumers' preferences is also 'given', in the sense that it is strictly determined by those preferences plus the stocks of factors in existence and the possible results of combining them, though it is *not* given in the sense that anyone can look and see what it is. Enterprise decision-makers might allow their own consumer preferences to influence their decisions, but it could plausibly be asserted that this element is unnecessary. We are left with one important sense in which costs are subjective: that decisions rest upon judgments which may not be demonstrable. In the same way, choosing the best move in a new chess position may be said to be subjective. This is not to deny that there is, objectively, one best move. It is merely to say that the chess-playing community and its analysts may require a century or two to determine that best move, whereas the player must now decide, using trained judgment. (While chessplayers may eventually come to a final decision on whether to take the pawn in the Poisoned Pawn variation of the Najdorf, most business decisions will never be finally evaluated, because many of the conditions of the decision are irretrievably uncertain. Also, business has more pieces and more squares than chess.)

When we look at economists' cost curves, it is easy to forget that these curves are conjectural. It makes the analysis easier to follow if we tacitly, and falsely, assume that anyone can look and see what costs are. But costs are counterfactuals. Costs are estimated by decision-makers who survey a wide range of possible course of action, and select what seems to them the best. They do this in terms of future income foregone. A business decision results from the comparison of a number of alternative production plans. It is possible to check on whether the production plan conforms to announced expectations, but it is not possible to check on how its outcome compares with the outcomes of the plans which were not implemented. As Thirlby and Wiseman show in detail (Thirlby 1946b; 1952; Wiseman 1953), actual business decisions involve comparisons of alternative ways of doing things, in circumstances such that no marginal rule which is independently checkable can be applied.

iii. OTHER COMPROMISE SYSTEMS FROM THE 1930S

Lange's system is often associated with other systems first advocated in the 1930s, and incorporating into socialism elements traditionally associated with capitalism. The best-known are Hall (1937), Dickinson (1939), Lerner (1937; 1944), Durbin (1949), and Beckwith (1949). That all these proposals are often lumped together has helped to reinforce the notion that Lange's system is a 'market' or 'competitive' system. Some of these systems were proposed earlier than Lange's, and possess a more plausible claim to feasibility, but they have lacked the charm of Lange's simulated market, with its 'accounting prices'. All of these schemes are attempted compromises between capitalism and earlier conceptions of socialism.

In some ways the various proposals of the 1930s differ in tone and flavor. They range from Lange's, which it is almost impossible to seriously believe anyone could ever try to implement, to Durbin's, probably the most 'realistic'. When we read Lange, we breathe "the air from another planet". When we read Durbin, we never stray far from British nationalized industries. Yet in other ways, all these proposals are remarkably unified in approach and methodology. They all accept that the textbook model of capitalism can be employed as an operating scheme for socialism. They all, in fact, explicitly make the argument that since we have a good theory of what determines prices in the market, it must follow that there is no theoretical obstacle to having factor prices determined without any factor markets. They all accept, as a matter of practical recommendation, that there must be a market for consumer goods.

On the crucial question of whether there will be factor markets under socialism, or whether the authorities will fix 'prices' without buying and selling, the writers vary. Thus, Hall (1937), like Lange, takes it for granted that socialism excludes factor markets. Aside from consumer goods, "there are no payments and no receipts". Durbin clearly supposes that nationalized industries will buy and sell their inputs and products. Dickinson equivocates: though much of his discussion seems to be compatible with an administrative simulation of the market, like Lange's or Hall's, near the end of his book, he makes a strong declaration of the financial independence of socialist enterprises, which he says "will be managed very much as separate enterprises are under capitalism" (213). Lerner is more concerned to get the formal conditions correctly specified than to describe the institutional conditions. Although Lerner enters the discussion as an apparent advocate of socialism, it emerges that he actually views the choice of private or state ownership as a matter to be decided on the merits of each case (Lerner 1934; 1936; 1937; 1944; see Friedman 1947).

Although all these works very emphatically proclaim that Mises is clearly wrong and that socialism is entirely workable, on close inspection they all (except possibly Beckwith) allow the possibility that socialism will perform poorly. This results from their argument that the 'theoretical' possibility of socialism follows from standard price theory. Since this conclusion is derived by excluding 'practical' issues from economics, there has to be some admission that the "practical" questions do have some relevance to the problem of administering socialism. Thus, Hall states that the practical difficulties of socialism "are unknown" (74), and frequently reminds the reader that he is excluding 'practical' issues. At the same time most of his discussion conveys a confident assumption of practical feasibility. Lange surprisingly states (120) that in privately-owned industries where competition prevails, the outcome will be better than under socialism, so these industries should not be socialized (though he thinks that competition has disappeared in most of private industry and cannot be restored).

8

PROPERTY RIGHTS AND THE LIMITS OF MARKET SOCIALISM

Very few of the many socialists who responded to Mises in the 1920s failed to agree with his assumption that socialism was incompatible with factor markets. But by the 1940s, the majority view, at least among Western economists who paid any attention to 'comparative economic systems', was that socialism could encompass factor markets. Any doubts about this could be silenced by the example of Soviet Russia, where 'socialism' prevailed (most of industry was nationalized and purportedly administered through a society-wide plan) and yet where factor markets survived (state enterprises paid each other sums of money for the factors they used).[1]

How can we make sense of this? One obvious tack would be to say that, for some reason or other, many writers on socialism before 1940, including Marx and Mises, rashly assumed that socialism necessarily excluded factor markets; but then wiser heads somehow came to realize that this assumption was unwarranted, and it was therefore dropped. Today we are enlightened enough to understand that socialism can incorporate factor markets. On this account, it is puzzling why so many people made that particular unwarranted assumption, and there is the further puzzle of why the actual discussion did not proceed at all along the above lines: there was instead a search for NFM procedures which might simulate the effects of factor markets, and then, with no fanfare, a rapid slide into the position that factor markets were, of course, indispensable in any advanced industrial economy, including a socialist one.

If socialism means abolition of private ownership of the means of production and its replacement by 'common' ownership, and perhaps if the level of output required of 'socialism' is allowed to be somewhat less than that provided by capitalism, then Mises's argument seems to be refuted by the actual existence of nationalized industries. This commonsense objection helps to explain why the Mises argument was so widely rejected from the 1930s until the 1980s. It is a serious objection because although the scope of his argument is not *confined* to fully-nationalized economies, it certainly is intended to *include* them.

Mises replied to such arguments by pointing out that nationalized concerns were able to draw upon price and other information from the surrounding private-exchange economy. And when it became clear that Soviet Russia had adopted a stable system in which the great bulk of industry was nationalized and allegedly 'planned', Mises argued that 'socialist' Russia too could survive by drawing upon price and other information from the surrounding world (1981, 118). (He also kept on insisting, when it was in gross bad taste to do so, that mass poverty was an invariable feature of Soviet-type economies.) Whatever the merits of this as an argument about feasibility, it doesn't address the point that state ownership and a functioning market are apparently compatible, as a matter of observable fact. Mises's response to this is his insistence on the necessity for financial markets. While this is a shrewd reply, it leaves a hazy zone in the theoretical territory being fought over. It is possible to imagine an industrial system with well-developed markets in virtually all factors of production, considered as discrete goods, but no financial markets. Without too much straining of the evidence, such a system could be approximately identified with some actual economies, such as Yugoslavia between, say, 1950 and 1980, or Hungary from 1968 to 1989.

i. The Puzzle about FM Socialism

a. How is Market Socialism Even Conceptually Possible?

The term 'market socialism' may be applied to trade among independent self-managed co-operatives or communes. Here, the 'socialism' component arises from the internal organization of enterprises, the 'market' refers to the relations among enterprises. The situation here is basically similar to, if not a species of, private property: comparatively small groups 'own outright' the assets which they offer in trade. In that case the economic calculation problem doesn't arise. From a Misesian point of view, such a system is feasible if the groups are small enough, and on the understanding that the group members may have accepted some sacrifice of output (of goods other than co-operative living) for the sake of co-operative living. There are, of course, other questions that arise, notably: how can it be ensured, without suppressing the 'market', that the internal organization of these autonomous trading enterprises remains 'co-operative'?

Alternatively 'market socialism' may denote a system in which all industrial enterprises are owned by 'the community' (or the state) and at the same time, these enterprises trade with each other. Although in this chapter I sometimes refer for simplicity to state ownership, the discussion applies equally to any form of social or community ownership, where the owning entity ('society', 'the community') is conceived as a single organization or administration. It's convenient to discuss the issue in terms of state ownership because of the abundance of real-life examples of state-owned industrial enterprises, which do engage in trade.

On the face of it, there is something puzzling about this 'market socialism'. It is generally conceded that it's impossible—or at least utterly pointless—for an individual to conduct a market transaction with himself. Trade requires two independent transactors. If all of industry is owned by the state, how then is it possible for trade to occur between state enterprises?

I am a property owner and I authorize two agents, Peter and Paul, to trade on my behalf. Peter and Paul go to market, they happen to meet, and they conclude a market exchange: gold for bananas. Both items exchanged belong to neither Peter nor Paul; they belong to me, in the sense that I alone am legally recognized as the owner.

This looks like a genuine market exchange, yet the gold and the bananas remain 'my property'. We need to distinguish between a. the case where I have instructed that precisely this transaction shall occur, and b. the case where it happens independently of my immediate initiative or knowledge. In case a., some special explanation is demanded, for example: Peter and Paul, acting as my agents, might be bound by certain covenants which forbid me simply to order the transfers; or I might believe it to be useful for accounting purposes to balance Peter's transactions with Paul's in this way. In the absence of some such special explanation, we would have two remaining options: 1. I have taken leave of my senses; 2. the transaction, while it looks like a market transaction, is really not a market transaction, but an element in my plan. In that case, what is going on is essentially the same as if I had asked one employee to carry the gold from one warehouse to another, and asked another employee to carry the bananas in the reverse direction. Or, an even closer parallel, it is as though I had arranged a meeting with Peter and Paul, and announced: 'Peter, heretofore it has been your job to take care of my gold; from now on you will be responsible for looking after my bananas. Paul, you have been entrusted with the task of taking care of my bananas; henceforth you will please concern yourself with my gold'.

The second case, b., is more interesting, and can be explained in the following way. Peter and Paul have certain general goals as my agents. They are each, let us suppose, seeking to increase my profits (for example, because they like me, or because they are on a profit-related bonus, or because I pay them a wage and might fire them, or because their performance with me will help them get a job with someone else). But they have some discretion as to how they employ my resources. They can even sell my assets without my explicit permission in each case.

Peter and Paul exchange bananas for gold because each believes that the other commodity will be more useful to him in pursuing his own goals as an agent of mine. Inherent in this explanation is the assumption that Peter, Paul, and I have three different 'information-sets'—we know different things. The relevant knowledge of each of us is not identical, and in all probability, each knows some relevant facts that the other two don't. It is especially likely that Paul knows many things, unknown to Peter or me, relevant to his specialized section of my administration, and that Peter knows many things, unknown to Paul or me, relevant to *his* section. If this assumption of variation in knowledge is not made, it's difficult to see why I would divide my business enterprise into at least two departments (headed by Peter and Paul) and permit them to make their own decisions, within limits, as to the disposition of my property.

When I give Peter a general license or permission to buy and sell assets on my behalf, it is because I think that this may benefit me. Peter may see chances to improve my position, chances of which I may be ignorant. It may be too costly for him to inform me and wait for my decision. I may have given Peter this authority expecting him to trade with other firms than mine, but if he concludes a similar transaction with my other agent Paul, I have every reason to be gratified, for it indicates that the one who gives up bananas for gold can better pursue my purposes with gold than with bananas, while the one who gives up gold for bananas can better pursue my purposes with bananas than with gold. Both divisions of my firm have benefitted (if Peter and Paul are both correct in their judgements) and therefore the firm as a whole has benefitted, and therefore I have benefitted. It wasn't necessary for me to perceive (or even agree) that the outcome was beneficial. I may be unaware of the reasons that Paul can better serve my interests with bananas than with gold, and vice versa for Peter. I may never even discover that the transaction has occurred, yet I still benefit.

When they engage in trade, Peter and Paul are delegates of the 'owner' of the traded assets. They are able to act, within limits, like 'owners', and the more liberty I permit them to dispose of my assets, the more like 'owners' their behavior may become. They do have rights to dispose of 'my' assets, including the right to transfer these assets to others. These rights are dependent on my authorization, and hence are derivative of my property rights, but still, these agents' rights are themselves in some ways like property rights. They indeed can and should be viewed as property rights. *Any individual who has the right to deploy any resource in any way is the owner of a property right in that resource.*[2] It would be possible, alternatively, to call all such rights by some new term, say 'resource-deployment rights', and to define 'property rights' as a subset of resource-deployment rights. Although this would take us closer to the vernacular in many situations, it would be ill-advised, because the very notion that there is something self-evidently different about property rights, contrasted with other resource-deployment rights, is a source of confusion. I use the neutral term 'deploy a resource', to mean roughly 'help to determine what will happen to this resource under certain conditions', because I think it is a mistake to become involved, at the most elementary level of property theory, in making distinctions between 'use' and 'non-use', 'consumption' and 'production', and so forth.

Especially before the 1930s, many socialists and anti-socialists implicitly accepted some form of the following argument for the incompatibility of state-owned industry and factor markets. A market exchange is an exchange of property titles between two independent transactors. To bring all of industry under one organization dispenses with independent transactors. Thus internal market exchanges cease when all of industry is brought into the ownership of a single entity, whether the state or some other organization. It follows that ownership of all of industry (all non-human capital outside households) by a single entity abolishes all markets, except perhaps for consumer goods and labor.

This conclusion is belied by the fact that market exchanges sometimes occur between state industries, or for that matter, between divisions of the same privately-owned firm. It is also belied by thought-experiments like the one about Peter and Paul. However, although the argument as stated must be faulty, there really is something in it. People who tacitly accepted it were onto something which the later 'market socialists' missed.

The manager of one division of an organization (a private firm or a government-owned industrial sector) may conclude an exchange with the manager of another division of the same organization. In practice there are many such apparent exchanges which are not genuine market exchanges. Typically, one division of a privately-owned company takes supplies from another division, and a book 'payment' is made by the second division to the first division, in 'exchange' for the supplies. But this is not a genuine market exchange; such payments are often termed 'allocations' or 'transfers'. There is a prior decision by senior management that the supplies will be transferred in one direction and funds in another direction. This is an administrative parallel with a market transaction, which facilitates cost comparisons. It is in principle little different from the case where a supervisor has two subordinates, one of whom passes partly-made goods to the other. It might be helpful to the supervisor to suppose that the worker who supplies the other worker with goods is 'paid' by the latter, but this is purely notional. The worker who receives these goods cannot determine for himself to 'purchase' them somewhere else, still less to purchase a different kind of goods altogether (except by leaving that employment altogether). One can imagine that a supervisor might even institute such a system, where workers in the same factory can each choose for themselves which other workers to 'buy' from. According to the precise circumstances, this scheme might be a case of 'sub-contracting', in which the workers really do become independent firms, or it might be an internal procedure for capturing some of the features of that situation, for instance as this affects the behavior of the workers. Returning to the divisional managers, it is possible that they might be able to influence the 'allocation'. The manager whose division receives the supplies might complain to senior management that she could buy equally good supplies more cheaply outside the firm, and this might persuade senior management to permit her to do so, or to reduce the financial magnitude of the transfer as displayed by book entries.

I do not claim that there is a simple test for the presence or absence of a genuine market exchange (as opposed to a simulated or notional market exchange). To the contrary, actual situations are frequently subtle and obscure. But there is a clear conceptual distinction—the presence or absence of a spontaneous pattern that emerges because of the autonomy of the agents involved. And most interdivisional allocations are not predominantly analyzable as market exchanges, since the transactors at the divisional level are substantially following the plan determined by their superiors.

Aside from these instances, there may occur uncontroversial cases of genuine trade between divisions of the same organization. The divisional manager may be authorized by higher management to make certain purchases anywhere he can find them, and may in fact find them by buying from another division of the same firm. In most cases the division will be rejecting possible purchases from other suppliers outside the firm, but we can imagine the firm growing until most or all of the available suppliers of some items are other divisions within the same firm. These are undoubtedly genuine market exchanges. There is therefore a functioning market within a single organization, or within a single unit of ownership. Since this is so, should there be any difficulty in supposing that we can have a wholly state-owned economy in which there are factor markets—especially since that is precisely what we do see when we look at most economies with a large nationalized sector?

The divisions' authority to transfer assets is normally limited in two ways: 1. There are some assets they cannot transfer (they cannot raise funds from outside the organization by offering claims upon future earnings of the division) and 2. Their authority to transfer assets is dependent upon senior management, which can indeed go so far as to abolish any division. This suggests two ways to modify the argument for the incompatibility of a single owner and a functioning market: a single owner is incompatible with a market in all assets, in which those able to transfer assets can capture the full changes in asset values which result from their actions. If this is a tautology, it is an illuminating one.

As another instance of market compatibility with a single owner, we may consider nationalized industries which compete with each other for customers, as well as bidding against each other for resources. Thus nationalized British trucking ('road haulage') and railroads competed against each other in the business of moving freight. The fact of having 'the same owner' (the government) no more prevented these concerns competing than it prevented their trading with each other. Countries with large nationalized sectors such as Britain have traditionally administered each industry in one organization, headed by a single board. They could instead, following nationalization, have left the firms as separate entities, apparently no more connected with each other than when they were private. But if they do that, in what sense are the state firms not private? (The firms are officially declared to be state property, but what difference does this really make?)

One answer to this question might be that they are not private because the government can intervene at any moment and (exercising its rights as owner) combine one state firm with another, or close down a state firm, or split it into two firms; the government could also intervene in the firm's operations in any way the government chose. But this answer is not satisfactory, because governments have done any and all of these things to nominally private firms.

Some writers have indeed maintained that if the government assumes the right to intervene in private property, then the property is no longer private but has become state property in fact. Mises characterizes German National Socialism in this way. More recently, Bajt points out the possibility that some nominally private firms heavily regulated by the government may have less independence than some nominally state-owned firms (Bajt 1974, 254). This suggests that the concepts "state-owned" and "privately owned" may not always be clear-cut, mutually exlusive categories.

b. Property Rights

Property consists of rules governing the deployment of resources. *Some* system of property is inescapable in all human societies (for examples of the range of observed property systems, see Forde 1934 and Hoebel 1968), because there will always be frequent occasions when two or more individuals will wish to use the same resource in mutually exclusive ways. This clash of purposes can be resolved by a rule specifying how the resource will be used, or at least specifying a decision-procedure to determine how the resource will be used. Because of the need for responsiveness to local circumstances in the deployment of resources, such rules often prescribe, not how a resource will be used nor even a procedure by which its use will be determined, but simply which individual or small group can decide. In such cases, property rules are property rights.[3] (The use of 'right' here is evaluatively neutral. It describes what is customary within a specific population.)

Property rights may be fleeting and severely limited. Among the Eskimoes, one man has no right to possession and exclusive use of two spears if a kinsman has no spear at his disposal: one of the spears must be given to him. Among the Yurok, someone owning a boat is obliged to ferry a passing traveller across the river—that traveller has a right to a limited, fleeting use of both boat and boat-owner's labor (Hoebel 1968, 57).

In the course of social evolution there is a conspicuous tendency for occasional, limited, and transitory rights to become arranged into the system known as 'private property'. The essentials of this system, which seems to have arisen in many times and places independently, are: 1. that an individual can count certain goods as 'her property', because she has come by them in an approved manner; 2. that she is entitled to do with these things as she pleases, within a very wide range, and especially that she can freely 'abuse' them (use them in ways which other people dislike); 3. that these rights are perpetual; 4. that she can freely 'alienate' her rights to these goods, transferring her rights over them to other individuals, either by exchange on mutually-agreed terms, or by gift (including posthumous bequest). Private property may rarely have existed in a pure form throughout an entire society, but it has frequently appeared recognizable as an important systematic tendency within the whole property system of a society.

Private property tends to emerge and expand its scope because of superior efficiency, potentially benefitting everyone. Thus, if a patch of ground can be used by any member of the tribe at any time, or by each member in turn on consecutive days, then no individual or group (short of everyone unanimously) can safely plant and reap crops on that patch of ground. The Eskimo custom of being obliged to give away one's second spear restricts the potential for capital accumulation and economic growth. This does not matter where such accumulation and growth are largely ruled out for other reasons, as is true in traditional Eskimo society. In a society of greater complexity, such a property rule would be crippling. The Yurok custom of being entitled to a free ride across the river may work well in traditional Yurok society, where weeks may separate each consecutive traveller. But as Yurok society develops more complexity and greater population density, the rule can be expected to place such a burden on owners of boats that availability of boats would be reduced to an extent highly inconvenient to a great many non-boat-owners, so that even they would benefit from the abolition of this custom.

A property system may work well for a society with a specific technology, population density, and so forth, and may have to be modified as these features change. People raised in societies in which private property is highly developed may tend to hold a simplistic view of the nature of 'ownership'. Since 'ownership' (a typical bundle of rights related to some resource) becomes standardized, and incorporates the lessons of centuries of legal cases in tending to bring all the most relevant aspects of a single good under the same owner, 'ownership' comes to be seen as a straightforward, unproblematical relationship between a person and a material thing. Of course, we are all aware that ownership is frequently modified, as for instance, ownership of a piece of land by government zoning regulations, but there is a tendency to think of these regulations as leaving something called 'ownership' essentially unchanged.

Without prior education, someone coming from a technologically-advanced culture in which private property is prominent may be confused by the property rules found in more technologically primitive societies. She may find, for example, that the system of property rights in land is unlike that of private property, and she may be tempted to say that 'they don't have a concept of land ownership' or alternatively that 'their concept of land ownership is different to ours'.

The same person will, however, frequently also have an over-simple view of the meaning of 'ownership' in her own culture. Consider two adjoining pieces of land 'owned' by different individuals. Ownership of one of these pieces of land may or may not give one the right to: burn a fire sending smoke over the adjoining land; pump water from an underground reserve, lowering the water availability in the adjoining land; allow animals (mice, rats, lions) to proliferate on one's own land and thus invade the adjoining land; erect a tall building blocking out sunlight from the adjoining land; shine a light (a candle or a floodlight) that can be seen from the adjoining land; and so forth. According to such variations, the exact meaning of 'owning a piece of land' varies.

Two property systems may effectively be the same, even though the legal descriptions differ. Imagine a society in which the 'king' owns all the land and permits individuals various rights in the land, as long as they pay him a rent calculated on the value of their holdings. Individuals are allowed to buy and sell these rights in the land. The king decides not to intervene very frequently in the administration of most of the land, even though no one dreams of denying that it is the king's property. Now imagine a different society in which people conceive of themselves as owning land directly as individuals. However, these people accept the theory that a government is necessary, so they appoint one person as 'protector', and pay him taxes related to the value of their land-holdings. Furthermore, the 'protector' is granted the right to occasionally move in and appropriate land for the use of the government. The people in the first society may regard the people in the second as rootless, atomized zombies. The people in the second may regard the people in the first as grovelling slaves entirely lacking in self-respect. Yet the two property systems may be identical; that's to say the actual rights of individuals to make use of resources may be identical.

The idea that 'ownership' represents a simple relation between an individual and an asset is sometimes a useful simplification, but it can easily lead to fallacious conclusions. In the above fable, it might be tempting to say: 1. that the property system of the first society has to be analyzed in terms of royal ownership, and that of the second in terms of individual ownership; 2. that in the first society the people as individuals 'really own the land'; 3. that in the second society the protector 'really owns the land'. One might want to defend 3. by saying that the real owner is the person who has the ultimate say. A lord might go on a journey, like the lord in the parable of the talents, but he may return at any time, and do what he likes with his property. Yet this would seem to commit us to saying that a society in which the government is accorded the right to intervene in the administration of property, and does so very occasionally, say once every 500 years, must be treated as a system of 'government ownership', though it functions nearly all the time very much like a system of pure private ownership. As an alternative, one might want to defend 2. by saying that, after all, the 'effective' owner is the person who makes the decisions about the use of a resource, and if individuals do so most of the time, then they are the 'real' owners. But this ignores the fact that the king does have some rights which might have belonged to the individual landowners. Consequently, what it means to say that a person owns a piece of land is different from the case where there is no kingly involvement.

Yet again, one might want to say that ownership is a matter of degree, and that individuals partly own the land while the king or protector partly owns the land in both systems. This comes closer to the correct approach, but it is inexact. The ways in which the king is accorded rights over the land may vary. In one society he may intervene in land sales but have no say in land use; in another, *vice versa*.

The correct approach is to say that individuals own rights relating to assets (or resources). When we say that someone owns an asset, say a house, we mean that he has certain rights relating to that house. The specific bundle of rights may be understood from the context. Thus, what it means to be the owner of a house in the United States is roughly understood, for many purposes, without further explanation. But in some contexts it is appropriate to point out that what it means to own a house—the precise bundle of rights—is changing continually. It changes with every piece of legislation by Congress, by state legislatures, and by municipalities, and with every decision of the courts, insofar as these modify the rights of house-'owners'. The fallacy is to suppose that there is some ghostly entity 'ownership' which remains intact amid all these changes.

In our two hypothetical societies, the individuals own certain rights in the land, and the king/protector owns certain rights in the land. In order to analyze the property systems, we have to specify those rights. The question of 'who is the owner of the land', independent of the question who owns particular rights in the land, is a will-o'-the-wisp which dissolves upon examination. 'Ownership', as a relation between person and 'owned' object is always imprecise; it refers to ownership of a bundle of rights. There is no unique bundle of rights which can be shown to qualify as 'ownership'. We can say, however, that provided individuals are at liberty to transfer each and every right separately or in aggregate, typical rights-bundles will tend to evolve for people's convenience (to internalize externalities and reduce transactions costs). Given that there are typical rights-bundles, there are further economies in standardizing these rights-bundles, even extending the typical rights-bundles to cases where, taken in isolation, they would not be especially convenient. It is this development which helps to account for the popular inexactitude of considering 'ownership' to be a simple relation between owner and owned resource.

According to the conception outlined here, all social rules without exception are property rules, and all rights without exception are property rights. A rule of a religious ritual, that only a priest wearing green robes can touch a certain sacred object, is a property rule. The rights to 'freedom of speech' or to privacy, are likewise property rights. Not only are all property rights human rights (a truism), but all human rights are property rights. They all specify ways in which individuals are entitled to use resources (including their own bodies). The demand for the abolition of slavery was the demand that certain property rights in an adult person's body should generally be owned by that person, and not by someone else.[4] All government regulations are property rules, instituting property rights. The right of a government inspector to close down a restaurant with a dirty kitchen is, according to this definition, a property right. (Although all these rules can be analyzed as property rules, this doesn't raise the specter of seeing all human activity as preoccupied with property. There are many contexts in which a rule's property aspect would not be material, just as, for example, all sentences can be analyzed syntactically, but the majority of discussions of the sentence 'Give me Liberty or give me Death!' will not draw upon the theory of syntax. We are most likely to be interested in social rules as property rules when their broad, systematic consequences for the deployment of resources are under discussion.)

In line with this analysis, we say that all derived rights are property rights. Thus, the tenant of a house owns certain rights in that house, and these rights are property rights. We don't forget that the tenant's rights are in a sense dependent on the landlord's rights, and that this dependence is referred to in the vernacular and in legalese by saying that the landlord's rights are property rights while the tenant's rights are not. As property theorists we observe that this is the way people in some societies talk, and we remain alert to the likelihood that such ways of talking will affect the society's property system, but we don't have to always talk that way ourselves.

The hired manager of a firm is entitled to do certain things with the firm's property. Acting as agent for the 'owner', he may sell some of the firm's property. This means, according to our way of talking, that the manager owns certain property rights in some of the firm's assets. That the manager could at any time be dismissed by the 'owner', or ordered by the 'owner' to do or not to do certain things with the firm's assets, is an important part of the description of the manager's and the 'owner's' property rights.

Bajt sees the need for some such analysis, but is misled by his conviction that we have to establish who the 'real owner' is:

> The legal owner, let us say, of a house, may be one person, and the economic owner quite another person. For instance, the tenant who, as a result of legal restrictions, does not pay a rent which is higher than depreciation, does not pay, in other words, any price for services he enjoys. He is, in effect, the economic owner of the house. (Bajt 1968, 1–2)

Bajt is on the track of a significant distinction. But as his own wording betrays, the tenant's rights are also legal in origin. The true distinction is that between the actual property rights—individuals' rights in fact or 'in effect'—and the different ways in which these can be perceived or described. The tenant does in fact pay a price for the services he enjoys, and a below-depreciation rent might even come about within the free market (in a town suffering from heavy emigration, or following the mass production of disposable paper palaces). But even if he resides there rent-free, the tenant is hardly an owner in the usual sense. He cannot sell the house and if he demolishes it he will probably be put in jail. On the other hand, if the tenant leaves or dies, the landlord may move in or sell the house (a thought that persistently crosses the minds of landlords in such circumstances). Rent control does remove some rights from the landlord and give some rights to the tenant. They each own a bundle of property rights in the house. But it is futile to endeavor to determine which of them is the 'owner' of the house. The rights-bundle previously labelled 'ownership' no longer exists.

We are now in a better position to explain how market trading among state enterprises is possible. There *is* a connection between markets and property, and markets prevail where property titles are exchanged. Managers of divisions of firms and of departments of state industries do own property rights in assets, including rights to transfer some of these rights to others. It is indeed true that genuine markets among state enterprises cannot exist without those enterprises having property rights in their assets. Thus, the argument for the incompatibility of state-ownership and factor markets (the impossibility of 'market socialism') does embody an important insight; it goes astray because of an obscurity in the usage of 'ownership'.

If we return to the case of Peter and Paul, we can see that their autonomy in the deployment of resources arises from their property rights. Those rights are acquired by permission of the 'owner' who finds it advantageous to transfer those rights because of differences in knowledge. There is a parallel between the 'owner' giving rights to Peter and Paul, so that the owner can benefit from their autonomy, and society, as metaphorical owner of all resources, giving property rights to all individuals. This is a rough and suggestive analogy—the notion of 'society' as 'owner' compounds the muddle of 'ownership' as a simple relation between person and object with the muddle of 'society' as a kind of person. But in its very inadequacy, this analogy bears thinking about: it suggests, for instance, that 'society' can never actually own things, in the sense of hands-on control, for reasons roughly parallel to the fact that an individual cannot exercise 'ownership' of a billion-dollar corporation in the same way that she can exercise 'ownership' of a pen.[5] Thus there is a similarity in the reason why private property (in the broadest sense) exists and the reason why a large organization always has to give autonomy to subordinate officials—the larger the organization, the more autonomy to more officials. Property rights have to be given to sections of the whole, because the sections have to be able to exercise autonomy in the deployment of resources. They have to be able to exercise this autonomy because of their specialized knowledge.

Very broadly, the same principle explains why I benefit from transferring property rights to my agents Peter and Paul, with the result that they may trade with each other, why a large corporation transfers property rights to its divisions, who may trade with each other, why widespread nationalization always evolves into 'market socialism', in which segments of the state-owned industry trade with each other, and why market socialism is not enough.

c. Mises's Property Theory and his Statement of the Economic Calculation Problem

The non-tradability of factors under socialism was something that most early twentieth-century socialists both took for granted and viewed as desirable. The fact that nationalized concerns did trade with one another was viewed as confirmation that these firms were not yet socialist—because they operated amidst privately-owned firms, and because governments had not subordinated their state-owned concerns into a planned whole. In 1920, the Bolsheviks were still attempting to administer Russian industry as a single unit with no internal trade, and when this attempt was abandoned in 1921, the abandonment was seen as a regrettable and temporary retreat from socialism. Nonetheless, that abandonment and the introduction of NEP did once again demonstrate the practical possibility of state enterprises engaging in mutual commodity exchange, a possibility which seems to be swept from view in Mises's earliest discussions of socialism.

Mises distinguishes (1981, 27) between ownership as a "sociological and economic" concept and ownership as a juristic concept. He identifies the former ("natural ownership") with "a purely physical relationship of man to the goods, independent of social relations between men or of a legal order". Mises contends that ownership of consumption goods is different from ownership of production goods (factors), in that the latter form of ownership "can be divided in the natural sense" (30). Further, with production goods "the *having* [ownership relation] is always two-fold: there is a physical *having* (direct), and a social *having* (indirect). The physical *having* is his who holds the commodity physically and used it productively; the social *having* belongs to him who, unable to dispose physically or legally of the commodity, may yet dispose indirectly of the effects of its use . . ." (30). Mises's point is that the 'owners' of production goods in an exchange economy are the consumers, since it is the consumers who determine how means of production are deployed: "if we are disinclined here to speak of ownership as shared between consumers and owners of the means of production, we should have to regard consumers as the true owners in the natural sense and describe those who are considered as the owners in the legal sense as administrators of other people's property" (31). Mises immediately adds that this "would take us too far from the accepted meaning of the words", so that he does not propose to habitually speak of consumers as owners of production goods.

In the light of the theory which I have outlined above, we can see that Mises's theory is inadequate. Perhaps for some purposes, it may be useful to distinguish the mere fact that someone 'has' something from any property rule or right, but economics and sociology must analyze property rules, which generally take the form of property rights, and which can be distinguished from both the theories held by the individuals in the society under study and any purely physical relation between persons and goods.

Mises's distinction between ownership of consumption goods and of production goods arises because Mises, while observing in passing that "consumption goods" are strictly production goods, does not deign to incorporate this fact systematically into his analysis. A ham sandwich is just as much a factor of production as a steel mill; for many purposes it is harmless to classify the ham sandwich as a 'consumption good', as it is so close to final consumption. One buys a sandwich in order to eat it. Eating it is a technique for producing utility by combining certain factors (the sandwich, one's mouth, and so forth). One buys a steel mill in order to produce steel which will then be fashioned, usually after many further stages, into steel articles which will eventually yield utility. A steel can of soda pop is one of the factors required to produce utility by the production technique of drinking the soda from the can (or, for those who like a more roundabout production structure, by first pouring the soda into a glass). All material goods are, strictly, means of production. Their point is to yield services (utility) to the consumer.

A thief who steals an apple and eats it is, on Mises's account, the "natural owner" of the apple (27). On my account of property, we might want to take this view. Normally, as a preliminary sketch of the property sytstem, we would view the thief as non-owner, but following through remorselessly the principle that property rights are to be analyzed insofar as they are effective—do in fact determine who gets what—we might have to view the fact that society does not take measures to reduce theft to the point where this particular thief would not have the apple as a part of the society's property system. Which line we would take would depend upon the specific purpose of the analysis. It is inadvisable to rule out in advance the designation of the thief as property owner, because historically there are many cases of gradual shading from illicit possession to socially approved ownership. The proceeds of piracy may become 'tribute', or lawful taxation. Or illicit trading of goods in the black market may have important consequences for allocation of resources. (As every viewer of 'caper movies' knows, big heists usually go wrong, from the standpoint of the perpetrators, because thieves fall out. Thievery on an elaborate scale cannot proceed successfully without a strong system of property rights among the transactors in stolen property.)

It is certainly an important fact that in an exchange economy one normally derives income from the ownership of production goods, not by consuming the products oneself, but by selling the products to others. But this hardly justifies calling those others the owners of the production goods. Mises argues that a self-sufficient farmer "can call his fields, his plough, his draught animals his own", whereas the farmer producing food for a market is owner in a different sense, because the consumers rather than the farmer "control production" (30). However, in the former case the farmer gets food, in the latter, money. The farmer in both cases is fully entitled to determine what to produce and how to produce it. In all likelihood, he will have considerably more room for choice in the latter case, though in both cases, of course, there will normally be a unique optimal choice. Mises's account has the perverse corollary that a subsistence farmer who gets the opportunity to produce for the market, and seizes it because this makes him richer, thereby loses ownership of his farm. If the 'owner' of a good is always to be counted as the person who can offer some inducement which will encourage the immediate 'owner' to deploy that good in a particular way, then numerous strange consequences follow: for example, that free laborers do not own their own human capital, but are themselves slaves owned by the consumers of their products.

The shortcomings of Mises's property theory arise from his insistence that 'ownership' be conceived as a simple relationship between a person and a thing owned, and not as a bundle of rights which may change its composition. Mises perceives that different legal formulas may give rise to fundamentally similar property systems. He therefore points out that what we mean by 'state ownership' can arise without formal expropriation. Increasing state regulation of production may be tantamount to nationalization. Private property can be abolished in fact whilst preserved in name (45). Mises seems blind to the converse: that insofar as the state's central organ of industrial planning relinquishes actual control or direction of industrial activity, devolving it to lower levels, individuals at these levels thereby acquire *de facto* property rights. Because of this blind spot, his arguments in the 1930s were less convincing than they might have been. He could have pointed out, as Michael Polanyi did (1940), that Soviet Russian planning, judged by its purported function, was a sham, and that Russian industry was far from Lenin's "single office and single factory". It would have been possible to argue that the necessity for money payments between state enterprises showed that socialism in the Marxian sense did not prevail in Russia (Rothbard 1991, 73). (This would not have prevented Mises from also observing that the actual system of Soviet industrial administration, due to its inefficiency, was holding the Russian masses down in unnecessary poverty.) But Mises could never countenance 'degrees of socialism', and he accepted Russia as socialist.

Mises's standpoint was more defensible than it might have been— and more defensible than most of his critics noticed—because of his focus on financial markets. From 1932, Mises in practice identified socialist societies by their enforced absence of capital and money markets. (Presumably he would have accepted that wartime Britain, with its stock exchange closed, was temporarily a socialist society.) It is difficult to read some of the eloquent passages in which Mises indicates the productive role of capital and money markets in an industrial society (notably 1981, 120–21 and 1966, 517–523, 705–710) without being impressed by his perspicacity. Mises was saying these things *before* Lange propounded his socialist scheme, and for that matter, before Berle and Means made such a stir, essentially by ignoring the role of capital markets.

But a society without financial markets is not necessarily a society in which means of production are *res extra commercium*. Nor is industry in a society without financial markets necessarily as inefficient as that of a society which abolishes all trade in means of production. It is not true that state allocation of capital necessarily "signifies elimination of the market" (1981, 122), for enterprises may still be able to buy and sell factors. And Mises insists upon referring to trade between state enterprises as "the creation of an artificial market for the means of production" (119). This is mistaken: markets for factors in state-owned economies may be genuine, functioning markets, though they will have different outcomes from those markets where different property rights prevail.

Mises's position is vulnerable in another respect. Arguing for the indispensability of capital and money markets, Mises maintains that a socialist society could not incorporate these institutions:

> it is scarcely to be assumed that socialists of whatever persuasion would seriously propose that this function should be made over to some group of people who would 'simply' have the business of doing what capitalists and speculators do under capitalistic conditions, the only difference being that the product of their foresight should not belong to them but to the community. . . . no socialist would dispute that the function which capitalists and speculators perform under Capitalism . . . is only performed because they are under the incentive to preserve their property and to make profits which increase it or at least allow them to live without diminishing their capital. (1981, 122)

Here Mises resorts to an incentives argument, whereas elsewhere he characterizes the economic calculation argument as applying irrespective of people's motives. It is true that Mises is merely dismissing the hypothetical proposal that a socialist society would arrange for securities trading, banking, futures markets, and all the other paraphernalia of financial markets, with the traders in these markets handing over any gains to "the community". Mises believes that no socialist would seriously advance such a proposal. But something like this has been suggested by Carens, whose scheme I consider in the next chapter.

d. The Difference between State and Private Ownership

The early Marxists and many other socialists saw the socialist revolution as the transfer of 'ownership' of industry from individuals to 'society'. The underlying notion is that 'society' can have something of the same relation to industry as each private capitalist had to that portion of industry which she owned. But since industry is much bigger than the biggest of the private firms which constitute it, state-owned industry has to be divided into sections which have to be given some degree of autonomy. 'Market socialists' point out, quite correctly, that this autonomy permits functioning factor markets within state-owned industry, thus generating market prices for factors. Although this position successfully sidesteps the Mises argument in its original literal formulation, it is susceptible to pressure from two sides, like the jaws of a vise.

1. The more autonomy is given to the state enterprises, the more like private enterprises they become. To call for state enterprises to be made 'more autonomous' *is* to call for them to become 'more private'. 'Autonomy' means nothing apart from property rights. That conclusion is a creature of my terminology, yet it is also true that autonomy for state enterprises means abandoning some of the expectations that used to be commonly vested in socialism (for example, a guarantee that planning would eliminate the trade cycle).

2. If state enterprises are to remain state enterprises in anything more than pious declaration, there must actually be some difference from private firms, some difference in organizational relationship to the government. Whatever this difference may be, it will make a difference to the operation of the state enterprises. Their prices will not be the same as those which would prevail in a private-exchange market. Their managers will not have the same information. This raises the possibility that output will still be lower, and lower for Misesian reasons:

'Market socialism' or FM socialism means factor markets without financial markets. It has two problems: it is too capitalist to appeal to most socialists, and not capitalist enough to work.

It has often been pointed out that the acceptance of FM socialism from the 1930s on constitutes a renunciation of most of the earlier hopes vested in socialism, especially the notion that the market allocation of factors could be replaced by 'conscious social control'. We can now see this somewhat differently. FM socialism, in the sense of divisions or segments of state-owned industry operating as autonomous firms, trading and competing with one another and therefore helping to form genuine market prices, entails the ownership of property rights by these state firms. The closer these property rights correspond with the property rights which would prevail in a private-exchange market, the closer will the prices which emerge from this market also correspond. The more the property rights diverge from those of 'private property'—the more palpable content there is to 'socialism'—the more will the prices diverge, and therefore the more the allocations will diverge.

Whenever there is state-owned industry for any length of time, there always arises the call to make it more efficient by emulating private industry. Sometimes there are campaigns to bring in managers from private firms, and exhortations to the state firms to stay on their toes, and so forth. Aside from such superficial measures, there may be attempts to redesign the institutional structure of state firms, short of 'privatization'. The state concerns may be given complete freedom to fix prices and output; they may be warned that they have to make a positive rate of return on investment—perhaps even a commercial rate of return; and the state concerns may have all their monopoly privileges withdrawn, so that it is legally possible for anyone to open up in competition with the state firms and possibly put them out of business.

If we ask why such a firm, with more independence than many nominally 'private' firms, is not yet defined as private, the reply will be that equity in the firm is held by the government. The firm may be a public company like British Petroleum in which it just so happens (so to speak) that the government owns a majority of the shares. This seems to be almost as close as a state-owned firm can get to a private firm (we don't forget here that, because of other measures like subsidies and controls, many 'private' firms appear much more statified than BP) except that no one in the government could have much incentive to sell those shares.

Most state-owned firms are owned by means more direct than majority ownership of publicly-tradable stock. Some kind of government organ, under the immediate control of an appointed official responsible to the parliament, owns the concern outright. There is commonly also a legal monopoly prohibiting competition and an understanding that losses will be covered out of receipts. The chief consequence of this for economic calculation is that a value of the concern as a whole (the present value of its expected future income) cannot be fixed in any way that draws widely upon the expertise of dispersed minds throughout society. Since there is no such accurate value, there can be no gearing of activities to maximize that value. Although the government may make efforts to 'decentralize' and 'marketize' state industry, this can hardly go so far as to permit individual enterprises to raise their own funding by offering stocks and bonds, with effective control over the enterprise passing from one group to another either by direct sale or by acquisition of stock. For if that happened, every claim to 'state ownership of industry' would be abandoned. Developed capital markets cannot co-exist with a state-owned economy, and the role played by the financial markets in co-ordinating production is therefore unavailable to 'market socialism'. It is therefore not feasible for government employees to operate an industrial concern in the same way as it could be operated under 'private ownership'. The information cannot be made available to them.

One could describe this situation by saying that the property rights are apportioned in a particular way, or one could say that the relevant property rights (including the right to transfer equity) simply don't exist. Either formulation might be a useful approximation, a rough description of some prominent features of the society's property system. In using terms like 'transfer of equity', there is always the danger that we will be misled by the descriptions of property prevalent in the society, which may be inaccurate, and may be mixed with evaluative judgements. On the other hand, before we can describe the property system it may be necessary to describe the property theories applied in the society's legal system.

Consider: 1. the idea of all of industry's being 'owned' by a single individual; and 2. the idea of all of industry's being 'owned' by all the people collectively. Certainly both of these can exist and doubtless have existed, in the sense that these propositions might be generally assented to by many individuals in the societies in question. It is also possible that in such societies, these formulas really do mean something important about the property system. But we have to ask ourselves what rights the single individual owner, or all the people collectively, can be said to possess.

In 1., the individual will have to delegate authority over the day-to-day disposal of resources to thousands or millions of other individuals. These thousands or millions of officials will actually own important property rights. The individual 'owner' may be said to have the power to tell any of these officials what to do. But she cannot have any idea what most of them are doing, except in a very general way. We can be confident that in such a society the officials will have far more say in determining the use of resources than will the individual 'owner'. This doesn't mean that her ownership of everything is an empty phrase—it could really mean something, but it cannot mean that she has the same relation to all the world's industry as I have to my briefcase.

In 2., the situation is the same. We may suppose that everyone has a voting button in the home, and that 'all' decisions on the use of all resources are made by everyone's voting. Even if everyone did nothing but deliberate and vote, it would be necessary for most actual decisions to be delegated to officials (who would therefore not be able to spend all their time deliberating and voting). These

officials would own property rights and would proximately determine the use of resources.

In 1., the single owner might sell most assets to other individuals.
How could these individuals pay, since the single owner owns
everything? They could pay by promising some of their future
income from their newly acquired assets. What would be in this for
the single owner? The fact that the former single owner's income
might become larger, because output would be greater following the
termination of single ownership. Analogous reasoning applies to 2.,
where the single owner is the 'whole community'.

ii. THE PRODUCTIVE ROLE OF FINANCIAL MARKETS

A best-selling novel by a conservative writer has its protagonist, a
bond trader, embarrassed because he is unable to explain to his little
daughter what product he makes (Wolfe 1987, 237–241). This novel
appeared at just that point in history when the rulers of the majority
of the world's population had finally been driven to acknowledge that
they had to permit capital and money markets if their subjects were
to extricate themselves from crushing poverty and build up their
industries on a sound basis. It would hardly seem so telling to have
an administrator in a hypothetical socialist planning bureau (or, say,
an air traffic controller) discountenanced because of a similar question: the administrator's reply might be that he helps to make
everything, by telling everyone where their efforts can most usefully
be directed. The difficulty in appreciating that an unusually successful bond trader is making a greater contribution to human welfare
than any hundred farmers or auto workers is merely a natural
consequence of the Marxian 'economic calculation blind spot'—
implicitly, the view that technical production ratios are self-evident,
and that therefore problems of industrial co-ordination are trifling.

In any form of society with complex technology, the whole pattern
of production has to be harmonized so that the composition of total
output is appropriate to the resources of society and to people's
wants. Of course, society cannot produce more than it can produce,
but it could very easily produce too much of some things in relation
to others. As one example, society could undertake particular lines of
production which would make perfect sense if resources were greater,
but would be inappropriate or even impossible to complete given the
actual constraints. The total amount which people want to save out
of their incomes must be equal to the total amount invested in

production for the future, while the total amount which people want to spend currently must be equal to the total flow of consumer goods becoming available.

Resources are allocated to different productive uses in *factor markets*, such as markets for labor, real estate, and capital goods. For example, any downtown area has a highly-organized market for office space, and when publishers go to press with a book such as this one, they choose among dozens of possible suppliers of printing and binding services. There are markets for chemistry teachers, temporary secretaries, recording studios, tankers, cranes, potassium permanganate, and spliced genes. There are many hundreds of such factor markets, each usually divided into several sub-markets, each one out of anyone's control, and each one so subtle and complex in its workings that a lifetime's close involvement in that market would enable you merely to make more informed guesses about what was going on.

If we picture society's entire stock of available resources as one vast warehouse, and ask ourselves how the contents of that warehouse are allocated among all the millions of enterprises which might like to employ them, it becomes clear that looking at factor markets alone leaves out a large part of the picture. Once production decision-makers have somehow come by a certain number of vouchers, so to speak, entitling them to claim portions of the capital goods in that warehouse, we can explain their decisions by analyzing factor markets. But factor markets don't fully explain how the decision-makers were awarded those vouchers. Here we have to turn to *financial markets*, notably the 'capital' and 'money' markets.[6]

Saving makes resources available, but savers are not automatically production decision-makers (entrepreneurs) and if they are, their savings may not completely fit the line of production in which they are engaged. For instance, some savers strongly value a high degree of assurance of maintenance of the value of their principal and will buy this by accepting a low rate of return, while others are prepared to bear greater risks given the likelihood of a higher rate of return. Some savers save for a long period, others for short. On the production side, for example, a business which is profitable, but currently experiences a substantial net outflow of funds, must be able to cover that outflow from somebody's savings.

Some entrepreneurs start with virtually nothing except an idea. The entrepreneur therefore raises the necessary funds from someone else: by approaching a particular individual who has savings; by getting a loan from a bank, which pools numerous people's savings;

by selling bonds or stocks. When an entrepreneur gets funds in any of these ways, the entrepreneur acquires 'command over resources', or, as I have metaphorically expressed it above, vouchers exchangeable at the great warehouse. There is a stock of real resources or real capital, the result of everyone's saving, and there is a stock of funds (financial capital), whose disposal is usually delegated by savers to various intermediaries. Someone who acquires the use of funds acquires a claim upon a portion of the stock of real resources, and insofar as the funds are actually spent to acquire the use of real resources, those resources are denied to other entrepreneurs for other uses. The entire intricate structure of financial markets is largely concerned with matching up the available savings with the available production opportunities.

Socialists commonly make two mistakes in thinking about financial markets. First, when they encounter a reference to 'providing funds' for investment, they judge this to be an illusory contribution. In order to make something, we need real resources: labor, raw materials, machinery, and so forth. The *money* is merely permission to go ahead—it reflects the fact that the capitalists control resources and no production can take place without their say-so. (This sometimes goes along with the notion that 'profit restricts production'. See below, 12.ii.b.) The illusion that 'providing funds' is a contribution to production therefore arises from the distinctive institutional character of capitalism.

This chain of reasoning is mostly correct; it goes wrong by overlooking the wider context. Providing funds is, in effect, giving permission to use real resources for a particular project.[7] But the number of such desirable projects greatly exceeds the capacity of the resources available. Hence, to give permission for some projects to go ahead is concomitantly to deny permission to other projects. Allocation of investment funds is a way of rationing out scarce real resources among competing projects. This competition of potential projects and the consequent need for rationing of real resources are *not* products of capitalist institutions. Furthermore, production of real resources has been made possible by people consuming less than they earn. Savers are the ultimate providers both of real productive resources and of the funds which constitute 'vouchers' or claims upon those resources. It is very much to the benefit of the whole population that resources be invested where they will yield the highest return—which in view of inescapable uncertainty means that resources be continually re-assigned from less promising to more promising projects. When we say that a bank, for instance, provides funds for various projects, this is not the whole story. The bank denies funds for other projects; to the extent that the bank skillfully chooses the profitable projects and rejects the loss-making projects, it increases future total output of real goods and services.

The second mistake is, strangely enough, almost the reverse of the first: it is to confound financial capital with real capital, the vouchers with the contents of the warehouse. Suppose that someone has a sum of savings which she may use either a. to finance the building of a new factory, or b. to purchase stocks, issued long ago, in existing companies. The mistake is to think that a. adds to production, while b. diverts resources from production into the barren sphere of coupon-clipping and paper-chasing. In fact the determinants of total investment[8] are not affected by such a decision.

Total saving always and automatically equals total investment, so the total amount which some people save without investing must be 'covered' by a corresponding amount which people—usually other people—invest without saving (by borrowing or otherwise incurring obligations in exchange for the use of funds). When stocks or bonds are purchased, claims are transferred from one person to another. Neither total resources available for investment nor total funds for investment are reduced by such transactions.[9]

By extension of this second fallacy, institutions like the stock exchange are supposed to divert vast sums of 'capital' from productive uses into purely 'financial', unproductive uses. Now, financial intermediaries hire labor, they rent office space, they pay bills for heating, lighting, telephones, computers, and so forth. These costs of running financial markets constitute all the resources such markets 'divert' from other uses, and they 'divert' them in the same way that hospitals divert resources from bakeries. It is a blunder to add to these actual costs the money, securities, bills, futures, and other instruments held or traded in financial markets. These are claims on real wealth; they do not somehow 'absorb' real wealth, or siphon it away from non-financial uses. (In much the same way, the accounting department of a firm employs resources such as accountants, computers, and so forth; it would be foolish to imagine that accounting also takes away the resources from all the other departments, because these are described in accounting statements.) Similarly, profits made by speculating on the stock market in no way represent a deduction from 'productive' earnings—any more than stock market losses represent an addition to those earnings. In the aggregate, stock market incomes constitute interest on savings: they are payment for provision of a productive service. All production is inherently speculative, because no one can know in advance (under capitalism or under any other conceivable institutions) whether any project will turn out to be worth while. Profits are made by those who do better than 'the market' at anticipating outcomes, and who thereby hasten the adjustment of production to real conditions; losses are made by those who do worse.

Financial markets perform a number of vital services:

1. Funds for investment funds have to be saved by someone, and it is efficient for savers to make their saving decisions in the light of the real costs and benefits to them of their savings. Thus, for example, the frequent socialist proposal to arbitrarily determine a rate of saving for society as a whole must *ipso facto* be inefficient, because individuals are no longer free to increase or decrease their personal savings. This reduces their individual utilities in much the same way as any restrictions on their choice of consumer goods. The stock and bond markets enable savers to move their savings about, or to dis-save quickly, thus increasing the utility which savers can derive from a given amount of savings.

2. Somehow, society's total stock of resources must be allocated to a selection of all the various proposed projects which, taken together, are vastly greater than those resources would permit. Since the fate of any project is uncertain, resources must be able to be swiftly moved or re-assigned from disappointing projects to be made available for more promising projects.

3. A flexible control must be exerted on those in charge of projects. They are using scarce resources, thereby automatically limiting what's available for other desirable projects. The control is flexible in the senses that: a. it takes the form of access to financial capital rather than specific lists of capital goods; b. amounts of financial capital can be available on diverse conditions; and c. it allows heterodox thinkers to invest in projects which most people, including most experts, consider unpromising (this is an important feature of the pattern of investment: projects embarked upon must not be limited to those approved by any organization, committee, or assembly). If investments turn out badly, the investors make losses.

4. Like all markets, financial markets transmit information in the form of prices. Stock prices, for example, draw upon the judgments of thousands of dispersed individuals, and signal to the entire market the current state of opinion about particular projects (a fall in a stock makes it harder for the issuing company to get funds). Since all production is a speculative gamble, these judgments are continually being revised in light of new information.

Financial markets would *not* play a very important role if the projects to go ahead were predetermined, and if savers' utility from their saving were disregarded. Financial markets don't merely match up a given amount of savings with a given list of production projects; financial markets help to determine which projects will be begun or continued, and which will be abandoned, which will be expanded, and which curtailed. They also help to determine who will save, and how much, by providing savers with information about how beneficial their saving is. In helping to determine the total amount of resources available and the uses to which these are put, financial markets generate information which it is beneficial for *any* form of society to take into account. However, humankind doesn't yet know of any feasible way to elicit, transmit, and bring to bear this information, in a technologically advanced society, other than by substantially free financial markets in a milieu of substantially private ownership of the means of production.[10]

9

MOTIVATION AND INFORMATION

i. ECONOMIC CALCULATION DISTINGUISHED
FROM INCENTIVES

The most popular argument against socialism is that it cannot offer adequate incentives.[1] This is normally understood to mean that individuals will know what to do, but will lack strength of motivation to do it, because the rewards they will receive for efficiency-promoting behavior will not be sufficiently powerful inducements. Taken by itself, the incentives argument implies that socialism might work if people had different motivations or 'natures', and fits in snugly with the conservative view that socialism would, in an ideal world, be wonderful, but cannot work because of original sin. According to this typical conservative view, people aren't good enough for socialism, and it is socialist hubris to maintain that people can become better. By contrast, the Mises argument doesn't appeal to any reduction in the strength of people's motivations under socialism. According to Mises, individuals under NFM socialism cannot know what to do. Unfortunately, most anti-socialists have been convinced that the incentives argument is irresistibly persuasive, so that they have tended either to ignore the economic calculation argument or to assimilate it into the incentives argument.[2]

a. Mallock's Criticism of Socialism

Of the many attacks on socialism on grounds of motivation, an excellent example is Mallock 1907. The later part of Mallock's work centers on what he calls "the ultimate difficulty" with socialism, the "problem of motive" (94–135). Observed "human nature" teaches us that people do not generally work for idealistic or self-sacrificing motives, but require some more tangible inducement. Mallock's argument is inconclusive. He doesn't consider the many humdrum types of unpaid work, such as routine charitable and social work, regularly and competently performed by thousands of people with little or no payment. The range of observation from which his generalizations about "human nature" are drawn is not exhaustive, and doesn't rule out the possibility that in a sufficiently different environment, people might behave sufficiently differently.

Mallock devotes most of a chapter to a difficulty which he considers only "proximate", the selection of "able men" to run industrial enterprises (73–93). This chapter remains eloquent over 80 years later, but it misses the problem of economic calculation. Mallock explains how competition between commercial enterprises removes the inefficient and incompetent directors, in a continuous weeding-out process, and how this process could not occur under socialism. It is easy to see that his reasoning would cut little ice with socialist readers. Mallock mentions "incompetence" and "inefficiency", but assumes that purely technical efficiency is at stake. He envisages directors failing because they are "incompetent", and because their products fall short in some demonstrable way. This surely suggests that *some* socialist monitoring system ought to be able to be devised. Mallock apparently does not see that the director might be brilliant and conscientious, and that the products might be technically excellent, but that they might still constitute atrocious waste because costs were too high. The issue of *the information conveyed by prices* is absent. The problem Mallock sees is how we shall get people to do what needs to be done. He does not perceive the possibility that if everyone could be assumed to be powerfully motivated, and also alert, able, and industrious, a non-market organization of industry might mean that they could not know what to aim at.

b. Motivation and Knowledge

Motivation and knowledge dissemination are conceptually distinct. "Even with the best will in the world," states Hayek, "it would be impossible for anyone intelligently to choose between various alternatives if the advantages they offered him stood in no relation to their usefulness to society" (Hayek 1944, 124–25). But someone with the best will in the world merely has to be aware of the usefulness to society of alternative courses of action. These comparative usefulnesses do not also have to be linked with the "advantages" to the individual—unless 'advantage' be defined in such a way that Hayek's statement becomes circular.

For purposes of analysis and discussion, we should distinguish between motivation and knowledge dissemination, but this does not imply that we can have the market performing the latter task without the market also carrying out the former task in its own fashion. If there is a functioning market, then it determines people's incomes, and thus induces them to make choices guided by income opportunities. Only through determining people's incomes does the market disseminate the information necessary for economic calculation. There are two distinct points here. 1. It might be that efficient production does not require market incentives in order to motivate people adequately, but that efficient production does require a functioning market for information dissemination, and that a functioning market requires people to be motivated by market incentives. Incentives may be necessary for a *market* economy, and a market economy may, for reasons independent of motivation, be necessary for efficiency. 2. There are many cases where it might actually be difficult to elicit the information required for efficient allocation unless units of calculation are identified with units of decision-makers' income. This arises because of the irreducible element of subjective individual evaluation in some allocational decisions. A couple of examples will illustrate this second point.

Consider a project which requires that a number of workers live in isolated conditions in Antarctica. In the market, the promoters of such a project would have to pay wages sufficient to induce enough suitable workers to volunteer, that is, sufficient to attract enough workers away from other jobs; there will be a tendency for the Antarctic jobs to go to those individuals who can do them *and* who place an especially high valuation on increased money wages by comparison with the valuation they place on working in a warm environment with easy access to the amenities of an urban center. Those who can cope easily with Antarctic conditions, including those few who relish these conditions, will be more likely to apply for the Antarctic job. In each worker's mind, a unique combination of pecuniary and non-pecuniary factors determines his[3] decision to volunteer or not. Thus the worker is able to compare the benefits to the rest of society, as revealed in his wages, with the sundry non-pecuniary benefits and disbenefits of diverse jobs.

Now suppose that a communist system is in operation. (Essentially the same argument applies to any system in which people's incomes are determined in a way that takes no account of the supply and demand for different kinds of labor.) When workers are required for a particular project, the administration announces the fact, and individuals volunteer. (It doesn't affect the point whether individuals are free to work or not, without this affecting their incomes, as in free-access communism, or whether they are compelled to work, but free to choose their type of work, as in labor-voucher communism.) Individuals may volunteer out of a combination of motives: to enjoy themselves by being productive, to be active in a primary group, to gain the approval of others, to make a contribution to social wellbeing, and so forth. The administration decides to proceed with the Antarctic project and announces the fact. A person considering whether to volunteer may not relish Antarctic conditions, but may feel some tug of social responsibility, let us say. How can this person compare the inconvenience to himself with the social benefit? If the number of qualified volunteers exceeds the number of positions, who should drop out? How can I tell if you mind Antarctic conditions more or less than I do? (If I know you very well, I might have a good idea, but I can't make the same judgment about thousands of people I've never met.) I don't merely have to estimate how much you mind Antarctic conditions, but what your comparative valuation of Antarctic conditions and increased output is, for in the market both are considered, and each person's judgment influences the terms for the other persons' judgments (the more people dislike these conditions, the higher the wages will be and the fewer people will be employed in Antarctica). Notice that the very few who positively relish Antarctic conditions should not automatically volunteer for the Antarctic jobs. They might produce more elsewhere, and they might value the difference between their higher product elsewhere and their product in the Antarctic job (as displayed to them in the difference between the wage rates) more highly than they value the difference in job enjoyability.

Someone might say that it does not matter who volunteers as long as enough volunteers appear, but this is not so: there is no reason to privilege the utility people derive from the products of the Antarctic project at the expense of the utility people derive from enjoying their work (or reducing its unpleasantness). Nor would it be relevant to offer the comment that under communism all jobs would be made as enjoyable as possible. In response to this we can observe that: 1. making work enjoyable competes with other objectives for scarce resources, and people are injured if they are not free to choose a combination entailing less enjoyable work and more products (other than the product 'enjoyable work'), and 2. even if all jobs are made enjoyable, they will not all be equally enjoyable for every individual, and choosing an enjoyable job which is less satisfying than an alternative job represents a sacrifice, which will be inefficient unless compensated by utility in another form, for instance, higher output (of goods other than job-satisfaction).

For my second example, suppose that, instead of household water being sold at market prices, it is provided free to every home. This seems at first glance like a pure bonus to the water-consumer, since water is 'free'. But it does not alter the fact that resources are diverted from production of other goods to expand the production of water. The water-consumer is also a consumer of these other goods, and so, if she is an average sort of person, she is still paying just as much for the water by not having those other goods, goods which are not produced because resources have been allocated to produce water. But since water is provided gratuitously to the immediate consumer, she will increase the amount of water she uses. Thus, her situation is decidedly worse than it would have been if she had had to pay the market price for the water, since she would prefer to use less water and have more of other goods instead—but that option has been made unavailable.

At first sight, the option does seem to be available, and the difficulty seems to be one of incentive alone. For after all, if each person were sufficiently motivated by a general concern for social welfare, and thus for economic efficiency, to reduce her water consumption by the required amount, then the effect on production would be the same. But here we run into the problem that *she cannot know* what is the 'right' amount by which to reduce her water consumption, because she cannot know how much production of other things would be increased by any given reduction of water consumption, nor how much everyone in society would evaluate the benefits of those other things by comparison with the amount of water sacrificed to get them. So even an acutely altruistic person with a tiny streak of self-interest will be tempted to use just as much water as she personally wants (or to move 'too close' to that point), because at least she *knows* that, whereas she is highly uncertain about the social costs. And an entirely altruistic or benevolent person, without a trace of self-interest, will try to guess at the correct trade-off, but in the absence of market prices will make mistakes, with inefficiency resulting.

A different point is well-recognized and much-discussed: that a 'self-interested' person will tend to 'free-ride' on others if those others voluntarily restrict their water consumption. Since one person's enlarged consumption will have an imperceptible effect on the availability of other goods, that person has little inducement to restrict water consumption voluntarily. The fact that some persons free-ride encourages others to free-ride too, since every additional free-rider makes it the more futile for anyone to refrain from free-riding. This fact is well-recognized and much-discussed, as are the prima-facie counter-instances like payment of subscriptions to public radio. But, as I have indicated, there is a knowledge problem which arises independently of self-interest, however defined. Some references to 'incentives' are made by people who may understand the need for the communication of information, and intend the word 'incentive' to include that function. But in some contexts it's helpful to keep the distinction in mind, and I therefore confine the term 'incentive' to motivation, excluding information dissemination.

The classic case of an incentives argument is Aristotle's response to Plato on child-rearing. Against Plato's proposal that children be raised in common, so that parents come to regard all children as their own, Aristotle (1992, 394) replies that "anybody will be equally the son of anybody, and will therefore be neglected by all alike", an argument lately endorsed by sociobiology. These arguments have been repeated for centuries, and have no doubt been seen as speculations about individuals' motivations. But one could make a point rather similar to Aristotle's on purely informational grounds. Bringing up a child is an exacting job, and many decisions have to be made about an individual child that can best be made by someone specializing in that child. Instead of having all children raised in common by everyone, each adult could be allocated a few children, from birth to adulthood. By specializing in a few children, each adult would be able to learn much about those children, and would be able to take effective actions impossible in a situation of amorphous responsibility. It is not difficult to extend the informational argument to show why biological parents should very often be the persons specializing in particular offspring: the mother feeds the baby and therefore learns much about its personality, knowledge unavailable to anyone else. And because of the genetic variability in all humans (except monozygous siblings) a person's store of insights into human behavior may well be peculiarly adapted to understanding the behavior of close kin. (As well as the motivational and informational aspects, we should also note the interactions between them, the most obvious being that information is required to turn motivation into concrete action; another being that without the appropriate kind of information, motivation may atrophy; yet another being that motivation and knowledge are often marginal substitutes.)

The practical inseparability of income determination and incentives has another aspect. It is sometimes suggested that the market can be retained for the benefit of its 'incentive' effects, while income can be 'distributed' without regard to the market. In its simplest form this has to be rejected. If the market works at all, then to that extent the market (and not some person or group) determines incomes. If the market does not determine incomes then, to that extent, it cannot function. It is feasible to have a market with some piecemeal 'redistribution' measures, though these will generally reduce efficiency, that is, they will impoverish. Some people, without inconsistency, willingly accept some impoverishment for the sake of redistribution (for instance Okun 1975), but the extreme case is impossible.

Rigid application of some independently-arrived-at assignment of incomes would paralyze the market: the market would no longer exist, and there would be no price signals. For example, if it were decreed that all individuals' real incomes were to be strictly equal, then any market change that would affect the fortunes of any individual, A, would have to be anticipated and stopped. If A saw a chance to get something at a lower price, or sell something at a higher price, thereby increasing his real income, this would have to be either prevented, or exactly and instantaneously compensated by a deduction from A's income. But if A knows that will happen, then the 'lower' or 'higher' price is no longer a lower or higher price to him.

ii. AN EQUALITARIAN SIMULATED MARKET

a. Carens's Proposal: the ESM

Carens has proposed an equalitarian system combining a kind of market with elements appealing to socialists (Carens 1981). His proposal differs strikingly from other such amalgams. Carens hopes to show that motivational considerations do not preclude the feasibility of a regime of universal income equality, but in the course of his exposition, he raises issues worth study even to those unattracted by his proposed system or convinced of its impracticability. There are two features of Carens's argument which make it both important in the history of thinking about 'alternative' social systems and peculiarly relevant to the economic calculation issue: 1. If correct, Carens's argument shows that the Mises argument must rest upon considerations of motivation. Misesians would then be mistaken in their contention that the unfeasibility of NFM socialism can be demonstrated independently of people's motivations. Thus, Carens's system would have implications for the Mises debate even if Carens's contention that suitable motivations could prevail were to be rejected. 2. Carens's system comes closer than any other to giving a plausible rendering of the notion, touched upon in many socialist writings, that socialism can simulate, or as Mises scoffingly puts it, "play at" the market.

Carens refers to the traditional kind of market as a "private property market (PPM)", and I will follow him in this (though some would say that his system preserves a large element of private property; this semantic issue need not detain us). His own proposal he calls "the egalitarian system"; I will call it 'the ESM' (for 'equalitarian simulated market').

In Carens's ESM, things exchange at more or less freely determined market prices. Everyone receives the same actual measurable income for personal consumption, that is, the same nominal total of money and in-kind income available for spending on one's own consumer goods. There is thus fairly strict universal equality of consumption incomes, in a commonly-understood sense. Carens accepts that some divergence from perfect equality is unavoidable; he views some kind of tolerable approximation to measurable equality as intrinsically worthwhile. Appreciable inequalities will arise in the ESM from at least three sources: 1. non-pecuniary income which cannot be precisely adjusted for by the tax authorities, such as the pleasure derived from a view or from congenial companions;[4] 2. 'household entrepreneurship', such as an individual spending his money wisely or luckily; and 3. saving of consumer goods, in order to have more of them later.

How are income equality and a functioning market to be reconciled? We now come to the key idea of Carens's proposal. In his ESM, people receive incomes which they can spend as they please on their own personal consumption. These incomes, consisting of money and those in-kind payments which can be identified and valued in money, are decreed equal for everyone. I shall throughout refer to these compulsorily equal consumer-goods incomes as 'post-tax incomes'. Alongside these post-tax incomes, each person has a known "pre-tax income" (Carens, 25), which may be greater or less than her post-tax income. If a person's pre-tax income is higher than her post-tax income, the excess cannot be spent on personal consumption. If a person's pre-tax income is lower than her post-tax income, her post-tax income is made up to the same level as everyone else's.

It might seem at first that the pre-tax incomes are entirely fictitious, but this is not so. The most noticeable effect of pre-tax incomes is that people with pre-tax incomes above their post-tax incomes could freely use that excess (or a large part of that excess—Carens's account is slightly obscure here, but the difference doesn't matter for the present discussion) for any purpose whatsoever, except adding to their personal consumption.

For example, in the ESM as under the PPM, a multimillionaire might exist, many times 'wealthier' than the average person. In the ESM, this wealth would give such a person all the 'power' and influence over resource allocation available to a person with the same amount of wealth in a PPM. Such a multimillionaire could buy and sell businesses, hire and fire workers, invest her capital freely according to her own judgement (see Carens, 27–35). She could thus do virtually everything with her money and her other assets that she could do within a PPM, *except* increase her consumption of consumer goods above the compulsorily equal level.

In the ESM, individuals might strive to get 'rich', in the sense of maximizing their pre-tax incomes. They would be free to pull off major real estate deals in the manner of Donald Trump, to engage in hostile takeovers in the style of T. Boone Pickens, to win or lose a fortune speculating in stocks, options, or commodities. Not only could they do all these things; they would be expected to do all these things. Carens's system relies for its effective operation on people doing such things, just as they would do them in a PPM. Individuals would not be free, however, to allocate any part of their business gains (above their post-tax incomes) to their own personal consumption.

Why should individuals in Carens's system bother to try to increase their pre-tax incomes? The beginning of a reply might be that even today, especially once they have accumulated enough to provide a certain minimum of personal security, investors frequently may not be motivated primarily by getting more to spend on their own personal consumption, narrowly defined. But Carens's basic answer is that individuals will try to maximize their pre-tax incomes because they will derive social-duty satisfactions from so doing. In Carens's system, individuals derive "social duty satisfactions" from their pre-tax incomes. In order to maximize their social-duty satisfactions, they are impelled to maximize their pre-tax incomes, even though they are unable to spend any increments to their pre-tax incomes 'on themselves'. Carens likens their position to that of trustees (29–30).

Similar motivations prevail in the labor market (39–48). In the PPM, a worker decides which of several available jobs to apply for by comparing the whole array of benefits provided by each of those jobs. Thus, a worker might prefer working as a secretary to working as a bricklayer, even though the bricklaying job paid $100 per month more than the secretarial job, but might be induced to take the bricklaying job if it paid $200 per month more than the secretarial job. The worker makes a trade-off between the money income and other benefits, such as how much he likes or dislikes a particular kind of work. In the ESM, the trade-off would be similar, except that the place of variation in money income would be taken by variation in pre-tax income. Nothing could change the worker's income available for personal consumption, since this would be compulsorily equalized across society, but there would be variations in pre-tax income, and workers would respond to these variations, because additional pre-tax income would yield additional social-duty satisfactions.

In Carens's ESM, increased social-duty satisfactions take the place of increased personal consumption as an incentive. One might deny that people could be motivated by changes in pre-tax income, when these changes could not affect the goods available for these people's 'own consumption'. Carens expects many readers to be skeptical about this, and offers arguments to show that people could be changed by "socializing" influences to respond to social-duty satisfactions with the same reliability that they now respond to income-consumption satisfactions. He takes it for granted that the PPM works because people pursue what he calls "income-consumption satisfactions" (25), that is, purchasable consumer goods for their own individual consumption.

Carens's scheme is a unique departure in socialist theory. Whenever socialists have admitted some role for the market, they have thereby acknowledged, usually regretfully, a greater role for what Smith termed "self-love". Carens is the first to attempt in a detailed way to make use of the invisible hand to serve consciously benevolent motives.

I will argue that Carens's system is unfeasible for Misesian or informational reasons. My main argument will be in three stages: 1. The efficiency of Carens's system depends upon allocations being the same as those which would be made in a PPM; 2. Contrary to immediate appearances, and to Carens's own view of the matter, the only way that the same allocations could be made would be by individuals accurately imagining how they would behave if they were in a PPM, and then actually behaving in an identical manner; and 3. Individuals in Carens's system could not, for various reasons, know how they would behave in an imaginary PPM.

b. The Efficiency of Carens's ESM

Carens is concerned to combat the widely-held view that efficiency is incompatible with income equality (1–3). He aims his argument mainly at those, like Okun, who presumptively disapprove of income inequalities, but reluctantly accept them because they acknowledge that there is, as a matter of ineluctable fact, a trade-off between equality and efficiency: the more equality you obtain by interventionist measures, the worse off people must be, on average and in general (Okun 1975). Carens holds that such a trade-off can be avoided. He contends that his system, incorporating equality of incomes, will be equally as efficient as a PPM.

There is a sense in which Carens's claim that his system can be as efficient as a PPM is meaningless. If we move from a PPM to the Carens system, there are gainers and losers. Some people have their incomes reduced (a restriction on how you can spend your money income is a cut in your real income), and other people have their incomes increased. Comparison of these two systems for their efficiency is therefore ruled out. Since there are losers in his system, compared with the PPM, he cannot say that his system is as efficient as the PPM, in any widely accepted definition of economic efficiency. In the ESM, some people have their incomes reduced by force, against their wishes. (If this were not so, the equivalent of Carens's system could come about by peaceful persuasion and voluntary donations in the PPM, and would not need to be politically enforced.) But we can pursue his efficiency argument further.

Efficiency may be analyzed into two categories: production efficiency and allocation efficiency. Production efficiency exists when, of all the goods being produced with given resources, it isn't possible to increase the output of one good without reducing the output of any other good. Thus, even with just two goods, there will normally be an infinite range of combinations of these two goods that are production-efficient. From the point of view of consumers' wants, the best outcome will be one of these combinations, but most of the range of combinations will be comparatively undesirable (and many combinations which are *not* production-efficient will be preferred by the consumers to many that are production-efficient). In order to

have efficiency, there must be both production efficiency and allocation efficiency.

Carens's ESM cannot be compared for efficiency with the PPM,
but perhaps it can be compared for production efficiency. Here we
run into a further problem. If post-tax incomes are equalized, the
pattern of demand will change. There are two reasons for this: first,
the people whose incomes are made up to the equal level will not
want to spend the addition on precisely the things which the people
whose post-tax incomes have been reduced will choose to cut out;
second, Carens's system calls for people to be motivated very
differently, and, hence, to have very different preferences. If, for
instance, millions of people are guaranteed, not only an income
sufficient to live on, but an income the same as anyone else's, whether
they work or not, and if not a single one of these people chooses to
work one minute less as a result (one of the requirements of Carens's
system, if its efficiency is to equal the PPM's), then there must have
been a thorough transformation of many people's wants, and since
all wants are inter-related through the price system, it is unlikely that
there will not be changes in the demand for various goods on sale in
the stores. Even though total money demand stay the same, its
composition (in quantities of specific goods) will change. But then,
production will be shifted into new areas, and it becomes difficult to
discuss how the new outcome compares with the PPM, in terms of
production efficiency.

The obvious way to proceed then is to ask: 'Will the ESM be as
efficient at producing the things demanded in it as the PPM is at
producing the things demanded in *it*?' The simplest way to approach
that question is to imagine that, just by coincidence, total demand
for all goods is identical in the two systems. This is what Carens does,
when he assumes that "there is the same pattern of demand in both
systems" (24). Although such a coincidence is practically impossible,
this is an acceptable assumption for purposes of discussion. If Carens
shows that, given the same pattern of demand, output would be the
same, he will have gone some way towards showing that his system is
no less 'efficient' than the PPM.

c. The Identity of Behavior in the Two Systems

Carens develops his argument mainly by means of hypothetical
examples or thought experiments, in which he compares what would
happen in the PPM with what would happen under corresponding
circumstances in the ESM (see especially 27–29). That is, he

proceeds by comparing the outcome of a hypothetical PPM situation with the outcome of a hypothetical ESM situation which is in all possible respects the same (the same individuals, with the same demands for goods, the same technology, and so forth). The only differences are those which unavoidably flow from the requirements of the two systems.

Carens seems to claim that his system will produce the same market decisions, the identical behavior, as the PPM, and therefore will be no less efficient than the PPM. All factor prices and quantities will be the same. An entrepreneur who would open a factory in the PPM will open a factory in exactly the same way in the ESM, employing the same number of workers at the same wages (though these would be merely pre-tax wages in the ESM). A worker who would change from one job to another in the PPM will do exactly that, in a corresponding ESM. This identify of behavior in the two systems is necessary for Carens's argument, and it does appear to be what he claims for his ESM. He states, for example, that individuals in the ESM "place the same relative value on the satisfactions derived from performing their social duty to acquire pre-tax income" as individuals in the PPM place on personal-consumption satisfactions (25). It is natural to suppose that when Carens says "the same" he means *the same*, that is, that in every situation where someone in the PPM has a choice involving a trade-off between personal-consumption satisfactions and some other satisfactions, in the corresponding ESM situation, he will come to precisely the same decision (whether to take a particular job, sell so many stocks at a particular price, and so forth). At the conclusion of his first example, Carens states: "In short, his behavior will be exactly the same in both systems" (29). The words "the same" frequently recur throughout Carens's book, when he compares a situation in the PPM with the corresponding situation in the ESM, and it is natural to take this literally, especially since the reader can perceive that without a literal reading, the inference of equal efficiency does not hold.

Yet Carens sometimes readily admits differences between decisions in the two systems, and appears not to notice that this contradicts one of the steps of his argument. Actually, it is quite easy to show that many decisions in the ESM could not be the same as they would be in a corresponding PPM. Some of the differences can be eliminated by modifying Carens's system, preserving its key principles, but some cannot. Carens sometimes discards the requirement of identical decisions quite casually. Can his argument be reframed to reach the same conclusion while dropping this requirement? Perhaps it would suffice to have decisions in some way roughly analogous (rather than identical) to those decisions that would have been made in the private property market?

No, Carens's argument falls if he cannot show that behavior will be precisely the same as it would have been in the PPM. This does not entail any assumption that the PPM is efficient. It's simply that, the way Carens sets up his argument, the only grounds for judging his system efficient are that it accurately simulates the PPM. There are a few cases where Carens does claim that the PPM is inefficient and that his system would do better. Aside from these, Carens doesn't offer some practical criterion of efficient allocation as an alternative to that of the PPM.

Any difference strictly invalidates Carens's argument, by contradicting the step which asserts the identity of allocations under corresponding circumstances in the two systems. In most cases where a difference can be predicted, it can also be stated specifically why the decision in Carens's system must be less efficient than the corresponding PPM decision. A refutation of Carens's argument would show that he hadn't *proved* that his system would be at least as efficient as the PPM, but would leave open the possibility that his system might *be* at least as efficient as the PPM. While refuting Carens's argument, I occasionally go further by presenting arguments that his system would be less efficient than the PPM.

Carens envisages considerable government curbing of, and piecemeal supplanting of, the ESM market by government action, parallel with government intervention in a PPM. The question of a *free* market is not an issue here. Carens does maintain the indispensability of a *functioning* market, and his reasons for this (195–200) are quite similar to those of Mises or Hayek. An interesting feature of Carens's system which he doesn't mention is that it could imaginably be more efficient than the PPM, in those cases where it would be more efficient for individuals to follow pre-tax rather than post-tax income. (It would be wrong to say that this could happen in the PPM by having people change their attitudes to pre-tax income, because in the PPM, where everyone is free to use any part of income for either personal consumption or investment purposes, individuals' actual control over resources, their wealth ownership, is necessarily governed by past post-tax incomes.) Taxation is liable to distort price signals and reduce output. Furthermore, various injurious interventions in the market, like rent control or a minimum wage, might more easily be scrapped in the ESM, and their impoverishing effects avoided, since many of the goals these measures are intended to attain would presumably be attained by the equalization of post-tax incomes.

Some readers might think that, whatever Carens says, my insistence on the identity of decisions in the two systems is illegitimate. Can't we simply say that people have their preferences, and these must be respected, whatever they are? If, in Carens's system, people's social-duty satisfactions differ from what their income-consumption satisfactions would have been in the corresponding PPM, can't this be defended as equally efficient? Isn't it introducing a bias in favor of one kind of motivation ('selfish' pursuit of personal consumption) to say that the outcome in the ESM must be judged by whether it matches the outcome in the corresponding PPM?

The answer to all these questions is 'No'. Only the choice made in the PPM is a prima-facie indication of efficiency. 'Efficiency', as Carens acknowledges, is a matter of maximizing everyone's satisfactions, defined independently of social-duty satisfaction or pre-tax income. The satisfaction someone in the ESM might get in the form of social-duty satisfactions is entirely derived from the knowledge that this helps other people maximize their income-consumption satisfactions. So the amount of social-duty satisfaction someone should get in a particular ESM situation is not, so to speak, free to shift at the individual's whim. It is governed by other people's income-consumption satisfactions.

When, for example, a worker in the PPM chooses one job over another because the first job pays better, even though it is less pleasant to perform, that worker is in effect comparing the additional product for consumers from the first job with that job's additional unpleasantness. The improvement in the worker's monetary compensation represents the bigger (more highly valued) product for consumers—it ultimately represents what the consumers are prepared to pay for the difference in the worker's output. The consumer is prepared to pay the worker enough to persuade the worker to do the work, because the product of the work is worth more to the consumer than the money the consumer pays to the worker (The employer is, as Walras first clearly stated, essentially an intermediary between the consumer and the worker). Both consumer and worker make direct comparisons of utilities they know. Turning to the ESM, things are not quite parallel. The worker knows how much each job pays (in pre-tax income), even though this makes no difference to his command over consumption goods. But there is nothing to tell the worker the trade-off between dislike of the work and increased pre-tax income. If the system is working as it should, pre-tax income does represent satisfaction of consumers' wants, and the worker knows that he ought to value that, since he wants to do his social duty. But if he values it too highly, or not highly enough, the outcome will be inefficient. He must value it precisely as he would have valued it in the PPM.

If a worker in the PPM moves from a lower-paid job to a higher-paid job despite disliking the higher-paid job more (say, because he finds the work less pleasant), he judges that the difference in money income more than compensates him for the difference in pleasantness of the work. If, now, part of that worker's income is confiscated and given to someone else, or part of someone else's income is confiscated and given to that worker, the circumstances of his choice are changed, and there is no reason to suppose that he will make the same choice. Nonetheless, it is vital for Carens's system that he does make the same choice. Take the case where his income is above the equal norm, and where he does in fact choose to switch jobs in the PPM. This signifies that, where he has a choice in the matter, the increased wage income outbalances the decreased job-satisfaction income. If, in the corresponding situation in the ESM, he fails to switch jobs, then total output of goods-other-than-job-satisfaction has been reduced, while he is enjoying a higher level of job-satisfaction. But this higher level of job-satisfaction he would gladly renounce in exchange for more of other goods. So the outcome is inefficient, in the restricted sense of efficiency which we have accepted for purposes of this discussion. In other words, because he cannot avail himself of the opportunity to give a portion of job-satisfaction for a portion of other goods, there is an aggregate loss, a social loss: the consumers of end-products are worse off because he stays in the lower-paid job, where his labor is less productive—and they are able and willing to pay him enough to compensate him fully, in his own judgment, for moving to the more productive job. If we reverse the situations, and suppose that in the PPM he would stay in his present job, but in the Carens system he 'overestimates' his social-duty satisfactions and changes jobs, then this is a net gain to other people (to 'society'), but he is suffering a loss. If we imagine all wage-workers erring in the same direction, then the population as a whole will have fewer job-satisfactions, and more other goods, than they would wish—that is, they would, if they could, choose to give up some of those other goods for more job-satisfactions. But even if the divergencies are random—if as many people overestimate as underestimate—the errors don't cancel out. All the errors represent losses.

Carens sometimes asserts that the ESM would make some aggregate magnitude "at least" as great as the PPM. For example, he refers to the problem of ensuring how his system "could generate at least the same level of savings as the PPM" (67). However, that is not good enough. His system must generate exactly the level of savings of the PPM, no more and no less, or his argument for efficiency fails.

Savings are a deduction from current consumption; they are not costless. Discussing incentives to effort in his system, he mentions the possibility that too much effort might be forthcoming: "it could be argued that the system would be *too* efficient" (147). Again, effort has a cost: the reduction of the utility which could have been derived from taking things easy. Too much effort is inefficient.

d. Some Modifications of the ESM

Some of my criticisms of the workability of the ESM refer to features of the system which could easily be removed by modifying it, without affecting its essential character. For that reason, I propose to mention some of these criticisms first. This will lead me to discard certain features of the ESM, features introduced by Carens for *ad hoc* ethical reasons. If I am right that these features are unworkable, then the modified system which results from discarding them has a stronger claim to feasibility—if the modified system is unfeasible, then an unmodified ESM is all the more clearly unfeasible. I will discuss only two of these features: 1. the link to "earning capacity"; and 2. the use of prior probabilities in evaluating investment decisions.

The ESM presupposes that everyone will care much less than they do today about their own personal consumption, while they place enormous importance on 'efficiency'—the sum of all individuals' personal consumption. The ESM might fall foul of the 'paradox of total altruism'—the fact that wanting to benefit other people presupposes that they can be benefited, and therefore that they want something other than benefiting others. Obversely, if everyone cares so much about their social-duty satisfactions, as derived from pre-tax incomes, and if people hold egalitarian values, won't envy be aroused by differences in social-duty satisfactions? The ESM multimillionaire is 'spending' her pre-tax income on social-duty satisfactions, which she values with something of the same intensity that some people now value yachts, racehorses, and elite education for their children. In a society dedicated to equality and preoccupied with social-duty satisfactions, won't the demand arise to 'redistribute' social-duty satisfactions, even if this meant introducing new personal-consumption inequalities? (see Schoek 1966.)

An appreciation of this difficulty leads Carens to make an adjustment in the rules of his system. Instead of striving to maximize their pre-tax incomes, individuals must strive to maximize their pre-tax incomes as a proportion of their "earning capacities'—the maximum amounts they *could* possibly earn (36–38). This enables Carens to incorporate in his system a moral principle from Bellamy (Carens, 153; Bellamy 1960, 76), that people should be praised and rewarded, not for what they do, but for what they do compared with what they could do.[5] Thus, in PPM societies, a habitually lazy genius whose occasional bursts of creative effort generate enormous benefits, may be rewarded far above a dogged, disciplined plodder of below-average talents. Carens thinks this judgment should be reversed, since the latter person does better by comparison with his potential.

As Carens acknowledges, his introduction of 'earning capacity' requires individuals to make calculations which have no counterpart in the PPM (37–38). In the PPM, people do have earning capacities, defined as the maximum nominal income they could possibly obtain, and they do receive some percentage of this, less than 100. But they do not generally give this maximum figure any thought, and no doubt many people would have to deliberate for a long time before they could confidently guess approximately what their 'earning capacity' was—and they could still be wrong. Although the use of earning capacity "may seem to create an unwelcome and unnecessary complication", it is "essential if the egalitarian system is to avoid replacing the inequality of income-consumption satisfactions in the PPM system with an equivalent inequality of social-duty satisfactions" (38).

Carens writes as though earning capacity really will make a difference to behavior. This seems to mean that people who, in the PPM, get a high proportion of their earning capacity would, in the ESM, respond less to price changes, and people who get a low proportion respond more. The lazy genius will be induced to put out more, and the untalented plodder will be induced to take it easy. The lazy genius in this case would have to be someone who could increase his output by being less lazy. The genius who requires a lot of lazing around to come up with an occasional good idea (I have someone in mind) would be able to carry on as in the PPM, though his observable behavior might be identical with that of the genius who just happens to be lazy. Similarly, the untalented plodder would have to be truly untalented. The person who, in the PPM, chose to excel at an undistinguished job while she secretly knew she could make much more money by being adventurous, might be impelled to change her life in Carens's system, assuming she decided to go along with the system.

Carens's aim in introducing earning capacity is foredoomed. In the PPM, individuals' incomes indicate the contributions to output made by the resources they own (notably their labor services). This contribution is inescapably unequal. If people's real incomes cease to represent their individual contributions to output (for example, by being made equal), then efficiency would require that people respond to some indicator that *does* represent their contributions to output, and this indicator would necessarily give unequal scores to individuals. If people are to respond to that indicator, then they must feel strongly about those scores, and it therefore follows that people must feel strongly about something that cannot be equalized.

Carens notices that it might be held that, if earning capacity causes people to behave differently, it must thereby cause them to behave inefficiently. This is correct, but Carens presents an argument against it, which illustrates the unsoundness of his general approach. Carens uses an example (43–48) in which "Jane" chooses, in the PPM, to make $5 per hour as a bricklayer, rather than $6 per hour as a plumber. The plumbing wage rate rises to $7 per hour. As Carens points out, this creates an incentive, in the PPM, for Jane to move from bricklaying to plumbing, but we cannot tell whether she will move or not (that depends upon her precise subjective trade-off between work satisfaction and money). It creates a similar incentive in the ESM, and here also we cannot tell whether she will move or not (that depends upon her precise subjective trade-off between work satisfaction and social-duty satisfaction). Carens's tables summarizing this have a bottom line, "Effect on incentives", showing a plus or a minus under the three occupations considered, and the pluses or minuses are the same in corresponding PPM and ESM outcomes.

However, Carens has to show that the precise magnitude, not merely the sign, is the same. He has to show that in just those conditions where Jane would value work satisfaction more highly than money in the PPM, she would value work satisfaction more highly than social-duty satisfactions in the ESM. This is obscured by Carens's statement that in the ESM "the price change has equivalent effects"—equivalent to its effects in the PPM. If "equivalent" means having the same actual outcome, the statement is false.

If consideration of earning capacity makes a difference to behavior, then it will sometimes cause Jane to take the plumbing job where it would be efficient not to take it, and sometimes cause her not to take it where it would be efficient to take it. Furthermore, Carens doesn't seem to notice that people's estimates of their earning capacities are bound to be inaccurate. So if they make different decisions according to those estimates, then even if it were true that decisions according to a correct estimate would be efficient, actual decisions will be inefficient.

Another case where Carens's system departs from a strict parallel with the market is his view of risky investments. In the PPM, if someone makes an investment that has a 0.9 probability of a profit of a million dollars, and a 0.1 probability of a profit of zero, and the investment turns out to make zero profit, the individual's failure is not reduced by the fact that the investment had been more likely to succeed than to fail. And if the investment turns out to be profitable, the individual's profit is not reduced because the investment had a one-in-ten probability of being unprofitable. Carens proposes that in his system, people's social-duty satisfactions be related, not to the actual outcome, but to the expected income, discounted for probability. Thus, in the example just mentioned, the individual in Carens's system would be credited with $900,000 (in social duty satisfactions) whatever the outcome. His pre-tax income would remain at one million dollars or zero, whatever the actual outcome, but his social-duty satisfactions would in either case amount to those from a pre-tax income of $900,000. (Carens doesn't propose that the pre-tax income itself be adjusted. This would be unworkable, because the market for factors must reflect the actual outcome in particular cases. Awareness of the actual income provides an incentive for individuals to search out the reasons why the actual outcomes occurred, and thus change the prior probabilities in subsequent similar cases. Furthermore, adjusting pre-tax income would require that the government could ascertain people's economic capacities and the probability of success of every venture.)

Where probabilities are ascertainable, institutions can develop in the PPM to remove the risk, usually by some form of pooling or insurance. In many market decisions there is no ascertainable, publicly inspectable probability. There are numerous conflicting theories ascribing differing probabilities. Individuals often embark upon an activity because their assessment of the probability of success differs from that of other people, perhaps all other people. The recommendation that individuals proceed according to probability can hardly mean other than that they should proceed according to their own estimate of the probability, which is not amenable to any objective test. This is an invitation to everyone to indulge their own wishful fancies. Thus, someone whose investment fails may feel that it was as good as a success, since in her estimate the probability of success was high. Chronic overoptimism about one's beloved projects, persistent indulgence of one's pet theories when the evidence of actual outcomes accumulates against those theories, is one of the most common and serious disorders of human action, and specifically of business behavior. It would be difficult to think of a simpler recipe for prompt industrial collapse than the proposal that people be encouraged to think of failure as though it had been success.

Like his proposal on earning capacity, Carens's proposal on risk weakens the link between pre-tax income and social-duty satisfactions. Social-duty satisfactions can no longer be inferred directly from pre-tax income, and this is hazardous for the workability of the ESM. The fact that individuals are to be guided, not by the indications of pre-tax income, which would be objective and public, but by modifications of pre-tax income which they individually make according to their personal evaluations, invites the likelihood that they will make errors which will not be corrected properly: the entrepreneur, convinced that his mistake was not a mistake, will be more ready to make the same mistake again.

Alternatively, it could be argued that a tendency would be bound to arise for people to take little notice of the adjustments to pre-tax income, since an entrepreneur's command over the future disposition of resources wouldn't be affected by them, but only by pre-tax income. A person who persistently scored his performance above his actual results would still be deprived of any investable funds, if she persistently made losses. Her subsequent opportunities to derive social-duty satisfactions from investments would be curtailed, and this would be more decisive than her immediate subjective response to her losses.

e. Motivation in the Two Systems

Carens is aware that most objections to his ESM will come from those who deny that incentives would be adequate, and he devotes much attention to the problem of securing adequate motivation. Carens's position can be summarized as follows. In the PPM, individuals are largely motivated by pursuit of "income-consumption satisfactions". For the ESM to work, the main motivational requirement is that people should come to attribute an importance to "social-duty satisfactions", derivable from pre-tax income, equivalent to the importance people in the PPM attribute to "income-consumption satisfactions". In all societies, every individual's goals and values are "determined by the prevailing culture".[6] Socialization is the process which makes individuals in the PPM value income-consumption satisfactions, and socialization can be relied upon to make individuals value social-duty satisfactions in the ESM. This follows from Carens's view that "given the proper conditions of socialization, almost any goals could be adopted on a widespread basis in a society" (104).

Here again we see the paradoxical nature of Carens's system: he relies on the notion that it is possible to give people any goals, by socialization. But the force of his argument is that it is iniquitous for there to be differences in income, and these differences in income could hardly matter unless it were the case that people cared deeply about the absolute and relative levels of their incomes. If it's possible to make people hold any values, then there is no point in equality of nominal incomes, for we can merely socialize people to be entirely satisfied with whatever they get, and their real incomes, measured in subjective utility, will then be equal, or as 'equal' as they could conceivably be made by any arrangement. (One can imagine someone holding that people ought to be given equal portions of goods, without any reference to the subjective utilities those goods might yield, and that the moral rationale for equality of goods does not extend to equality of social-duty satisfactions. Such a position would lose most of the persuasiveness of Carens's equalitarianism, and it's difficult to imagine a coherent defense of it. An alternative would be to delete any reference to social-duty satisfactions, so that individuals felt impelled to maximize pre-tax incomes, without gaining satisfactions in proportion to the amounts of those incomes—much as someone tries to get an arithmetic problem right, without feeling any better about it if the correct solution is a bigger number. This might place a further strain on the plausibility of supposing people to have the desired motivation.)

While I have no wish to conceal my opinion that it is fantastic to suppose that people's goals and values are determined by the prevailing culture,[7] I will concentrate here on the way Carens conceives the task which socialization would have to solve in order to cause people to possess the motivations required for his system to function as he wants it to function. There may be a temptation, encouraged by some of Carens's turns of phrase, to conceive the problem in these terms: In the PPM, people are motivated by a desire to increase their personal consumption, by increasing their real income after tax. In the ESM, people will instead be motivated by a desire to increase their social-duty satisfactions, by increasing their pre-tax income. One motivation replaces another. The only serious question then becomes: Is the new motivation powerful enough? But this misconceives the comparison between the two situations.

It suggests that, for the PPM to work, a special kind of motivation is required: that people desire 'personal consumption' (or "income-consumption satisfactions"), whereas they might *conceivably*, in this or some other system, desire something else. In market theory, the ultimate aim of all behavior is characterized as consumption of utility, but this is a broad category covering every possible way in which anyone might get gratification from any behavior. If we describe the PPM by saying that individuals want "income consumption", then we must include in income consumption the satisfactions that come from going to church, giving to charity, committing suicide, overthrowing the government, self-flagellation, feeling a sense of solidarity as part of a community, or acting in bizarre ways in a deliberate attempt to refute economic theory. The range of motivation in the PPM includes all that we would normally understand by the motive of 'social duty'. Hence, statements that people in the PPM are motivated by personal consumption, and in the ESM by social duty, are misleading. 'Social duty' may mean what the term, used in the vernacular, seems to evoke, in which case, there is no limitation of people's social-duty motivations in the PPM: they can be entirely as socially-dutiful as they please. Alternatively, 'social duty' may be a specially-defined term referring to a kind of motivation which can exist only in the ESM. 'Income consumption' may mean what an economist would take it to mean, in which case it encompasses all social-duty motives, including those in the ESM; social-duty motivation is a species of income-consumption motivation. Alternatively, it might mean a curious type of motivation existing only in the PPM—but there is no such type of motivation. Or thirdly it might mean, say, something like 'desire for the kinds of consumer goods one finds in stores, to be used personally by the desiring individual for her own gratification'. But in that case, the motivation will continue in the ESM, as Carens acknowledges.

Of course, the reader could interpret 'income consumption' as self-interested motivation and 'social duty' as altruistic motivation. Although his references to 'moral incentives' might encourage such an interpretation, Carens himself disavows it, claiming that behavior in the ESM is just as self-interested as in the PPM (120–23), so I will not expatiate on the difficulty of classifying observed behavior as self-interested or altruistic. People's behavior in the PPM may be as altruistic as they like. It is sometimes supposed that economic theory presupposes, or the PPM requires, predominantly selfish or self-interested behavior, but this is mistaken.[8] The ESM requires, if it is to work as Carens envisages, that most of people's *altruistic* motivations have to be scrapped along with most of their self-interested motivations (the point holds however we make the division). People cannot be allowed, for example, to give gifts (218–19), to operate charities, or to 'look after' those they love (by providing for them materially).

It is, then, misleading to think that the ESM's motivational problem is one of getting people to care more about social duty and less about personal consumption, in any sense that the use of these terms will immediately evoke in the reader. The problem is rather that of getting people to care far less about all the infinite range of their personally-chosen purposes in life, and far more about their (individually minuscule) contributions to the efficiency of the whole economy through maximizing pre-tax income.

Consider an individual in the ESM, with a fixed post-tax income. Would such an individual have a preference to increase this income? Leave aside the question of whether this preference is effective. By an ineffective preference here I mean a preference that does not issue in action—the action that would satisfy this preference may be currently impossible or too costly, but if such an action became possible or cheap enough, the preference would become effective. It is clear that individuals in the ESM would definitely prefer increases in their post-tax incomes. Carens acknowledges as much when he provides for economic growth, so that welcome increases in incomes are possible. There is also no reason to doubt that individuals would continue to prefer leisure to work. (This is sometimes discussed in terms of whether people are 'naturally lazy', but that misses the main point. 'Leisure' may be more strenuous than 'work'. Leisure is 'free time', doing what one feels like doing because one feels like doing it. Work, in this context, is doing what one does not necessarily feel like doing, or not at that time and place, under those conditions, except for some non-intrinsic compensation.)

One portion of the motivational task of the ESM is to ensure that individuals keep on working the same hours at the same intensity, even though this has no effect upon their post-tax incomes. Consider, for example, those whose pre-tax incomes are below their ESM post-tax incomes. There is no question that under present PPM conditions, providing lower-than-average-income people with a welfare check *equal to or less than* their income from work, will cause a drop in the amount of labor supplied. Empirical research confirms what common sense suggests.[9] This observed effect is quite dramatic, despite all the restrictions on such payments: there is a lot of time-consuming and even humiliating effort involved in claiming them, and 'going on welfare' damages one's future prospects for employment by reducing one's aptitude for work. In the ESM, by contrast, the payments will be automatic and for life, and will constitute, for over half the population, a sum *higher* than the pre-tax payment. There is no doubt that, *with present motivations*, a guaranteed income to all, unconditional upon effort, and equal to the average supply of consumer goods per head, would cause an immediate and catastrophic drop in labor supplied. Many people would simply cease work altogether. Now suppose that this catastrophic drop could be halved in the ESM. This would be a staggering, miraculous success for 'socialization' but it would not make the ESM efficient in the sense of equalling or approaching the output of the PPM. (This conclusion is not seriously qualified if everyone is legally obliged to go to work. The fact that people's incomes were unrelated to their output would cause people to change their behavior.)

Even people with a major commitment to social-duty satisfactions, and a minor interest in increasing their personal consumption will behave inefficiently in the ESM—in the sense that they will not work so much, or will not change jobs in response to changing pre-tax wages. Why this asymmetry between the two systems? In the PPM people can make their own trade-offs between personal consumption and other satisfactions; this is consonant with efficiency. In the ESM, *any* responsiveness to changes in personal consumption must result in an inefficient outcome, because of the income-leisure trade-off. If people get goods without the necessity to work, and cannot get more goods by working more, *any* regard for goods and for leisure will cause them to work less than they otherwise would, or to gravitate to work they find more congenial.

The fact that individuals will continue to place *some* value on income-consumption benefits has innumerable ramifications which menace the integrity of the ESM. I will here briefly mention two of these. First, this fact implies that people must be hurt by the restrictions on saving—these must reduce people's wellbeing and therefore social efficiency. Individuals are not permitted to reduce their present post-tax incomes, in order to reap a return in the form of higher post-tax incomes later. There would presumably be nothing to stop someone, say, accumulating large stocks of canned food, then living off these and buying better accommodation, but saving for productive purposes, with a view to higher personal post-tax income later, would be outlawed. This prohibition, essential for the survival of the ESM, appears blatantly unjust, and is certainly inefficient. Second, people will adjust their business affairs to get more 'income-consumption' satisfaction out of what they do. For example, an entrepreneur, faced with a choice between a plan that requires him to work in a grim milieu (whatever he regards as grim) and a plan that requires him to work in a picturesque bungalow on a leafy hillside overlooking a shimmering lake, will give the incidental personal benefits of the latter location more weight than he would in the PPM. And who could blame him for then being so dedicated to his work that he chose to live there?

f. Knowing What To Do in the ESM

Carens claims to show "that social-duty satisfactions would perform the same functions with respect to resource allocation [in the ESM] as income-consumption satisfactions perform in the PPM system" (38). But if "perform the same functions" means 'lead to the same outcome', he doesn't show this.

Carens's example is that of a worker, Jane, choosing among three jobs with different rates of pay and different degrees of work satisfaction. (In considering this example above, we were looking at the feasibility of individuals calculating their 'earning capacities'. Having discarded the earning capacity feature of the ESM, and thus made it more closely parallel to the PPM, we now consider the pure question of whether people could make the same decisions in both systems.) Jane chooses the one with intermediate pay, because it has greater work satisfaction than the one with highest pay, and she values the difference in work satisfaction more than the difference in pay. Carens claims that Jane "places the same relative value on social-duty satisfactions in the egalitarian system that she placed on income-consumption satisfactions" in the PPM (39). If these are the same, the outcome will be the same. The question is how plausible it is to suppose that they could be the same. The only way for the ESM to simulate the PPM is for individuals in the ESM to try to act as they would in the PPM. This is because the estimation of the social benefit must correspond to the valuation placed on consumer goods in the PPM, or the simulation is lost. Would it be possible for individuals to accurately determine what they would have done in the PPM? Picture the individual, in a society without individual variations in personal-consumption income, without anyone's being able to increase his personal-consumption income above a fixed level. Faced with the possibility of an increased pre-tax income in exchange for decreased work-enjoyment, the individual has to decide how he *would* decide if the increased pre-tax income could be spent in any way he pleased—on increased personal consumption and on giving away to others.

Would it be possible for people in the Carens system to accurately imagine how they would behave in the PPM, and then behave that way? There are several reasons for thinking this would be impossible.

There is the limitation of imagination. People sometimes play poker for real money, and sometimes for matchsticks. Their behavior is different in each case. Someone could try hard to play poker for matchsticks exactly as he would if he were playing for money, but he would be unlikely to have complete success. However, if he has never played for real money, has never had any experience of winning or losing real money at any time, and cannot look around at any examples of people playing for real money, it is even more difficult for him to imagine how he would play for real money.

Some of the choices made by factor-owners involve their own subjective preferences. Laborers compare, in the PPM, their non-pecuniary income from work with their monetary payment, or, in the ESM, their non-pecuniary satisfactions with their social-duty benefits as revealed by their pre-tax income. This requires experimentation or trial and error. An individual in the PPM might take a congenial job at comparatively low wages, fully believing that the non-pecuniary satisfactions would compensate for the difference in wages. After a spell in this job, he might discover that the compensation was insufficient, and quit that job for a less intrinsically satisfying but higher-paid job. Even an individual who doesn't do this himself (a lifestyle entrepreneur) may be influenced by the reports of those individuals who do. Thus, people have to be free to vary their monetary incomes, including their personal-consumption incomes, or they will be unable to learn about the most efficient gratification of their wants. People in Caren's system cannot know how much weight to give to social-duty satisfactions unless they have some way of determining how much they would have valued the higher consumption they would have gotten in the PPM.

No one can be sure *exactly* how he would behave in different circumstances, and the stranger the circumstances, the greater the uncertainty. It might be thought that if I can't know how I would behave in certain specified circumstances, then to that extent there's something quirky or irrational about that choice in those circumstances, that it doesn't reflect my 'true preferences'. But people often like to be quirky and there is a reduction in efficiency if they aren't permitted to be quirky. And decision-making is guided by the skilled use of intuitive algorithms dependent on subliminal clues. A pianist may not be as good at improvizing by moving his fingers in the air in front of him, imagining he is playing the piano, as he would with a real piano, even if he does know as he makes each motion, what the notes would have sounded like. A marksman may not be as good at aiming at an imaginary target as he is at aiming at a target he can see. The fact that some of the determinants of a decision may be unconscious, or dependent upon subtle clues from minute nuances of the immediate environment, does not necessarily mean that they do not make the decision more effective. Thus, whether we see the situation-bound determinants of decisions as ultimate consumables or as intuitive algorithms, changing these determinants changes the decisions and may reduce efficiency.

One cannot know how one would react to the prospect of more or less money income, except by knowing how one would react to the prospect of more or less of the things money can buy. The rule, 'Respond to an increase in pre-tax income as you would if you could spend it freely', calls for imaginative guesswork. Frequent and substantial mistakes would be made in this process and could not be tested or corrected.

— 10 —

DIVISION OF KNOWLEDGE

All organs of a socialist economy will work, so to speak, within glass walls. (Dickinson 1939, 9)

i. Spontaneous Order

In Mises's view, modern industry is too complicated to plan. Mises in effect claims that an intricate, complex industrial structure requires what Marx calls "anarchy of production"—absence of overall planning. It has seemed to many people as though this claim *must* be wrong. There is something baffling in the notion that we, the members of human society, can do something without thinking about it, and yet be unable to do at least as well by 'conscious' design and goal-directed organization. How can it be that we must sometimes rely upon unplanned processes to deliver the goods?

a. Spontaneous Order in Nature

Orderly patterns can occur without being designed. In some cases such natural order is useful to human beings. Sometimes the only way to bring about a certain state of affairs is to set up the conditions in which a spontaneous process will lead to the desired result. An example is the growing of crystals, which people may wish to use for various purposes, but which they are incapable of arranging molecule by molecule. Appropriate conditions are prepared, and a natural process then 'arranges' the molecules in crystals of predetermined shape. This process can be broadly described, but cannot be traced in detail: we cannot predict the path of each molecule, but this isn't necessary to benefit from the process. The ordered complexity of crystal formation is especially impressive where *several* substances dissolved in the same container of hot water build up separate crystals of each substance as the solution cools. Michael Polanyi observes that to attempt a task of the same complexity by conscious planning (such as sorting out millions of mixed marbles into batches of the same color) "would keep the whole of humanity busy for years; yet a similar result is accomplished spontaneously in a few seconds" (Polanyi 1951, 155–56). Another example is the formation of snowflakes. Billions upon billions of snowflakes have been produced, and every one of them has a six-sided shape, all different and all fairly intricate.

The most striking instances of spontaneously-produced order are living organisms, spontaneous both in their origin (natural selection) and their interaction (ecology). Frequently those most hostile to a laissez-faire approach to the spontaneous order of the market are most supportive of a laissez-faire approach to the spontaneous order of nature. It was once thought that living organisms were so intricately and efficiently structured that they could only have been invented by a conscious mind. It is now commonly held that they are *too* intricately and efficiently structured to have been designed by a conscious mind (Dawkins 1986).

Orderly patterns come about, without being contrived, because of regularities in the behavior of the elements making up the patterns. We focus our attention on examples where the resulting order somehow 'looks as though' it might have been designed. Less impressive examples include the formation of sand dunes and the distribution of water molecules in a glass container. By extrapolation, any natural regularity (such as spatiotemporal extension and duration) is a case of spontaneous order; to exist is to exhibit spontaneous order and *vice versa*. Cases of designed or intelligently imposed order can be subsumed under spontaneous order, since the mind works anarchically, consciousness being a spontaneously precipitated focal area, like the Chicago Board of Trade in world commodities markets.

b. A Remark about Spontaneous Order in Engineering

Hayek traces the socialist preoccupation with planning society to the Saint-Simonian admiration for science and engineering (Hayek 1979), but this appears to be exactly wrong. It seems rather that this preoccupation arose from a revulsion against science and technology; in this the Saint-Simonians took the opposite attitude to Saint-Simon (Iggers 1972, xl). If so, that would be appropriate, for, contrary to what Hayek alleges, engineers tend to prefer machines that are self-correcting and, best of all, self-controlling.

(The paradigm here is the so-called 'Watt's governor', actually employed in medieval times.) One might perhaps therefore expect engineers to favor the setting up of social institutions which would work best by requiring no further 'conscious' intervention, a policy of laissez-faire. It would be easy to give anecdotal examples to suggest that the mechanical or engineering approach to human society will be one favorable to laissez-faire, including the influence of engineering models upon Herbert Spencer, Léon Walras, and John Muth.[1]

c. Spontaneous Order in Society

Orderly patterns, consciously intended and deliberately brought about, abound in the human world. Yet spontaneous order is conspicuous everywhere in human interactions. The regularities in the behavior of individuals may often give rise to systematic consequences not planned by those individuals. In nature, spontaneous order means that complex, orderly structures emerge without design. Things which may 'look' planned have come into being without any planning. In society, spontaneous order also means that complex, orderly structures emerge without design. But in this case, there may be plenty of planning going on. It's just that the spontaneous process makes the numerous planners' actions together result in a complex and orderly structure which none of them planned, independently of any success they may enjoy in fulfilling their plans. It is a truism that, from the point of view of the development of society, these 'unintended consequences of human action' may be far more important than success or failure in the goals which loom so large in the minds of the individuals concerned.

A simple example of spontaneous interpersonal order is the way in which people will 'distribute' themselves in a train or theater, where each person is free to pick any vacant seat (Polanyi 1951, 115). Not only does the resulting 'distribution' possess many of the same orderly properties that could be attained by assigning each person a seat in advance; it also has some properties which a system of assignment would find more difficult to achieve: a tendency for people to sit nearer those they like the look of, and for those who care more about their seat locations to get better locations by arriving earlier. In many cases, however, the advantages of seating assignment may outweigh the advantages of free choice of seats.

There is no reason to assume that a spontaneous order will be welcome. A cancer is a spontaneous order. The fact that buses leave the depot at regular intervals, but arrive at your nearest bus-stop in convoys of five; the fact that a kitten playing with a pen will eventually result in the pen's being deposited in the best hiding-place on the sitting-room floor; the fact that slow traffic always moves by alternating rest and movement—these are familiar instances of usually unwelcome spontaneous orders. Yet the possibility exists that a spontaneous order may have a desirable outcome, and that this outcome may be unachievable except by permitting the spontaneous order.

An oft-cited case where spontaneous order draws upon the knowledge of many individuals is the formation of paths in country areas (see Hayek 1979, 40–41). An individual takes what seems to her the best route. This beats down the foliage and makes it more likely that someone else will take the same route. A network of paths is formed, which is orderly, which draws upon the knowledge of many thousands of individuals, which serves people's purposes well, but which was never preconceived in anyone's mind. The network of paths was made by individuals many of whom have never met each other, perhaps separated by thousands of years, geographically by hundreds of miles, and zoologically by orders or classes.

Some of the knowledge which went into forming the paths could not have been explicitly formulated and indeed, in this case, the paths would most commonly have been partly formed by beasts, who might have taken advantage of knowledge not available to humans. Each person who uses such a network of paths is being guided by the knowledge of numerous individuals she has never met, and it is possible that the network could never be designed from scratch to be equally good—numerous trials may be necessary to find the best way to negotiate dangers like steep drops or marshes. It is conceivable, though somewhat unlikely, that someone surveying the land and making a thorough study could design a better network of paths.

While paths develop over generations, some spontaneous orders may emerge within minutes or even seconds. Traffic responds to radio broadcasts about traffic conditions. Analysis of responses to such broadcasts would show an orderly response, with the aggregate more predictable than the individual. Each driver interprets the news in the light of his own knowledge and intentions, including what he can see with his own eyes, his past experience of such broadcasts, and the particular goal of his journey. Upon hearing that traffic is very slow on a particular road, some drivers avoid it, others wait, a few may even change direction towards it (if the holdup is due to an accident and they are physicians or reporters). The outcome can be compared with a procedure by which a single agency instructed each driver on what to do. This might be too cumbersome to be practicable. A single agency, such as a traffic police force, might intervene piecemeal to supplement and correct the outcome, but this would depend upon the independent rationale of the spontaneous process. Such 'interventionist' modification of a spontaneous order should not be confused with replacement of the spontaneous system by direction, and should be limited so that it does not excessively impair the spontaneous system.

Spontaneous order in human groups, and in all animal groups, is a matter of information or knowledge. Because of spontaneous social order, all the individuals can make use of knowledge which none of them singly possesses. Knowledge is scattered among many different individuals. Each individual can use not only his own knowledge but knowledge which he does not possess, because other individuals' actions, guided by their knowledge, can reveal to him those aspects of their knowledge which require him to modify his own actions. Their actions are perceived by him as abstract signals which may show him just that aspect of their knowledge which is relevant to his own plans. In turn, his consequent actions may emit abstract signals which help to modify the actions of numerous other individuals.

When this happens in very simple cases, it is so trite that it seems scarcely worth analyzing. A group of animals is approached by a predator. One animal spots the predator and gives a characteristic danger call. The whole group moves off. The knowledge possessed by the individual who made the call may be of two sorts: 1. The individual perceives signs of the approaching predator. Since no two individuals perceive precisely the same things, every individual always has special, personal, privileged knowledge, arising from his 'point of view'. 2. The individual possesses background knowledge. He has a 'theory'. This tells him what constitutes signs of danger. He is able to distinguish leaves rustling in the wind from leaves brushed by a big hairy beast. An individual's background knowledge is also always unique to that individual—no two individuals share precisely the same theories of the world. It is possible that this individual's background knowledge may be superior to that of other individuals —perhaps that is why he gave the danger call before others did. The animal group may have a system for individuals with such superior background knowledge to place themselves at the periphery of the group.

ii. THE USE OF KNOWLEDGE IN SOCIETY

How can the combination of fragments of knowledge existing in different minds bring about results which, if they were to be brought about deliberately, would require a knowledge on the part of the directing mind which no single person can possess? (Hayek 1948, 54)

a. Leonard Read's Pencil

In an amusing little piece, written as if in the first person by an ordinary lead pencil, Read (1958) captures one of the fundamental qualities of modern production. Although millions of pencils are manufactured every day, strictly speaking no one knows how to make them. Many thousands of different people know partial aspects of how to make little bits of them. Thus, the graphite miner doesn't know much about the making of the wooden stem or of the eraser, and the miners of zinc and copper (for the brass ferrule) are largely ignorant of the production of factice (for the eraser) by reacting rape seed oil with sulfur chloride. All the millions of people engaged in the production of a given line of pencils, people who for the most part don't meet, don't know each other, and are not aware of each other's existence, effectively co-operate in producing pencils.

This "intellectual division of labor", as Mises calls it, is present in virtually all market exchange. A community of pastoralists makes contact with a fishing community. Meat, milk, and horns are exchanged for fish. Both pastoralists and fishers benefit by the trade. The pastoralists are benefitting from the art of fishing, of which they are ignorant, and the fishers benefit from the art of herding cattle, of which they are ignorant. It may be tempting to some to suppose that there is something accidental about this intellectual division of labor, that it is due to the rudimentary state of co-operation through exchange. We may easily imagine that the leading experts of the two communities sit down together and discuss the possibilities for the two forms of production. It's even conceivable that they may come up with something useful. A pastoralist may learn a lot about fishing, and a fisher a lot about cattle herding. But if we jump ahead to a modern society, where there are many thousands of specialized branches of knowledge, it is out of the question for anyone to master more than a handful of them. Of course, a diligent person can read summaries of the chief principles and findings in many fields. A journalistic specialist can gain quite a respectable knowledge of many fields, by reading the industry journals and frequently meeting people in those industries. In such cases the 'most important' facts about an industry are formulated and learned. Important though these facts are, they omit much fine-grained detail, they omit exceptional oddities, and they omit peculiar concrete "circumstances of time and place" (Hayek 1948, 80). Furthermore, they will always incorporate 'indisputable truths' which are in fact false, and which someone, somewhere, believes to be false and is right now proving to be false. Even within a single industry, no one knows all those facts about the industry which would determine its response to some change in the information.

b. Adam Smith's Pin Factory

To take an example, therefore, from a very trifling manufacture . . . the trade of the pin-maker; a workman not educated to this business . . . could scarce, perhaps, with his utmost industry, make one pin in a day, and certainly could not make twenty. But in the way in which this business is now carried on . . . it is divided into a number of branches . . . . One man draws out the wire, another straights it, a third cuts it, a fourth points it, a fifth grinds it at the top for receiving the head; to make the head requires two or three distinct operations; to put it on, is a peculiar business, to whiten the pins is another . . . . if they had all wrought separately and independently, and without any of them having been educated to this peculiar business, they certainly could not each of them have made twenty, perhaps not one pin in a day; that is, certainly, not the two hundred and fortieth, perhaps not the four thousand eight hundredth part of what they are at present capable of performing. . . . (Smith 1981, 14–15)

What is Smith driving at here? Many writers suppose that Smith is emphasizing the productive potential of specialization (division of labor) within a workshop or factory, and that he finds the example of pin-making an apt and eloquent example of this potential. Much ink has been spilled on Smith's choice of pin-making. Clapham (1924, 68) expresses deep regret "that Adam Smith did not go a few miles from Kirkcaldy to the Carron Works to see them turning and boring their cannonades instead of his silly pin factory". Ashton (1925, 281) approves, observing that in "text-books and examination scripts the pin trade of a hundred or more years ago has been given a prominence which is far from justified by its true rank among economic activities. . . . the manufacture of pins does not afford the ideal illustration of the division of labour". Others point out that the pin-making example was already well-known when Smith wrote, and that he lifted it from earlier literature, pruning it of detail in the process. I could cite many more examples of this surprising myopia. Very few writers show any awareness of Smith's actual intention here, and these few do not make it fully explicit (Blaug 1985, 220).

Pin-making can be defended on expository grounds, as a graphic, comprehensible example without equal. Smith introduces it as "a very trifling manufacture; but one in which the division of labour has been very often taken notice of" (14). However, Smith's chief object in introducing the pin-making workshop is to use it as an analogy with the whole of society. The transition is made with the words: "The separation of different trades and employments from one another, seems to have taken place, in consequence of this advantage" (15), and the remainder of Chapter I focusses on this unplanned, society-wide division of labor. Chapter II begins with the words: "This division of labor, from which so many advantages are derived, is not originally the effect of any human wisdom, which foresees and intends that general opulence to which it gives occasion. It is the . . . consequence of . . . the propensity to truck, barter, and exchange one thing for another" (25). There is an implied contrast here with the pin-making workshop, where division of labor *is* the "result of human wisdom". Trade inadvertently turned the world into a huge integrated factory in which millions reaped the benefits of increased output, before people paid much attention to the deliberate contrivance of factories with internal specialization.

In the workshop, 18 different specialist workers are deliberately arranged in a planned division of labor, resulting in an enormous increase of production through specialisation and co-operation. In society as a whole, what Smith called "the Great Society", many thousands of different specialist producers are somehow 'arranged' in an unplanned division of labor, resulting in an enormous increase of production through specialization and co-operation. The organizer of the workshop can *see* the rationale for specialization and co-operation, and can experiment with new arrangements. The "sovereign" or government *cannot see* the rationale for specialization and co-operation among the many different "trades" in the whole society, and it is "the utmost folly and presumption" for that sovereign to think that it can adapt this Great Society to a design of its own contriving.

How can this be possible? How are the various industries selected and adapted? The whole of *The Wealth of Nations* is concerned to answer questions such as these, and that is why the pin-factory example occurs at the beginning. The great purpose of *The Wealth of Nations* is not merely to systematize and extend the existing corpus of economics, but to do so in the context of a single great insight. The laborer taking part in making pins has personal expertise not shared by the other persons with whom he co-operates. Yet his part in the making of pins is selected by the employer. When we come to the whole of society, however, the individual producer has personal expertise which helps him to choose what occupation to pursue, what goods to produce, and how to produce them. In making a decision, the producer draws upon his own personal knowledge, knowledge which is frequently available to no one else. Unlike the arrangement of workers in a workshop, the arrangement of producers in the whole society draws upon the expertise, the private knowledge, of each of them. Anyone seeking to interfere in the arrangement that results is therefore likely to bring about unexpected and probably deleterious repercussions, because the intervener does not know the full circumstances that were taken into account in arriving at the arrangement.

iii. THE HEURISTICS OF INSTITUTIONS

a. The Design of Institutions to Facilitate Discovery and Dissemination of Knowledge

Institutions may be designed for their heuristic qualities. An elementary example is the 'meeting'. A meeting may be called to come to some sort of conclusion, to decide what to do or what to think. In one of the simplest cases, a decision-maker calls a meeting of her advisors and asks them for their comments on a particular issue. One of the advisors may think of something which the decision-maker would not have thought of, but which the decision-maker finds relevant to the decision. It is also possible that a decision may be taken by vote of the meeting. The vote is usually preceded by a debate, and the debate may affect the outcome of the vote. Debating and voting draws upon the separate knowledge of the various participants.

A special kind of debate is a trial in a court of law. In Anglophone countries, this is conducted by the 'adversary' system, in which prosecution and defense each present admittedly incomplete and biassed cases, in competition with one another. It is not self-evident that this is the best system, but in evaluating it, we should not overlook the fact that this system will elicit some information that no other system would elicit.

A technique for eliciting information which is now routinely used in the Anglo-Saxon world, but which might have seemed grotesquely inappropriate in some other and earlier cultures,[2] is that of brainstorming. In brainstorming, a group of people meet together and throw out ideas in an unihibited fashion, however unworkable, crazy, or silly these ideas may appear. No one need fear censure or ridicule for advancing an idea which is hopelessly ill-advised. Someone writes down all the suggestions. Then the group carefully scrutinizes each suggestion. Sometimes the apparently inappropriate suggestions turn out, on close examination, to be more plausible. Sometimes they suggest other possibilities. Sometimes, by conveying a sense of the limits of what is feasible, they make for a more confident and balanced choice among the more prosaic alternatives. Brainstorming can be performed by a single person, and is a more explicit enactment of the way in which individuals always make new discoveries (see Campbell 1986). Yet group brainstorming draws upon more knowledge than a single person possesses; it simulates a kind of amplified or group mind by linking up several minds through a specific procedure or set of procedures. It may seem unnecessary to point out that the institution of brainstorming is employed because it produces results that alternative procedures will not produce.

The traditional way to conduct a conference or convention is something like the following. There are several sessions, devoted to different topics and attended by everyone. Usually, someone is nominated as a speaker, to give a presentation which opens the discussion in each session. Sometimes there is a second speaker, who may criticize the first. Sometimes one or more speakers will 'wind up' by summarizing the earlier speeches and the discussion, and perhaps evaluating the points made. More intimate and close attention to details is often left to the informal breaks between sessions, and is unplanned (though it is sometimes where the 'real business' of the conference is transacted). Sometimes more detailed matters are left to narrow 'committees', which meet during a break in the full sessions of the conference, and report back.

An alternative method, which has become more common in recent decades, is to begin with a presentation or two to the entire conference, and then immediately to split up into many small groups. A conference of 100 individuals may split up into 20 groups of five members each. Each group elects a spokesman, and then discusses the matters raised in the initial presentations. There are numerous variants of this technique. Sometimes each group will be allocated a specific specialized topic; sometimes half of the groups will all deal with one aspect, the other half with another. The spokesmen make a note of the main points and later the full conference re-assembles, and the spokesmen make their reports.

It is not necessary for us to accept that this second approach to the organizations of conferences is ever well-advised. Leaving that aside, two things can be said about it: 1. it has obvious disadvantages; and

2. it has advantages which may conceivably outweigh its disadvantages. Indeed, these perceptible advantages are the point of the procedure. It would therefore be an elementary blunder to cite some of the disadvantages in the belief that this disposed of the procedure. Among the disadvantages are that some valuable points will be made that, due to the imperfect filtering of the spokesmen, will not be available to most of the participants, and that there will be duplication, with different groups expending effort and time in covering identical ground. Among the advantages are that more people will contribute their ideas, that a more balanced picture of everyone's views will emerge (because the discussion is less likely to be dominated by a few flashy attention-huggers), and that more close attention will be given to various topics (because a group of five is less likely to wander far from its members' interests for long, and therefore less likely to send them to sleep).

There is a trade-off in such conferences between the gains of greater division and the losses of the spokesmen's reports. The information elicited must have a certain character, with manifest criteria of relevance, otherwise people will feel that they are losing more by relying upon spokesmen's fallible reports than they are gaining by more detailed coverage of the ground. Once again, it may seem unnecessary to state that these two institutional forms, the traditional and the subdivided conferences, will not produce the same ideas or the same conclusions.

A conference is a spontaneous or polycentric order. There is no point in holding a conference where everyone knows in advance exactly what everyone will say. That would be a play, not a conference. Conferences are also components of wider spontaneous orders. In a series of conferences, the problems raised in one conference may help to determine the content and the conduct of subsequent conferences. Even an apparently isolated conference will be part of some wider pattern of information: newsletters, journals, libraries, and so forth.

Wherever knowlege is incomplete, there may be disagreement. To establish the truth, or the best candidate for a provisional surrogate for the truth, we may wait until there is agreement or may let everyone go their own way, and see which works. According to circumstances, it *may* be best to divide up the task of acquiring knowledge. Suppose that six individuals are searching an area of ground for something they believe to be somewhere within that area (a bird's nest, or a lost necklace). It could be best for the six to cover the whole ground together, but it may sometimes be best for them to divide up the territory, perhaps into six segments, with each person alloted a segment to search. Given certain assumptions, the second procedure will be more efficient than the first—the probability of the object's being found within a short period of time may be far greater.

The above example is one where the 'territory' is spatial. But other illustrations can be considered. A group of individuals with varying theories or areas of expertise can be given the same problem. They can all work on it together, or they can each work on it separately. In some circumstances, the second approach will be better. If individuals are each given different segments of the problem, they can report their progress so far to the other individuals, and this may enable the other individuals to modify their approach. In this procedure, each individual reports her progress, and reads the reports from all the other individuals. These reports, singly or in combination, may prompt her to change direction, and hence make a difference to her future reports. There are obvious applications of this scenario in scientific research, the growth of law by precedent, or the evolution of myth and folksong. It applies to any broad tradition of enquiry, such as that of which this book is a part. It is trite that the course of my thinking has been affected by the results of other people's enquiries, and this work in turn, along with others, will change the direction of subsequent writers' thoughts. But it is sometimes overlooked that every one of the individual writers in this collective process has knowledge unavailable to some of the others, and even some that is available to none of the others.

Outside economics, little has been made of the dispersal of knowledge, and the fact that each individual has privileged knowledge. Kitcher (1990) describes the "division of cognitive labor" in science, and argues that the pattern of scientific change in which die-hards cling to old theories, while the avant-garde discards them, is desirable. Yet he neglects the fact that every scientist has unique knowledge or information, and that therefore it is impossible for all scientists to see a theoretical problem identically, and therefore always to agree upon when change is due. (Thus there is no need to do anything to promote disagreements or disputes; they cannot be avoided. On the other hand, once this is grasped, it seems pointless to artificially stimulate further disagreement.) Kitcher implicitly assumes that all scientists in a given field have the same information, and therefore that any differences in their judgments are noise generated by the individuals, viewed as receptacles for a common "science". He overlooks the fact that the institution of science is a community of interacting individual minds, each unique in its knowledge. This is similar to the illusion that all members of a single linguistic community have learned 'the same' language, when in fact (as everyone who has reared a child knows) they have each developed a different and individually unique language, though hopefully each one may have some overlap with those of other individuals (see Hattiangadi 1987).

b. Different Institutions: Different Information

If institutions are different, then information will be different. If this be true, then it is always wrong to assert or assume that one set of institutions will have access to the same information as another set of institutions. Statements to the effect that some theory is true of more than one institutional system, and *a fortiori,* of all institutional systems, should be viewed with deep suspicion when the content of that theory is information-dependent.

Different procedures may produce the same information only under very restricted conditions. If we wish to multiply two large numbers, we can follow different procedures which may give the same result. We can do it in our heads, we can use a calculator, we can employ logarithms, we can write out a 'long multiplication' computation, and so forth. These should all produce 'the same answer'. Even here the outcome in the broadest sense is not the same. Some methods take longer than others. The frequency of errors varies, and the characteristic errors are different with the different methods. In certain areas, where there is not 'one right answer', or where, if there is, there is no confidence that anyone knows it, an identity of results is even less to be expected from different procedures. This is particularly the case where several individuals' knowledge must be drawn upon, and where each person's knowledge is both limited and unique to that person.

If someone objected to a brainstorming session by saying: 'Let's save the time and just get a secretary to make a list of the points that would come up in the session—it should only take her a couple of minutes to type out', we would be flabbergasted. A brainstorming session is conducted because it is a way of getting the information. It would be even more strange if someone said: 'Skip the stage of listing suggestions—just write out the final answer.' These alternative institutions cannot produce the same information. Of course, it might be argued that, in particular circumstances, they would do as well or better, but that is another matter.

A social institution, such as a corporation or a market, is not bricks and mortar, nor a collection of specific persons, but an assemblage of practices. A social institution can always be evaluated as a set of procedures for eliciting certain results, though this doesn't require the assumption that the institution was set up with that purpose. Brainstorming or the structure of a conference are procedures which can be employed, say, by a private firm or by a state corporation. But there are other procedures which cannot be so employed, because they define these institutions. Or, to put this another way, a private firm is a set of procedures, and a state corporation is a different, incompatible set of procedures. When we distinguish a private firm from a state corporation, we do so in terms of the permissible procedures involved.

In the writings of many socialists there is the assumption, tacit or explicit, that decision-makers in socialism will possess at least as much information as decision-makers in the free market. That they will have as much is stated by Lange as though it were self-evident (1938, 61). It is equally obvious to Dickinson that they will have a lot more). It is clear why Dickinson thinks the socialist managers will have some information that the private entrepreneurs don't have. In a phrase that Dickinson uses more than once, the socialist economy operates within "glass walls" (Dickinson 1939, 9, 20). Dickinson supposes that everyone will be able to see what everyone else is doing, because all will be part of one common effort, and there will be no industrial secrecy. But why does Dickinson believe that the socialist managers will also have all the information that the private entrepreneurs have? He, like Lange, thinks this is self-evident.

When a private firm becomes a government 'enterprise' or part of some government organization, information is lost, for quite simple and demonstrable reasons. Before nationalization, the firm maintained its position by doing better than its competitors, actual and potential. Anyone was free to woo away the firm's customers and put the firm out of business. (When I say 'anyone', I use the term in the sense in which anyone is free to write a best-selling novel. The great majority of people do not possess the acumen to do either of these things, but they are free in the sense that no one is empowered to use coercion to stop them.) Under nationalization, the enterprise is usually given a coercive monopoly and thus protected from those who can do better. Despite this privileged position, the enterprise is usually not allowed to fail; its losses may be indefinitely covered by the taxpayers.

If I ask a question of a group of 50 people, I will stand a better chance of getting the right answer than if I pick one of the group and ask only her. Industry will have access to more information about production if anyone is allowed to enter the industry and try to do better than the existing producers. If 'anyone' is to be allowed to enter, there must be some way of evaluating the performance of rivals, and no single person or group can be permitted to control the industry. Individuals must be free to enter an industry even if the government, the experts, and the consensus of respectable opinion are solidly united against them.

It might be objected that a state-owned industry can canvass 'answers' from everybody, and these can be chanelled to the appropriate responsible officials. This misses the point by taking the metaphor too seriously. A teacher asking a question of a class of 50 students already knows the answer. In industry nobody can know the answers in advance. (Or at least, if someone does know, there is no way that the rest of us can know in advance who that person is.) And the correct answer may not be immediately recognized as such. 'Supplying the right answer' may mean forming a team of people to act with dedication over a period of years, after which it becomes clear that this team will survive whereas others have to be dissolved.

Alternatively, it might be argued that a publicly-owned industry can provide opportunities for new entrants, regardless of their respectability or qualifications, just as the free market does. But this is precisely what a state-owned industry cannot do. It's not possible or desirable that everyone who feels like it shall be permitted to use up valuable resources in pursuit of each person's pet project. The market's solution is to let anybody try, on condition that if they turn out to be wrong, they make losses. Apparent losses may be accepted as long as enough savers or savers' delegates can be persuaded to continue funding the project. This system entails that numerous savers or their numerous delegates make the immediate decision as to which projects are abandoned, which maintained, which curtailed, and which expanded. Ultimately, to the extent that savers or intermediaries pursue the highest returns, these matters are decided by the consumers. To introduce anything approaching such a system is to introduce private ownership of factors and functioning financial markets.

iv. PRICES AS INFORMATION

a. Uncentralized Knowledge in Market Adjustments

When any change occurs in the market, there are thousands, and ultimately millions, of resulting changes. Suppose that a new application is discovered and implemented for copper. The price of copper rises. As a result, all those using copper in thousands of different existing applications will find copper more costly, and will value copper more highly in relation to other factors. They will therefore seek to substitute other factors for copper. For example, in electrical applications they may substitute aluminum or silver for copper—thus raising the price of aluminum or silver. Or they may use less conductive metal and compensate with more of other materials or labor. There will also be increased output of copper mines, and a movement of factors into copper mining.

In such cases, the response to the original price rise will become more pronounced with the passage of time—it may be slight over the first few months, but quite marked after a few years. This is due to four reasons: 1. it requires time to make design and other changes to reduce the use of copper; 2. some equipment appropriate to the earlier price, though no longer worth replacing, may be worth using as long as it lasts; 3. some producers may require time to be convinced that the rise is more than fleeting; and 4. it may take time to *think of* production changes which will reflect the new price ratios.

Any one change, in this case a rise in the price of copper, stimulates thousands of consequent changes, and each one of these in turn stimulates thousands of consequent changes. (Part of the genius of Walras was that he was able to see that these millions upon millions of repercussions of a single price change do not go on reverberating or oscillating endlessly, but converge upon a unique equilibrium of the whole system. Although this occurs only in the theorist's imagination, because in reality fresh changes emerge every moment, the insight is important in showing that the repercussions of change have a coherent shape and direction, and, given some simplifying but by no means bizarre assumptions, do not involve pointless or self-defeating elements.)

Some changes may be limited or neutralized by other concurrent changes, or may even be outweighed by those other changes. For example, an increased demand for copper may be outweighed by improved mining or recycling technology or the discovery of new copper deposits. This doesn't mean that the increased demand for copper disappears in a blur. This increased demand makes the price of copper higher than it would otherwise have been. The actual price reflects many simultaneously changing influences, each of which must have its effect if the price is not to be misleading.

All this is elementary price theory. The crucial point which is often not especially emphasized is that each step in the adjustment process, each link between any price change and one of the price changes caused by it, requires decisions by one or more minds which are not also involved in other steps. Typically, one of these decisions will draw upon specialized knowledge—knowledge that is not known to many people remote from the scene. There will even be knowledge known *only* to the individual decision-maker—though this condition is not necessary to support the argument. All that is necessary is that the knowledge is somewhat specialized—that all the knowledge in all enterprises in all industries is not simultaneously available to any one individual, group, assembly, or organization. This fact is, once stated, hardly likely to be disputed. But there are a few elaborations which may easily be overlooked.

A great deal of the knowledge drawn upon is not formulated. Some of it just happens not to have been formulated; some of it could not be formulated. A person experienced in working with certain equipment may have a hunch or a feel for what can be done with that equipment, and this experienced hunch or feel may be a useful pointer, if not necessarily always correct. Even if all the local formulable knowledge could be formulated and made easily accessible to some outside party, there would remain the hunches and feels, the experienced noses—what Michael Polanyi calls 'tacit knowledge'. These cannot be centralized, because they are predispositions or skills, inseparable from the bodies of the individuals who house them.

Even if tacit knowledge is overlooked, and we imagine that all the relevant knowledge were to be formulated, it is easy to underestimate what this would entail. Knowledge is brought to bear upon a particular situation, a particular constellation of prices and techniques. It would not suffice to have, written out somewhere, instructions for what to do in that situation, for it is only one of an infinity of situations which might have come about. So the knowledge would have to be cast in a very general form, and this once again means that the formulation, if it could be made, would have to be decoded by someone thoroughly familiar with what it meant.

Yet even if this difficulty could be overcome, and all the knowledge which local decision-makers draw upon could be unambiguously formulated and presented to the administration, they would not be able to process all of it simultaneously, so they would have to delegate this job once again, back to the local decision-makers. These local decisions are made day by day, and even second by second, so they cannot all be made by a single body. (It might be supposed that the body could use a large computer, but this overlooks the fact that large computers are now used by many of the local decision-makers, for there is no limit to the subtlety and complexity of the analyses *they* can make, if the means to make them become cheap enough.) Furthermore, we have seen that part of the response to a change in prices is a redirection of attention, a shifting of the focus of learning and discovery. Much of the full response to a price change will be discovered gradually in the years following that price change. Here is another indication that the decision-making task would have to be delegated back to the enterprises by the administration.

Finally, market allocations may embody 'knowledge' which is subjectively known to no one, even in tacit or subliminal form. This can come about by various scenarios, the simplest and best-known of which is the interaction of luck and emulation. One firm may hit upon a superior approach unthinkingly, perhaps by following a false theory. If we suppose that this approach has real but unnoticed benefits, then it is only necessary to assume that a. the benefits cause a firm to be more likely to survive or grow, and b. all firms are likely to copy practices from firms which survive or grow. It then follows that efficient practices will be selected over inefficient ones even though all market agents are ignorant of these effects, let alone the reasons for them, though such a selective mechanism could be combined, in varying degrees, with some actual insight into the reasons.[4] These considerations do not demonstrate that uncentralized decision-making using the abstract signal of price must be superior to society-wide planning by a single administration. *A priori*, it is conceivable, for instance, that local enterprise decision-makers are prone to aberrations and delusions to which central administrators are immune (and this might or might not outweigh the advantages of uncentralized decision-making). It is also conceivable, and has often been suggested, that the undirected totality of interactions among decision-makers might generate a kind of noise, due to the proliferation of futile moves and counter-moves, that could be eliminated by a central authority (and again, this might or might not outweigh the advantages of non-centralization). As we shall see below (10.iv.c.), this possibility seems less likely after a bit of thought than it seems at first blush.

Consider a different arena of the spontaneous dissemination of information. Every day millions of people send messages, by telephone, telegraph, fax, E-mail, or letter. This is 'blind' anarchy: there is no central authority empowered to instruct everyone where to send their messages, let alone the content of the messages. We might consider the proposal for a central message authority, which would replace all these haphazard messages by a single daily message, on the scale of a multi-volume telephone directory, assigning to every household exactly the correct piece of information. By comparison with this hypothetical system, we can detect inefficiencies in the present anarchic system. Two letters about the same matter may cross in the post. Two or more messages may go from different individuals carrying the same information to the same recipient. Such inefficiencies could be corrected by the central message authority—assuming that the authority has immediate access to all the information available to all senders and recipients, plus costless computational capacity. But if we suppose that the authority cannot be immediately aware of all this information and cannot immediately perceive all the relevant relationships among the numerous pieces of information, then we may entertain doubts that the introduction of the authority would actually improve communications.

The role of prices in conveying information by reflecting the specialized knowlege of numerous market agents means that various descriptions of the market process are unlikely to be successfully transformed into operable planning mechanisms. A good example is 'input-output tables', which are useful for picturing the inter-relationships among different activities. In an input-output table, industry is divided into various categories, which designate the rows and columns of a table. For instance, if we look up 'iron' and 'coal' in such a table, we can find what quantity of iron goes to produce what quantity of coal, and *vice versa*. Ideally, there would be billions of rows and columns, designating all goods, and we would have a complete picture of an economy. In practice, groups of goods have to be aggregated, and this automatically loses much of the coherence and 'sense' of the economic system. Aggregation aside, the tables could be used for planning purposes only if we could move determinately from one table to another given a change in some of the quantities. But with any such change, the 'coefficients' (quantities of various goods used as inputs in the production of other goods) would change in ways that the tables can never specify, because these changed coefficients draw upon the specialized knowledge of individuals scattered throughout the system.

b. The God's Eye View

Much that goes on in the existing industrial system is obscure to observers, who try to make sense of it as though they were investigating an alien and largely unknown world. Marx and his followers consider this fact reprehensible: Since humans have created the industrial system, they ought to know all about it. But if the market is a complex system that performs feats of information transmission unattainable by 'conscious' means, then the maintenance of at least the existing level of output may be inseparable from the 'unknown' character of the system.

The unknown character of the economy sometimes gives rise to the theory that something is obscuring the view. This is captured in Dickinson's metaphor that under socialism the economy will operate within glass walls. The administration will just look at what is going on, and will see everything. If we apply this metaphor instead to our example of the transmission of messages, we immediately notice the error. It's not that something gets in the way of our perception of the whole system: the whole system is far too large and intricate to be seen as a whole. It's a misunderstanding to suppose that there is something that can be stripped away, leaving all the interconnections clearly visible.

Furthermore, the market is an arena for competing theories. If there are 20 firms in an industry, they may each have different views of industry conditions. The administration may come up with a twenty-first view, which will be imposed upon all 20 firms (or whatever 'firms' have become after socialization). Writers like Dickinson seem to assume that we know some way to ensure that this twenty-first view is more likely to be correct than one of the other 20 picked at random, but there is no ground for such an assumption. Instead of 20 competing theories, some of which may be comparatively corroborated and others refuted, there is now only one theory being tried out, and this will now be more difficult to test, since no alternatives have been permitted. In any case, it is likely that enterprises closer to the correct theory will be forcibly made to comply with an inferior theory.

c. Rivalrous Withholding of Information

Anarchic or polycentric processes can sometimes achieve results unobtainable by deliberate organization, but there is no guarantee that they must do so in every case.[5] A popular approach is to think of a way in which the spontaneous system might go wrong, then assume that this is bound to happen and that some other system will avoid the problem.

O'Neill 1989 is a rare example of a Marxist trying to meet the

Mises-Hayek case for the market on its own terms. O'Neill argues that self-interested competitors have no incentive to inform one another of relevant information, even though it would be beneficial for all of them if information were shared (1989, 205). As a result, firms do not receive information about their competitors' plans. Hence, when demand for a product increases, each firm increases production without knowing what its competitors will do. There is therefore overproduction, some of the products cannot be sold profitably, and a slump ensues.

Like many such conjectural accounts, O'Neill's argument, even if entirely correct, does not conclusively show what it is supposed to show. The market may have shortcomings which are outweighed by its benefits, and an alternative system may cure the shortcomings at the expense of losing the market's benefits. O'Neill seems to accept that some relevant information is transmitted cheaply and quickly by prices, but although his alternative is not spelled out, it is clear that he wants to abolish prices.

O'Neill's argument proves too much. If true, it would show that markets were frequently in severe crisis. Any acceptable theory has to account for the fact that millions of market adjustments are made every day, smoothly and harmoniously, without a trace of 'crisis', even if we are inordinately generous with that term. Marx is aware that the bare fact of autonomy of enterprises alone cannot explain the trade cycle, but only the possibility of a trade cycle. In the drafts which Engels worked up into Volumes II and III of *Capital*, Marx tries to develop other explanatory forces: the underconsumption of the masses, the falling rate of profit, the instability of the relations among 'departments'. But in these drafts Marx never gets to the point of making clear whether he has the sketch of a complete theory of crises in his mind or whether he is still fishing. O'Neill ignores the problem.

O'Neill is mistaken to think that he has given any explanation for a cycle of boom and slump. Suppose that each of 100 producers are ignorant of the plans of the other 99, and therefore their uncertainty about the future is increased. This yields no bias towards 'overproduction'. Each producer knows that there are 99 others, and makes some attempt to estimate their responses, perhaps guided by past experience of similar market adjustments, or by what industry analysts are saying. O'Neill gives no reason why inaccurate predictions are not equally likely to be overcautious as overoptimistic. So we might expect that about 50 producers will overproduce (increase output too much) and about 50 underproduce (increase output too little), after which they rapidly converge on the correct response. Even if, for some reason, all 100 overproduce, then in some other industry, a corresponding 100 would be underproducing, so there is no general tendency to overproduction.

Producers increase output because they notice that the price of the product has risen, or the number of orders coming in has increased, or both. 'Overproduction' can only mean that each producer assumes that the whole of an increase in the demand for his individual products will be maintained, when in fact part of that increase will be short-lived, since other producers will increase their output. But each producer is well aware that some changes are short-lived and that other producers respond to changes in demand. A producer may just as easily overestimate as underestimate his competitors' responses.

The first responses will be short-run, and will most often be effective quite rapidly. Enterprises will increase output quickly, without making major changes such as building new plant. As far as short-run changes go, then, it is, in many industries, quite misleading to think of a long period in which each firm increases output without seeing the effects on quantity demanded. They find out within months or weeks, and make further adjustments accordingly. Long-run changes, such as building new plant, will not be entered upon lightly. Firms may be hesitant to add new plant which they know will result in losses if the increased demand turns out to be transitory.

A model of the market showing alternating overproduction and underproduction does not necessarily produce anything so dramatic as 'crisis'. After all, we can model the behavior of a thermostat by alternating overproduction and underproduction of heat. Unplanned self-correcting mechanisms (homeostats), as distinct from planned organizations, can only work in some such way. O'Neill doesn't notice that some of the things he objects to about the market follow from *any* spontaneous, uncentralized system.[6] How much overproduction or underproduction will occur before correcting tendencies set in? Even supposing producers to be blindly responding to demand and paying no attention to the broader picture, the period of uncorrected overproduction could not be much longer than the time from the first implementation of an increase in output to the offering for sale of that increased output. O'Neill offers no evidence that this period is long, or the amount of overproduction great.

What remains of O'Neill's argument, then, is that because of lack of information about competitors' plans, there will be inaccuracy in guessing the future. O'Neill adds (208) that even given this information, there will not be proper co-ordination, because the producers will still be competing, and therefore will be unable to co-ordinate their actions. O'Neill may have overlooked the fact that even if all the production plans were known, it would still *not* be known a. what the desirable total output would be, nor b. what the best division of that output among the firms would be. These cannot be known in advance—in fact this is strictly implied by what O'Neill says (201). They have to be discovered in the course of production itself. Hence, if the firms did have some way to deliberately contrive their individual and total output, that could only involve the imposition on all the firms of an almost certainly false theory of desirable total output and division of that output. Of course, O'Neill could reply that aggregate output and the division of that output among the producer organizations would somehow be known, for this and all other industries. But this amounts to acceptance of the idea of a single great plan, formulated in advance, which O'Neill says he rejects (201, 209n). Is it true that the market has informational difficulties of the sort described by O'Neill? The mere fact that such difficulties are imaginable does not show that they exist and are serious. O'Neill appears to under-rate the market's co-ordinating tendencies. He claims that if a firm knew that aggregate planned production of a good would "exceed demand", then still "no adjustment by any particular actor of his or her own actions will necessarily lead to co-ordination" (208). Production "exceeding demand" presumably means that prices fall so that they do not cover costs. It's true that if a firm 'knows'—or rightly believes—that this is going to happen, that firm will probably be powerless by itself to completely correct the situation, but the firm can be expected to respond in a way that tends towards correction. In practice, 'knowing that this is going to happen' may not literally involve knowing the correct or equilibrium industry output and the actual projected output, but may be a more informal judgment that producers are over-reacting to an increase in demand.

Someone might object that knowing the best aggregate output doesn't tell a firm what its share of that output ought to be. This is quite true, but it is independent of the problem we are discussing. It's inseparable from competition, in the broad sense of letting all comers try their hands at something and then finding out who does it best, that total output is not deliberately divided up and assigned to various producer groups. Take the imaginary situation where there are 100 firms, each one of which knows that in equilibrium there will be 90 firms. Disagreement remains over the identity of the ten which will have to quit. No one can be certain who the successful producer groups will be. The only way to find out is to let the 100 contend. It is inseparable from complex industry, and not a product of capitalist institutions, that situations may arise where this kind of knowledge is lacking, and this is independent of any problem of aggregate overproduction, but might be superimposed on an industry which was also experiencing aggregate overproduction. Insofar as knowledge of the correct aggregate industry output is a guide to the firm's correct output, the firm will be induced to move in a co-ordinating or equilibrating direction. Insofar as it is not a guide, this is primarily due to forms of uncertainty which could not be removed without a plan specifying in advance what everyone must do—a proposal which O'Neill categorically dismisses as unworkable.

Is it true that firms seriously lack information about their competitors' plans, information whose absence causes them to be more inclined to misjudge future demand? A great deal of information about what firms do is public knowledge. If they ask their workers for overtime or start hiring additional workers, news gets out. Ex-employees of one firm are hired by another, and take with them knowledge of procedures at the old firm. And people in an industry engage in deliberate sharing of information through conferences, seminars, and the industry press. There are also independent consultants and writers specializing in each industry, who make it their business to find out what firms are doing and communicate it. We must add to all these the fact that firms' future plans are themselves tentative and revisable. A firm's present plan to increase next year's output by 20 percent will be revised in the course of the year. This revisability reduces the value of knowing a firm's plans.

Another important consideration is that if two firms can increase their joint output by sharing their plans (which may or may not involve merger), they will do so. 'Competition' is not a state of affairs in which given firms are compelled to compete. Competition refers to a situation where there are no artificial barriers preventing people from competing or collaborating as they please. In any industry, therefore, the surviving firms or groups of firms who do not share certain kinds of information are those who have not found it profitable to do so, suggesting that no significant output gains can be achieved by pooling those kinds of information.

That all goes to show that the problem of firms keeping their plans secret may be less serious than a first glance might suggest. Still, it's hard to deny that situations may arise where one firm refrains from conveying information to a competitor and where conveying that information would improve co-ordination.[7] This can be defended on the grounds that no one has described a system which would capture the benefits of market prices whilst simultaneously preventing firms from keeping some information to themselves. It is analogous to the fact that if we practice brainstorming, some time is spent on foolish and foredoomed options, or that if we allow people to send each other messages, A will sometimes tell B what B already knows, or that if we permit trials on the adversary system, prosecution and defense will sometimes keep relevant information from each other and from the jury, or that if people obey traffic lights, they will often wait at intersections quite needlessly—or that if we travel by air, our coffee is sometimes spilled. All these features are inefficient if we place ourselves in the position of an omniscient, omnipotent onlooker who can adjust details of a process without any further repercussions, but may be efficient given the actual choice among institutions.

What O'Neill wants is an uncentralized system which communicates as much information as the price system *and* conveys additional information, withheld by firms in the market because of competitive rivalry. But we ought not to take the possibility of such a system for granted, at least until someone has given us an outline of it.

— 11 —

PLANNING AND THE MARKET

i. The Sense in which the Market is Incompatible with Planning

With this recognition, at last, of the real nature of the productive forces of today, the social anarchy of production gives place to a social regulation of production upon a definite plan, according to the needs of the community and of each individual. (Engels 1954, 387–88)

a. Planning of Parts versus Planning of the Whole

The unplanned nature of the market has often been described, sometimes with approval, sometimes with hostility, and sometimes neutrally. Smith rejoices in the "invisible hand" (Smith 1981, 456), while Marx is offended by the allocation of resources "behind the backs of the producers" (Capital I, 108). A classic, evaluatively neutral description of the market's unplanned character is given by Knight (1965, 31–35).

Within the market, there are always numerous plans. In this sense there is no incompatibility between planning and the market; they are symbiotic. A family plans what to get from the supermarket. A business enterprise plans for the coming year. A worker plans a vacation. An impresario plans a concert. Planning flourishes within the market to a far greater degree than it has done in any non-market order. When people object to the planlessness of the market, its 'anarchy of production', its chaotic and haphazard behavior, or when they praise the market's spontaneous, automatic quality, they are referring to the market's total pattern or overall outcome. The replacement of 'the market' by planning means the replacement of many plans by one plan, a "single great plan" in the words of Engels. These two forms of planning are not only distinct; they are at odds. The more that is decided by a single great plan, a society-wide plan, the less can be decided by individuals or by groups (other than the individual or group which makes the single great plan).

The households in a street spend various amounts of money on different items of food. Each household, we will assume, plans its purchases of food for the week ahead. *Precisely for this reason*, the total purchases of food by all the households in the street cannot be planned by anyone. Planning of that total must at least severely limit the planning by each household of its own purchases.

This holds true independently of how the plan for the street's purchases of food is arrived at. If the plan is determined by vote of all the households in the street, this does not give back to the individual households the power to plan they have lost by having to conform to the street plan. As the number of households becomes larger—say, more than a couple of dozen—the situation facing the individual household becomes almost indistingishable from one in which that household has no say in its choice of food. Democracy is no substitute for freedom.

The planning of the whole of society's industry from a single center is sometimes termed 'central planning'. However, every plan (in the relevant sense) emanates from a single center (in the relevant sense). A business firm is planned from its center (or, in cases of firms with autonomous divisions, there are several planning centers and to this extent the board of directors renounces planning of the whole). What is different about 'central planning' is not that it is 'central'; it is the scope of the plan: the plan covers the whole of industry, or it covers a very large section of industry (as in the case of some proposals for planning which permit an independent sector, usually a minor part of society-wide production). What is sometimes called 'central planning' was variously called by Marx "conscious social control" or "a definite social plan" (I, 83) and was later termed (usually by its opponents) 'collectivist economic planning'. In this work I generally prefer the term 'society-wide planning'.

The word 'plan' has many shades of meaning, but here we are interested only in those plans which embody intentions and the means to execute them. Traditional Marxism is identified with a kind of planning which replaces the "anarchy" of capitalist production with a "single vast plan" (Engels 1954, 411) for industry. This means that all those activities which are not planned under the market (planned, that is, from a single center for the whole of society) will be planned under communism. While other kinds of 'planning' of the whole of industry, which do not necessarily abolish the market, have been proposed, it's desirable not to describe one kind of planning in terms that imply a different kind of planning. If we abolish the market, we cannot then expect to have the information provided by spontaneously-generated market prices, and if we do not abolish the market, we have to accept that many activities will be determined in detail within that market and therefore cannot be specified in our plan.

The Marxian conception of 'conscious social control' implies 'the planning of the composition of output'. Over a given period of time, there will be some output: consumer goods of certain kinds in certain quantities, and capital goods of certain kinds in certain quantities. In the market, nobody attempts to make that complete list of goods correspond to some predetermined list, not even roughly. Though economists may observe and analyze the 'list' as it emerges, or talk about some hypothetical list, the market will work even if no one pays any attention to any such list. Under Marx's communism, the population as a whole, through some sort of democratic structure, deliberately selects the composition of output, and then directs industry to achieve that composition. This doesn't necessarily imply that the communist administration will not be flexible or will not modify its industrial plan in the light of experience. It does imply that the coherent shape of the inter-relations of different sectors will not be left to automatic forces in a spontaneous system, but will be consciously aimed at by people who see why it is required. In the market, crucial features of the inter-relation of sectors may never even be noticed.

b. The Hierarchical Structure of Planned Organizations

Assume that we want to co-ordinate the activities of a number of people by planning. The actions of the individuals are to be co-ordinated in such a way that they all co-operate to realize a preconceived goal. Assume also that the task of attaining the goal is a complex one, that has to be broken down into a number of sections in which different people are to specialize. Given these assumptions, the fundamental pattern for planning is a hierarchy of command.

The diagram depicts the structure of planning within an organization, as conceived by the 'classical' school of organization theory represented by Fayol (1949), Urwick (1935), and Graicunas (1937), a framework adopted by Michael Polanyi and Paul Craig Roberts. Orders flow downward from apex to base. Information flows upward and is condensed at each level (but there need not be a symmetry of orders and information). For simplicity, only four levels of command are shown and each supervisor (represented by a square) has two

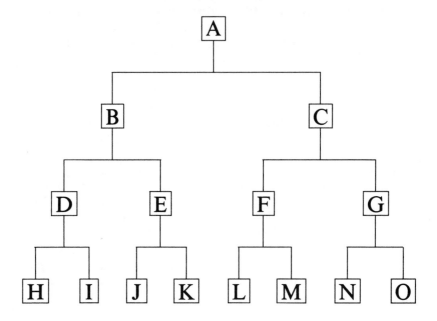

subordinates. The number of levels of command could be increased. The number of subordinates under each officer (the 'span of control') could also be increased. Generally, it's desirable to restrict both the span of control and the number of levels, though these are substitutes. It used to be argued that the span of control had a universal upper limit of six or so, but the trend has been to emphasize the diversity in this upper limit according to various features of the situation. The plan specifies tasks, broken down into sections at each level. This organization is 'hierarchical' in two senses: 1. order is imposed from above by commands, and 2. the organization is divided into sections or divisions, sub-organizations, as it were, whose linkage together constitutes the whole organization. Each unit in the hierarchy does what it is told to do by the unit above: there is a 'chain of command'. As with the example of a street's grocery shopping, it does not diminish the hierarchical quality of the organization if the sovereign body formulating the plan is a democratic assembly of all the individuals involved in executing the plan. The subordinate doesn't in the slightest degree cease to be a subordinate because he has an equal vote with his superior in deciding the plan. (As Michels points out [1962], in any large, complex organization, numerous decisions must be left to leaders or officials, but this fact need not concern us here.)

The above is the basic pattern of organization of a firm (or division of a firm), an army (or division thereof), a 'planned economy' (as we saw in Soviet Russia, often called a 'command economy'), or any other planned organization with complex tasks. There are good reasons for thinking that this is the only practicable pattern of planning under the assumptions stated. In the command model of planning, the rationale of the process arises and is maintained because someone at the top has a picture of the objective, and because the objective is susceptible of being broken down into a number of component objectives, each objective consisting of several smaller objectives. Division of knowledge plays a major part in the actual operation of most command planning organizations. A does not know as much about C's objectives as C does, and C does not know as much about G's objectives as G does. Because of division of knowledge, G must make many decisions without awaiting an explicit instruction from C, yet the decisions G may make must not contravene C's instructions, and there are some decisions G is not authorized to take without B's approval. This may give rise to frustrations, especially when G sees, or thinks he sees, that C's instructions are not the best way to achieve A's objectives. (In the military, this is the celebrated borderline between 'initiative' and 'discipline'.) One naturally tends to sympathize with people in that situation, but G cannot be left free to improvize beyond the limits of his authority and C's instructions, because this might destroy the co-ordination of the organization, which arises from the plan. Individuals may occasionally expedite the plan's objectives by flouting the chain of command, just as a motorist may, once in a while, save a life by flouting a traffic signal. But plan-derived rationale and coherence are abolished if the chain of command is not respected generally. Furthermore, it would be mistaken to suppose that everyone single-mindedly pursues the objectives of the plan as they perceive it, or that they perceive it perfectly accurately. Therefore unplanned horizontal or diagonal collaboration can easily subvert the plan. In the simple model of the diagram, all relationships are vertical. In practice, numerous horizontal (D—G) or diagonal (B—G) relationships occur, sometimes helping the aims of the organization and sometimes hindering them. It has long been known that, whatever the formal structure of an organization, an informal structure will also develop, and that informal structures can be powerful. (The classic case is the Hawthorne Bank Wiring Room. See

Roethlisburger and Dixon 1939, 379–548.) Formal structures should therefore be designed to accommodate and utilize informal structures (or sometimes to suppress them), and individuals operating organizations should be sensitive to informal structures. But there are limits to the positive role of informal structures. The fact that informal structures may sometimes be very helpful, and may sometimes be thwarted by the formal structure in cases where it would be better (for the goals of the formal structure) if they were not thwarted, does not show that the informal structure should always prevail or that it is the embryo of a more effective and radically different formal structure.

There are organizations which suffer because people's tasks and responsibilities are ill-defined. As in 9.i.b. above, we can distinguish motivation problems and knowledge problems. Among the motivation problems, the individuals may try to take advantage of the lack of clarity by 'passing the buck' ('That's not my job') or by taking advantage of the ambiguity to expend time and resources on 'empire-building', which may not always further the goals of the organization. But, assuming single-minded devotion to the goals of the organization, individuals may be ignorant of the best way in which they can act, in the context of the actions of others. (A shrewd and energetic person who is ready to frustrate pursuit of the organization's goals if it suits his own purposes may be more useful to an organization, and therefore to its members, than a member who is loyal yet dull-witted.)

Knowledge is scarce, and there are benefits of specialization; C, for instance, specializes in seeing the way to combine F's and G's activities to fulfil A's instructions, and may therefore understand that more completely than G does. This may not always be the case; perhaps G would do better than C in C's job. Specialization in knowledge arises partly because knowledge is scarce, and it is therefore sensible to specialize, and partly because simply by doing any job you usually come to know more about some crucial aspects of that job than anyone else, including your superiors and subordinates.

It is often claimed that an organization will work better if each individual has a grasp of the 'big picture'—the goals of the organization and her part in achieving them. But this is neither necessary nor sufficient for the organization to operate. And the organization cannot permit every individual to go her own way according to her grasp of the big picture—at least, the organization must place limits on this. Different parts of the organization will have different ranges of authority: if my grasp of the big picture leads me to think that something ought to be done differently in another department, I have to persuade someone at a high enough level in that department.

In organizations, different segments have some autonomy. A divisional manager doesn't merely carry out the literal instructions of senior management. Even someone asked to do the simplest of tasks, such as typing a document, normally has to interpret this request, and normally has some room for discretion, to do the job in the best way ("the best way" includes consideration of the person's own human capital; therefore the same job would be best done differently by different people). Even the most superficially rigid organizations therefore depend upon division of knowledge and autonomous initiative. An organization does not differ from a market in ruling out segmentary autonomy, but in the manner in which the segments are co-ordinated.

Is hierarchical structure an imperative of all planned organizations? This depends upon the specific situation. To take an extreme example, a few years ago thousands of people all over the world agreed that on a particular day they would hum, as a means of establishing harmony and peace in the world. All that is required for executing this plan is that everyone involved agree to do it. There is no need for a hierarchy, because each person's role is easy to grasp and, once grasped, requires no modification. Individuals do not have to keep adjusting their actions to precise details of the environment or of the actions of their fellows. But if we consider erecting a large building or fighting a war, the advantages of a chain of command are very strong. (Hierarchically organized armies have generally defeated loosely organized fighters unless the latter possessed truly spectacular advantages in numbers or other assets.) If thousands of people humming have to do it in specific numbers at specific locations, a hierarchy would be essential: some central body would have to draw up a list of volunteers, assign them to specific locations, make contingency plans for the failure of some to comply, and so forth. Some complex 'tasks'—the stock example is feeding a large city—are not planned at all; they are left to the market. But if feeding a city really became a task, a goal to be achieved by the deliberate arrangement of numerous people's efforts, hierarchy would be unavoidable. It would not do to let people go their own ways, because there has to be someone to unload the ship when it docks, and someone to take the cargo into town. Nor would a desire to help out plus a universal grasp of 'the big picture' be enough, because people's interpretations of what needs to be done and who needs to do it will vary considerably.

Apparent counterexamples may be due to the fact that the outlines of the 'plan' are taken as given, because the 'plan' broadly follows some conventional or traditional model. Great scope can be given to sections or departments of the organization, to go their own way, or to interact freely, if the goal and the way to achieve it are determined outside this process of autonomous interaction. The most obvious source of 'givenness' of the basic plan is tradition. A less rigid hierarchy would have been required in building a medieval cathedral than in constructing a newly designed factory. One of the reasons why the early Marxists were able to combine (in their imaginations) a single great industrial plan with a loosely federated non-authoritarian structure is that vast areas of decision-making which we can see would have to be put into the plan and translated into instructions to subordinates, the Marxists saw as being self-evident and hardly requiring any administrative attention.

c. The Logic of the Market

> Nobody ever saw a dog make a fair and deliberate exchange of one bone for another with another dog. Nobody ever saw one animal by its gestures and natural cries signify to another, this is mine, that yours; I am willing to give this for that. (Smith 1976, 26)

The market is made up of interconnected trades or exchanges. The feature of a trade or market exchange which distinguishes it from an 'exchange' more loosely conceived is that the two individuals engaging in the trade are each free to conclude the trade or not to conclude it, and possess a similar freedom with respect to numerous other possible trades. Consequently, either of the two individuals may say: 'If you give me x, I will give you y'. Thus the trade has to satisfy both individuals, not in the sense that they view it with a warm feeling, but in the sense that, at the time when they conclude it, they choose it over the available alternatives. The market's spontaneous order is like that of a game. The total outcome is always unpredictable in detail, because it depends upon decisions by many autonomous individuals. Yet it is also orderly in ways that these individuals may not notice.

Generally, trade is an exchange of titles to ownership or of other transferable rights. We may form a mental picture of two men handing each other objects, and then walking off in opposite directions, each carrying the object formerly carried by the other. But this may not be a trade at all (they may both be carrying out the instructions of a third person who may own both objects at all times, or they may be acting in a play, or practicing a ritual). And a trade may occur when two people exchange two plots of land which neither of them has visited or ever will. In some cases where goods are sold, they may remain in the same position in the warehouse, the warehousing firm merely recording the fact of the change of title in its books.[1] The items exchanged may be services, including the service of not performing some action.

The definition of the market does not logically require the existence of money, but it is doubtful whether there has been a market without money, and the existence of money demonstrates the existence of a market. Money emerges spontaneously from any routinized trading. As soon as individuals are motivated to exchange A for B even partly because they know that B is highly desired by others and is therefore a useful thing to have for its general acceptability in future exchanges, then B has the quality of moneyness. 'Moneyness' is a property possessed by different goods in different degrees. A car has more moneyness than a house, and a certified diamond more moneyness than a car. However, people's desire to acquire a good for its moneyness immediately gives that good even more moneyness. A chain reaction occurs, with only a few goods acquiring an immense amount of moneyness by comparison with other goods, and usually one good becomes clearly established as the outstanding repository of moneyness—as 'money'. The notion of a 'barter economy', in which individuals regularly swap things without 'inventing' money, is no doubt pure fiction, though people from a culture in which money has some peculiar characteristic may hestitate to recognize money in other cultures, where money lacks that characteristic, just as they may hesitate to recognize religion or property for analogous reasons. Money is a good that people desire entirely or partly because they regard it as an instrument for acquiring other goods by exchange. To recognize money historically, however, we do not have to intuit a distinctive element in people's consciousness. We can look for characteristic monetary phenomena, for example: Do food prices rise in terms of the putative money following a disappointing harvest? Does price inflation follow an increase in the supply of putative money—as when Alexander spent the gold in the Persian emperor's treasury?

d. Comprehensive Planning Excludes an Internal Market

Marx considers that 'conscious social control' (comprehensive society-wide planning) and 'commodity production' (production for sale) are incompatible, and Marx's position is endorsed by all the early Marxists. More recently, various forms of society-wide planning compatible with the market have been advocated by some Marxists, though usually as a form of administration transitional to the ultimate abolition of the market.

Marx perceives that the logic of planning and the logic of the market are different. He is aware that 'bourgeois relations of production' (commodity production) entail consequences incompatible with the aspirations of socialists. Bourgeois socialists, who advance proposals for the retention of commodity exchange while hoping to bring about a harmonious and just social order are, in later usage, looking for a cat that barks. Marx is able to see that, as it was later put by Neurath, "every completely administered economy is a natural economy" (1919, 216).

Comprehensive society-wide planning cannot have any use for a market, and must rule out any possibility of a market. For if, on one hand, the planners can specify in advance the actions which all the individuals are to take, they do not need the information provided by the spontaneous adjustment of market prices. On the other hand, if individuals follow the planners' instructions, the individuals cannot simultaneously be making up their own minds on the basis of their own information about what to do. The administration might require that individuals pass around pieces of paper marked with certain denominations, in a parallel with 'buying and selling'. But this could only be a pointless charade. To suggest that they might do so in order to 'keep accounts' or to 'check the plan' would make sense only if there remained a process outside the planners' control which resulted in ascribing to goods numerical values that could not be found in any other way. But a spontaneous process which determines the prices of various goods must also determine the physical quantities corresponding to those prices, and the amounts of goods allocated to different uses. In that case the spontaneous process, and not the plan, makes the allocations. If, however, all the transfers of pieces of paper are foreseen by the planners, they must have foreseen the numerical values, and they achieve nothing by the charade of pretended buying and selling.

e. Forms of Planning Compatible with a Functioning Market

A government may intervene in the market, and may co-ordinate its interventions in a planned manner, to achieve certain goals. This kind of planning does not achieve the aims of Marxian socialism, and must always have numerous unplanned repercussions which the planners may not like. It does not replace the market as the major determinant of allocations, and therefore does not have to offer some technique for doing so. The whole system is overwhelmingly unplanned, though the planners may, of course, achieve some of their main objectives.

Mercantilist planning is the system against which Adam Smith protested, and which now dominates most of the world. Mercantilists do not want to abolish the market. Piecemeal interventions are conducted at the behest of various powerful interest-groups, and a reigning ideology rationalizes this with rhetoric suggesting that the interventions are parts of a grand scheme to enhance the welfare of the population. Politically, Detroit (stockholders and employees) has a more focussed organization than the aggregate of all car-buyers, so Detroit can easily get the government to attack the welfare of all car-buyers for the benefit of Detroit, for example by tariffs on imported cars. This measure can then be represented to the unsophisticated as part of a plan to benefit everyone except foreigners.

Mercantilism is threatened by ideological instability. If mercantilists fail to recognize that there has to be a spontaneous area of human social life, which must be left alone even when it has identifiable evil consequences, because it has gigantic beneficial consequences which cannot be precisely specified in advance, then they will recognize no limits to their interventions, and they will be tempted to launch upon ever more ambitious interventions, not only by the need to tackle the problems caused by existing interventions, but also by the demands from an endless supply of new interest-groups who want privileges comparable to those already showered upon other groups. But this leads in the direction of society-wide planning, which abolishes financial markets and factor markets, and renders industrial civilization, with high living standards for the masses, an impossibility. Yet if the mercantilists respect a line which signifies 'Thus far and no further', that calls into question the already established interventions, which benefit special interests at the expense of the rest of the population.

Indicative planning has been tried in France and Britain.[2] The theory is that if the government collects a lot of statistics from firms and then publishes a projection of trends for the next few years, the projection will give firms some guidance by eliminating the uncertainty arising from each firm's being unsure of what all the other firms will do.

The incoherence of this scheme is evident. The 'plan' does not contain any 'teeth' (or few and insufficient teeth). The firms are not compelled to play their part in the plan, and in a competitive industry it is not even clear what 'their part' is. At best, the plan summarizes and averages out the guesses about the future which firms made some months earlier. Why should a firm pay any attention to such a meaningless exercise, especially as it will not be compensated for any losses it makes by conforming with the plan?

Indicative planning confuses targets and forecasts. The publication of a forecast doesn't make the forecast outlook more likely, nor does it diminish uncertainty, unless everyone has good reason to think the government forecast is more reliable than any of the hundreds of other forecasts which abound. In Britain, the planners wanted faster growth, so they asked firms what they would do if the growth rate were higher. The planners then put the answers to these questions together, to compose a scenario of faster growth. U.K. production figures generally fell below the plan. This caused some economists to call for more modest targets on the grounds that 'planning' would then be more 'realistic'. Some Labour politicians called for direct coercive intervention to make planning effective, but they omitted to explain how real planners would know where to intervene. The mainstream planners made no serious attempt to seek adherence to targets different from what the market would achieve, because they knew that they had no way of determining which targets would be better. So they contented themselves with guessing what the market would do. In France, output of some goods greatly outstripped the 'plan'; the unfazed planners commented that the plan was 'flexible'.

Macro-economic Planning, the effective legacy of the 'Keynesian revolution', refers to the manipulation of money supply, credit controls, taxes, and government spending and borrowing, in order to achieve certain broad objectives, notably to reduce unemployment just before national elections. Macro-economic policy does not attempt to determine the composition of output. Faith in macro-economic policy reached a peak in the 1960s, but it is now recognized that, while governments can push unemployment down temporarily, this tends to create an increase in unemployment later. The secular or 'natural' rate of unemployment[3] is determined by slow-to-change factors like minimum wage laws, welfare payments, taxes on investment, and leisure preferences, not by fiscal or monetary policy.

Soviet-style Planning occupied much more space in early drafts of this work. The basic method of Soviet planning emerged from the first five-year plan. Each enterprise was given an instruction from above, to produce a target, usually expressed in some physical magnitude, such as weight or quantity of articles. For overshooting its target, the enterprise receives financial and other rewards. For failing to reach it, the enterprise was penalized. Each enterprise had its own profit-and-loss account, and was instructed to maximize its profits, some of which it was permitted to retain for its own purposes. But sheer size of output was the main conern of the plan. The planners' job was apparently to draw up and communicate a single plan of national production, in which the physical outputs and inputs of every enterprise were meshed together. The plans had to be formulated in broad categories—so many rivets, so many girders of such-and-such a length. The planners could not know all the various subdivisions, styles and models appropriate to each task. The broad aggregates in which they had to deal were not very informative about the real interconnections among enterprises. As Michael Polanyi observed:

> It is as if the manager of a team of chess-players were to find out from each individual player what his next move was going to be and would then sum up the result by saying: 'The plan of my team is to advance 45 pawns by one place, move 20 bishops by an average of three places, 15 castles by an average of four places, etc.' He could pretend to have a plan for his team, but actually he would be only announcing a nonsensical summary of an aggregate of plans.[4] (1951, 134)

According to Polanyi, and as elaborated by Roberts (1971), the fundamental rationale of Soviet pretense of planning was that the planners asked the enterprises what they intended to do, and then instructed them to do it. Later, other writers came to adopt the view that the Soviet economy was not really planned (Ticktin 1973; Zaleski 1980).

The Soviet economy never was planned in the sense that a group of people at the top were able to work out what everyone should do and then tell them to do it. 'Plans' were published: five-year plans, which generated yearly, quarterly, and monthly plans, and, of course, the attempts to implement these plans did have major effects. But the plans were usually issued after the commencement of the period to which they applied, and were always amended repeatedly in the course of 'implementation'. When the government triumphantly announced that the five-year plan had been fulfilled, this was a drastically different document than had been first published under that name about four years earlier (Pejovich 1976; Zaleski 1980).

Official doctrine proclaimed that the Soviet Union had become 'socialist' in 1936, and was moving towards 'full communism'. It was repeatedly proclaimed that the Soviet Union was about to overtake the United States in output, and that the abolition of money was only a few decades away. In 1952, Stalin stated that money remained in existence only because of the non-state sector, the collective farms (Stalin 1972, 16). After Stalin's death, the proliferation of 'commodity relations' was openly welcomed, but it was still held that commodities and money were soon to disappear. Under Krushchev in the 1960s, it was confidently predicted that moneyless communism would arrive within the lifetime of the present generation (Jacobs 1962, 245). Although the coming of full communism was repeatedly postponed, its imminence remained official dogma almost right up to the point where socialism was abandoned and the Soviet Union dismantled.

The vast internal black market and the ability to copy prices and technology from the West enabled Soviet industry to avoid collapse, but the system was unable to make substantial improvements in the living standards of the majority of people, whose incomes fell further and further behind those of workers in the West.

Planning in broad outline is, I have found, an idea at the backs of the minds of many people who favor society-wide industrial planning. Such individuals do not find objections to society-wide planning fatal because they interpret such objections as applying only to planning of all the fine detail. Surely, they reason, it ought to be possible to plan the broad lines of industrial development, and allow local communities or enterprises to flesh out these skeletal plans with detail drawn from their experience.

Such an approach cannot work, because there is no broad outline apart from the aggregate outcome of the fine detail. Thirty years ago, it was believed by all the experts and by those members of the general public who took any interest that the cotton industry was in for a steady decline. New, cheaper, stronger, more versatile (for instance, crease-resistant) artificial fibers would gradually replace cotton. In this climate of opinion, any world industrial planning committee would have directed a long-term running down of cotton production. The committee would have planned new lives for millions of cotton growers. Either new crops or capital would have had to move to the cotton-growing areas or cotton growers would have had to migrate to other areas, where new industrial capacity would have had to be built to complement their new activities. The by-products of cotton (high-protein oil, animal feed, building materials, and fuel) would have had to be substituted from other sources. This decision to run down the cotton industry would have affected every industry and every individual's daily life.

Yet it would all have been a vast blunder. Cotton experienced a surprising revival.[5] I recall watching, in the late 1970s, a TV sit-com in which a person's willingness to entertain the idea that there could ever be "a substitute for denim" was represented as clear proof of his gullible stupidity. The most important of the easily-identified reasons for cotton's revival were: 1. consumers' resistance to the new fibers; 2. newly developed 'open-end' spinning machines; 3. new methods of treating cotton cloth to make it flameproof and crease-resistant; 4. buoyant demand for the by-products; 5. augmented yields per acre because of chemical fertilizers, irrigation, and new plant varieties; 6. the effect of oil price increases on production of artificial fibers; and 7. the development of rapid mechanical pickers. To itemize these factors is to give a false impression of simplicity derived from hindsight. Open-end spinning, for instance, is suitable for only some kinds of cloth, is expensive to install, and experienced many teething troubles before proving its superiority. Nicely balancing advantages and disadvantages was a protracted, complex process of discovery, dependent on the fact that everyone was free to improvize and was constantly informed by market prices.

Such surprises are by no means rare. The growth of mini-mills in the U.S. steel industry in the 1980s was not predicted by industry experts a few years earlier. Such major unpredictable developments will always characterize industrial civilization, but they merely dramatize the fact that the broad categories applied to industry by observers are rather like the subject categories in libraries, matters of administrative convenience rather than identifications of separate entities with lives of their own.

An attempt to plan in broad outline means that most details are settled outside the plan. If they are settled by the market, we have a system of government intervention in the market. If they are not settled by the market, we need to be told how they are to be co-ordinated. In either case, the aggregate of unplanned details creates its own broad outline, posing the alternatives of disorganization or abandonment of the plan.

f. Was Marx a 'Central Planner'?

In a well-known passage (I, 336–37), Marx contrasts the division of labor inside a workshop with the society-wide division of labor under capitalism. Within the workshop the division of labor is preconceived 'a priori', whereas in society as a whole, the division of labor is "an a posteriori, nature-imposed necessity"—the unplanned outcome of competition among independent commodity-producers. Marx considers this contrast a scandalous paradox, and does not allow the possibility that there might be any rational justification for it. That view has been endorsed by successive Marxists, most famously in Lenin's assertion, just before taking power, that social-ism means turning society-wide industry into "a single office and a single factory" (LCW 25, 479).

Marx does not like the way workers are treated in nineteenth-century factories, and does not advocate the "despotism" of the factory for the whole of society. But he does want to see at least this aspect of the factory adopted by the whole of society: the "*a priori* system*" (336), in which a preconceived plan is worked out in advance, and then implemented. When Marx says here of capitalism that the "constant tendency to equilibrium, of the various spheres of production, is exercised only in the shape of a reaction against the constant upsetting of this equilibrium", it is clear that he finds this indefensible. Like many of Marx's descriptions of the anarchy of the market, this wording applies to any conceivable unplanned sys-tem, and expresses Marx's absolute commitment to comprehensive society-wide planning. So well-known and well-hated are the per-nicious concomitants of 'central planning' that one finds anti-Marxists accusing Marx of aiming for those pernicious concomi-tants, and defenders of Marx denying that Marx wanted central planning. An example of the former is Walicki 1988 and of the latter Elliott 1987.

Marx commits himself to 'central planning' in the sense of a single industrial plan for the whole society, but he doesn't envisage the trappings of central planning, no matter how obvious these may seem to us. With his blind spot about the role of the market, Marx underestimates the scale of the task facing the communist adminis-tration. Marx does not want a totalitarian state or a society over-run by bureaucracy, but what has since come to be called "participatory democracy" (Hunt 1984, 162–265). His view of the individual's life under communism, as far as we can tell, was one of immense freedom and opportunity. Yet he wants society-wide industry to be ruled by a single great plan.

g. Proposals for Socialism without Market or Plan

Within the ranks of socialists, the main result of the Soviet fiasco has been decreased respect for society-wide planning and a strong revival of FM socialism. Only a tiny handful of socialists have clearly opted for a socialism which rejects *both* society-wide planning and the market—though many of the non-market socialists are hazy on the kind of 'planning' they envisage.[6] I here exclude anarchocommunism, which entails village autarky and the abandonment of an integrated world-wide industrial structure (see Chapter 13 below).

Aside from the Lange system, which soon lost its non-market character, the one serious and extended advocacy of non-market socialism purportedly without 'central planning' is that of Albert and Hahnel (1991a; 1991b). Consumers' councils propose what they shall consume during the coming year, and producers' councils propose what they shall produce. By a series of back-and-forth amendments to the proposals, a plan emerges, with the help of an office of experts in planning techniques. By this means, Albert and Hahnel hope to avoid both a market and authoritarian controls. Unlike other socialists who dislike both markets and central plans, Albert and Hahnel accept the need for budgets and restrictions on consumption, and for indicative 'prices'.

The system appears to lack the drive to reduce costs which is a vital part of maintaining and increasing mass living standards. Cost reduction occurs effectively in the market because if one producing organization is undercut by another, the latter may acquire the business and the former may disappear. In the market, producers are answerable to consumers. If producers make something unwanted (even if they work hard at it), they cease to be paid for it. It is not clear whether anything parallel to this will occur, but if it does, the plan would have to be abandoned, because there would have to be a direct link between producers and consumers. If it does not occur, there will be a loss of efficiency, because there is no pressure for producers to turn out what the consumers want.

Like the Lange scheme and all simulations, the Albert-Hahnel system is most compatible with a static framework in which nothing changes. How will it be decided when a new organization will open or an existing one close down, or move into a different line of production? Such issues of dynamic change raise questions about the responsiveness of the system to the consumers' wishes. The Albert-Hahnel scheme is an adaptation of the mathematical techniques for 'iterative' planning developed by several writers including Hurwicz (1973) and Malinvaud (1967). It's generally agreed by those working on these techniques that they are not 'yet' ready for implementation. (For a skeptical and very readable account, see Machlup 1984, 195–201.)

Further problems are raised by the egalitarian wage system enforced by the Albert-Hahnel proposal. Without wage differentials, enterprises experiencing an upsurge in demand for their products will have no accurate way of signalling that they wish to attract labor from other enterprises.

ii. The Scale of Production Plans within the Market

The trouble with competitions is that somebody wins them. (Orwell 1968)

a. Marx's Theory of Centralization

The theory that monopoly arises inevitably from competition, because bigger firms can generally 'beat' smaller firms predates Marx, but he did a lot to promote it. *Capital* is filled with eloquent depictions of the growing size of firms, and reminders that this inexorable trend is the outcome of competition. In his pithiest expression of this theme, Marx writes that "One capitalist always kills many" (I, 714).

Marx draws a terminological distinction between 'concentration' and 'centralization'. 'Concentration' is growth in the size of firms with growth of output. Centralization occurs where the size of a firm grows by uniting several existing firms: it is "transformation of many small into few large capitals" (I, 586). In non-Marxist parlance, Marx's 'centralization' is a form of concentration. I will use the term 'centralization' to refer to Marx's theory that concentration must show a long-term increase under competitive capitalism.

Marx does not specify any circumstances where growth beyond a certain size might impose net disadvantages on a firm. He identifies bigness with advancement, technological and social (see I, 588). "The smaller capitals crowd into spheres of production which modern industry has only sporadically or incompletely got hold of" (I, 587). He expects that the smallest firms will disappear completely, followed by somewhat larger firms, and so on until at least entire industries are controlled by single firms. Marx states that: "In any given branch of industry centralisation would reach its extreme limit if all the individual capitals invested in it were fused into a single capital. In a given society the limit would be reached only when the entire social capital was united in the hands of either a single capitalist or a single capitalist company" (I, 587–88). There are only a few ambiguous remarks hinting at any forces tending to counteract centralization, short of complete monopoly (III, 246; IVc, 311).

For Marx, centralization—and *not* 'the class struggle'—is the fundamental reason why capitalism leads to communism. Centralization tends in the direction of a single great plan for the whole of society, and therefore lays the basis for society-wide industrial planning. Centralization implies the breakdown of the rationale of capitalist production according to the law of value, and by putting the whole of industry in the control of a tiny handful of redundant coupon-clippers, invites a take-over by the increasingly pauperized and furious majority (I, 714–15; III, 439). Centralization also tends to make Marxists incurious about the administrative requirements of socialism, because they assume that the longer the revolution is delayed, the closer administration comes to being socialist, in the sense that ever larger segments of world industry are planned as single units. Marx hails the joint stock company as "the abolition of capital as private property within the framework of capitalist production itself" (III, 436) and, along with workers' co-operatives, as transitional to communism (440). In a later work purportedly read and approved by Marx, Engels says of the new business 'trusts': "the production without any definite plan of capitalistic society capitulates to the production upon a definite plan of the invading socialist society" (1954, 384). Engels believes that one industry after another will be monopolized by trusts, so that the bourgeois state will "have to undertake the direction of production" (385).

Marx has two major arguments for his prediction of centralization: economies of scale and the falling rate of profit. Because of advantages of scale, "the larger capital beats the smaller" (I, 586). Marx is so convinced of an irresistible process in which more capital-intensive production and economies of scale go together, that he probably doesn't notice that these are at odds: nearly all the examples he gives of economies of scale are capital-saving economies: they reduce the amount of capital per worker, making production less capital-intensive (see Leijonhufvud 1986, 210).

Marx argues that a tendency for the rate to fall is inherent in capitalism. This tendency can be checked and even occasionally reversed, but the actual long-term trend, in Marx's stated view, must be for the rate to fall. It is now recognized by virtually all Marxist economists that Marx's theory does not in fact demonstrate a falling rate of profit, and that there is no reason to expect the rate to fall.

Marx frequently points out that while the rate of profit falls, the 'mass' of profit may rise. He sometimes writes as though he believes that the increased mass of profit will compensate the capitalist for the reduced rate, and thus enable bigger capitalists to endure lower rates than smaller capitalists, thereby accentuating centralization. It's not absolutely clear that Marx wholeheartedly embraces this simple error, though his words often suggest it (for instance III, 259). In fact, the mass has no significance apart from the rate. No investor would put a million dollars into one firm to get $40,000 per year, passing up the opportunity to put $100,000 into each of ten firms to get a total of $50,000 per year. If the rate of profit were lower in bigger or more capital-intensive firms, this would imply a trend to smaller and less capital-intensive firms, the opposite of that envisaged by Marx. (In any case, when Marx suggests that the mass can compensate for the rate, he is forgetting another part of his theory, which states that the profit actually realized by a firm is the common rate of profit on the firm's whole outlay. Big firms with high OCCs never see the lower rate of surplus value which they generate: they automatically get some of the surplus-value produced by lower-OCC firms. So mass compensating for rate just cannot arise.)

Marx carelessly assumes that centralization implies increasing inequality of wealth ownership: that fewer and bigger firms implies fewer and bigger owners of firms—"the constantly diminishing number of the magnates of capital" (I, 715; and see II, 360; III, 246). There is no necessary relation between the number of firms and the number of capitalists. (It is arithmetically possible for the whole of industry to be owned by one big firm with every member of society holding an equal share in it.) There is no evidence of any long-term trend to greater inequality of capital ownership, but in any case this is independent of whether centralization occurs.

b. Historical Evidence of Concentration Trends

The centralization theory is extraordinarily tenacious, both inside and outside Marxism.[7] *Looking Backward* has a vivid passage depicting socialism as the culmination of ever bigger business corporations (Bellamy 1960, 51–55). Berle and Means 1939 enjoyed a spectacular popular success in the 1940s. The authors warn that, extrapolating current trends, the 200 largest U.S. corporations will have absorbed practically all industrial activity by 1969. (As it turned out, the share of the leading 200 nonfinancial corporations in all nonfinancial corporate assets fell from 57 percent in 1933 to 39.5 percent in 1975. See Brozen 1982, 309–311.) Even anti-socialist opponents of Marx frequently concede that centralization has occurred and is inevitable (for instance Conway 1987, 128).

If the centralization theory were right, we should expect to see a long-term trend towards increasing concentration in all industries. Absent any special circumstances, we should expect to find industry much more concentrated today than a century ago. The historical record since Marx's day does not show any marked trend towards greater concentration of industry. United States industry, for example, is not much more (and perhaps no more) concentrated today than it was 100 or 150 years ago; some evidence suggests a modest decline in concentration during this span of time (Nutter and Einhorn 1969; see Brozen 1982, 91–98). Centralization seems to be refuted by the historical outcome, but two possible objections need to be borne in mind: that the modern figures don't measure what Marx was talking about and that the decline in concentration is due to the antitrust laws.

It is true that the statistics cited in modern discussions are skew to Marx's concern. Modern economists are concerned with the possibility of excessive concentration as a source of inefficiency. Neoclassical economists have been intensely suspicious that firms making a large contribution to an industry's output will be able to exercise 'monopoly power', raising prices and reducing output, an issue that doesn't concern Marx, who assumes that bigger means more efficient. Yet there is some relation between the modern figures and Marx's theory. Different ways of measuring industrial concentration can give widely diverging verdicts on the same situation (see Stigler 1983, 29–36). But they should all have increased if Marx is right.

Writers and researchers on concentration lose interest once it is demonstrated that there is no concentrating trend in a particular area. They always focus on that area which seems a promising candidate for growing concentration. At one time there was concern about the proportion of total U.S. nonfinancial business assets owned by the 50, or 100, or 200, largest firms. Attention has shifted away from this figure, because the declining trend is quite marked. Writers in search of a centralizing trend have fastened on manufacturing. The contribution of the top 200 manufacturing firms to total manufacturing output (shipments) rose from 41% in 1937 to 45% in 1977 (while the contribution of the top 50 fell from 28% to 25%). This is hardly solid evidence for centralization, since manufacturing itself fell steadily in relative importance during this period, and is now below one-quarter of U.S. national output, while manufactured imports rose considerably (see Brozen 1982, 311–314).

Can the historical outcome be explained by antitrust legislation? It has been argued (Stigler 1983, 259–271) that antitrust has had a slight effect in reducing concentration. On the other hand, many industries have experienced a decline in concentration unrelated to antitrust. Furthermore, Nutter's figures show a decline in concentration for the period 1899–1939. The first antitrust law, the Sherman Act, was passed in 1890, and its provisions were not very severe. Countries with less intrusive antitrust laws, like Japan, do not have unusually high levels of concentration. There are ways in which antitrust laws might increase concentration, the most obvious being that 'collusion' is easier to deter than increasing size, and inter-firm collaboration is sometimes a substitute for merger.

In the 1890s there was a great clamor over the rapid growth and alleged power of the 'trusts' (though there were only six which were nationally organized and long-lived). The trusts were founded mainly because U.S. state laws didn't permit the existence of holding companies. Trusts were primarily an attempt to get round these restrictive laws, but within a few years virtually all such laws were repealed (Chandler 1977, 315–334). Trusts often also represented attempts to cartelize industries, but such attempts enjoy little success without government backing. Most of the great business combinations which achieved a large share of their respective industries' outputs around the end of the nineteenth century had these shares reduced within a few years, predominantly by normal competitive developments unrelated to the (then still rudimentary) antitrust laws (Brozen 1982, 209–219).

By World War I it was clear to leading Marxists that centralization was proceeding so slowly that they could not rely on it to form the organizational basis for socialism. But since capitalism had to create that organizational basis, some Marxists shifted their attention to two hopeful signs: the apparent domination of industry by a few big banks and wartime industrial regulation, both of these especially pronounced in Germany. By 1917 it was a commonplace to many Marxists that the immediate road to socialism lay in control of the big banks and in German-style state controls.

c. The Implausibility of Centralization

Historical evidence fails to corroborate the theory that competition creates monopoly. However, the fact that industry[8] is probably no more concentrated than in Marx's day (and certainly not much more concentrated) could be attributed to temporary factors which may come to an end. I will therefore offer some reasons why, on the basis of everyday facts and reasonable conjectures, we ought to be able to perceive that ever-increasing concentration is not to be expected. Even if there had to date been a pronounced concentrating trend, we should still be fairly confident that it could not continue indefinitely.

First, a simple fact of arithmetic. If the bigger firm doesn't 'beat' the smaller firm every time, but only has an enhanced probability of being the 'winner', then we do not get an indefinite trend to increasing size. (We can translate 'beating' as taking one percent of the 'loser's' sales per year.) Even if there were always economies, and never diseconomies, of scale, that would be insufficient to yield a centralizing trend. Size might always be an advantage, but smaller firms might be better managed than bigger firms, say, 30 percent of the time. As long as smaller firms *sometimes* maintain themselves or grow in competition with larger firms, Marx's 'limit' of one firm per industry will not be approached.[9] If the rate of formation, survival, and growth of new, small firms and the probability of a bigger firm 'beating' a smaller firm remain unchanged, then an equilibrium will be reached, with a range of firms of various sizes. If some of these variables change, then the equilibrium 'spread' of firm sizes will shift. But in order to get a trend to ever-increasing size, bigger firms must 'beat' smaller firms 100 percent of the time, or there must be a tendency for that to become true (for example, by a steadily increasing minimum size of viable firm).

Marx has at least an inkling of this. He refers to "new offshoots of capital", but supplies no clue as to how these new offshoots could, even temporarily, be successful, if big, established firms always have the edge.[10] He claims that the minimum outlay required to start a firm rises in the long term (I, 293; 586–87). If it were true that the minimum capital needed to start a business were rising, if this were a reflection of an indefinite rise in the minimum viable size for a business, and if this rise were occurring faster than the growth of incomes, there would eventually (though perhaps not for a long time, if we start with firms larger than that minimum) have to be indefinitely increasing concentration. But Marx fails to give any reason why the minimum size of firm must always rise, except to suggest that a falling rate of profit hits small firms harder than large ones, a variant of the fallacy that mass can compensate for rate.

A puzzling question for the centralization theory is: Why does centralization proceed so slowly? Many industries are not monopolized by one big firm, some of them in countries where government policy has been to encourage concentration. In the U.S., the leading firm in the average manufacturing industry produces 17 percent of its industry's output. This simple objection is serious, because any candidate for a 'temporary counteracting tendency' is also a candidate for a permanent counteracting tendency or even the main tendency 'counteracted' by the impetus to concentration. Some industries have experienced pronounced long-term declines in concentration. U.S. Steel's 66 percent of domestic steel production in 1901 fell to 20 percent by 1982 (Brozen 1982, 91). Brozen lists several examples of such declines in concentration. Many industries either begin with a single firm or soon after their origin come to have a single firm producing all or most of the industry's output. Yet frequently, as with IBM in the computer industry, that firm's share of output subsequently declines.

Even where industries show increasing concentration, this doesn't necessarily corroborate the centralization theory. For example, the theory implies that if we find 30 firms in an industry and come back 20 years later to find 25 firms in that industry, the 25 must be drawn from the original 30. If this is not so, then the centralization theory is challenged rather than corroborated. For the theory supposes that bigger firms always 'beat' smaller firms. If we find a pattern of fluidity, with new firms coming in and old firms going out of business—if we find that 'the top is a slippery place'—then the centralization theory becomes suspect, regardless of any increasing concentration trend. Just such a pattern of fluidity is observable in many highly concentrated industries, tobacco being a good example (Brozen 1982, 19–21; see also Jewkes 1977).

Firms obstinately refrain from possible integration.[11] The car industry is "dominated" by a few large firms (as the somewhat misleading metaphor goes—more aptly, the car industry is dominated by people who buy cars, and these people have made purchasing decisions which, in the aggregate, mean that most output will be produced by a handful of firms), but these big firms depend upon the supplies of many small firms. Thus a GM car is really produced, even in the restricted sense of manufacturing the components and putting them together, by a kind of coalition of dozens of firms related through the market. Why don't the car firms absorb their smaller suppliers? To erect a large building is usually undertaken by a major firm which then assigns the work to several (often more than 20) sub-contractors. Why don't the construction firms absorb these small sub-contractors and form one firm to handle every aspect of erecting a building? Traditionally, distillers of Scotch whisky would malt their own barley, but increasingly they now choose to buy malted barley from specialist maltsters. A century ago book publishers typeset and printed their own books, but now they almost never do (despite the fossil word 'Press' in the names of some of them), and typesetters and printers, once synonymous, are now separate firms. Why do large retailing chains often sell franchises, rather than having employees run each of their branches? Why do department stores frequently sublet specialties within the store to independent merchants (a practice which casual observation suggests is growing)?

Why do firms often lease equipment instead of buying it outright (or manufacturing it)? Without a theory to account for the observed fact of persistent, systematic avoidance of merger, a prediction of all-consuming merger must appear less than compelling. The fact that similar patterns of concentration turn up in corresponding industries in different countries (Pryor 1972) suggests that these patterns are not arbitrary.

Managers often face the 'make or buy' decision. Will the firm produce a required service inside the company, or buy it from an outside supplier? This decision is perpetually under review—it commonly happens that a firm which has been performing a function 'in-house' for many years decides to close down that department and buy the service from outside. From the Marxian viewpoint, or almost any that favors the centralization theory, this fact is hard to account for. In this light, the large scale of Russian firms before 1913 takes on a different significance. Some Bolsheviks argued that large firm size showed Russian industry to be more advanced than the West's. But Russian firms may have been larger because, lacking the Western environment of numerous suppliers, the manufacturers had to produce many items in-house.

There must be potent reasons why multi-person firms exist yet show no tendency to indefinite expansion. Coase (1937) points out that transactions may be conducted within the firm or through the market, each option having advantages and disadvantages. The firm will expand as long as internal transactions are cheaper than external ones. The market therefore provides the optimal amount of planning. Coase offers suggestions as to why the costs of organizing transactions within the firm may rise as the size of firm increases, one being that the entrepreneur is more likely to make mistakes the more transactions he determines.[12] Alchian and Demsetz (1972) argue that firms arise because of team production and the need to curb shirking by team members. A person employed to monitor team members to control their shirking might himself shirk; the solution is to make the monitor of team efforts the 'residual claimant', the person who collects what is left of revenues after all expenses have been paid. This is an informational argument, since it turns on the existence of situations where it is comparatively difficult to accurately gauge individual contributions to output. In later work, Demsetz (1988, 144–165) puts even more emphasis on information, in the form of specialized knowledge. Since knowledge of making steel is generally different from knowledge of making steel goods, steel producers usually sell steel rather than making steel articles.

A popular theory is that since organizing transactions within a firm sometimes has benefits, it must pay for any firm to expand indefinitely, the point being that the expanding firm can supposedly allow as much autonomy to its components as it chooses to allow, and head office can selectively intervene only when it is very confident that this is advantageous. However, the information available to a person who owns a company cannot be the same as that available to a person who runs the 'same' operation as a division of a larger company. Williamson (1985, 135–162) gives more detailed reasons why 'selective intervention' is sometimes not feasible.

ABUNDANCE AND THE PRICE SYSTEM

I. The Conquest of Scarcity and the Obsolescence of the Price System

a. Capitalism's Role in Developing the Forces of Production

> Fanatically bent on making value expand itself, [the capitalist] ruthlessly forces the human race to produce for production's sake; he thus forces the development of the productive powers of society, and creates those material conditions, which alone can form the real basis of a higher form of society. . . . (Capital I, 555)

Marxism holds that communism has not been possible until recently. There was a time when capitalism was more efficient than any alternative, but since some date in the nineteenth century, capitalism has been less efficient than communism would have been. According to Engels (MECW v6, 348–49), as long as there is not more than "enough for all", there has to be a ruling class and a poor, oppressed class. The reason for this is not given (nor any specification of what counts as "enough"), but even if it were true, a planned, non-market organization is compatible with a ruling class and a poor, oppressed class. One would think that someone might have an interest in that system of production which would maximize output. Engels goes on to assert that the productive forces have so outgrown private property that they provoke violent disturbances. The metaphor of the productive forces 'outgrowing' private property implies that there is some superior alternative, and the question remains why the superior alternative was not superior earlier.

Imagine a communist society which has been flourishing for a thousand years. Earth is hit by an asteroid, which abruptly reduces the level of output to that of 2,000 years earlier. It follows from the

Marxist position that society would have to revert to capitalism, because this would be more efficient than communism at (once again) raising the level of output to the required level. If the market price system is now dispensable, why was it once indispensable? The most obvious reply would be that, once output has been raised to a particular level, we no longer have to be so concerned about economizing. But although this reply is sometimes evoked by various Marxian turns of phrase, it would concede that the market *is* superior at economizing, and would therefore contradict the Marxist contention that the persistence of the market holds back the productive forces.

The next reply would be that communism could have been more efficient at any time, but its preconditions didn't exist. For example, people had not developed the techniques of administration and planning required to operate communism. Yet if an effort were made to substantiate this position by discussing all the administrative prerequisites of communism, we couldn't know in advance that we wouldn't find these prerequisites still unfulfilled. Marxists have traditionally claimed that the administration of communism would be far simpler than the elaborate financial apparatus of capitalism. And although planning techniques were more rudimentary in earlier ages, the task facing planners of society-wide production would also have been far simpler. There is no clear criterion to determine when and how the historical transition was made from the market's necessity to its obsolescence. (Similar suspicion attaches to the Marxist view that communism is not feasible in a single country. If planned production for use really is superior to anarchy of production, then this ought to hold for segments of the world economy. The obvious retort, that such segments would be buffeted by the winds of the capitalist environment, is weak, since ability to weather such storms is an index of general flexibility and responsiveness to change.)

b. Abundance and the Obsolescence of the Market

Two claims link abundance with the obsolescence of the market: 1. Rising output makes the price system unnecessary. 2. The price system involves waste, which can be eliminated by abolishing the price system. Though frequently advanced together and not clearly distinguished, these arguments are mutually independent. I evaluate 1. here, and 2. in Sections ii. and iii. below.

Marx's view of the transition from labor-voucher communism to free-access communism may seem to illustrate the theory that part of the rationale for prices and wages is to ration out the available products. Yet this theory, so widely embraced by twentieth-century Marxists, is not Marx's. Marx holds that 'distribution' always adapts to the organization of 'production', and that anarchy of production is a necessary and sufficient cause of commodity production. The view that money must survive until there is superabundance of consumer goods (Mandel 1968, 633) is therefore a serious departure from Marx.

After the 1870s, economists accorded greater importance to the notion of 'scarcity', and began to see the function of the price system as the allocation of scarce resources. Eventually some Marxists adapted this idea, as in the argument of Buick and Crump (1986, 132), which runs as follows: 1. "Conventional" (non-Marxist) economic theory "admits" that if there were "abundance" (absence of scarcity) there would be no need for prices. 2. There is now, or possibly soon could be, abundance. 3. Therefore there is now, or possibly soon could be, no need for prices. This argument relies upon equivocation. The sense of 'scarcity' in which economists say that the need for a price system arises from scarcity is distinct from the sense in which Buick and Crump claim that scarcity has been, or possibly soon could be, abolished. Economists do not 'admit' that abundance in Buick and Crump's sense would eliminate the need for prices. Buick and Crump draw attention to this themselves: they attack the economist's definition of scarcity as "unreasonable" and state that abolition of this kind of scarcity is "impossible" (132), without noticing that economics does not then offer any support for their claim that we no longer need the price system. They hazily define "abundance" as a state of affairs where "resources exceed needs" (137), and their discussion occasionally seems to suggest that "needs" means all wants. But most of the time they recognize that strict abundance is nowhere in sight: their proposed communism will continue to "be concerned with using resources efficiently and rationally" (137), something that makes sense only where there is scarcity.

Scarcity was made the defining feature of economics by Robbins (1932, 15). Some writers deny that all of economics can be encompassed in the scarcity principle, but they don't dispute that this principle covers a major segment of economics (Kirzner 1976, 161–62). The special, technical definition of scarcity applies to any goods where the decision to use a unit of that good entails giving up some other potential use. Thus there is a choice between alternative uses, and there is a cost to any use chosen—the cost is the best of the uses that were not chosen, as a direct result of the fact that the chosen use was chosen. If I have a plot of land, and choose to use it for a golf course, and if in the absence of using it for a golf course it would be used to grow strawberries, then this land is scarce, and the ungrown strawberries are the cost of the games of golf. Without scarcity there is no cost; without cost, no scarcity.

A good is scarce when the use to which it is put displaces another potential use. When steel is used to make a car, one can imagine perhaps millions of alternative ways in which that steel might have been used. But we can be confident that production of *some* other steel article is reduced because the steel was used to make that car, or that the resources used in making the steel could have been used to make something else. If this were not so, steel would be free: its price would have fallen to zero. A conceptual test for the existence of scarcity is to ask oneself whether a use could be found for an additional, gratuitous unit of the good—say, if this unit miraculously appeared out of nowhere. Only if that free additional unit would have to be ignored or thrown away as unusable can the good be said to be abundant (unscarce) in the strict sense.

A commonly-held view is that if incomes keep rising, there must eventually come a point where the price system will no longer be necessary. Surely at some point everyone ought to be content with what they have! If the price system is necessary because of scarcity, this means that people want more than they can get. Once a certain level of income is attained, 'wanting more' becomes explicable only as pathological greed. Many individuals, as David Friedman has noted (Friedman 1989, 100) suppose that an income about double their own is as much as anyone can reasonably want. This view arises partly because people tend to think of a higher income as meaning more of the same goods, when in fact it may mean different goods. Not many people want 100 cars, but most people would love a car with qualities that would make it 100 times as costly to produce as their present car, if they could have that car at the same price as their present one.[1]

If it were true that rising incomes were about to lead to the onset of 'abundance', in which people would cease to want more, we would expect to see some signs of this in the behavior of whole communities of people living at 'high' income levels. Switzerland has an average real income higher than the U.S. and many times the average world income. Yet we observe no sign that the Swiss are ceasing to want more, even in the nicest suburbs of Zurich. The theory that people's wants level off once they reach a certain level of income is not corroborated by any observation of actual behavior.

As income rises, certain things, formerly highly desirable and cherished, become taken for granted. Attention focusses on new desirabilia. A thousand years ago no one actively 'wanted' a camera or a telephone, but many people would have wanted either one if it had been offered to them cheap enough. I don't waste my time 'wanting' a car that would take me cheaply and safely to the bottom of the ocean or to another planet, but I would be very interested if one became available, as I expect it might to my great-grandchildren.

The notion that rising incomes will or could soon reach a point where people cease to want more is not as persuasive as it seems at first glance. Yet the use of this notion in arguing for the obsolescence of prices is mistaken in a more fundamental way. The Mises argument suggests that the rationale of the price system lies, not primarily in rationing out consumer goods, but in organizing production. The standard defenses of gratuitous provision—that people don't bloat their stomachs on hundreds of gallons of water from public drinking fountains, don't take more sugar than they like in their coffee whenever a coffee house provides sugar free, and so forth—therefore miss the main point. If we accept that there is some attainable level of income at which everyone would cease to want more of anything, it might still be the case that that level of income could be maintained only by efficient allocation of factors in production, which requires production decision-makers to make comparisons of cost. Society's stock of factors may imaginably be sufficient to maintain a certain level of income (which, for the sake of argument, we may suppose to entail that people don't want more of anything), but this might be so only on condition that economizing in the use of resources can be continued. A society where everyone has 'enough' TVs and cars may still be one in which cost comparisons have to be made of inputs into production of TVs and cars.[2] (Because, hypothetically, the level of income has only to be maintained and not increased, it should not be concluded that the conditions of production can be frozen, and no further production choices made. Some exhaustible resources will be used up, or the richest reserves will be used up, requiring a new combination of factors to extract them, at a higher cost. Such increases in costs would change all prices and therefore all input combinations, even if compensated by innovations and adjustments elsewhere.)

c. Piecemeal Communism

Even if we could all have bread for nothing, we should not want more than a quite limited amount. (Russell 1919, 98)

In Marx's free-access communism, everyone will take as much as they please from the common store of goods. Proposals have been made to introduce the system of free access for only a limited number of goods (Beckwith 1976, Chapter 3, provides a historical summary of proposals for gratuitous provision, whether free-access or rationed). One of Bertrand Russell's potboilers gave this idea wide currency and presents the classic argument in its favor: that there are certain goods which people already consume in the maximum quantity regardless of price—they already consume the same amounts of these goods that they would consume if the goods were provided gratuitously. The suggestion was taken up by Lange, who concluded that "Marx's second phase of communism may be gradually approached" (Lange 1938, 138–141). Mandel (1968, 658) presents a similar argument. A detailed treatment is given by Beckwith (1976), who presents many other arguments for free distribution.

Whether or not a price is charged for bread, there is a cost to producing it. Resources are diverted from other possible uses to produce bread, thus reducing other forms of consumption. If people don't pay for the bread by means of a price, they pay for it in taxes. There is therefore no net gain for the average person merely from having the bread 'free'. If we accept the premiss that everyone is already consuming the maximum amount of bread, then no one is enabled to afford more bread by free distribution. So the effect of free distribution is merely to distribute income from those who pay higher taxes to those who pay lower taxes (the people who pay lower taxes increase their purchases of things other than bread). If this is the desired outcome—to diminish some people's incomes and increase others'—there is no need to confuse the issue by free distribution of a good. Of course, someone may regard free distribution purely as a way to help the poor by enabling them to have more bread. But this abandons the argument that everyone is already consuming the maximum. And in that case, it is better to give the poor cash than to provide them with free goods, and better to give them free goods in limited rations (bread-vouchers) than to give them unlimited free supplies.

A fallacy is tacitly implied in much advocacy of free distribution. The discussion usually starts with a good like salt, which is admittedly consumed by almost everyone in quantities which vary little with incomes or with the price of salt. It is then suggested that if provision of other goods, like bread, is increased, along with generally rising incomes, people's desire for more of such goods must at some point 'level off'; these goods will then become like salt—people won't increase their consumption of such goods even if they're free. But household salt is a highly unusual good; it has two properties, both of which together will never apply to any of the great majority of goods: 1. its purchase takes only a minute portion of a person's total income; 2. it has no close substitutes. As a result, consumption of household salt is highly insensitive to price; a 100 percent price increase (or a move to free provision) might barely affect consumption.[3] Having been sold on the salt example, the reader is then asked to imagine that, as people's incomes rise, their consumption of bread levels off, and that bread therefore becomes more like salt. But neither of the two conditions has become true of bread. If there is an observed levelling-off in bread consumption, it's probably because, for some people at their current incomes, bread is an inferior good.[4] Be that as it may, it's unlikely that bread, while continuing to be desired, will come to have no close substitutes.

If the quantity consumed appears to level off historically, the price of that good is still performing an important function, and free provision of that good will cause people to increase their consumption of it. Free provision of bread would cause people to substitute bread for other foods that they would actually prefer to have if prices accurately represented production costs. Thus free government provision of a good is inefficient; it reduces the satisfaction of people's wants from the available resources, just as surely as if physical goods were needlessly destroyed. Whether or not there is manifest 'waste' to a commonsensical observer, there must always be waste in the strictly economic sense, whenever some good is provided at a price below its cost and the amount consumed is responsive to price changes.[5]

The idea behind advocacy of free provision is that it is justified once satiety has been attained, and it is supposed that, with increasing output, satiety will be attained for goods one after another. But the fact that consumption of some good has levelled off doesn't indicate that satiety has been reached for that good—merely that additions to income are more satisfactorily spent on other goods. (Many economists hold that general satiety can never be achieved, because potential human wants are unlimited.[6] Socialists often claim that this view arises from a narrow and unwarranted conception of human nature. It is possible that such socialists have not exercised their imagination on the notion of satiety, or don't grasp that satiety would mean a state of affairs where no one could think of any improvement. But this is all somewhat redundant, since the impossibility of satiety is not required to pursue the argument. Once it is accepted that there is not vast waste within the market, that the market is more productive than any alternative framework, that the richest communities on Earth show no signs of approaching satiety, and that most of the world is far below the income levels of those richest communities, the possibility of satiety, thousands of years hence at best and not capable of being hastened by political intervention, has no bearing on any policy discussion. For all practical purposes, the consequences of the thesis that satiety is a long way away are indistinguishable from the consequences of the thesis that satiety is unattainable.)

The use of gratuitously-provided goods would have to be regulated: bread can be used as animal feed (and regularly is, in countries where bread is subsidized), and salt in many chemical processes (as a production input, sodium chloride doesn't conform to the two conditions, and its use is therefore sensitive to price changes). Further problems would be generated by the government's role in intervening between the producers and consumers. 'Bread', for example, will have to be defined by the government, with a list of qualifying characteristics. Producers will have an incentive to drop any unlisted characteristics, but will lose any inducement to offer an innovative product which drops listed characteristics.

ii. Restriction of Production by the Market

In this section I consider the claim, often made by socialists, that there is something in the market's system of production for profit which results in holding the volume of output below the technical potential. In the next section (iii., below) I consider the claim that many activities or occupations prevalent in the market are unnecessary, and therefore wasteful. Both of these claims support the conclusion that output of useful products could be increased by abolishing the market. In both cases, of course, I discuss only a few characteristic examples of these claims.

a. Restriction of Production by Cost

Frequently, a desirable and technically feasible project is not implemented because it would be too expensive. This fact is sometimes adduced, without further argument, as evidence that something is amiss. It appears that 'costs', or the juggling of figures concerned with mere money, are choking back the output of useful goods. Costs, then, evidently restrict production.

Costs do restrict particular lines of production, but costs do not restrict the aggregate of all lines of production. Different lines of production compete for the available resources. If any one line is expanded, this curtails production in other lines. Production of each good is 'restricted' by the inescapable requirements of producing all the other goods. If a desirable project has to be abandoned because 'it would cost too much money', this means that it would cost too much in real resources, and this in turn means that it would cost too much in reduced output of other desirable projects. A financial cost represents a resource cost; a resource cost represents a want-satisfaction cost.[7]

Consider, for instance, the claim that a particular kind of dirty and dangerous work (such as coal-mining) could be abolished by additional mechanization. This is true, but it means allocating costly resources to make machines. Other human wants would go unsatisfied, other sufferings unrelieved, in order to eliminate underground mining by humans. One consequence would be that other kinds of dirty and dangerous work would tend to be increased (as lower output generally tends to reduce opportunities to substitute machines for humans or to change the nature of the work for the benefit of the workers). The complaint about 'mere costs' is sometimes made by referring to the fact that *labor* is used because it is 'cheap'. A typical statement is Bookchin's: "I shall not belabor the fact that the cost factor—the profit motive, to state it bluntly—inhibits the use of technological innovations. It is fairly well established that in many areas of the economy it is cheaper to use labor than machines" (Bookchin 1971, 96). It is more than fairly well established, but it is not well established that there is anything wrong with it.

Even a communist society which had dispensed with prices, would have to take into account the 'cheapness' of labor (though the link between the laborer's income and the cost of his labor would have been severed). Such a society would have to employ labor where its cost was less than that of a machine, and employ a machine where its cost was less than that of labor. A determination not to use labor 'merely' because it was cheap would mean a decision by the administration to allocate labor regardless of its opportunity cost. When a decision is made, in the market, not to install a robot, because 'labor is cheaper', this reflects the availability of the labor in question and the resources (including labor) required to produce the robots in question. Unless the information 'labor is cheaper' can be transmitted in some form, robots will be installed where their use represents too high a cost. In practice this could apply only to isolated, particular cases. If the determination is made, across the board, not to use labor 'merely' because it is cheaper, then numerous decisions will be made to install robots where robots do not exist and cannot be produced quickly enough in sufficient quantity. The administration would be making decisions which physically could not be followed. The actual installation of robots would then be determined by a spontaneous process of waiting in line, influence-peddling, and other mechanisms less efficient than prices.

Some may grant that the requirement for an enterprise to cover its costs, or break even, is not a restriction of production, but may point to the 'profit' which goes to owners of enterprises or other investors. By 'profit' they generally mean the regular return on capital, what Marx calls "average rate of profit" and what I call interest.[8] Socialists generally believe that people are not entitled to an income 'merely' because they have invested their savings, but even if capitalists should not be paid for the use of resources purchased with their savings, the question remains whether the administration would have to continue to view these resources as costly, and, so to speak, charge itself for the use of these resources, as a computational device to ensure efficient deployment of those resources.

d. Restriction of Production by Interest

> . . . the capitalist mode of production . . . comes to a standstill at a point fixed by the production and realization of profit, and not the satisfaction of requirements. (III, 258)

Is the adjustment of production by means of an interest rate an overall restriction of production, or is it like the cases examined in 12.iii. above, one in which 'restriction' of individual sectors of the economy is part of the determination of the shape of total output (and compatible with maximization of total output)? An enterprise or project pays its way when the proceeds cover all the costs *plus interest* (or all the costs including interest, if we adopt that way of speaking). Would the administration be able, without injury, to rate any project as 'paying its way' if the benefits of the project just covered its non-interest costs?

1. Interest in the Market

Any future stream of income may be 'capitalized', and regarded as interest. Hence, if a plot of land yields rents of $1,000 per year indefinitely, and the prevailing interest rate is four percent, then the market price of that plot of land will be $25,000. Given the interest rate, any future stream of income can be represented as a 'present value', and an asset which yields that future stream of income will sell at that present value. The same principle determines the selling price of a machine, a building, a ship, a taxicab medallion, or any asset.[9]

In order to know how expected future income determines the value of an asset, we have to know the rate of interest. The rate of interest could conceivably be zero (there would be 'no interest'). In that case, any asset with a perpetual return, such as a typical piece of land, would have an infinite value. Another consequence would be that any asset expected to yield something of value in the distant future, no matter how distant, but yielding nothing else before or after, would be worth the full expected value of that future yield.

In the market, we nearly always observe a rate of interest greater than zero. This reflects 'positive time preference', the fact that people generally prefer something desirable in the near future to a similar desirable thing in the remote future. There is still disagreement about the exact reasons for positive time preference. The most influential interest theory today is that of Irving Fisher (1930), which combines time preference (or as he calls it, "impatience") with "investment opportunity". Though Mises admired Fisher, his own view was closer to that of Fisher's critic, Frank Fetter, who espoused a 'pure' time-preference theory. Some Misesians have attempted to revive the debate over the merits of Fisher's and Fetter's theories (see Fetter 1977).[10] According to Mises, positive time preference is a sufficient explanation for a positive rate of interest and positive time preference is inseparable from human action (Mises 1966, 483–490, 524–537).

The rate of interest helps to determine which production projects will be embarked upon. At first glance, it might appear that a lower rate of interest would simply lead to 'more investment', that additional projects would become viable the lower the interest rate. But this is not the case (Fisher 1930). A fall in the rate of interest makes some projects worthwhile and others not worthwhile, as does a rise in the interest rate. Any change in the interest rate raises the present value of some projects and reduces the present value of others. Thus, a change in the interest rate, or the persistence of the interest rate at a particular level, has innumerable intricate effects upon production.

In production we are confronted by choices between a certain amount of output in the near future and a greater amount of output in the distant future. A farming community may, for instance, build an irrigation system which, once completed, will increase output of crops. But while the community is building the irrigation system, the resources employed for that purpose are not producing current output of crops, so for the time being they reduce their agricultural output (or their output of some other good, such as leisure). These longer-term, ultimately more productive methods Böhm-Bawerk called 'roundabout'. (It is not that roundabout methods are necessarily more productive than more direct methods. If a more direct approach is also more productive it will be adopted. The interesting choices which remain are those between direct methods which yield a certain amount soon and indirect methods which yield a greater amount after a delay.) Thus, there is a choice between a certain amount of goods in the near future and a greater amount of goods in the more distant future.

The notion of interest restricting production, like costs restricting production, is an illusion. A fall in the interest rate, due to a fall in time-preference (if, for instance, people become more confident about the future, and therefore more prepared to save) means that people save a higher proportion of their income. Production changes its shape, becoming more oriented to the more distant future as compared with the near future. It is not the 'amount' of current production which changes, but the fact that output of final consumption goods is reduced in the near future and increased in the distant future. This can be seen from the fact that labor and capital factors may be just as 'fully employed' with the former high rate of interest as with the new, lower rate of interest.

2. The Unavoidability of Interest under Communism

Let us now picture, by way of a change, the administration of a communist society, faced with the task of allocating resources to their best uses, according to the consumers' wishes. The administration will have to determine how much to sacrifice the near future to the distant future or *vice versa*. For its own purposes, the administration will require a 'price of time', so that thousands of different projects with varying time-shapes of future output can be compared, to identify those with the highest present value. The administration will discount benefits the more, the remoter they are. To take an obvious case, the administration will not treat two production processes as equivalent if they produce identical flows of benefits, one commencing immediately, one commencing in 500 years. Slightly less obviously, two similar machines which will each last 15 years will be considered more valuable than one otherwise similar machine which will last 30 years, because the total output of the two machines is available sooner. Numerous non-obvious and far more complex cases would confront the administration every day.

Various subtle and conflicting theories have been advanced to account for positive time preference as an observable market phenomenon. Justifying positive time preference to the communist administration is a simpler matter. 1. The future is uncertain, and its uncertainty increases with its remoteness. The longer the time before the fruition of a project, the greater the likelihood that circumstances will have changed to render the project unworthwhile. 2. The current population will not see it as their destiny to tighten their belts indefinitely purely for the enrichment of remote future generations. 3. A zero rate of interest would have bizarre results: for instance, numerous projects with slight but perpetual yields would all have to be accorded an infinite value. In practice, the attempt to pursue such a policy would have to lead to the splitting of production into two parts: one part (including an interest rate) to feed and maintain the current population, the other part a kind of inter-generational 'pyramid' building, presumably limited by estimates of when the human species would die out.

c. Unused Capacity as a Symptom of Restricted Production

A special version of the argument that profitability restricts production is the appeal to 'excess' or 'unused' capacity. An industrial plant sometimes has measurable 'excess capacity'. Suppose that, geared up to the maximum possible, the buildings and basic equipment can produce 30 percent more output. In that case the plant has '23 percent excess or unused capacity'. Frequently the implication of such statements is that something must be wrong. Sometimes people even add up all the 'excess capacity' at all the different plants in a country and say that the country has a whole has 'such and such excess capacity', with the implication that the country could conceivably produce at 'full capacity'.

Whenever a factory expands production to come closer to full capacity, it draws resources away from other areas of production, reducing output in those other areas. Typically, the factory will employ more workers, more raw materials, more manufactured inputs, more energy, and more capital in the form of comparatively mobile equipment. Even if some part of these additional inputs were formerly idle, some, and normally the great majority, will not have been idle. Expansion of production to full capacity involves a cost. To the socialist administration, as to the market, there is no reason to assume that this cost is worth the extra output from this particular plant. Adding together the excess capacity of all plants is a fallacy of composition. Expansion of output at one plant reduces output in other plants, because of the drawing away of complementary factors (see Hayek 1984, 163ff).

It may be asked whether there is ever anything wrong with excess capacity.[11] There may be something wrong with it, but the inefficiency which may be involved may very well lie entirely in the past. In the late nineteenth century there was much railroad-building which, with hindsight, was found to be unwarranted. It would have been inefficient in the early twentieth century to operate the railroads at full capacity, sending things by rail that could more cheaply be sent by other means. The only efficient thing to do was to operate railroads below full capacity, and refrain from fully replacing them, closing some lines and scavenging the track for removable assets, and allowing other lines to deteriorate.

Overinvestment which occurred in the past may have been the best possible decision given the knowledge prevailing at the time, even though it can now be seen to be suboptimal. Alternatively it may have been a mistake, about which nothing can now be done. But there may be a third explanation for excess capacity: it may actually represent the optimum, even with hindsight. This would arise because at some point in the history of the plant, it was used to full capacity. Since no plant can be used at more than 100 percent of capacity, all 'play' in the industrial structure must take place by variations in output below 100 percent. Most people have a commonsense awareness of this: they don't see it as an attainable ideal to have every office desk and every car in use 24 hours a day, 365 days a year.

iv. Wasteful Activities in the Market

a. Wasteful Occupations

A common way of arguing that capitalism wastes resources is to make a list of activities or occupations held to be unnecessary except under capitalism. The proportion of these in the total workforce is then estimated, and the conclusion emerges that the revolution will speedily increase output by the indicated amount. It is then further deduced that the average working day can be greatly reduced. In the classic example of this style of argument, Lafargue (1975) infers that the workers could easily reduce their working hours to three per day "reserving the rest of the day and night for leisure and feasting" (48–49) and still consume far more goods than they do under capitalism. The editor of the 1975 edition of Lafargue's work keeps the tradition alive by implying that "we can surely produce the necessaries and comforts of life" in a working day of less than half an hour (24). In Lafargue's view, though the entire population will consume their fill, it will be a difficult enough problem to find everybody a few hours' work: "to have work for all it is necessary to apportion it like water on a ship in distress" (59). The outstanding problem for capitalist production "is no longer to find producers and multiply their powers but to discover consumers, to excite their appetites and create in them fictitious needs" (56).

Lists of 'wasteful' occupations can be found in numerous socialist writings, such as Owen 1844, 10–30; Engels MECW, v4, 247–252; Lafargue, 53–54; and Kidron 1974, 41–46. Such lists automatically include all activities having anything specifically to do with buying and selling.

At least a large part of financial activities corresponds to operations which would have to be carried out in any imaginable society with advanced industry—for example, measuring the costs of resources used up in particular lines of production. It is mistaken to suppose that all these activities could simply be eliminated in a non-market system. It may be contended that some costs of financial controls arise only because of the existence of a market. But any alternative, non-market system would also involve activities unique to that system. An authority which tried to plan the economy by solving simultaneous equations would have to employ thousands of people to gather the information to provide the 'constants' for the equations, and to compute the solution. A similar point applies to labor-hours, energy units, a simulated market, or any other socialist planning scheme.

It is rash to conclude that resources allocated to financial operations could be released for other uses. The employment of accountants, for example, is one of the costs paid for in each enterprise or firm. There can be too many accountants employed, just as buildings can be too well-insulated, quality inspection too stringent, or inventories too high. If the number of accountants employed is excessive, then it will be possible to improve profitability by reducing the number of accountants: there will then be less accuracy in financial controls (and a consequent fall in output per unit of input, aside from the input of accountants' labor) but this fall will be more than compensated by saving in accountants' wages. Notice that if too many or too few accountants are employed, there is a waste of real resources: we are all poorer. Accountants are productive workers, not only in the trivial sense that someone wants to pay for their services, but in the wider sense that their efforts expand the quantities of food, clothing, shelter, and other final goods that can be made available given the existing stock of resources. They do this by preventing waste: by helping to adjust production so that the most profitable use is made of the resources at society's disposal.

As an example of a cost which might be saved by free distribution, Beckwith cites the practice of putting price stickers on goods. Manufacturing and applying price stickers does use up resources, but this can be justified if it saves on other resources. In this, it is no different from building a road or fertilizing crops. Not all goods are stickered: for instance, the prices of some goods are given in a list which can be consulted. The *precise method* of identifying a good's price varies according to cost and benefit. It is not the precise method which is at issue, but the mere fact of spending resources to inform consumers of the prices of goods they might want to buy. But without some such technique, consumers wouldn't be in a position to allocate their incomes among different goods taking into account the costs of those goods. The intensity of demand for a particular good cannot be communicated except by reference to the other goods consumers are prepared to renounce. Unless *some* resources were expended to communicate prices, there would be misallocation, resulting in a suboptimal mix of final goods. We would all be worse off.

b. Planned Obsolescence

The opinion that 'planned obsolescence' is wasteful was given wide popularity by Packard (1960), who develops at length suggestions thrown out by Galbraith (1958). In order to think clearly about this issue, we have to distinguish two conceivable scenarios: 1. The range of options facing a firm includes two ways of producing a similar sort of article. One way results in a less durable product, which is less costly to produce. The firm compares the difference in durability with the difference in cost, and decides that the second way will be more profitable, because potential consumers will prefer a less durable article at a cheaper price. 2. The range of options includes two ways of producing an article. One way is less durable without being less costly to produce. The less durable way is chosen at no saving in cost. Most writing which criticizes built-in obsolescence pays no attention to this distinction. Scenario 2. is scandalous, while Scenario 1. is laudable. Planned obsolescence is often held to be wasteful, but if costs matter—if costs represent reductions in output of other goods—then *refraining* from planned obsolescence could be wasteful, because the gain in consumer wellbeing from making the article more durable may be outweighed by the loss in consumer wellbeing due to the reduction in output of other products. Scenario 1. is commonplace, while no one seems to have come up with a well-attested instance of Scenario 2. Yet Galbraith and Packard tend to blur the distinction, thus insinuating the notion that planned obsolescence is likely to be wasteful, when, for all we know, any reduction in planned obsolescence would be wasteful.

Packard's discussion is based on his Fourierist view that "Man throughout recorded history has struggled—often against appalling odds—to cope with material scarcity", but nowadays all that has changed, and "The great challenge . . . is to cope with a threatened over-abundance of the staples and amenities and frills of life" (1960, 7). Thus, the market has devised methods of waste-creation to avert the menace of plethora. Packard substantiates this, as he does many of his propositions, by a handful of quotations from individuals giving their own opinions; many of these individuals are marketing men and writers in advertising journals, speaking during the recession of the late 1950s, and preoccupied with reducing inventory.

Packard's discussion does distinguish cursorily among various types of planned obsolescence, but gives no more than a one-line nod (58) to the possibility that some of them might be justifiable. Packard's rhetoric assumes that it must be bad for things to have shorter lives. His book gives the impression that product lives are getting shorter, that this is due to threatening superabundance, and that it entails waste. Yet despite the appearance of supporting evidence, not one of these key propositions is unequivocally corroborated by any of Packard's sources. Packard mentions the fact that some household articles, such as socks, have become more durable (56) but doesn't make even a sketchy attempt to assess the overall trend. If the typical cases of planned obsolescence cited by Packard are justified by cost-saving, then the title of his book should have been *The Waste Preventers*. Among Packard's examples, the best substantiated ones tend to be most easily defensible on grounds of cost-saving. The undeniably objectionable cases seem to be no more than legends, like the potato peeler which was deliberately made the same color as potato peelings, so as to be more frequently thrown away by mistake (47–48).

Galbraith and Packard took their cue from controversies in the 1950s engineering literature (see Packard, 61–67). Asked to plan for a definite product-life, shorter than was technically feasible, some engineers had qualms about this, and a discussion ensued over the propriety of doing such a thing. Typically, there would be a product, such as a refrigerator, made from many components. For many of these components, there would be a trade-off between longevity and cheapness. The whole appliance would be difficult to repair, or consumers would be unwilling to have it repaired, preferring to junk it and buy a new model. Given that the expected life of some of the components of the refrigerator would be, say, 20 years, it made sense for the management to approach the engineers and say: 'This product has an expected life of 20 years, and for cost reasons, an optimum desired life of 20 years. But we have inherited traditional methods of making some of the components, so that they will last 50 or 100 years. If the extra longevity of those components implies extra cost in making them, then the extra 30 or 80 years' life represents a waste. Therefore, we want you to look closely at some of these unnecessarily durable components, to see if you can reduce the longevity to 20 years with a saving in costs.'

If the circumstances were akin to this, then planned obsolescence was a strategy for reducing waste. If a component in a refrigerator, junked after 20 years, has another 30 years' life, and is thereby more expensive to make, then that cost increment is a waste. Implementing planned obsolescence will make refrigerators cheaper. There will be an increase in output, both of refrigerators and of other goods. Another possibility is that the management guesses that consumers would prefer the product life to be reduced from 30 to 25 years, if, say, there could be a five percent reduction in price. If the management guesses right, and can achieve that life-shortening with that cost reduction, then this too is a way of eliminating waste. The qualms that some engineers had about this were based on the idea that it is discreditable to aim deliberately for a short product-life, though presumably these engineers would not have urged that toilet-roll holders be made of platinum.

With economic development, there is a trend for labor-time to become more expensive in relation to equipment and materials. Some older products were 'built to last', but required much repair and maintenance during their lives. Changing cost relations may mean that it becomes more important to have a product that will operate trouble-free with little labor input for a short period, rather than having a much longer ultimate life requiring larger labor input. When someone decides to throw away a radio rather than buy a new one, because the cost of repair would be as great as the cost of a new radio, this is no cause for regret. Both the repair costs and the purchase costs represent real resource costs.

Though Packard doesn't wholeheartedly endorse the assumption that costs don't matter, he is not untouched by it. He quotes an "engineer-executive" as stating that designed product life "would undoubtedly vary from one product to another and perhaps be reviewed and changed from time to time as economic or other conditions change". Packard's comment: "A reader might wonder why a product's life expectancy should change simply because 'economic or other conditions' change" (68). As we have seen, no one who has given any thought to the basic economics of the situation would wonder this for a moment. Packard also contends that a company is culpable if it sells a product which could have been made with a "much longer" life "for the same cost, or only a little more" (58), but he offers no evidence that any company has ever done this.[11]

The Man in the White Suit is a popular movie made at Ealing in 1952, starring Alec Guinness as a young scientist who invents a kind of cloth that never needs washing and never wears out. The Guinness character finds that capitalists and unions are united in opposition to the new material, because of the threat of closing down all the textile mills. It is implausible that such would be the outcome, but even if it were, it would take time, and some firms could be occupied profitably for many years replacing existing garments with the new material (if any such material existed, it's doubtful that clothing would be among its more urgent applications). The story implies that there is no competition: every firm will sacrifice its own interests for the sake of the clothing industry as a whole. If that were really so, the inventor could have gone into business independently, making a fortune from the established producers' reluctance to use the new fabric. More likely, one of the producers would have 'cheated' by hiring the inventor. (Such stories also tend to overlook the fact that if people could buy everlasting clothes at the same price as the old, degradable garments, one consequence would be that people would want to own more clothes.)

In one scene, Guinness, eagerly anticipating the launching of his new invention, falls into conversation with a group of factory workers, one of whom predicts that the material will never be marketed: "What do you think happened to all the other things—the razor blade that never gets blunt, the car that runs on water with just a pinch of something in it?" Such urban legends used to be rife—I encountered the cheap fuel story in the form of 'the car that will run on potato juice' several times in Britain in the 1960s. The appeal of such myths to the imagination is helped by the enormous gulf in durability between the imagined 'everlasting' product and what we are used to. If instead we imagine a slight increase in durability, and beyond that, another slight increase, and so on, the scenario is less credible, especially since we know that light bulbs *do* last far longer than they used to, that cars *do* get better mileage, and that textiles firms *have* repeatedly introduced new, more durable fibers—have, in fact, spent millions to develop such fibers, and then marketed them with heavy emphasis on durability (and then often been disappointed by the consumers' stubborn preference for less durable natural fibers). Durability is observably a competitive weapon. Major retail clothing chains owe their existence, in part, to the consumers' desire for some guarantee of quality. Since apparel manufacturers are so numerous and constantly changing, the retail chains offer their services as guarantors of quality, enforcing strict controls on suppliers, and readily exchanging consumers' purchases. In the days when Japanese and Hong Kong firms produced inferior imitations of western brands, they were not very successful as exporters. Their subsequent manufacturing success has been associated with a reputation for quality.

The most robust of the legends is 'the everlasting light bulb'. In Britain, the allegation that light bulbs are made in order to burn out unnecessarily quickly was investigated by the House of Commons All-Party Select Committee on Science and Technology, which produced its report in 1978. The report concludes that "the various companies expend considerable effort and funds to promote more efficient and longer-lasting lamps" (House of Commons 1978). In the months immediately prior to the committee's investigations, two individuals became media heroes by their confident assertions that bulbs were deliberately made to cease functioning sooner than they should. These two gave evidence to the committee and were questioned at length (the entertaining cross-examination is reproduced in the report).

Their arguments were found unconvincing. However, the argument of one of them, S.J. Prais, is quite sensible and remains worthy of being discussed. It is less sinister in its implications than the popular story. Physics tells us that there is a trade-off between luminous efficiency (brightness per unit of electricity) and long life: if a filament illuminates it will burn out, and the more it illuminates with a given current, the quicker it will burn out.[13] Prais doesn't claim that there is scope for making bulbs last longer without losing luminous efficiency, but that optimally bulbs should last somewhat longer and provide somewhat less illumination per unit of electricity.

c. Cohen on the Output-Leisure Trade-Off

Alongside complaints that the market restricts production, we find complaints that the market excessively expands production. In my preferred usage, it makes no sense to speak of 'too much production' of all goods. An allegation of 'too much production' usually arises when output of some good is not counted in 'production'. The allegation then means that this valued good is underproduced, because all other goods are overproduced. In the argument of G.A. Cohen, the valued good is leisure. Cohen contends that in "advanced capitalism", there is a bias towards producing goods other than leisure (Cohen 1978, 297–325; similar claims are made by Black ca. 1985, 29 and Schweickart 1980, 82–89). Cohen uncontroversially points out: 1. that there is under capitalism an unprecedently rapid increase in productivity; 2. that an increase in productivity leads to a growth of output, a growth of leisure, or some combination of each; and 3. that under capitalism it leads to some combination of each. Cohen further claims 4. that capitalism is biassed towards too much output and too little leisure (310).

There is a trade-off between 'output' and 'leisure': it is always possible to have less output and more leisure, or less leisure and more output. Inefficiency exists where a possible shift in the combination of output and leisure would increase utility for the members of society. Since workers' wages represent the value of their output for external consumers, the most natural understanding of any allegation of inefficiency would be that workers are somehow prevented from choosing lower-money-incomes-and-more-leisure. Suppose that there were a statute requiring that all employees work at least an eight-hour day. This would mean that no one would be free to work a five-hour day and have correspondingly less wage income. This would be inefficient, and the abolition of the statute would be an improvement.

Some might say that workers should not be free to choose the combination of wages and leisure they prefer: their choices are just wrong, independently of their wishes. Cohen seems to hold *both* 1. that 'capitalism' forces upon workers too much wages and too little leisure (meaning more wages and less leisure than they would like) *and* 2. that 'capitalism' operates on workers' minds, mainly by advertising, to cause them to want too much wages and too little leisure (meaning more wages and less leisure than they should want, by some standard independent of their preferences). Cohen's only discernable argument for 1. can be pieced together from remarks on pages 311ff. It is that the bias suits the interests of firms. An unstated premiss is that whatever suits the interests of firms occurs. Since firms want to make as much money as possible, and will always make less money if they reduce their output, they will always be opposed to reducing their output—and a shorter working day entails reduced output. This approach leaves a number of loose ends—such as why it is that firms don't just insist that all their employees work for nothing. It confuses the individual and the aggregate. Suppose that all workers work 40 hours a day and would prefer to work 30 hours a day with correspondingly less pay. A profit-seeking firm would offer 30 hours a day, immediately giving that firm a strong advantage over other firms in attracting labor. Other firms would be induced to move to the 30-hour day, and a 30-hour day would soon become essential for any firm's survival.

The trade-off between output and leisure is chosen by workers, and as output rises, workers determine how much of the gains to take in the form of output, how much to take in the form of reduced working hours, and how much to take in the form of more congenial work conditions (see below, 14.ii.b.). These three are substitutes—at any given level of output, an increase in one of these three means a decrease in at least one of the other two, probably both. Cohen says that "the system demonstrably possesses an output-expanding bias" (317), but no demonstration is cited. Further: "the textbooks which present the arguments in favour of capitalism do not devote attention to [the output-bias of capitalism]. Its neglect by established economics needs to be explained . . ." But the explanation is straightforward. No one has produced any evidence that the imagined 'bias' exists. Working hours have fallen steadily with rising output. Hours at work per head have also been reduced by longer schooling, longer vacations, and earlier retirement. From 1870 to 1979, output per U.S. worker rose by 1,100 percent, average hours worked per year fell by around 40 percent, while real income per head in the form of goods other than leisure increased over sevenfold (Baumol et al. 1989, Chapter 3; see the statistics in Maddison 1991).

Cohen doesn't explain how we know that workers were mistaken to make this particular division of their productivity gains between leisure and other goods, nor how we would know if the workers had been right.

When government or union regulations place a ceiling on working hours, we observe various attempts by workers to 'get round' the regulations. Generally, we observe that 'moonlighting' is common, signifying that for many workers the 'standard package' offers too few hours. If working hours were being kept artificially high, against the wishes of workers, we would expect moonlighting to be very rare, we would expect to witness numerous surreptitious deals between workers and managements to reduce hours, we would expect large numbers of people to seek part-time work as their sole source of income (whereas actually many part-time jobs are taken by people who have other employment, or temporary motives such as a course of study), and we would expect many self-employed people to reduce their hours below the average. None of these things occurs, so there is no reason to doubt that the prevailing combination of hours and output arises from the workers' choices. We are therefore left with Cohen's claim that workers are duped into wanting things they ought not to want (317).

d. 'Consumers' Wants are Wrong'

Alongside the charge that the market is wasteful in throwing away resources which could be used to satisfy people's actual wants, there has always been the charge that the market is wasteful in stimulating wants that people ought not to have. The contention that consumers' actual wants are wrong further divides into two variants: 1. The claim that what consumers want is against their own interests, or different to what they would want if they had better information (that their instrumental wants are not effectively geared to their ultimate wants). 2. The claim that what consumers want is just wrong, whether or not they would want something different if they had better information. I will ignore 2., except insofar as some comments on 1. are also relevant to 2. Nearly all arguments for 1. appeal to the influence of advertising (Galbraith 1958; Cohen 1978; Schweickart 1980).

Galbraith (1958) thinks that advertisers can "compel" (157) people to want whatever is advertised. If advertisers could compel anyone to buy, this would indeed be alarming, though it would still be open to people to avoid becoming exposed to such ads (for instance, by buying only those magazines which adopted a voluntary code excluding ads utilizing the techniques of compulsion). But since firms advertise competing products, the way in which consumers choose among the advertised products cannot be explained entirely by the fact that they are advertised. Many firms spend large sums on research-and-development (finding new ways to give the consumers what they want) and market research (finding out what the consumers in fact want). These sums could be saved if there existed a method to make consumers buy any advertised product. Products sometimes fail after being nationally advertised; more commonly they are withdrawn after local field-testing suggests the consumers won't go for them; and more commonly still they are withdrawn at an earlier stage because of research findings. Sometimes new products exceed all expectations and experience runaway demand. It's difficult to explain such occurrences without acknowledging that consumers have some independent influence in determining their purchases. Instead of compelling consumers, I propose that ads offer suggestions, which consumers are free to accept or reject. To say that ads compel people to buy is like describing the gift of a bouquet of roses as an act of rape. It is obvious enough, and has frequently been pointed out, that people who say that consumers don't make genuine choices are really just grousing because consumers make choices the critics don't like. It is also conspicuous that, when it comes to implementing their own social policies, those who rhetorically denounce advertising as a magically effective means of compulsion place more reliance on the policeman's billyclub than the chirpy jingle.[14]

Advertising is productive. I see a product advertised, and decide to give it a try. I like the product, and begin to consume it regularly. My utility has been increased by the ad: it has made me better off. If the ad had not been placed, I would be just as badly off as if the product did not exist. This is the typical and intended scenario; other scenarios are of lesser importance. I may see an ad, try the product, and not like it. I therefore do not buy it again. Still, this is part of my constant search for information about the availability of goods. The quantity of such unsuccessful tries is held in check both by the producers' prior planning (an unsuccessful try is unsuccessful for both parties) and by the consumer's evaluation of the situation before the purchase (he doesn't buy everything he sees advertised). It could *conceivably* be wasteful—there could *imaginably* be too much of this sort of thing.[15] To demonstrate this, one would have to outline an alternative institution which disseminated the same amount of information more cheaply, or gave the same amount of consumer satisfaction with less information-seeking. One would then have the problem of explaining why that institution had not emerged voluntarily on the market and therefore has to be forced upon people.

People sometimes object to the fact that different advertisements 'cancel each other' by recommending alternative products. Another criticism is that ads sometimes mislead us: Schweickart cites, as his sole example of what he calls "nonrational" techniques, claiming something for one's own brand which is in fact true of all brands, thereby allowing the consumer to infer that it is not true of the other brands.[16] From this Schweickart concludes that ads sometimes work against consumers' interests, and from this that ads are sources of inefficiency and that there is no consumer sovereignty. Some enemies of advertising even argue as though the ideal were for producers never to influence consumers' decisions at all: the case against ads is instantly proved, since ads obviously make a difference to consumers' behavior.

We often allow contending views to be expressed, as the most appropriate way to get at the truth. This occurs in political, religious, and scientific debate, and in the contest of prosecution and defense in a law court. If opposing points of view are expressed, they frequently 'cancel each other'. This is right and proper, and in any case unavoidable given opposing recommendations. Is it wasteful? The opinion that it is 'obviously' so presumably arises from tacitly assuming that the search for information is really over before it starts, that somewhere all the right answers are already written down, and merely have to be consulted. In a trial, we don't expect the defense counsel to volunteer the fact that his client has the habit of kicking stray dogs, and, insofar as this is relevant to our assessment of the defendant's character, the defense's conduct is misleading. We can even admit that it must happen from time to time that misleading rhetoric by the prosecution or defense procures a wrong conviction or acquittal. This doesn't prove that the adversarial system is an ineffective means of arriving at the truth. This system elicits information which would not be elicited by any alternative, and the *net outcome* may lead to right verdicts in more cases than other procedures. The same applies to advertising. And how can we take seriously the suggestion that my sovereignty as a consumer is infringed because I am free to listen to the suggestions of other people, including producers, and follow these suggestions if they appeal to me? Isn't it clear that my sovereignty would be infringed if I were *not* free to do this? Is freedom of religion abridged by permitting the existence of churches?

Nothing can be concluded about advertising as a whole, without a comparison of advertising with some alternative institution for performing the necessary functions of advertising. No one has decreed that producers take the initiative in disseminating information about products; this arrangement, to the extent that it prevails, is a spontaneous outcome of people's voluntary choices. A consumer can decide to ignore ads and hire a team of experts to evaluate products. The more consumers adopt this technique, the less it pays producers (except for the expert product evaluators) to advertise. Such a system does exist, in the shape of *Consumer Reports*, road tests of cars in auto magazines, media product scandals, magazines' vetting of their advertisers, and the like. But most of this function is undertaken by retailers such as mail-order firms and department stores. Since these retailers take upon themselves part of the function of evaluating quality, advertising of the goods themselves directly to the consumer by brand is correspondingly reduced.

Yet this approach shows no sign of expanding to supplant ads completely. One explanation is that consumers don't always know what standards of evaluation to apply: producers have conjectured that consumers will find a product gratifying in a way that consumers have not yet thought of. Ads are a natural outgrowth of a system in which producers try to conjecture people's potential wants and take the gamble of producing to satisfy the conjectured wants, as contrasted with a system in which goods are made to consumers' specific instructions. For most goods, most consumers prefer the former system, because it makes possible mass production and enormous cost reduction. They may also prefer it because they find that producers can guess consumers' wants better than the consumers can themselves.

Advertising can make large numbers of people aware of a product within a short space of time, and thus make economies of scale possible. By enabling economies of scale and by giving consumers more information, ads can lower prices (Benham 1972; Steiner 1973). Consumer advertising is generally heaviest at the launching of a new product, and then tapers off. There are signs (such as coupon promotions) that much marketing of consumer products is primarily designed to persuade us to try them once. Some critics have no objection to ads in the form of dull bulletins, but object to the attention-catching or entertaining qualities of some ads. This position is strictly absurd: to first admit that ads should convey information and then say that they should do so in the most ineffective way imaginable. But perhaps it is merely a kind of category mistake, like dismissing 'Ode to a Nightingale' as sloppy ornithology. The function of many ads is not to make out a reasoned case for the superiority of the product—this would be to waste our precious time, when the proof of the pudding is in the eating—but to catch our attention, to offer a mnemonic in the form of a cluster of associations, and to give a coded summation of the kind of virtues we may expect to find in the product. (Such a summation may be subtle: it may, for instance, draw attention to the kind of personal lifestyle into which the product would most probably fit, by focussing on some symbolic demarcation of what counts as self-fulfillment among practitioners of that lifestyle.) Some object to the attribution of symbolic or vicarious qualities to products, like the suggestion that an elegant car will help a man to attract women, or to enhance his status. One can easily surmise what searing indictments of the soulless functionalism of commerce would be delivered if ads did *not* address the human appetites for symbol and status. It is not to be expected that ads, any more than conversation, or theater, or the writings of those who excoriate ads, will be free of bad taste, lack of candor, or attempts to mislead. But ads are habitually greeted with skepticism. Everyone understands that ads are paid for by producers to persuade us to buy their products.

The fact that I wouldn't want something I do want if someone hadn't persuaded me to want it is no grounds for viewing that want as less respectable than any other. Enemies of advertising often tacitly compare the influence of advertising with a situation in which people's wants owe nothing to the surrounding culture. But that is an impossibility, and the fact that someone wants something because of cultural influences does not make her desire for that thing a matter of no consequence, her wishes fair game to be trampled on by anyone who thinks he knows better. The favored policies of the foes of advertising do not try to cut individuals loose from social influences, but rather to replace voluntary, commercial influences by coercive, political ones.

Cohen (318) argues that advertising promotes output at the expense of leisure, because goods are advertised and 'leisure' is not. Cohen acknowledges that leisure-related goods are advertised, but dismisses this with the statement that "rising income is required to procure them, and the advertisements do not mention the sacrifice of leisure needed to sustain that income" (318), the population evidently consisting of hydrocephalous cretins unequipped to figure this out for themselves. Cohen maintains that people in general don't know what's good for them: they pursue objectives which don't satisfy them (319). But Cohen offers no argument to counter the common-sense view that people can find out what gives them satisfaction and adjust their goals appropriately, though they may, of course, make mistakes. People experience variations in their amounts of leisure at different periods, and they can observe the lives of friends and neighbors with varying work/leisure ratios, and varying leisure pastimes. They have plenty of material to form conclusions about the comparative yields from work and leisure.[17] All consumer advertising operates within a stream of information from many sources: personal experience, word of mouth, journalism, and expert opinion.

iv. THE MEANING OF WASTE

If you do carpentry, you may incidentally create sawdust, shavings, and chippings. Superficially considered, these incidentals of wood-work may be described as 'waste'. What criterion is here being applied? A reduction in the creation of sawdust is *prima facie* desirable. But an alternative method of carpentry may reduce the amount of sawdust, while increasing the amount of labor expended. Suppose that the value of the increased labor is greater than the value of the wood saved from being lost as sawdust. Has waste been reduced by resorting to this method? Clearly not, for more labor is now used up, and the value of the labor used up is greater than the value of the wood saved. Thus there has been an increase in waste, in the very act of reducing a specific visible kind of apparent waste.

But, someone may say, the sawdust is waste, in the sense that if we could *costlessly* reduce the loss of wood in the form of sawdust, this would be an unmitigated gain. However, if we could snap our fingers and cause tables and chairs to spring into existence without using up any wood, or tools, or labor (except the modest chore of finger-snapping), that would be an unmitigated gain, too. It would follow that all production were pure waste. 'Waste' is only waste when there is a feasible way to prevent it *profitably*. 'Preventing waste' at a loss is wasteful. (By 'profit' and 'loss' in this context, I refer to the difference between benefits obtained and benefits foregone.)

Another possibility is that the sawdust may be collected and used in some further production process. The sawdust may be 'recycled'. But recycling too is wasteful if it is done at a social loss—if its cost exceeds its benefit. At the time of writing there is a great deal of public concern about the desirability of increasing the volume of recycling, but little awareness of the fact that for each material there is some optimum amount of recycling, and that more recycling than the optimum is just as wasteful as less. This implies that we should find some way of ensuring that actual recycling neither exceeds nor falls short of the optimum amount of recycling.

When a building is heated, some heat is always lost to the atmosphere. However much we increased the building's insulation, it would always be possible to increase the insulation yet further and 'waste' less heat, but there has to come a point where more resources would be consumed in providing the insulation than would be saved in generating 'wasted' heat. At that point, it becomes truly wasteful to prevent 'wastage' of heat. During the energy crisis of the 1970s, there was some talk about 'energy accounting'. Even using energy accounting, an increase in insulation could be excessive, since it takes energy to produce insulation. Similarly, constructing solar power facilities can easily use up more energy than these facilities will produce during their expected life, and energy consumed in construction of subway systems can far exceed the energy subsequently saved in reduced automobile use (Baumol and Blackman 1980). But application of 'energy accounting' alone is always misleading and tends to encourage waste, since the most efficient combination of resources will never be the most efficient in energy terms alone. It is always possible to save energy by using more non-energy resources.

Another source of apparent waste is the residue left in containers of food and other materials. Packard (44) insinuates that producers have an interest in increasing this 'waste', but if any producer could offer packaging of the same convenience and the same cost, enabling more of the contents to be retrieved, the producer would have a clear interest in selecting this option. Packard relates how his son punctured used-up aerosol cans of whipped cream, and retrieved several spoonfuls of cream per can. Packard comments: "Now we whip our own" (45). Such a reaction is foolish: the amount of cream thrown away with the container is irrelevant, even if it were 99 percent. What matters is the total cost of getting a quantity of cream into the consumers' mouth. Some proportion of food or other consumable material is always lost. If one method of delivery increases the amount of material lost, while offering the remaining material more cheaply (taking into account the consumer's valuation of his time and trouble in preparing the material for final consumption), then this is the efficient, or non-wasteful, method. To enforce greater retrievability of materials from packages than is freely chosen by individuals in the market is to increase actual waste, in the very act of reducing apparent 'waste'.

A coherent and defensible usage of the word 'waste' is 'any use of resources in other than least-cost production combinations'.[18] Thus, 'waste' means the same as 'economic inefficiency', as discussed in Chapter 1 above. The whole of economic theory relating to 'efficiency' could be reworded so that it referred to 'waste avoidance'.

The conclusion of the economic calculation argument can similarly be reformulated: In the absence of factor markets, a socialist administration would possess no reliable indication of waste and therefore couldn't implement any effective system of waste avoidance.

— 13 —

ANARCHY, STATE, AND COMMUNISM

i. How Anarchist was Marx's Communism?

Marxists are anarchists in the literal sense that they purport to aim at a stateless social order. If Marx and his friends had not become involved in a faction fight with Bakunin during the late 1860s, when the term 'anarchist' became the convenient label for the Bakuninists, Marxism might well have entered the twentieth century calling itself 'anarchist'. It was common ground among Marxists and Bakuninists that the imminent socialist society would dispense with the state, just as it would dispense with private property, money, wages, and social classes. The two main issues which appeared to separate Bakuninists and Marxists were the organization of the revolutionaries before the revolution and the need for a transitional regime to usher in the new society. Bakuninists contended that the state must disappear at once with the revolutionary uprising, or it would perpetuate itself. Marxists argued that the revolutionaries must first take over the state, after which it would "wither away", ceasing to exist because no longer required.

Is it then true to say that Marxists and anarchocommunists agree on the objective, disagreeing only on how to get it? I don't think so. The most remarkable aspect of the Marxian view is surely not that the state is expected to wither away, but that this withering away is to be prepared by an enormous expansion of the state's power. The state takes over the ownership and administration of all the industrial means of production, whereupon the state gradually ceases to exist, although central administration of all industry remains. In the thinking of Marx and Engels, the state is to become an enormous, all-powerful organization, and this organization is to remain indefinitely. When Engels asserts, for example, that the whole of society's production is to be governed by a "single vast plan", he is not speaking of the transition but of full-blown, stateless communism. The existence and implementation of such a plan is continuously claimed to be the great merit which communism possesses, compared to the bourgeois order. The very pages immediately preceding Engels's statements about the necessary disappearance of the state (1954, 369–388) are filled with unequivocal declarations to this effect. We have no clear indication that Engels or Marx countenance the possibility that society-wide planning will ever cease to be the framework of communist industrial organization.

What does Engels mean by the withering away of the state?[1] The gigantic unified apparatus of administration is to remain, but is in some way to change its nature so that it ceases to be a state. Marx and Engels want everything to be taken over by the state, not as an end in itself, but purely as a preparation for the taking over of the state and production by "society". The takeover by society is not seen by them as a way of talking about a state takeover, but rather as incompatible with the continuation of the state. "The proletariat seizes political power and turns the means of production into state property. But, in doing this, it abolishes . . . . the state as state" (Engels 1954, 388). In the very process of turning the entire means of production into state property, the proletariat abolishes the state! The state is to be abolished only *as a state*. The administrative entity which is the state is to survive, but transformed, so that it is no longer a state. How is the placing of all power over industry in the hands of the state supposed to help the state to wither away? Engels explains that the state will at last be the representative of the whole of society, that there will no longer be class conflict and anarchy of production. Without classes and anarchy of production, there will simply be no need for a state; it will be redundant.

a. The Marxist Definition of the State

Marxists have frequently explained their position by the following syllogism. All states are instruments for the oppression of exploited classes by exploiting classes. The revolution will dispense with exploitation and with classes. Therefore, after the revolution, the state will disappear. In the most celebrated Marxist work on the state, Lenin repeats the traditional formula that the state is necessary when one class exploits and oppresses another, but Lenin's "socialism" retains a state, although there is no longer class exploitation or oppression. One might try to defend Lenin's position by saying that a few remnants of the old classes would still be around, but Lenin doesn't take this line. Instead, he argues that the state continues to be needed because there is not yet free access to goods, but payment according to work—and this is a "law", and law requires a state (LCW 25, 476). This argument is intelligible: if people can take what they want from a superabundant store, there is presumably less cause for conflict than if their access to goods is restricted to a modest payment for work done. But it follows that a state may be needed when there is no class exploitation or oppression. In Marx's higher phase of communism, theft is hardly conceivable, but in Marx's first phase, or in Lenin's socialism, theft would have to be deterred by penalties (though Marx does *not* envisage a state in his first phase). It follows that even where we see the state being utilized as an instrument of class exploitation and oppression, it is conceivable that, intermixed with or alongside its class function, the state may be fulfilling a non-class function similar to that in post-capitalist society. After all, the great majority of acts of theft or robbery in the U.S. today are committed *by* people who are neither wealthy nor in any danger of extreme hardship *against* other people who are neither wealthy nor in any danger of extreme hardship.

The assertion that a state can only be an instrument of class oppression could be a definition or a sociological theory. If it were a definition, then a supreme administration equipped with armies, police, and jails would not qualify as a state unless it were used by an exploiting class or classes against an exploited class or classes. In that case, the prediction of the state's disappearance would turn out to be less extraordinary than it first appeared. If, to the contrary, the assertion that the state can only be an instrument of class oppression is not a definition of the word 'state', but a statement about what occurs in human societies, then it must be the claim that a 'state', defined in some way other than as an instrument of class oppression, as a matter of fact can only be an instrument of class oppression, and hence cannot exist where there are no classes. It is clear that the Marxists' assertion must be understood in this second sense, but what is this other way of defining 'state'? What is the Marxist definition of 'state', a definition which must make no reference to class oppression if the Marxist assertion about states being instruments of class oppression is to be saved from vacuity?

The state is often defined as a unified coercive organization claiming an ultimate monopoly on the use of force within a geographical area, this claim being widely accepted among the population of that area (but see Nozick 1974, 23). According to this definition, the three characteristics of the state are unity, coercion, and legitimacy. Since the communist administration is obviously intended to possess legitimacy (widespread popular acceptance) and will have to preserve unity in order to exert "conscious social control" by means of a "single vast plan", we might suppose that the communist administration will cease to qualify as a state because it will no longer need to employ coercion. Some remarks by Engels do suggest that the administration will cease to be a state because it will no longer *force* anyone to do anything (Engels 1954, 389). But although Marx and Engels regard communism as a system with very little coercion, this is not the key, defining notion which makes them view communism as stateless, as can be seen from Engels's discussion of the Iroquois confederacy. Engels takes a generous view of traditional Iroquois society, yet he doesn't deny that it is characterized by legitimized coercion, and he praises it for its statelessness:

> No soldiers, no gendarmes or police, no nobles, kings, regents, prefects, or judges, no prisons, no lawsuits—and everything takes its orderly course. All quarrels and disputes are settled by the whole of the community affected. . . . Although there were many more matters to be settled in common than today . . . yet there is no need for even a trace of our complicated administrative apparatus with all its ramifications. The decisions are taken by those concerned, and in most cases everything has been already settled by the custom of centuries. (Engels 1942, 86)

Engels's discussion of the Iroquois is tinged with anticipation of communism, echoing the turns of phrase he employs to describe communism. Engels and Marx write of the state as being peculiarly alien from, and apparently above, society. The root idea seems to be that separate specialized agencies, especially police, prisons, and judges, mark the presence of a state. At times they seem to mean that once the state is removed, anyone and everyone will spontaneously enforce social rules, in the way that customers in a bar might intervene to restrain someone who loses his temper. Yet other passages—especially Marx's notes on Bakunin (MECW v24, 513–522)—show that they advocate a formal electoral structure, though one in which the elected remain living and working among the electors.

When Engels says that the Iroquois have no soldiers, gendarmes, police, or judges, to be scrupulously accurate he should qualify these nouns with the adjective 'full-time'. As Engels sees it, a state run by amateurs ceases to be a state. Marxian communism is to be stateless in the sense that it has no specialized organizational structure separate from the rest of society. There is to be thoroughgoing 'participatory democracy' (in the language of the 1960s) in which "those concerned" with anything make the decisions about it. Hunt accurately characterizes the Marxian communist administration as "democracy without professionals" (1984, 161, 365).

To spell this out is immediately to raise questions about its feasibility. Even the two reasons given by Engels to help explain why "there is no need for even a trace of our complicated administrative apparatus" (decisions by "those concerned" and regulation by "the custom of centuries") could not apply in any industrial society. "Those concerned" in any decision are difficult to separate out, and very numerous. Those concerned in the location of a factory, for example, include those who will consume the factory's products, those who would have consumed the products of an alternative installation at that location, those who live or work nearby, those who live or work near the alternative locations, and so forth. Centuries-old custom can set the framework for resolving disputes, in other words can constitute the fundamental principles of the law, but cannot say whether to generate electricity by nuclear fission or the burning of fossil fuels.

Removal of social classes would not remove all conflicts of interest requiring coercive means of settling disputes. To what extent should pesticides be used to increase food production and incidentally poison wildlife? To what extent should aircraft noise be reduced, with concomitant reduction in the quality or quantity of air travel? To what extent should the fact that method of production A is more irksome, for those involved in it, than method of production B count against the fact that method of production B is more effective in satisfying the consumers' wants? To what extent should animals suffer so that some human wants can be satisfied? To what extent should some neighbourhoods which are picturesque for natural or historical reasons be preserved from changes which would reduce the esthetic satisfactions of those who live there, when this preservation reduces the output of goods desired by millions of other people? Such questions must always impinge differently on some groups than on others. Some groups have an interest in selecting one point on the trade-off curve; other groups have different interests. Such conflicting interests are automatically present in any industrial society (including any 'post-industrial' society) and cannot be eliminated by any change in the system of property, or by changes in any institutions.

b. Society-wide Planning and the Withering Away of the State

These difficulties become multiplied if there is to be a "single vast plan" governing the world's industry, replacing all the allocations now made spontaneously through the market. Even to draw up such a plan to be voted on would require so many arbitrary options—arbitrary from a democratic point of view—that it would be difficult to be sure that the plan adopted actually was the most widely preferred of all possible plans. (Indeed, it's hard to say what 'most widely preferred' actually means, without an element of the arbitrary. Even supposing that the countless billions of possible plans could all be voted upon, there is no reason to suppose that the plan which gets the most votes is 'most widely preferred' in any interesting sense—for a number of well-known reasons, perhaps the simplest being that a vote doesn't register the intensity of preference.)

It is unhelpful to suggest that matters be sorted out by "those concerned". Almost everyone is concerned to some extent with most things, and precisely those who feel themselves to be most acutely concerned are those who will most violently disagree. And if no one has to pay for anything, and all votes are equally cheap, people will be encouraged to vote, on issues where a very small cost would have been enough to stop them voting, to over-ride the votes of others, where those others would have paid a high price to get their way. Once adopted, a plan might be strenuously opposed by a small minority. If the plan calls for flooding an area where some people dwell, they might not like the choice between leaving their homes and being drowned. Since under any selected plan there would be thousands of groups in analogous positions, these groups would form coalitions, and seek out potential new groups, with the offer: 'If you support us on this issue, we will support you on that.'

Since the world industrial plan would have to be articulated by a single sovereign body, and since it is hardly likely that this body could do without a specialized administrative staff, Marxian communism could not avoid retaining a state, whether defined as a unified, coercive administration or as "a special public power separated from the body of the people" (Engels 1942, 85). Nothing could be further from the aspirations of Marx and Engels than an oppressive state or a meddlesome bureaucracy, but their commitment to society-wide comprehensive industrial planning requires that the communist administration be an omnipotent state. This is not apparent to Marx because of his unawareness of the problem of economic calculation. Marx sees the communist administration as a federation of self-governing groups, largely concerned with their internal affairs, and collaborating for the comparatively few purposes that concern all the groups. Such an organizational form can be made to seem compatible with the Marxian insistence on 'planned production for use' by assuming that the task of planning is child's play, and this in turn must require the assumption that most allocative decisions are obvious and undebatable.

ii. KROPOTKIN'S ANARCHOCOMMUNISM

In Kropotkin's proposed system of anarchocommunism, as in Marxian communism, groups of producers govern themselves and federate for occasional common purposes. In some ways, Kropotkin's utopia looks quite similar to Marx's, and Kropotkin's attacks on Marx often relate to views held by Marx's followers rather than Marx himself, and to questions of the revolution rather than the ultimate social order aimed at. But in Kropotkin's scheme, unlike Marx's, there is no overall plan determining the whole of society's production.

Kropotkin cites numerous contemporary examples to demonstrate that central direction is unnecessary even for major undertakings: the European railway system, the Dutch canals, the English Lifeboat Association, the Red Cross, and even the German societies for propagating military knowledge (Kropotkin 1907, Chapter 11). (A communist anarchist who, because of his horror of German militarism, ended up giving full support to the Allies in the First World War here argues that German military excellence is due to private rather than state initiative.) Sizeable slices of Kropotkin's writings could be taken for the arguments of a *laissez faire* liberal. Yet Kropotkin is a communist, insisting on the total abolition of the market and denouncing even the suggestion that workers be paid in labor-vouchers—for Kropotkin merely a survival of detestable wage-slavery.

All Kropotkin's examples of inter-group co-operation, like the European railways, are made possible by a clear system of property rights. Kropotkin takes this background of private property so much for granted that he does not consider its importance for the kinds of inter-group federation he describes. Many different companies worked together to construct the European railway network, but at least they were each fairly sure where railroads could be built; they bought the land or bought the right to put rails across someone else's land. In Kropotkin's utopia, construction of a railroad would require co-operation among many local communities. There would be disputes over the use of land, and the resolution of these disputes could be facilitated in two ways: some higher authority could be established, perhaps a committee elected by numerous communities, or clear lines of land ownership could be drawn between the territories of neighbouring communities. The first would require giving the authority compulsory powers against the communities. The second would permit the emergence of a market among communities.

Kropotkin's proposed system dispenses with the market, but does not replace it with society-wide planning. Because Marxists favor society-wide planning, much of the debate about economic calculation has focussed on problems which would confront the planners. But Mises's argument is not fundamentally directed at society-wide planning; it is directed at the proposal to abolish buying and selling of factors of production. The Mises argument therefore applies just as much to Kropotkinism as to Marxism.

a. Anarchocommunism Implies Local Autarky and Low Output

In the market, world production is integrated; all its parts are interdependent. The making of any simple object such as a light bulb or a watch involves the co-operation of millions of people, many of them separated by thousands of miles. Marxists are aware of this worldwide integration, acknowledge that it is bound up with high output, and propose to retain it, substituting conscious direction for commercial anarchy as the ordering process. True anarchist communism like that of Kropotkin proposes instead to abandon worldwide integration of production by making every locality self-sufficient. Kropotkin is chiefly renowned for his advocacy of combining farming with factory work, eliminating the geographical division into manufacturing and farming regions. But the logic of his position goes much further, to remove all specialization by region, so that each locality is self-sufficient in everything, or nearly everything (Kropotkin 1968, 22–23, 74–78; 1907, 205). Kropotkin apparently does allow some small inter-regional movements of goods, but gives no attention to how this "exchange" might be regulated without trade or prices.

It is not clear whether Kropotkin has noticed that his opposition to regional specialization follows inescapably from his opposition to both the market and society-wide planning. More likely, he arrived at these positions independently. But whether or not one accepts the Misesian claim that only the market can integrate world production, it is clear that anarchocommunism cannot do so. At least, no anarchocommunist has proposed a way by which this might be accomplished. So local self-sufficiency is not a matter of taste, but an unavoidable attribute of anarchocommunism.

Kropotkin misrepresents Ricardo's law of comparative advantage, which shows how regional specialization leads to greater total output.[2] According to Kropotkin, economists hold that "Hungary and Russia are predestined by nature to grow corn in order to feed the manufacturing countries; that Britain had to provide the world-market with cottons, iron goods and coal; Belgium with woollen cloth . . . . so it ought to remain" (1968, 20). He presents statistics showing (in 1898) the rapid industrialization of Germany, Russia, India, and Japan, and correctly predicts that this will continue until every country has a substantial involvement in manufacturing. But this in no way challenges the Ricardians, as Kropotkin imagines. They merely point out that specialization and trade are mutually beneficial wherever there are comparative advantages (which is to say, practically always). Ricardians don't deny that the pattern of specialization and the course of trade may evolve.

Kropotkin believes he can discern a trend away from "division" towards "integration". Like Marx and others who observe the development of industry with too rigid preconceptions, Kropotkin is so ready to see what he wants to see that, even in making his case, he presents facts which call it into question. He is so keen to demonstrate that the newly industrializing countries are overtaking Britain that he draws attention to the "constantly increasing quantities of machinery" being sent to "old Europe" from the U.S. (29), failing to remark that this shows trade between countries increasing even as the less industrialized countries become more industrialized, in flat contradiction to his argument. Kropotkin argues that if the quantity of Russian manufacturing output were to treble, Russia wouldn't cease to be predominantly agricultural, but "there will be no room for imported manufactured goods, because an agricultural country can produce them cheaper than those countries which live on imported food" (42). His conclusion is that once the trebling has occurred, Russia will no longer import manufactures.

"Manufacturing" is a general term encompassing thousands of different specialized activities and products. As Russian manufacturing increases, we would expect Russian manufacturers to specialize in those kinds of manufactures which it was least advantageous to import from England, and English manufactures to specialize in some of the remaining kinds of manufactures. Kropotkin also seems to overlook the fact that growth of industry is not a matter of shuffling factories from one country to another. With industrialization, the populations of both England and Russia produce more. They buy more manufactured products—both more of the same kinds of products and new kinds of products. So even if Russia's trebling manufacturing did replace exactly what was formerly imported, Russia would import new kinds of manufactured goods. But it is more to be expected that Russian manufacturers would find it cheapest to import some of the components they needed—manufactured inputs to further manufacture. Thus, we should not be surprised if growth of manufacturing in predominantly agricultural country increased foreign trade, and this is what we observe historically. As is well known, the developed or industrial countries now do most of their foreign trade with each other, rather than with the less developed countries. And today, for example, the U.S. is the world's largest producer of manufactured goods, yet is simultaneously a major importer of manufactured products and exporter of crops.

Even if Russian foreign trade ceased, there would still be considerable inter-regional trade within Russia. A century after Kropotkin wrote, large areas of Russia are still heavily agricultural. Looked at superficially, statistics on international trade are always misleading, since political boundaries are arbitrary from the standpoint of industrial efficiency. Russian 'self-sufficiency' would not guarantee the self-sufficiency of Khabarovsk, and the latter is a necessary condition for anarchocommunism throughout Russia.

Even when manufacturing capacity has been scattered across the Earth's surface fairly evenly in relation to population, large movements of goods from one region to another will persist and even increase. Deposits of minerals and climatic conditions vary, but there is more to it than that. Although economists have not contended that certain countries were "predestined by nature" to produce certain goods, they have frequently maintained that the division of labor arises because of differences in resources. This position is often still repeated as though it were self-evident (Mises 1966, 158). Yet it is mistaken. Let's consider this on the interpersonal and inter-regional levels in turn.

Suppose that a group of persons is confronted with a task requiring their co-operation, let us say, to move a horse-drawn wagon which has become stuck in the mud. Then, two persons may push from behind, one may try to move each wheel, and one may encourage the horse. This is a case of division of labor. It is very likely that the individuals will vary in their suitability for each of these tasks, but the division of labor does *not arise* from differences in individual capacity. If the seven individuals are genetic clones with identical training, it still makes sense for them to station themselves at different points in relation to the wagon. Or consider the pin factory cited by Smith. Although much of the gain in productivity arises from the eighteen different workers becoming well-practiced in their specialties, some of the gain arises independently of this. Even with 18 identical workers, or with workers so bored by continual specialization that they offered wage reductions in exchange for a system of rotation where each worker moved through all 18 operations over 18 successive working days, division of labor would still be more productive in pins per worker-hour than a system where isolated workers each made entire pins.

If we now turn to specialization among geographical regions (or 'nations') we reach the same conclusion. Suppose that natural resources were distributed perfectly evenly over the Earth's inhabited area, that all individuals in the world were identical in abilities, and that climate were the same everywhere. Regional division of labor would still arise. Perhaps the clearest way to see this is to consider that there may be certain kinds of factories where the entire world market provides sufficient demand for just one such factory. That factory must be located somewhere, though it would, initially, be a matter of indifference where. But once it is built and running, the region where it is located now specializes in that product. The same principle applies, of course, to kinds of factories where the world demand is sufficient for more than one, but for a number less than the number of 'regions' in which we are interested. Suppose we divide the world into 100 regions, and consider a kind of factory of which the world requires only 90. Then, although the 90 factories *may* go to 90 different regions, there is still regional specialization. The ten remaining regions will 'import' that product from the rest of the world, and will therefore specialize in some other product which the rest of the world will import from them. Thus, regional specialization may be beneficial even where its specific causes are fortuitous.

Regional division of labor doesn't depend upon differences in regional endowments of resources, though these obviously stimulate it. In the case we have just looked at, specialization would arise unrelated to prior resource differences, but this specialization would create resource differences, notably local skills and local installations of durable capital. In this case, division of labor would create local peculiarities in resource endowments, which would then further stimulate specialization.

Writing at the end of the nineteenth century, Kropotkin is right to expect the sharp division of the world into masses of backward peasants and a little European enclave of manufacturers to be overcome by the growth of manufacturing everywhere. Perhaps he is somewhat optimistic about this, failing to foresee that the growth of Bolshevism and other 'development planning' ideas would hold back so many poor countries in their pre-industrial poverty. No doubt Kropotkin was irritated by such conventional pieties of the day as that "German produce can *never* equal the English!" (1968, 20). But Kropotkin was wrong to attribute such views to Ricardian theory. He is further mistaken in thinking that this development will reduce the amount of inter-regional specialization and exchange. And he is therefore mistaken in believing that we are approaching a point where a move to local autarky would not necessitate a violent reduction in living standards. Imposing autarky even upon very large countries like Russia or China would be more devastating today than it would have been a century ago. But Kropotkin's system calls for autarky on a much smaller scale, therefore with greater devastation, though he envisages people living at something better than the income levels of nineteenth-century factory workers, while performing considerably fewer hours of work. It would be a very cautious estimate to say that the introduction of village autarky today would quickly kill 95 percent of the world's population. An obvious conclusion from all this is that anarchy, whether or not it is compatible with a private property and market system, is not simultaneously compatible with communism and affluence.

— 14 —

PROSPECTS FOR WORKERS'
SELF-MANAGEMENT

Co-operative factories furnish proof that the capitalist has become no
less redundant as a functionary in production as he himself, looking
down from his high perch, finds the big landowner redundant. (Capital
III, 387)

i. THE SELF-MANAGEMENT IDEA

The proposal that all the workers in a workplace should be in charge
of the management of that workplace has appeared in various forms
throughout the history of socialism. Its implementation has frequently been attempted, and has occasionally succeeded, at least in
the sense that firms managed in some such way have sometimes
flourished for several decades. Among the labels attached to this
form of organization are 'self-management', 'labor management',
'workers' control', 'worker control', 'industrial democracy', and
'producers' co-operatives'. 'Self-management' is now the most popular term. Each of these terms would be misleading if taken literally.
For the sake of brevity, I'll refer to self-managed firms as 'co-ops' and
non-self-managed firms as 'conventional firms', though both categories encompass a great range of possible forms, and some actual
enterprises might be hard to categorize.

The self-management idea has many variants. All the workers may
manage together directly, by means of an assembly, or indirectly, by
electing a supervisory board. They may manage in co-operation with
a group of specialized managers, or they may try to do without them.
They may manage in detail, or they may only set general policy, or in
the weakest versions, they may merely be consulted to vote on major
decisions. The workers may own outright the assets of the enterprise
or they may not. Advocates of self-management may favor commu-

nism, or some form of NFM or FM socialism, or they may envisage a substantially free market.

Modest or partial self-management schemes receive much lip-service in the political mainstream, under the labels 'participation', 'co-partnership', or 'codetermination' (see Thimm 1980). The notion of 'worker participation in management' or 'worker representation on the board' is despised as too little by many self-management advocates, though some of the arguments for it are similar to those for full self-management. Support for self-management arises from diverse motives: among some politicians it is considered a useful means of 'overcoming industrial confrontation' by 'giving workers a stake in the enterprise'; some socialists view it as the essence of 'market socialism'; other socialists see it as a way of exacerbating class confrontation and ultimately demolishing the market system.

Self-management has had a following among socialists since the early nineteenth century. Marx praises and welcomes the existing worker co-operatives of his day (Capital III, 387–88, 440). In his view they show that the capitalist is unnecessary, but the co-operatives suffer from limitations because they relate to each other and to the surrounding world via the market. They thus reproduce "all the shortcomings of the prevailing system" (Capital III, 440). Marx doesn't see any *intrinsic* value in substituting a collective capitalist for an individual one. The value of the co-ops is that they demonstrate the redundancy of the capitalist and thus prepare the way for communism. Marx sometimes cites the co-ops and the centralization of capital as two developments which together constitute the transition to communism, but he actually accords far more importance to centralization. Though Marx probably sees workplaces under communism as being operated in a democratic fashion, he never addresses the question of possible clashes between the democracy of the workplace and the democracy of the whole of society.

a. Self-Management in Yugoslavia

Yugoslavia came under Communist Party rule at the end of the Second World War, and rapidly adopted all the trappings of Leninist dictatorship and 'planning'. But in 1948–49 Yugoslavia ceased to belong to the Soviet bloc, for reasons which did not include any fundamental disagreements about the nature of the socialist system (Lydall 1984, 59–64). The Soviet Union failed to invade, and the

Yugoslavian Communists were free to develop their own variant of Marxism-Leninism (Johnson 1972). Industry remained nationalized, but the planning system was relaxed, and more authority given to local authorities. Enterprises became more autonomous, and subject to competition in product markets. Management by workers' collectives was introduced in 1950 and strengthened by further laws throughout the 1950s. It seems (Lydall 1984, 69–73) that the unsophisticated Yugoslav leaders decided upon the principle of self-management without noticing that it means greater freedom for the market (since it strengthens local workplace autonomy as against central directives). Yugoslav firms were allowed some freedom in the use of their assets, but ultimate ownership lay with the state, and the firm was obliged to maintain the book value of its assets. Central state allocation of capital to firms, on the Soviet model, was replaced with state control of bank credit to firms. Buying and selling among firms was encouraged. Each firm had an individual director, who was hired and fired by the collective, but also had obligations to the state.

The system prevailed until the 1990s. Yugoslav self-management was compulsory: it was imposed on the workforce by the government, and no other managerial form was permitted. It was illegal to advocate any alternative system of management. According to official descriptions, the assets of nationalized firms (the great majority) are owned by 'society' (the state) and managed by the workers in each firm. The workers control both by directly voting in workplace assemblies and by voting for the director of the firm. In practice, the powers of the workers' assemblies were limited by the one-party state, which made sure that the party-nominated candidate was always elected director.

At first the new system was widely hailed as an alternative to capitalism and Soviet-style socialism, but after some years unemployment grew and output flagged. Before the opening of hostilities among the nationalities of Yugoslavia, leading to the breakup of the federation amid great loss of life, the self-management system had already come to be seen as a disappointment.

b. The Mondragón Phenomenon

Mondragón is an industrial town in the Basque country of northern Spain, where, in 1943, Don José María Arizmendi-Arietta, a local priest imbued with 'co-operative' ideals, opened a technical training school. In the 1950s five of his former students, under his guidance, started a new factory, run as a workers' co-op, to make paraffin stoves. Other co-operatives sprang up in the region, and the co-ops then formed their own bank. The Mondragón co-ops are purely free-market institutions which have demonstrated their capacity to succeed and to expand rapidly in competition with conventional firms. By 1988 the system comprised 166 co-ops, with 21,000 workers, and combined sales of $1.6 billion (Morrison 1991, 8), and it continues to expand quite lustily. Most of the co-ops are in manufacturing, with a few in retail trade, housing, and agriculture.

The organization of the Mondragón co-ops has evolved and continues to do so. The co-ops are independent business units, but the internal organization of each associated co-op has to conform with a common set of rules, which is revised from time to time. (If it doesn't conform, then a firm can't associate with the other co-ops and with the C.L.P., the co-operative bank.) Ultimate authority rests with all the workers, who vote for a board which then appoints the managers. The Mondragón workers do not actually manage—they have come to believe that specialized managers are indispensable. 'Self-management' at Mondragón means that the workers appoint the board, and a 'watchdog council'; the members of both of these bodies are members of the co-op. A general assembly of the whole membership is held once a year, and may also be called under extraordinary circumstances; it has considerable but not unlimited powers. Initially, there was a strong egalitarian flavor to the Mondragón movement, and a rule of association fixed the maximum ratio of the highest pre-tax wage to the lowest at 3. After considerable debate, this has since been raised to 6. In conventional European enterprises the ratio is commonly around 10. Viewed in the Basque economy as a whole, co-ops have something of an elite quality, and don't include the lowest-paid, so the present range of pay may already be close to what would prevail in the absence of the co-op form and the 6:1 rule.

A co-op is allowed to hire some workers who are not members, but the rules of association restrict these workers to a small percentage of the membership.[1] With this exception, members, workers, employees, and voters are the same people. To be taken on as a member, a worker has to pay the co-op an 'entry fee' (it has been periodically increased and is now around $10,000), most of which is usually loaned to the new member by the co-op; that's to say, a deduction is made from his pay for several years after he joins. Most of a member's contributions go into his 'individual capital account', which may not be withdrawn except upon retirement or dismissal. Interest is paid to the members on their individual capital accounts, the rate being fixed by a general assembly each year. Part of this interest, up to a maximum of 6 percent, may be cashed by the member; the rest stays in his account. Part of any net surplus may also go into individual accounts. Further voluntary contributions may be added, and if the co-op makes losses, capital contributions may be required from members, in the form of withholding from their wages and interest.

All the co-ops are associated with a co-operative bank, which channels the deposits of the co-ops into the most auspicious investments within the co-operative system. In this way, co-ops may be able to invest some of their members' savings outside the immediate workplace.[2]

Since the co-ops have grown rapidly by recruiting young workers, they are only now approaching the point where large sums will be withdrawn by members as retirement pay; we can therefore expect to see further important adjustments in the rules and financial operations of the Mondragón co-ops by the turn of the century. The next 20 years will be a crucial phase, because research into co-ops which have done comparatively well in the past has found that they most often sold out and ceased to be co-ops upon the retirement of their leading members. Mondragón is an outstanding success for self-management—perhaps *the* outstanding success. It has incorporated more features of conventional business practice than many self-management enthusiasts would like, and will no doubt continue to adapt.

This brief look at the two most celebrated examples of self-management brings out an important fact. A widely-shared vision of self-management is one of all the workers actively engaged in managing their own activities from day to day, with specialized managers reduced to being consultants or facilitators. But in real-life examples involving sizeable enterprises able to survive for more than a few years, reality doesn't correspond to any such vision. There is a specialized management, and managers manage in much the same way that they do in conventional firms—though there are some differences. Both in Yugoslavia and in Mondragón, although some workers use the system to pursue an active involvement in management, a high proportion are little more involved than they would be in a conventional firm. Self-management enthusiasts may dismiss these examples as not being true self-management, but in that case these enthusiasts cannot truthfully claim that there is practical evidence that 'true' self-management works. Self-management is sometimes counterposed to 'hierarchy', but it seems that self-management which survives incorporates hierarchy: self-management takes the form of an all-workforce, last-resort authority over the hierarchy, rather than any attempt to dissolve hierarchy. It would be wrong, however, to conclude that in Yugoslavia, Mondragón, and other enduring instances, self-management is merely cosmetic and makes no difference, just as it would be wrong to suppose that political democracy makes no difference because important elections occur infrequently. The crucial difference between a Mondragón co-op and a U.S. firm with an ESOP (employee stock ownership plan) is that, with marginal exceptions, Mondragón workers and 'stock owners' must be the same individuals, all of whom have an equal vote in electing the board, as well as being able to vote on critical decisions in general assembly.

ii. THE EFFICIENCY OF SELF-MANAGEMENT

a. Work-Satisfaction and End-Products

In response to the suggestion that workers should democratically manage their own workplaces, the obvious retort is: 'Why don't they?' The co-op is not the predominant organizational form in modern industry. If it were, then most discussion of self-management would be redundant. Anyone interested in self-management should give some thought to the possibility that conventional firms predominate over co-ops because the former are more efficient.

Some proponents of self-management reply that 'efficiency' is not the only relevant criterion. We must also take into account the fulfillment the worker derives from his work or the emotional pain that the worker suffers in a conventional firm. According to this line of thinking, it doesn't matter too much whether self-management is efficient, because efficiency should be over-ridden in some cases. This, however, reflects a misunderstanding about the economic notion of efficiency. The satisfaction the worker gets from his work, or from the social structure of the workplace, is included in the estimation of efficiency, and no economist would ever ignore it (except deliberately and temporarily as part of a specially simplified model).

The utility the worker derives from the quality or organization of his work I will, for the sake of brevity, call 'work-satisfaction', and I will refer to such utility as 'internal'. The utility gained by consumers of the worker's end-product[3] I will call 'external' utility. The term 'external' here has to be understood in a special sense. If a worker makes TV sets, the TV sets contribute to the utility of the people who will watch them. Making TV sets uses various resources (land, metal, plastic, labor, energy, and so forth) and thus reduces the output of other goods, and hence, reduces the total utility derived from goods other than TV sets. This reduction in utility from other goods is the cost of making the TV sets. Efficiency consists in maximizing the utility of consumers. Production of TV sets reduces, among many other things, production of medical services (if production of TV sets were curtailed, there would be more resources to spare for production of medical services, which could be expanded). Efficiency exists when it is not possible to move resources from production of TV sets to production of medical services, or *vice versa,* and thereby increase utility. For this to be the case, production of TV sets must occur at 'least cost' in terms of lost production of medical services, and *vice versa.*

A worker takes part in the production of TV sets. The external consumers are the consumers of those TV sets and of other products, such as medical services. The worker producing TV sets may himself be a consumer of TV sets. He may go into a store and buy one of the TV sets he has had a hand in producing, and may therefore, purely on that account, be interested in the quality and price of the TV sets he helps to produce. Normally this effect is negligible. However, by my terminology here, that worker, when buying a TV set, would be an 'external consumer'. In exchange for his part in producing TV sets, the worker receives a sum of money, a wage.

The worker also, of course, has certain feelings about his work. Some economists used to discuss this topic under the heading 'disutility of labor', but this label is best avoided, since nothing in economic theory requires that workers dislike their work. As a matter of fact, some workers heartily despise their work, while some derive much gratification from it. But whether the worker likes or dislikes his work—or has feelings about it too complex to be captured in either of these phrases—he will generally not be indifferent to the way the work is organized. A change in the way the work is organized may increase or decrease his utility. To take some simple examples: a supervisor may issue brusque commands or polite requests; there may be rules, like not smoking on the job, or these rules may be absent; working hours may be rigidly fixed, with pay deducted for even a few minutes' lateness, or they may be flexible, with freedom to make time up whenever this is convenient to the worker.

Let us consider a proposed change which the worker would prefer. We may call this an increase in work-satisfaction; more loosely, the worker will enjoy the work more. There are three scenarios: 1. This change may increase the utility of external consumers. 2. The change may not affect the utility of external consumers. 3. The change may reduce the utility of external consumers.

Scenario 1 means that more or better TV sets are produced, or costs (to external consumers) are reduced, or both. In addition, the worker gets more work-satisfaction; internal utility is increased. The change would be profitable for the firm quite apart from the worker's gain in work-satisfaction. If the firm is maximizing profits, we would expect the firm to introduce this change, assuming that the possibility of the change were noticed and its effects judged correctly. (In reality, many such opportunities for increasing profits are missed, as are other kinds of profit-increasing opportunities. But still, on the face of it we can expect a systematic tendency for such changes to be implemented. I discuss below the possibility that firms might be biassed against a change even if it were profitable.)

In Scenario 2, the firm can implement a change which would increase the worker's work-satisfaction, without affecting the utility of external consumers. That is to say, the firm has the option of implementing a change which will not increase or decrease output of TV sets with given resources, but will improve the worker's satisfaction from his work. Does the firm have any inducement to introduce this change, 'just because it pleases the worker'? The correct answer is 'Yes'. The firm has an incentive to introduce a change which gives the worker more work-satisfaction but otherwise leaves the firm's output and costs unchanged, because this additional work-satisfaction amounts to an increase in the worker's non-monetary wage, an increase which (by our supposition) costs the firm nothing. The firm will therefore be able to pay lower money wages and still retain the worker's services, or, alternatively, will be able to reap benefits equivalent to those it could have reaped by paying higher money wages, without actually paying them. These benefits might include a choice of higher-quality workers, lower labor turnover, quicker replacement of workers who leave, and greater diligence by workers because retention of their jobs is now worth more to them. (Scenario 2 embraces two scenarios: the re-organization of work may have *no* effect on output for external consumers, or it may have two effects which just counterbalance one another: reducing output in one way while increasing it in another way—say, by causing the worker to be more enthusiastic and hence more diligent. In either case we assume that there is no net effect on external output, while the worker likes the job more.)

If a worker likes something about a job (speaking comparatively), he views that something as worth a sum of money to him. He is therefore prepared to give up money for it. This could actually be done by workers paying employers to organize the work in a way which the workers preferred, but it will nearly always be easier for the employers simply to pay a lower money wage. Either way, the worker is saying: 'I am prepared to sacrifice some income in the form of food, clothing, shelter, and other goods purchasable out of money wages, for the sake of additional income in the form of work-satisfaction'. Alternatively, workers can become their own employers, either singly or in groups, and accept less money income for the sake of increased work-satisfaction.

A worker does a job not merely for the money wage, but for the whole package of benefits associated with working at that job—and 'benefits' may be judged to be such purely by comparison with other jobs.[4] Out of all the jobs a worker might take, he frequently does not pick the one with the highest money wage, or even the highest money wage after adjustment for travelling time and other job-associated 'expenses'. Probably very few workers are actually in that job which, of all the jobs available to them, pays the most money. (It doesn't matter whether we classify the non-monetary benefits of a job as 'wages' in non-monetary form or as 'non-wage benefits').

It is always to the advantage of the firm to introduce any measure which makes the job more attractive to the worker, if the introduction of this measure costs the firm nothing. But cost, for instance, includes increases in administrative outlays due to reduction of predictability. In other words, there are cost savings in having a standard procedure and sticking to it 'insensitively'. These are real resource costs. We all enjoy more of the good things of life because supervisors are less sensitive to their subordinates' feelings than they might be.

Those categories of jobs which yield workers comparatively high non-monetary benefits will be paid less money; workers in particularly disliked jobs will be paid more for them.[5] People sometimes complain that employers are 'taking advantage' of workers because the workers have non-monetary motives for picking those jobs. In the U.K., nursing is reputedly paid less than other jobs with similar skill requirements, because many people who might be secretaries prefer to be nurses. Assuming this popular belief to be true, it is the consumers who ultimately 'take advantage of nurses'. Hospital care is cheaper and more of it is made available because nurses' services are cheaper. When the money wage in any occupation falls, this causes an increase in the number of people employed in that occupation. More people are employed in nursing, and fewer people in other occupations, because many people find nursing attractive for non-monetary reasons. This is efficient: where people are willing to buy more work-satisfaction, the quantity of work-satisfaction supplied will be increased.

Just as the purchaser of bananas with money can equally well be described as 'selling' his money for bananas, so the worker can be described as 'paying' labor services in order to buy a bundle of job-benefits, including a sum of money, but not confined to the money. Frequently, of course, workers have manifested a much higher relative preference for hard cash than they ought to have done, in the judgements of wealthier and more leisured observers, just as those same workers have, alas, persisted in preferring football to ballet. But it is difficult to find any firm argument for the view that workers are habitually at fault in this way. Take a single man who chooses a job which gives him a lot of work-satisfaction. He then gets married and switches to a job with less work-satisfaction and more money. His family are better off (they consume more goods purchasable with money). Society as a whole, outside himself and his family, is better off (the worker is producing more for external consumers, as indicated by his higher money wages). The worker himself is better off, by his own reckoning (he prefers the better life for his family to the better work-satisfaction in the old job). It's not obvious that the worker has made a morally or esthetically mistaken choice.

Before we proceed to Scenario 3, we need to be clear that this scenario cannot be dismissed out of hand. Some readers, for instance, may think that the firm ought always to introduce such a change, because this will cause the worker to be more productive. It may be supposed that if workers are happier they will produce more. Let's accept here that the effect of workers' being happier is to cause them to produce more. (In fact, there is absolutely no evidence for this. See Scott 1992, 61.) Still, a change that makes workers happier may have other effects that cause them to produce less. It is possible that a change may make the worker happier and more productive, but may more than cancel out this improvement by raising costs in other ways. If the increase in output due to increased enjoyment of work outweighs any decrease due to other effects of the same organizational change, then we have Scenario 1. If the increase is exactly compensated by the decrease, we have Scenario 2. We have seen that in both these cases, a profit-seeking firm which correctly appraises the situation will institute the change. The argument still holds if, for 'being happier at work', we substitute 'being less alienated', 'being empowered', or any similar description.

We now turn to the remaining possibility, Scenario 3. Here a change in work organization is better for the worker's work-satisfaction but worse, on balance, for the external consumer. The worker feels better at work, but his output for external consumers is reduced. It will therefore be less profitable for the firm, if the worker continues to be paid the same wage. Costs will be higher or output will be lower. The question to be decided now is: 'Does the increased work-satisfaction fully make up for the decreased satisfaction to external consumers?' This question can be answered by establishing whether the worker is prepared to take a lower money wage (or to give up some other element of the employment contract) sufficient to restore profitability.

There is sometimes discussion (Miller 1989, 326) of whether workers actually 'want' more 'say' in management. Though such enquiries may be useful, we should beware of an artificial issue, analogous to: 'Do workers want a free supply of peppermint-flavored beer?'. If they have to pay the cost of beer, people do want non-peppermint-flavored beer and do *not* want peppermint-flavored beer. The question whether workers want more say presumably means whether they would want more say if they didn't have to pay for it. If the answer to this question be 'Yes', it would merely invite the further question whether workers were prepared to pay enough for that 'say' to cover the cost. If and to the extent that some change in the organization of work is unprofitable, because it reduces the utility of external consumers, are workers prepared to take a suffi-ciently large pay cut to restore profitability? If they are, then profit-maximizing firms will offer their employees a new combina-tion of benefits, comprising less money and more congenial work-organization.

The fact that co-ops don't predominate suggests that the loss in utility to external consumers, which would arise from self-management, is not fully compensated by the concomitant gain in work-satisfaction. Supposing this account to be correct, self-management would be inefficient in the fullest sense: it would not be conducive to human welfare, defined to include work-satisfaction. If self-management were efficient in the fullest sense, we would expect to see it more widely implemented.

In thinking about this possibility, we have to remember that it is not a verdict for all times and places. Workers vary in their preferences, and maybe some of them urgently desire self-management while others don't. Furthermore, aside from self-management, the precise organizational structure of firms has varied historically and varies now from industry to industry. Perhaps self-management is less injurious to external consumers in some industries than in others. The conjunction of unusual workers, who urgently want self-management, and unusual industries, where self-management hurts production for external consumers less, may help to explain the spotty success of a few self-managed firms (where this cannot be explained more readily by tax concessions and other privileges coercively extracted from the rest of society).

The self-management movement is essentially a campaign for a change of tastes by workers, a recommendation of a different lifestyle, like the recommendation that we should read more books and watch less TV, or that we should become vegetarians or nudists. A mass change in workers' preferences, like the recent change to a higher-fiber diet, might occur with respect to self-management. A possible reason for expecting this is that as the real value of workers' money incomes rises, the marginal benefit to them of more real income in money form may well fall relative to the marginal benefit obtainable from greater work-satisfaction. However, there are at least three good reasons why this result may not occur, or may be negligible: 1. Changes in the organization of work other than a change in the direction of self-management may produce more work-satisfaction. 2. Changes in the organization of work which come at the expense of money income will also come at the expense of shorter working hours. People may prefer to work fewer hours than to have a more congenial organization of work. 3. Many of the benefits we might expect employees to derive from self-management may more surely be obtained by ceasing to be an employee and becoming self-employed.

Under present circumstances money wages are heavily taxed whereas work-satisfaction is less heavily taxed or not taxed at all. Thus, the existing structure of government intervention artificially stimulates the provision of rewards to the worker in non-monetary form. In this way the government is already inadvertently increasing the weight that workers attribute to work-satisfaction by comparison with money. This is *prima facie* inefficient, a reduction in workers' welfare.

I have been assuming that workers desire job-satisfaction and that job-satisfaction might be enhanced by self-management. Similar arguments apply to other features of the organization of production. For example, it is often held (Nove 1984) that there is something unpleasant about working for large, alienating organizations and that the government ought to do something to reduce the size of big corporations. However, the fact that large, alienating organizations exist suggests that, if employees dislike working for large, alienating organizations, they don't do so sufficiently to outweigh the increased production for external consumers made possible by large, alienating organizations. In that case, workers have chosen more of the things which money can buy rather than a smaller, cozier scale of organization. Further, smaller-sized enterprises and self-management are themselves substitutes: at a given money wage, one can have more self-management *or* a smaller-sized organization.

I have neglected the possibility that, whether or not self-management reduces output for external consumers, self-management reduces work-satisfaction. The details would depend on precisely what variety of self-management were considered, but there are clear reasons why many workers may not like self-management. In the case of a non-hierarchical system, the worker may prefer to be fired or awarded a raise by a single individual than by a vote of all his fellow-employees, who first debate his merits at length. Some workers may have a distaste for meetings, arguments, reading financial statements, and voting. They may prefer to get on with their specialized jobs and let others do the managing. (It often puzzles 'born activists' and people in the articulate professions that many individuals find participation in group decision-making a dull chore at best. One sometimes hears the theory that 'apathy' springs from 'powerlessness' or 'alienation'. However, this begs the question: my apathy about the details of chrysanthemum cultivation can't convincingly be explained by my powerlessness in the matter, nor by my alienation, unless the absence of alienation is absolute non-specialization. Furthermore, in a firm of 100 individuals, all of them equally active in group decision-making, the tangible 'power' to influence decisions experienced by one member of the firm would be close to zero. It is only when 90 or so members are apathetic that the remaining 10 or less personally have much in the way of perceptible 'power'.)

b. Workers as Consumers: The Choice of Institutions

Before proceeding, we should consider the objection that workers don't in fact choose the institutional structure of the firms that employ them. Most workers certainly don't give much thought to the self-management option, and many workers may evince little interest in the structure of the firm where they work.

If, however, we view workers as consumers, shopping around for the best job package, we see that their situation is similar to that of consumers in other fields. McDonald's offers a standard package of fast food, with a limited range of choice. The individual customer who enters the store and demands a radically different package will be disappointed. Yet McDonald's has to keep alert to changes in consumers' preferences—like the recent fashion for avoiding red meat in favor of salads. It is open to anybody to start a new fast food outlet, offering an alternative standard package, and it is also open to anybody to offer more choice—a less standardized package. Therefore, although McDonald's establishes a standard package, and the individual McDonald's customer can do little more than take it or leave it, millions of consumers actually determine what that standard package will be, and how important it will be as an element in the population's aggregate diet. If McDonald's did not pick a standard package which was popular, McDonald's would no longer be there.

Furthermore this entire system, in which McDonald's and other fast food firms vie for consumer patronage, is itself under the control and choice of consumers. Consumers could, if they desired, abolish it and establish a different system—say a system in which all restaurants were contractors producing custom-designed meals to individually-determined specifications. The system in which producers try to estimate what people will buy, and then produce large quantities of these things, leaving customers to buy them or not, is itself a product of consumer choice. It could not survive a day or an hour longer, if consumers decided that they preferred a different system. Even today, it is not universal, and different systems prevail in different contexts—such as the system where customers order precisely what they want before it is produced, or the system where customers sign a long-term contract with producers and then accept whatever the producers send them.

The 'standard package' of employment conditions offered by many firms is analogous to the standard package of food in McDonald's. Although a given firm may have a rigid set of employment procedures, some firms offer different (but still rigid) sets of procedures, and some firms offer flexible procedures in which there is much room for choice. Sometimes an employee goes to the management and requests a special arrangement (such as being able to do work at home part of the time, or being able to arrive and depart at times different from the standard ones), and sometimes the management agrees to the request. To the extent that firms maximize profits, they will endeavor to increase the attractiveness of the job to the worker, where this can be done cheaply enough. If they can provide an increase in work-satisfaction which is worth a dollar to the worker for less than it would cost them to pay the worker another dollar, then they will be inclined to choose the former option, securing the same result more cheaply.

We should not be deterred from this conclusion by the reflection that many workers may take the basic 'job package' for granted. There is sometimes confusion about the notion of 'freedom of choice'. The fullest freedom of choice necessarily entails the freedom to make choices in a sloppy, ill-informed, 'unconscious', and prejudiced manner. There is a reduction in human welfare if individuals who wish to do that are forced to 'make fully informed choices', that is, to divert precious time and other resources from other areas of their lives in order to become virtuosi of 'rational decision-making', thus gratifying some external observer.

Here we should distinguish two points: 1. In many cases it is entirely 'rational' (wise or sensible) to employ rough-and-ready rules of thumb, to proceed (as human beings do in the great majority of their actions) 'on automatic pilot'. That is, it would be crass stupidity to try to analyze every situation exhaustively and make what some theorists call 'rational' decisions. This would be folly comparable to that of the person who spends days driving around searching for the 'best' deal on an air-conditioner, ultimately 'saving' himself $50 on the purchase price. (The fact that the language of decision-making and choice is still appropriate in cases of 'automatic pilot' is demonstrated by the possibility that new information would cause the individual to come off automatic pilot and pay attention. Thus, I don't normally pay much heed to exactly where my feet land on the sidewalk, but if I heard credibly that terrorists had mined specific areas of sidewalk I would instantly become extremely attentive to this.) 2. In some cases, reliance on 'automatic pilot' may be mistaken. An individual may trust a decision to unthinking habit or prejudice when he ought to give it some thought. This is an error, but it's still free choice. (It is also still 'rational', in the broad, Misesian sense, and in the broad sense most common in ordinary speech, though perhaps not 'rational' in some narrower, specialized sense.)

I grew up in England, where it was taken for granted that milk was delivered door-to-door, usually with several competing dairies covering the same territories. I witnessed the decline, but not disappearance, of this system, and then moved to the United States, where it was already a dim memory. This change involved many influences, presumably including the growth of employment of women outside the home, the rise of supermarkets, universal ownership of fridges, and the switch from glass to paper packaging of milk. No single individual can now summon up the home delivery services of 20 or 50 years ago, but this change in the options facing individuals results entirely from the past and current choices made by millions of individuals.

The present predominant structure of the firm, or range of structures, was not mandated by law (though law has adapted to the evolution of firm organization). Like other market outcomes, the organization of firms has resulted from individual choices. To approach this slightly differently, if firms had been invented as self-managed entities, with members free to sell their self-management rights in exchange for higher wages, we would expect the self-management aspect to have become a legal fossil, a dead letter, and the actual organization of firms to be essentially what it in fact is today. Even if firms were today compelled to adopt self-management, but with the possibility of 'buying out' of self-management rights, we would expect a rapid transition to broadly the present state of affairs. (That sentence is somewhat stronger than the previous one, which is in turn somewhat stronger than its predecessor, but I can't think of any good reason why they should not in fact stand or fall together. And we now have an experimental test of that last sentence. In many parts of Eastern Europe the formerly state-owned factories are becoming the property of the workers, and in Yugoslavia all factories were formerly controlled by the workforce. We will be able to see how long these co-ops last in competition with newly-created conventional private firms.)

c. Obstacles to Free Choice of Workplace Institutions

There is no law that forbids co-ops. People are free to form self-managed business enterprises, and they sometimes do. The fact that conventional firms overwhelmingly predominate therefore suggests the possibility that self-management is, in most circumstances, an inefficient organizational form. As we have seen, this would mean that most workers don't desire self-management sufficiently powerfully to be willing to take cuts in their money wages big enough to compensate the firm for the income it loses because of self-management's inefficiency at serving external consumers.

There are various objections that might be raised to this way of posing the question. Many self-management advocates evidently believe *both* that self-management could potentially improve efficiency at serving external consumers *and* that workers would prefer self-management if they could get it. These proponents must therefore hold that there is something that prevents the spread of institutions which would benefit both the workers employed and the consumers (through increased output). As candidates for this obstacle I will now briefly discuss: legal restrictions; opposition from capital; opposition from banks; opposition from management; opposition from labor unions; entrenched opinion.

There are legal restrictions on the forms which business enterprises may take, but these don't seem to be any worse for co-ops than similar restrictions on other kinds of enterprises. Elster (1989, 104) states that British co-ops were not allowed limited liability until 1862, and that the U.S. National Labor Relations Act can be a hindrance to co-ops. Yet there is often nowadays special legal recognition of the co-op form, with tax advantages.[6] As well as the theoretical or advocacy literature on behalf of self-management, there is a practical, 'how to do it' literature, in which we can occasionally find references to the reasons why most co-ops fail (for instance Brandow and McDonnell 1981). These writers don't mention legal restrictions as a significant cause of serious difficulties or of failure. Furthermore the occasional instances of successful co-ops show that any legal barriers are not insurmountable. And conventional firms predominate in *all* societies which have moved beyond subsistence farming, despite great variations in legal systems and in other institutions. None of this is to deny that removal of government regulation of co-ops (and of conventional firms), allowing them to be structured according to freedom of contract, would be an improvement.

Some self-management proponents see the main obstacle to the growth of co-ops in the opposition of 'capital', 'management', or 'the banks'. These notions can be interpreted in different ways. Let us begin with the theory that there is a 'capitalist class' which has a grip on all 'capital', and will not let it into the hands of co-ops. The capitalist class can be identified with people who have substantial savings on which they receive an interest return, or perhaps with the richest segment of this group, according to some arbitrary demarcation. In neither case is this a closed club. There is continual entry to and departure from the capitalist class, and its members hold the full range of different opinions. Marx and Engels were almost pure capitalists, and revolutionary groups, including the most militant, usually manage to attract into membership a number of capitalists.

Capitalists are people who want an interest return on their savings. There is no particular reason why capitalists should object to co-ops, if these concerns can pay them the prevailing rate of interest. This raises the issue of whether 'true' self-management is compatible with paying interest on savings to investors who are not members of the co-op. Let's first assume that it is. Then investors can be expected, in the main, to follow the highest returns. If co-ops can pay the same dividends as conventional firms, there seems to be no reason for capitalists to oppose them. If co-ops could pay a higher rate of return, 'capital' (saved funds) would flow from conventional firms to co-ops, and co-ops would expand relative to conventional firms, until the rates of return were equal, or until conventional firms had disappeared. If we assume that capitalists' opinions tend to change in the direction of favoring what benefits them financially, then capitalists would tend to become warm supporters of self-management.

It is sometimes claimed that banks discriminate against co-ops, but we would expect this to depend upon the anticipated likelihood that their loans would be repaid. (I sometimes ask individual self-management enthusiasts how they would feel about entrusting their life savings to a co-op formed by the self-management activists of their acquaintance. The question usually elicits an instant smirk.) Brandow and McDonnell report that "Banks are often reluctant to give loans to collectively run businesses, especially new ones" (17). They do not state that the reluctance is any greater than for other businesses, though perhaps they intend to hint at that. I know of no evidence that banks are more reluctant to lend to self-managed businesses, but if they were, this might be an appropriate rule-of-thumb, if self-managed firms were in fact more likely to default. Vanek suggests that "conventional" banks "would hardly lend much to a producer co-operative, and the co-operatives themselves might shun such funding" (Vanek 1975, 455). He gives no reason why the co-operatives might take this attitude, but if they do, that is in itself an indication of inefficient management, if such funding would be helpful. Complaints about the difficulty of obtaining bank loans are rife among conventional small businesses too.

It is difficult to imagine any reason why a bank would refuse to lend to a co-op, if co-ops were able to pay their way and were therefore good prospects to repay the loans with the agreed interest. But if existing banks were reluctant to do this, then self-management sympathizers could pool their savings and form special co-op banks. If co-ops were even of normal profitability, co-op banks would have exceptional profit opportunities, as long as they were operating in a market avoided by conventional banks. (Even without discrimination by conventional banks, lending to co-ops might require specialized knowledge which would best be supplied by a co-op bank.)

It might be considered that the existing banks form a solid front against self-management, each altruistically renouncing profits for the sake of the conventional firm. Aside from the difficulty of conjecturing why they should wish to do such a thing, and the possibility of new entrants to banking, such an arrangement would be difficult to enforce. Indubitably successful co-ops are able to get bank loans, so there is no total boycott, infraction of which would be comparatively easy to detect. We don't observe that the banks giving these loans have their premises bombed, or that their directors are black-balled from golf clubs.

Whether we are dealing with capitalists (people who save and invest) or banks (associations of people who pool other people's savings and direct them into investment), a conspiracy against co-ops seems far-fetched. As Marx said, capitalists "care not whether they market bibles or whisky", a picturesque way of acknowledging that even if most of them do care, the competitive result will be much the same as if none of them did. Why then should capitalists care whether they market conventional management or self-management?

Miller (1989, 88–90), who argues that banks are bound to discriminate against co-ops, accepts that this is a reflection of the banks' accurate evaluation of the soundness of the loans, and yet still maintains that the discrimination is a manifestation of the market's "non-neutrality", and a good reason for having the government actively discriminate in favor of co-ops. Miller accepts that it is not non-neutrality (in the relevant sense) for the market to provide beer more cheaply than champagne (and thus 'discriminate against wine-drinkers'), because this depends only on 'natural' or 'pre-institutional' factors (80–81). He claims that by contrast "the exigencies of market competition are likely to pose a stark choice between economic survival and the non-material benefits of co-operation" (83). But these are not alternatives: it's a natural, pre-institutional fact that the way a local production association is organized will affect its productivity. Miller argues that a bank can see "that the co-operators have no incentive to repay their borrow-ings; [the bank] can predict that the co-operative will either have to borrow ever-increasing sums, or else be outperformed by the compe-tition and go bankrupt" (89). Leaving aside the question of whether Miller is right to say that this must happen (and it may be too sweeping—perhaps a co-op's members could be held personally liable for its debts, for instance), the question is whether this kind of consideration, if it holds, is pre-institutional or, alternatively, is an artifact of market institutions. It's hard to see any reason why we should deny that it is pre-institutional: if an organization's members identify so little with its future that they incur obligations they cannot fulfill, this is a 'natural' fact about the deficiencies of that organizational form. If banks somehow overlooked this failing and made loans to organizations with a high failure rate, this would be a true social cost; resources would be misallocated and output would be reduced. When he outlines the institutions of "market socialism" (309–312), Miller neither introduces any mech-anism to stop the co-ops behaving in the same irresponsible way towards the state banks nor gives any reason why they wouldn't do so.

Alternatively, it might be contended that co-ops should not have to pay for the use of other people's savings. We saw in 3.ii. and 12.ii.b. that no industrial society could do without interest (or some time-discount rate). However, in this context (the context of trying to account for the predominance of conventional firms by finding an obstacle to workers' voluntary choice of organizational forms), the dispensability or undesirability of interest is not relevant. Supposing interest to be an unjustifiable imposition, it wouldn't follow that co-ops which did worse than conventional firms when both had to pay interest on capital would be able to do as well or better than conventional firms when both were freed from interest charges. A further argument would be necessary to indicate why this might be the case, and it's difficult to imagine any such argument (compare: 'Co-ops do worse than conventional firms because, like those conven-tional firms, they have to pay for stationery').

The theory that managers may tend to be opposed to self-management is more persuasive than the similar claim about capital-ists or banks. Managers might not like self-management in the same way that typesetters do not like electronic publishing: the more thoroughgoing forms of self-management appear to threaten their continued existence as an occupational group. Yet those thoroughgo-ing forms seem the least credible: most of the viable co-ops employ managers, and have had no difficulty in finding sympathetic managers.

There are obvious reasons why labor unions might be suspicious of self-management. The more closely the entire workforce becomes identified with the management, the more it can be said to 'be' the management, then the less scope there seems to be for a an organization which represents the non-management workers *against* the management (the management representing the interests of the owners of the firm's assets to the rest of the workers). If the co-op's workforce itself owns the co-op's assets, then the workforce as a whole has to see to it that its recalcitrant individual members are disciplined to act in the interests of the co-op.

Labor unions exert little influence on developments in the present-day economy. If unions keep declining at their present rate, before long they will be as insignificant as workers' co-ops. In the U.S., despite legal privileges, union membership has fallen below 15 percent of the workforce and is still falling. Many industries are scarcely affected by union activities. Even in industries where unions are strong, they can normally do no more than delay or limit major changes in technology or work organization. If self-management became a major practice with a widespread following, we might expect to see some clashes between unions and self-management enthusiasts, but unions can hardly be a major obstacle to self-management, simply because unions are so weak.

Elster (1989, 98) views seriously a suggestion by Peter Jay that a major benefit of co-ops would be to eliminate collective bargaining, but that this benefit cannot be acquired until co-ops become universal. One advantage of a co-op is that it can (in the present ideological climate) more easily request the workers to take a cut in pay. But this should constitute a direct gain in flexibility and survivability for the co-op rather than an external effect. In any case, this cannot explain the failure of co-ops in most industries, where collective bargaining is either non-existent or almost so.

Vanek argues that "those who hold economic power—the entrepreneurs, top management, and most union leadership—feel fundamentally threatened by self-management. A whole body of doctrine has been developed to defend the *status quo*. This doctrine is by no means the only instrument of defence" (Vanek 1975, 29). Yet elsewhere Vanek concedes that "hostility and prejudice" can explain "only a part, and perhaps only a small part, of the difficulties of the co-operatives" (1975, 453).

In fact, there prevails tremendous goodwill towards self-management. It's difficult to find a trace of articulate hostility except among a few Marxist sects. For example, there has been a vast outpouring of books and articles on Mondragón, overwhelmingly voicing warm approval, and the small proportion of critical material mostly fastens on the question of whether Mondragón has admitted too many elements of conventional business practice. No measures have been taken against Mondragón by the government, even under Franco, and no hostility has been shown by European business. Whenever the mainstream media devote space to co-ops, they echo the views of the dedicated self-management activists, or they commission those very activists to write the copy (an example is Oakeshott 1973). The sociological literature is overwhelmingly favorable to self-management. Only in economics is there any serious criticism, but here too the majority of writing is by committed advocates of self-management. In the early and mid-twentieth century, there was enormous support for various forms of 'co-operation' among Roman Catholic intellectuals across the world and across the political spectrum, influenced by the papal bulls *De Rerum Novarum* (1890) and *Quadragesimo Anno* (1931). It was this powerful Catholic ideology which directly led to the formation of the Mondragón co-operatives (though it is no longer the dominant intellectual force in Mondragón). 'Co-determination' is legally enforced in Germany, and is an object of admiration by politicians and journalists in other countries, much as Yugoslavian self-management used to be (though the German form is less glamorous because less radical). The general failure of self-management occurs despite a powerful prejudice in self-management's favor, a prejudice which pervades the entire culture. Most critics are not hostile in the sense of wishing to artificially discourage self-management, but merely skeptical of its benefits and apprehensive that it may be imposed by force.

In any case, arguments about 'hostility' are unconvincing because, in a modern society with a significant functioning market and civil liberties, major developments frequently occur which are opposed by popular opinion or by the opinion of 'powerful groups'. The decline in church attendance, the enormous growth of TV viewing at the expense of other family activities, the growth of supermarkets at the expense of little stores, the predominance of women employed outside the home—such trends have occurred inexorably, in the teeth of widespread dislike. This is not to say that they couldn't have been limited or reversed, but any attempt to do so could hardly have been surreptitious. There is no sign of an organized effort to block self-management, but we would expect any such effort to fail, and to fail noisily, if self-management could substantially increase work-satisfaction without a major drop in output for external consumers.

An alternative approach is to appeal to externalities and market failure. Elster (1989) advances a number of arguments, suggesting that co-ops may be in a kind of Prisoner's Dilemma: 1. Successful co-ops may be tempted to introduce departures from self-management, without realizing that they will lead to the disappearance of self-management; 2. Co-ops train their members in entrepreneurial skills; conventional firms which hire former co-op members free-ride on this entrepreneurial training; 3. Conventional firms may be favored by "endogenous preference formation", meaning that the prevalence of conventional firms influences workers to prefer conventional firms; 4. Co-ops may suffer from "adverse selection", meaning that the sort of people attracted to some institution when it is unconventional will be the sort of people who cannot make a success of it. Elster's conclusion is that we can't get the full benefits of co-ops unless they are universal or at least preponderant, so there isn't a sufficiently strong incentive for individuals to form and join co-ops, so governments ought to penalize conventional firms.

Now it's too convenient for a proponent of x to claim that we can't really get the benefits of x until x is universal, therefore we should all be forced to adopt x, and only then will each of us find that we like it. Elster claims that co-ops are required by "economic justice" but doesn't explain why. Is it really unjust for me to be free to associate with another person in a venture where I agree to follow her directions in return for money, when I can terminate this association any time I wish? Or is it really unjust for me to be free to help someone make something, on condition that she pays me an agreed sum (whether she can sell the product or not) and on condition that she bears any loss or reaps any profit from the sale of the product? Although Elster's argument is recognizably designed to be unrefutable by observations within the present-day world, it is perhaps susceptible to being rendered into testable form. Thus, 2. implies that ex-co-op members get higher pay than former employees of conventional firms, and this could be tested. 3. and 4. could be approached by first looking at the many cases where unconventional practices do become widely preferred. It should then be possible to come up with an explanation for why self-management is an exception, and this explanation might have testable consequences. 1.

seems the most tricky, but there are plenty of cases where people make long-term contractual commitments because they're sensitive to the possibility of opportunistic erosion of some desirable pattern.

d. Why Self-Management May Be Inefficient

So far we have been discussing the implications of the possibility that co-ops may be inefficient. We have not touched upon the reasons why this may be so. Reasons why co-ops may be inefficient fall into two broad categories. 1. Management decisions may be *less competent*; or 2. Management decisions may be oriented to *less appropriate goals*. Most discussion has focussed on 2. rather than 1., because the forms of self-management taken most seriously do not dispense with specialized managers, nor do they substantially change the day-to-day authority relations of managers and other workers. I will therefore say little about 1: A chain of command and responsibility offers advantages; few would lightly board an airplane captained by vote of the crew, and any fighting force which abandoned the command principle would quickly be eliminated by a more hierarchically structured force of similar size and equipment. A single strategic vision may be more effective than a compromise among different visions. Management is a skilled discipline, and will be better done by specialists. Reflections of this sort are hardly decisive arguments, but they are suggestive.

Furthermore, we observe that in practice organizations with a formally 'democratic' or 'participatory' structure are run by an informal hierarchy (Michels 1962; Newman 1980). This occurs even where the individuals concerned are passionately devoted to an ideal of non-hierarchy, and where they introduce special devices like recall or rotation in an attempt to limit the power of the leadership. Hence, we don't have to compare hierarchy with democracy, but two alternative hierarchies—one formally recognized, and one informally generated. The likely lesser competence of the latter alternative looms as a possibility: leaders emerge because of their ability to carry a majority with them, rather than being recruited and dismissed on the basis of results, and empowered to give unpopular directions. It becomes more difficult to pin the responsibility on a leader when she is an unofficial leader.

In a Mondragón-style co-op, the worker has an ownership stake in the enterprise. If there is to be no drift away from self-management, the worker cannot be permitted to withdraw his entire stake and invest the proceeds somewhere else. A large element of a worker's savings has to be in the firm that employs him. This is inherently undesirable, since it increases the worker's exposure to risk. It also means that it's difficult for financial capital to be raised from numerous scattered adherents to a particular theory. If the occasional saver here and there believes that a project is worth backing, these savers cannot get together and support the project without also working on it full-time. The mobility of financial capital is retarded. Entrepreneurial flair is hobbled: it becomes impossible for one person with a clear, original vision to employ 20 others on a project in an attempt to demonstrate its success, without first convincing those 20 individuals to make a more profound commitment than merely accepting payment for work done, and without giving those 20 the power to thwart the vision by their own managerial decisions. Edison might never have been able to launch his innovations if only co-ops were permitted. (The history of Mondragón itself bears out the importance of entrepreneurial leadership. Accounts of Arizmendi's role in conceiving, inspiring, and steering the co-ops reveal his unique far-sightedness and his ability to get things done his way when few agreed with him. To legally charter the co-op bank, when he had no support for it from the members, Arizmendi presented the government with the minutes of a meeting which had never taken place, and forged the signatures of two co-op members who were in fact opposed to the bank [Whyte and Whyte 1991, 50].)

We might expect that an organizational form suffering from certain deficiencies would do comparatively well in an environment where those deficiencies didn't matter much. In the same way, races of animals that can't stand the cold very well might multiply during a temporary phase of exceptionally mild winters. Since some of the difficulties of a Mondragón-style co-op arise from workers leaving the firm, we might see such co-ops surviving for a while in communities where, for some independent cultural reason, workers' mobility between firms is reduced, and where most of the workers are young when first recruited. Alternatively, a co-op might survive by exploiting a special niche in the ecology of organizations.[7]

The owners of a firm seek to maximize the value of their assets, and it is best for 'society' (for the rest of us) that they do so. This may entail closing down the firm, or laying off a large segment of the workforce. One would expect the employees to vote against such measures, even when these are indicated by 'profitability', since (under most self-management proposals) any stake the employees have in the firm is inseparable from their role as employees. The employees are then placing their own interests before those of the enterprise, and indirectly before those of society as a whole. When profitability would indicate that a firm be shut down, its capital assets and its workers moved elsewhere so that they can be more productive, the workers might seek to delay this adjustment, 'milking' the firm for more wages in the short run.

In less extreme cases, the employees will still tend to underinvest in long-term developments, siphoning off funds that might have been better allocated to increasing future productivity. It's important to appreciate clearly why this is *not* true of shareholders, but *is* true of worker-managers: the worker may leave the firm, voluntarily or involuntarily. In that case he loses any gains from the future productivity of the firm. The shareholder may 'leave' the firm, by selling her shares, yet take with her the enhanced value arising from a long-term investment decision. (Among other ways of 'quitting', this applies to death: the shareholder making a long-term investment knows that, in the event of her death, the gains from that investment will go to her heirs.) On the other hand, the worker may want to quit the firm because, say, demand for his kind of labor has risen in another sector. If his current firm looks to be very profitable, he may decide to stay to reap the rewards, even though it is optimal that he move. The problem arises, once again, because he cannot separate his equity in the firm from his labor.

To prevent erosion of the co-op form, everything which could lead to a separation of owners from workers has to be severely contained. Hiring workers who are not full members, permitting workers to sell or cash in their 'shares', allowing some workers to make bigger investments than others—all these natural and convenient developments harbor dangers and must be curbed. The result is that no one can have a pure interest in maximizing the present value of the firm. The future income of the firm can be captured only by recipients of wages. This means that decisions by worker-owners must under some circumstances differ from decisions by pure owners. The co-op will, under some circumstances, tend to under-employ or under-invest, because the immediate effect of increased hiring may be to reduce the pay of the existing members, and because members may not be around to capture future yields from present investments.[8]

Partly because of such problems, some self-management advocates reject the idea of worker co-ownership. The ownership of the firm's capital, or the provision of its finance, should be 'external'. This means that a co-op would borrow the capital it required, and pay interest for it. The workers would manage the firm but would have no ownership in its assets. In practice, almost all the proponents of self-management with external financing advocate a virtual state monopoly of such financing. This amounts to the complete nationalization, if not abolition, of financial markets.

The abolition of the capital market would be far more momentous than any mere change in managerial structures. If the government passed and enforced a law saying that all enterprises had to be co-ops, this would appreciably reduce the welfare of workers (in the workers' own judgment), but probably no more so than many other varieties of existing government intervention. Within most firms a tacit conspiracy would arise to stretch the co-op form to provide the substance of a conventional firm. Abolition of financial markets would be vastly more damaging.

We don't yet possess a complete theory explaining why some organizational forms are more efficient or survive better than others. We can construct models predicting outcomes of various organizational forms, and then look to see if actual outcomes of organizations approximating to our models correspond with the models' predictions. But we can say that: 1. Overwhelmingly, co-ops fail in competition with conventional firms. 2. Contrary to the assumptions of self-management enthusiasts, there exists no good account of this failure in terms of any 'unfair' disadvantage suffered by co-ops. 3. Inasmuch as co-ops have had some limited success, they have done so in proportion to their closeness to conventional firms. (Self-management enthusiasts chalk up the successes, and lament the departures from true self-management, when it is likely that the latter help to account for the former.) 4. We do not lack good models predicting failure for co-ops. 5. Whatever the merits or demerits of co-ops, any proposal to help them out by having state banks pre-empt the functions of free financial markets is a cure far worse than the disease. We may not know precisely why co-ops generally fail, but we do have very good grounds for the view that substantially free financial markets are required by any growing industrial civilization.

— 15 —

IN DEFENSE OF SCIENTIFIC
UTOPIANISM

Let them stop the wheels of history if they can! (Untermann 1927, 252)

Most Marxists have not seen it as their primary role to make out a case for the replacement of capitalism by communism. They have generally dismissed as 'utopian' any suggestion that this should be a major concern of theirs. They have instead espoused the 'scientific' conception that human society is being borne in the direction of communism by momentous social forces largely beyond the control of individual human actions. Hence, the major activities of communists will, to those onlookers with a narrow bourgeois outlook, often appear to have nothing to do with communism; they may, for example, become involved in strikes by particular groups of workers.

This 'scientific' approach has frequently been associated with the view that it is illegitimate to discuss, in more than the sketchiest of terms, the organization of post-capitalist society. Yet if we wish to make a critical examination of the claims of NFM socialism, we do not have a choice about whether to discuss NFM socialism in terms of present tendencies or in terms of its inherent feasibility. As a matter of the simplest logic (the modus tollens), any argument that present tendencies will or might culminate in NFM socialism would be refuted by a demonstration that NFM socialism were unfeasible. And no argument about present tendencies alone can prove NFM socialism to be feasible.

i. MARXIST ANTI-UTOPIANISM

Marx and Engels claim that their socialism differs from earlier socialisms by being scientific rather than utopian. Anti-Marxists have often retorted that Marxism is utopian and therefore unscientific. Against both of these positions, I maintain that any scientific approach to a practical discussion of desirable future forms of society (and therefore any scientific approach to social policy) is utopian, and that some of Marxism's difficulties which have endangered its scientific status have arisen because it has shrunk from being utopian.

'Utopia' refers to an imaginary and desirable state of affairs, especially if it be elaborated in detail and expounded in narrative form. Sometimes the term 'utopian' is used dismissively with respect to some proposal that the speaker believes to be impracticable. However, if someone imagines a highly desirable future social order, distinctly different from the one we live in, it is unsound to assume that this order must be unfeasible. Just four or five lifespans ago, it would have been almost universally considered the ravings of a lunatic to propose that women have legal equality with men and that governments be elected by near-universal adult suffrage. The indignant incredulity with which most people would have greeted such fantastic proposals could have been, and in a few cases were, rationalized into plausible arguments. The utopians are sometimes right; the skeptics are sometimes wrong. It is illegitimate to dismiss some scheme merely because it is utopian (where 'utopian' means desirable and unlike the present state of affairs). Alternatively, if 'utopian' be so defined as to imply 'unfeasible', then the claim that some scheme is utopian requires a supporting argument about feasibility.

Sometimes the pejorative term 'utopian' characterizes the efforts of people who depict the sort of society they would like to see, paying little attention to its feasibility. Such a person may, for instance, collect together all the features she would like to see, without examining their interactions, and hence their possible incompatibilities. Now it is true that someone adopting this procedure runs a considerable risk that the society portrayed will be unfeasible. But still, this has to be shown in each particular case.

Marxists are usually averse to depicting and discussing the way post-capitalist society would operate. Whenever they do so, they nearly always do it sketchily and often somewhat defensively. Though this aversion was present in Marxism from the 1840s onwards, it became more pronounced around the turn of the century. If it was premature to discuss the particulars of socialist organization in 1865, one might expect to see somewhat more discussion in somewhat more detail by 1915, when socialism was 50 years closer. With the passage of time, the anti-utopianism of the 'scientific socialists' acquired something of a hollow ring. A contemptuous refusal to 'compose recipes for future cookshops' may sound reasonable when you have no immediate prospect of being appointed *chef de cuisine*. But when you are about to take up this appointment at six o'clock the following morning and already have your white cap freshly starched (the position of European Marxism after 1912), the remark is less apposite.

If one proposes to do something, it is only sensible to have a clear idea of what one is aiming for, and only in light of that is it possible to discuss intelligently the best way to get to the objective, if indeed that is possible at all. This is the 'scientific' way to proceed. No engineer applying scientific principles to, say, building a bridge, would say that he cannot supply a blueprint until the bridge is built. But even the most mundane activities—catching a plane or changing TV channels—are essentially 'utopian'. All rational action is utopian in the sense that it is directed to bringing about an imaginary and desired future state of affairs (defining this to include the maintenance in future of a present state of affairs, whose re-appearance in the future is, in the present, imaginary).

When it comes to disparaging utopianism the Marxist, at first blush, lines up with the conservative and the cynic, yet the substance of the Marxist's position is very different. He is committed to a future which, if he were to talk about it, would appear to most people as utopian, but he prefers not to talk about it. Instead, he talks about the present in terms which presuppose that it will be succeeded by his preferred future. When the Marxist declines to go into the workability of communism on the ground that such an analysis is 'premature', he certainly doesn't mean that it's too soon to be sure that communism is coming—exactly the reverse! Since communism is coming in any case, since all doubt about this merely evinces failure to grasp the meaning of the historical process, any discussion of its possible difficulties can only amount to useless speculation.

In examining Marxist references to this theme, one finds it related to the direction of history, and in particular, to the class struggle. This suggests one kind of Marxist position: communism is the necessary outcome of history, or of social evolution. On this account, it would be wrong to regard communism as an objective to be pursued and hence to be argued for and recommended. One doesn't for example *do* anything to bring about the next solar eclipse.

A position like this was attributed to Marx by Mises, and of course, by many others, but it is difficult to pin such a view on Marx. If I say that the outcome of a boxing match between Woody Allen and

Mike Tyson would be 'inevitable', I need fear no accusation of historical fatalism. This is an assessment of 'the balance of forces'. The one occasion when Marx and Engels appeal to 'inevitability' clearly derives from such a balance-of-forces appraisal (MECW v6, 496). Marx's expectation of communist revolution was based on a number of factual beliefs about capitalism: that centralization and the falling rate of profit were dictated by industrial technology, that the class war between workers and capitalists was irreconcilable, that capitalists were increasingly redundant in production, that communism would be more efficient than capitalism, and so forth. Given these propositions, the prediction of proletarian revolution is quite reasonable, and doesn't require any fatalistic philosophy of history.

Although Marx was no fatalist, he did endorse the view that communism was implicit in the development of capitalism. Before 1912, and to some extent even up to 1918 when they found themselves in office, German Social Democratic intellectuals did not, as one might have supposed, spend a great deal of their time discussing how socialism would operate. Nor did it greatly concern them that most Social Democratic voters were more interested in modest adjustments to capitalism than they were in socialism. The intellectuals were reassured by their knowledge that the class struggle was inherent in capitalism, that the class struggle could only tend to become more intense, and that it could never end until the workers were triumphant.

Because of their theory that communism was inherent in capitalism, Marxists did not see advocacy of communism *per se* as a top-priority task. It was more important to denounce capitalism and support the workers in the class war. But the theory that capitalism was preparing the way for communism always had to be re-interpreted according to the latest developments in capitalism. At every time, capitalism was by definition doomed, but it had evidently not been so immediately doomed some decades earlier. Every individual Marxist for the past 150 years has had the exhilarating experience of divining that he was living at precisely that point in human development—no earlier and no later—when everything was coming together to ensure that humankind would make the great leap from prehistory into true humanity. From the beginning, Marxism has looked at capitalism, observing its latest technological wonders and some of its recent cultural trends, extrapolated both, and perceived communism. "Socialism", wrote Lenin shortly before taking power, "is now gazing at us from all the windows of modern capitalism" (LCW v25, 363). These days we frequently hear that true socialism has finally been made possible by the development of computers.

Lenin identified "imperialism" as the "highest stage of capitalism'; there could be no more stages. Kidron proposed in 1966 that imperialism was "the highest stage but one" (Kidron 1974, 124). Trotsky wrote about "the death agony of capitalism". After World War II, Marxists came to refer to present-day society as "late capitalism", disregarding all the signs that capitalism was just learning to crawl. For decades past a rapid torrent of books—even if we count only those that proclaim the fact in their titles—has testified to the 'crisis of capitalism'. This fancifulness could have been kept within bounds if the Marxists had been more utopian and therefore more scientific.

ii. Historical Materialism

Marx and Engels developed a theory of history which their followers later called 'historical materialism'. Marx never presented a detailed exposition of this theory, but only scattered, brief remarks. Engels wrote more on the subject, but his account is often more superficial and less interesting than Marx's. Marxists have frequently put together a kind of composite theory of history, based on assorted dicta by Marx and Engels. Thus, Marx's statement that "In every epoch the ruling ideas are the ideas of the ruling class" has been taken seriously, though it requires only a few seconds' thought to see that it is either false or vacuous: It's trivial that the prevailing ideas among the population must be such as to permit the ruling class its ruling position, but there are numerous historical instances where, for example, the religious affiliations of the masses are different from those of the rulers.

The more specific doctrine of historical materialism is largely based on one brief passage in Marx (1970, 20–22). This theory has been effectively criticized many times (for example, see Federn 1939). I will not repeat all the standard criticisms, though I agree with many of them. I am interested here in the view that historical materialism offers some reason for expecting capitalism to be replaced by communism or by any form of NFM socialism.

a. Forces, Relations, and Superstructure

'Material productive forces' means (at least roughly) the productive techniques, equipment, and resources available to a society.

'Relations of production' means (at least roughly) the social relations governing the way in which individuals interact in production (often taken to be equivalent to the prevailing system of property). Marx states that these relations of production "correspond to a definite stage of development" of the productive forces. The relations constitute "the real foundation, on which arises a legal and political superstructure, and to which correspond definite forms of social consciousness" (1970, 20). In Marx's account, the productive forces —call them 'the forces'—develop or advance. This causes them to come into conflict with the relations of production—call them 'the relations', also well-known to Marxists as 'the base'. When that happens, the relations begin to hinder the further development of the forces. Then a social revolution occurs: the relations are modified or replaced, bringing them into harmony with the forces. When the relations are changed, "The changes in the economic foundation lead sooner or later to the transformation of the whole immense superstructure" (21). The superstructure includes at least the legal and political systems; many Marxists have taken it to mean all social institutions other than the relations, thus encompassing religion, philosophy, art, and morality. There seems to be a simple difficulty here: inasmuch as the relations (the base) are enforced by legal doctrines and institutions (part of the superstructure), as they virtually always are, the superstructure must change before the relations can change. One way out of this difficulty would be to define some aspects of law as part of the base rather than part of the superstructure. Another way is Cohen's 'functional' approach, discussed in the next section.

Marx's references to the "real" and the "material" are metaphorical. Marx doubtless understands that a church service is in a literal sense precisely as real or material as the ploughing of a field, and that both occur proximately because individual human beings harbor certain intentions. Since the motor of major social change is claimed always to be improvements in the forces, therefore largely improvements in knowledge, historical materialism could just as well be called 'historical idealism' or 'historical intellectualism'.

I will say little about the many problems involved in demarcating the 'forces', the 'base', or the 'superstructure' (I confine myself here to criticisms which apply regardless of the exact demarcation). But there is one problem which has been overlooked, arising from the implications of marginalism and subjectivism in economic theory.

All human activity may be seen as 'production', since it aims to realize desirable states of affairs. There is no clearly distinguishable 'economic' realm separate from human action in general, since no class of motives or of means is specifically 'economic'. The economic is an aspect from which all action may be viewed. From an economic point of view, a church service or a criminal trial are processes of production. Although Marxists would no doubt reject this, it is not clear on what basis, since, for example, Marx sometimes allows that production of immaterial services is production (he mentions schoolteaching [Capital I, 477] and transportation, [II, 153]). It's true that Marx has a theory of productive and unproductive labor, but this is so muddled that it is charitable to leave it out,[2] and in any case, Marx holds that each society has a different standard of productive labor, so this won't do for defining historical materialism, which applies to all societies. The economic base is sometimes related to 'subsistence', but if this is to be defined in some strictly biological sense, then much that is treated by everyone, including Marx, as 'production', is omitted. For instance, suppose that in the modern U.S., food production is 5,000 times that required for subsistence (measured by the value of resources devoted to it) and 50 times subsistence (measured by actual output of food). Then, according to one's interpretation, the proportion of agriculture classifiable as subsistence is two percent or 0.0002 percent. But which two percent? Or which 0.0002 percent? And if instead we insist on including all of agriculture, why not also include law, religion, philosophy, and so forth, which have just as little to do with 'subsistence' as does the majority of agriculture? Historical materialism rests on the preconception that there is some limited sphere of life unproblematically identifiable as 'economic' or 'production', but this preconception arises from a mistake. And since in a modern society the overwhelming bulk of production is not for subsistence in the sense that the population would die if it were taken away, a subsistence interpretation of 'base' implies that a very small portion of production somehow has a unique governing effect on the rest of society.

Marx adds that a "social formation" never disappears "before all the productive forces for which it is sufficient [Some translations: 'for which there is room in it'] have developed" (21). Since it's usually assumed, and does seem to be Marx's intention, that "social formation" = base plus superstructure, this implies that relations can never change until all the productive forces for which there is room in them have developed. The concept of "room" here is slippery, but if it's not to become vacuous, it at least implies that humans cannot deliberately speed up the process of introducing the new relations.

Marx's formulation rules out the possibility, for example, that a change in opinion (or at least, a change in opinion not strictly coincident with the advance of the productive forces) could lead people to amend their relations of production independently of the conflict between the forces and the relations—or even not independently, if they do it 'too soon'. Marx's theory, as he states it, rules out the possibility that a society encompassing slavery could, due to a debate about right and wrong, decide to abolish slavery (except where this coincides with a period where the productive forces have come into conflict with slavery), and it equally rules out the possibility that slavery could ever be abolished while it still permitted the productive forces to develop as well as any of the alternatives did.

Marx's theory implies that it is impossible for the relations to be modified except by their having come into conflict with the forces. No reason is given by Marx for this, and it's difficult to imagine any remotely plausible reason—unless perhaps we are supposed to accept two premisses: a. that people always lack the opportunity or the will to sacrifice some gains in the forces for the sake of their preferences anent the relations; and b. that there is such a tight fit between relations and forces that people never have the opportunity to change the relations without impairing the forces.

Marx also seems to insinuate the unlikely premiss that there is always a choice between precisely one set of relations which thwarts further development of the forces and precisely one set of relations which permits further development of the forces. A society may well face the possibility of several different sets of relations, including perhaps more than one which permit further development of the forces, but probably in different degrees. We wouldn't normally expect the members of a society to be aware of all these possibilities, much less aware of the precise degree to which they will permit further development of the forces—but this merely underlines the hardly disputable fact that the actual development of a society can be greatly influenced by 'intellectual accidents', by who happens to think of what, when.

Marx also says that the relations are inevitably entered into [some translations: 'are indispensable'] and that they are independent of the "will" of the people who enter into them. Why should that be? It could be a reference to the fact that individuals are bound by the social relations agreed upon by their fellows, who mostly tend to continue the traditions they have inherited. But it is unlikely that Marx would give such prominence to the merest truism, and it seems from the context that Marx is here explaining his notion of 'correspondence': he is claiming that the relations are indispensable and independent of human will because only one set of relations is harmonious with any particular state of the forces.

Marx's theory has the following consequence. Take some cultural element which might be supposed to have had some influence on social development—say the Stoic and then Christian notion that all human souls are of equal worth. Marx's theory seems to imply that it cannot have had much or any influence on European history, except insofar as it directly influenced the forces.

Marx's theory thus seems to require premises which we have no reason to accept, and which on reflection seem manifestly false. But we can go further. Marx's theory, with its "correspondence" between forces and relations, between relations and superstructure (implied in the assertion that a change in the base changes the superstructure), and between superstructure and "definite forms of social consciousness", seems to imply that if we know how a society produces its wealth, we will be able to deduce a great deal about all the institutions and beliefs of that society. We should then expect that if we compared a lot of different cultures for many different features including forces of production, we would find forces of production to be a reliable predictor of other institutional features.

Hallpike (1986, 146–182) looks at 113 societies classified according to 15 variables including "type of subsistence" (hunting, pastoralism, different types of agriculture, and so forth). He does this in order to test the 'cultural materialism' espoused by many anthropologists, which is more modest than its ideological parent, historical materialism. Hallpike finds that type of subsistence is a reliable predictor of four variables: permanence of settlement; population density; community size; and household form. It is a weak predictor of five variables: prevailing rule of descent; compactness of settlement; form and complexity of community political leadership; forms and prevalence of slavery; and community integration (solidarity). It is no predictor at all of five variables: residence after marriage; segregation of adolescent boys; intercommunity marriage; local political succession; and form of family. Most of the correlations which did appear were either due to the difference between hunting-and-gathering and all other types of subsistence, or could be seen on closer inspection to be spurious.

In his ensuing discussion, Hallpike makes many observations injurious to the cultural materialist hypothesis, and therefore also to historical materialism. He summarizes the considerable evidence refuting the widely-held theory that "oriental despotism" can be attributed to the need for centralized management of major irrigation works (260–66). He shows that groups of people with a common origin who take up different technological ways of life are, hundreds or thousands of years later, much more alike in their general culture than groups with different origins who have taken up the same technological way of life (206 et passim). As we might expect, Hallpike's findings do support some kinds of limitation of the relations by the forces.

No one would ever dispute that a change in the forces may sometimes lead to changes in the relations, and that these may lead to changes in the rest of society. What non-Marxists would say is that other routes for social change cannot be ruled out. A change in the superstructure may lead to a change in the forces, or may change the relations independently of the forces. For example, the victory of one faction in a political struggle (superstructure) may lead to a modification of the relations (base), which may then affect the forces.

There is nothing original or distinctive about Marx's view that changes in the forces may cause changes in the relations (at least roughly, that changes in technology may cause changes in property rules), which may then cause changes in the rest of society. Original and distinctive are the claims: 1. that all social revolutions are fundamentally nothing other than adjustments of relations to fit changed forces; 2. that relations can never change until all the forces that could have developed 'within' those relations have developed; 3. that new relations cannot appear except when and because changed forces have come into conflict with old relations. From 2. and 3. follows 4., that the relations can never be changed except because of conflict between relations and forces.

These claims define historical materialism. If they are abandoned, there is nothing distinctive left to defend. They are very restrictive, though in one particular very open: they say nothing about what causes the forces to advance. They don't rule out, for instance, that superstructural features might directly affect the forces (as when Babylonian astronomy, motivated by religion and politics, made it easier to plant crops at the appropriate time and to navigate ships). They *do* rule out any direct effect of the superstructure on the relations (or, taking the unusual interpretation that base and superstructure are not exhaustive of institutions, any direct effect of the non-base and non-superstructure institutions on the relations). Thus, for instance, all the changes in English common law over the centuries can only be explained by disharmonies between the forces and the relations. It is forbidden to explain any of them by autonomous intellectual changes in legal theorizing—or perhaps such an explanation could be admitted so long as these legal changes were somehow sealed off from having any direct influence on the relations.

Marxists have tended to assume tacitly that elements of the superstructure do not autonomously affect the forces, or not very much. The usual assumption seems to be that the relations affect the forces: in capitalism by stimulating their advance, in all earlier societies by retarding their advance. But this assumption is not allowed to extend to the notion that the relations could control the forces, which would threaten to scuttle the whole theory—especially if allied with the proposition that something other than the forces might affect the relations.

To contradict historical materialism, it's only necessary to claim that the relations changed *once* for some reason other than the development of the forces, or that the superstructure changed *once* for some reason other than the adjustment of the relations to the forces. To pick an example at random, one scholar of the origin of states, summarizing what is known about this momentous class of historical events, states that the formation of states had many repercussions for technology and the economy, but was not itself a response to technological improvement (R. Cohen 1978). The question for historical materialism is not whether Ronald Cohen is wrong about this, but why we should suppose, before we look at the evidence, that he must be wrong. Why *couldn't* spontaneous political processes—inter-group dynamics of disputes and war—give rise to a state, which then acts directly on both the forces and the relations, not to mention the superstructure? Why cudgel history to make it fit one pattern on all occasions, when no good reason has been given for the exclusion of alternative patterns?

The Indian caste system has survived for thousands of years, and has had enormous repercussions for every aspect of Indian life. It seems to have arisen because conquerors wanted to maintain racial distinctness from their subjects. No one can seriously claim that caste has arisen because of the forces or the relations of production. Numerous societies have had very similar technologies and property systems without a caste system. It appears that historical materialists have only one recourse, faced with examples like this: they must accept that the superstructure and the forms of consciousness corresponding to it are only a part, and may be only a small part, of any given culture. Historical materialism then ceases to be a master theory explaining the broad course of historical development, and becomes a more limited set of claims about the relations between forces and relations of production.

Many Marxist writers have tacitly or explicitly modified historical materialism to permit the autonomous influence of superstructural elements on the relations. But I don't know of any of them who have managed to do this while retaining a non-vacuous theory of historical materialism, a theory which would say something both interesting and not manifestly false. The usual practice is to declaim commonplaces about the interconnections of all the elements of cultural life. Weasel phrases like 'intimately bound up with' are freely employed to convey the impression that the writer knows something about such interconnections.

b. Cohen's Defense of Historical Materialism

Historical materialism depends upon there being a 'tight fit' between at least many of the important institutions of society. If, to take an extreme instance, any level of forces were equally compatible or 'friendly' with thousands of possible sets of relations, and *vice versa,* the theory would have little importance (even though it might still be true that occasionally a particular advance of the forces would collide with a particular inhospitable set of relations). But a tight fit implies much more than the absence of such a state of affairs. Just consider a development of the forces which puts it into 'conflict' with the existing relations. Whatever this means, it cannot mean that that level of the forces cannot co-exist with the existing relations—for they do co-exist. For there to be a 'conflict' in the sense Marx intends, it seems that there must be an alternative, 'better' set of relations, waiting to take over. But how is it brought about that this new set of relations—and only this set, not some spurious claimant—rises up to displace the old set? An obvious answer is that it depends upon somebody's noticing the superiority of the new relations, but this has two difficulties: 1. it undermines the drift of Marx's argument that the interaction of forces, relations, and superstructure occurs independently of human understanding; and 2. it admits the possibility, indeed the high likelihood, that mistakes may be made, that relations which just look as if they will help along the forces will be preferred to those that really do, or that possible relations highly beneficial to the forces will be overlooked.

In his defense of historical materialism, Cohen (1978; 1988) appeals to functional explanation—explanation of the sort 'birds have hollow bones because this makes it easier for them to fly'. Cohen rightly states that we may be entitled to give functional explanations even where we don't know the mechanism which causes features of some entity to serve a function. Thus, we were entitled to suppose that eyes were 'for' seeing, and to wonder what the lateral lines on fishes were 'for', even before we found a good explanation (Darwin's theory of natural selection) for why such things do serve a function. Yet there must actually *be* a mechanism causing things to be 'functional', and in cases where we have no other grounds for supposing functionality to be at work, we *would* have to know the mechanism before we accepted a functional explanation. The only reason, independent of natural selection theory, why we are warranted in thinking the eye must be 'for' seeing, is that the eye does so well at seeing because it is constructed in a way which is highly improbable to have come about randomly (Dawkins 1986). And the main impetus for supposing that the lateral lines were 'for' something was awareness of numerous cases like the mammalian eye where complex organs turned out to be 'for' something. The mere fact that any feature happens to have 'fortunate' consequences, judged by any imputed 'function' is no grounds for holding that the feature has appeared because it served the function (Williams 1966). There are cases where institutions have been designed for a specific purpose, or modified by trial and error, and there are invisible-hand explanations, such as theories of the market process, or of Darwinian natural selection, which show how some institutions can turn out better than people know how to design. Where such processes are absent, we do not find any intricate suitedness to a function, remotely comparable to the suitedness of the mammalian eye for seeing, or even of hollow bones for flying. Examples of 'maladaptiveness' or 'dysfunctionality' are rife throughout human cultures (Hallpike 1986, 113ff).

Functional explanation enables Cohen to deftly avoid one of the serious difficulties which has plagued historical materialism. Instead of finding it contradictory that the relations may affect the forces, when the theory says that the forces bring the relations into line, in Cohen's understanding, the relations do affect the forces, and precisely for this reason, the forces bring the relations into line: they do this by selecting those relations which affect the forces in such a way as to be most appropriate to the development of the forces.

Cohen's version of historical materialism is more in need of functional explanations than Marx's, for Cohen goes beyond Marx's assertion that developing forces sometimes come into conflict with relations, by claiming (160–61) that relations are in harmony or conflict with the forces according as they promote or fail to promote the development of the forces. Thus, forces and relations might get along quite nicely, without any exceptional stresses or strains; still, they must be described as 'in conflict' if the forces just maintain themselves without developing. Whatever the selective mechanism that adjusts relations to forces may be, it therefore has to 'look ahead' and make an evaluation, something which Darwinian explanations cannot allow for. (Alternatively, the selective mechanism must be allowed to 'make mistakes', since certain relations might apparently favor certain forces for a few years, decades, or centuries, but might prove a hindrance in the longer term.)

c. The Element of Truth in Historical Materialism

If we survey the broad outlines of human history, we can hardly fail to notice the cumulative improvement in productive techniques, nor that improved techniques often have many widespread repercussions for the social order, nor that various techniques have differing degrees of compatibility with various property systems, so that a change in techniques can (in some sense) demand a change in the property system or (in some sense) cause such a change. These are the facts which historical materialism emphasizes. These facts alone do not imply historical materialism. There is no reason to suppose that social change always occurs according to one scenario, or that there is any 'base' which has to be accorded explanatory 'primacy'. Any element of society—for example, language, or religion—can be viewed as 'basic' for certain analytic purposes. Such expressions are merely fleeting metaphors, of no theoretical importance.

The kind of relationship that may hold between forces and relations—or any other aspects of culture—needs to be scrutinized. A change in technology may lead to a change in property, but it doesn't strictly follow from this that the new property rights are in any way more conducive to the new technology. If, however, they are so conducive, the nature of the conduciveness may not be simple. Some relations may conceivably be absolutely incompatible with some forces—but in that case, the two just cannot co-exist, so a disparity between them cannot be a causal factor. Suppose that the forces change, and that in some way this causes friction or antagonism with the relations. It's not clear that there must be just one available alternative set of relations which removes the friction, or if there is, that people will know about. But if there is, people may prefer to change the forces to conform with the existing relations. (After using fire-arms for 100 years, the Japanese gave up all employment of them for over 200 years. This illustrates that people are capable of abandoning a particular technique if they want to. See Perrin 1979.)

If a change in technology leads to a change in the property system, there is no guarantee that this change will then stimulate technology. It may be that the invention of the cotton gin had the effect of strengthening and extending plantation slavery, which then had the effect of retarding the development of technology in the South. (The point of all such examples is not that they are necessarily accurate, but that there is no reason to dismiss them out of hand without an examination of the facts.) The Marxian scenario can happen, but there are other scenarios which can happen.

The most famous example of cultural innovation in non-human animals illustrates the point. Scientists threw grain and sweet potatoes on the beaches to attract the monkeys into the open, where they would be easier to observe. One monkey invented the washing of sweet potatoes and rice in the sea, and this was copied by others until it spread through the whole population. The way of life of the monkeys was transformed; they learned to dive for seaweed and to swim to other islands which they colonized (Wilson 1975, 170–71; Kawai 1965; Kawamura 1963). But although the food-washing technological innovation caused, among other things, the colonization of other islands, it would be incorrect to suggest that colonization of other islands selected food-washing, or that there is any functional relationship. It was just a fortunate consequence. If swimming to other islands had caused the monkeys to meet another population of monkeys who infected the first group with a disease and wiped them all out, we would not be tempted to invoke a functional explanation. That would just be an unfortunate consequence.

Along with other animals, humans pursue what seems to help them get what they want, and to avoid what seems to frustrate their getting what they want. This simple fact about humans explains much without bringing in functional explanations. Thus, it is quite plausible that if some members of a population discover a new technique that helps them find more game or grow better crops, they will implement this technique, and others will copy them, until the technique spreads throughout the population. It is also quite likely that the new technique will have repercussions for the property system. It is even entirely possible (but not always necessarily so) that these consequent changes in the property system will help the spread of the new technique, and perhaps even that it will then help the implementation and spread of yet-to-be-discovered techniques.

Cohen's discussion always assumes that the forces differ relevantly only in their 'level'. But two sets of productive forces might differ markedly while not being distinguishable as to 'level'. We can compare two communities one of which fishes, the other of which hunts. Or two alternative 'presents' (or 'futures') in which different technological discoveries have been made.

iii. MARX'S CASE FOR COMMUNISM

Thus from our study of the development of the capitalist system we can confidently deduce the following conclusions: THE NUMBER OF THE CAPITAL-ISTS GROWS SMALLER, BUT THESE FEW CAPITALISTS GROW RICHER AND STRONGER; THE NUMBER OF THE WORKERS CONTINUALLY INCREASES, AND WORKING-CLASS SOLIDARITY LIKEWISE INCREASES, THOUGH NOT TO THE SAME EXTENT; THE CONTRAST BETWEEN THE WORKERS AND THE CAPITALISTS GROWS EVER GREATER. INEVITABLY, THEREFORE, THE DEVELOPMENT OF CAPITALISM LEADS TO A CLASH BETWEEN THE TWO CLASSES, THAT IS, IT LEADS TO THE COMMUNIST REVOLUTION. (Bukharin and Preobrazhensky 1966, 66)

In the writings of Marx and Engels there is a clear argument that communism is desirable, that it is feasible, and that it is, in view of modern developments, likely. Contrary to what almost everyone believes, at no point does this argument require, or receive any specific support from, historical materialism. Historical materialism and the espousal of communism as the future of humankind are frequently found together, but there is no logical connection between them. Much effort has been misallocated to criticizing Marx's alleged historical fatalism, when Marx relies entirely upon specific, clear, non-fatalist arguments for communism as the culmination of trends generated inescapably by capitalism.

It is often supposed either 1. that the arguments for communism are derivative from historical materialism ('applications' of historical materialism, possibly), or 2. that these arguments have to be combined with historical materialism to yield a conclusion about communism. But neither of these hold. Marx and his followers advance arguments for communism, based upon such matters as the 'laws of motion of capitalism', the dynamics of the class struggle, and various moral judgments about alternative social institutions. All of these arguments can be (and often have been) advanced independently of historical materialism. If these arguments can be derived from historical materialism (which they can, by the addition of still further premisses), they can equally well be derived from other theoretical positions. All of these arguments support communism well or badly with or without historical materialism. And different arguments would cause historical materialism to be anti-communist. For example, if the Mises argument is correct, then modern forces cannot co-exist with communist relations. The need to maintain the conduciveness of the relations to the forces implies that we oppose NFM socialism. Hence, historical materialism is anti-communist.

Marx attributes crucial importance to the process of centralization of capital. If there really were a trend towards 'one big firm', this would offer some support for Marxian socialism, which requires the whole of society-wide industry to be governed by a single administrative structure. But this support is not strengthened by conceiving the centralization process as an application of historical materialism, nor is that process itself an application in that it follows directly from historical materialism. Centralization and historical materialism are each true or false independently of the other. The same goes for all Marx's 'laws of motion of capitalism'; they all stand or fall without reference to historical materialism.

Marx holds that communism will give most people higher living standards and better lives, because of its superior output. Further, communism is morally superior to the market because under communism society-wide production is planned, whereas under the market society-wide production cannot be planned. On the question of communism as the culmination of present trends, Marx presents a coherent, comprehensible series of arguments of the 'balance of forces' type. Among the propositions involved in this series of arguments:

1. The inescapable trend in the market is for ever-increasing size of organizational and ownership units (Marx's centralization thesis).

2. The inescapable trend in the market is for increasing inequality of wealth ownership (Marx mistakenly thinks that this follows from 1.).

3. Capitalism socializes production, while leaving distribution private. This is a 'contradiction' which can only be resolved by socializing distribution too—terminating the market and instituting 'production for use'.

4. Inherent in capitalism, there is an unavoidable class struggle between workers and capitalists, which could be terminated by the establishment of communism.

5. The condition of the workers under capitalism perpetually tends to get worse.

6. Production under communism will be immensely more efficient than production under capitalism, primarily because under communism there is a single great industrial plan, and no market.

These propositions form the bare bones of Marx's case for communism (leaving aside, that is, his strong but unargued moral revulsion against buying and selling). They could be added to at great length. For instance, we could add a statement about the trade cycle: according to Marx this is produced by the free market, not by government intervention, and can never be cured except by abolishing capitalism and replacing it with communism. But the statement about the trade cycle can be taken as implicit in 6. and to some extent in 5. above. We could add a statement that the capitalist becomes increasingly redundant, but we could regard that claim as implicit in propositions 1., 2., and 6.

Logically speaking, these six propositions owe nothing to historical materialism; that is, they are not derivable from historical materialism alone nor do they gain (in the sense of more strongly implying support for communism) from being linked to historical materialism. (Most if not all of them were advocated before Marx, by socialists who were not historical materialists.) Taken together, the six propositions would, if true, go a long way towards showing that communism were feasible, desirable, and likely. However, all six propositions are untenable.

We have seen (11.iii) that 1. is false and that 2. does not follow from 1. Empirical evidence also goes against 2. As to 5., the Marx of the 1840s thought that workers were literally becoming pauperized, their incomes driven down to near-starvation level. Later, Marx was careful to word his claims so that he could not be pinned down to such an interpretation, while continuing to insinuate it. The subsequent improvement in the wellbeing of the working masses—judged by food, housing, health, leisure, safety at work, or any other plausible measure—has been fabulous beyond Marx's dreams, and there is no reason why it should not continue indefinitely, as long as a substantially free market is permitted to function. 3. is an ambiguous claim, which seems to rest on equivocation as to the word 'social'. All the individuals in the world become increasingly interdependent through the market, and in this sense the world economy becomes a single organism. But this does not show that it will benefit from being placed under a single administration.

iv. THE CLASS STRUGGLE

Marx's analysis of forces, relations, and superstructure leads on to an analysis of class. A rising class is identified with relations that correspond to higher forces of production. The adjustment of relations to forces may therefore be achieved by political revolution, in which individuals acting in the interest of the class identified with the relations corresponding to higher forces take power and pursue policies encouraging the flourishing of these 'progressive' relations. These policies may or may not lead to the rising class becoming the ruling class.[3]

All I will say here about this theory is that it is somewhat less plausible than the exact opposite: that political revolutions are made in behalf of interest-groups which don't like recent changes. Therefore, revolutions are attempts at holding back developments, especially disruptive repercussions of improvements in technology. Revolutions constitute the coming to power of groups which strive to hinder or delay changes in the productive relations caused by changes in the forces. I don't claim that this theory is true, but it makes better sense of the English, American, and French revolutions, and offers Marxists the consolation that the Marxist-inspired revolutions of the twentieth century have been terrific successes. Such a theory is equally compatible with analysis in terms of forces, relations, and superstructure—in other words, the steps from that analysis to class and politics are many, often tenuous, and often unexamined.

Marx and Engels claim that there is a class struggle under capitalism, and that this class struggle will (or is likely to) lead to the victory of the working-class, which will then become the ruling class. This period of working-class rule will be brief, however, for the working-class government will introduce communism, and in doing so, cease to exist as a government, just as the working class will cease to exist as a class.

Marx formed his fundamental ideas at a time when the new industrial proletariat was still a small proportion of the European population, but rapidly growing. It was predictable that this class, for the most part politically unrepresented, would eventually become the majority of the population, and that such a development would help to transform the old political systems. Marx attached to this reasonable prediction the notion, no doubt suggested to him by reading Stein, that 'communism' (with its complete abolition of the market) was associated with the proletariat, whereas 'socialism' (with its attempts to reform the market) was associated with the middle class.

But communist ideas indigenous to the working class were very much a local, peripheral, and passing episode. As time passed it became clear that workers were no more likely to become communists than to become Mormons or Spiritualists—if anything, less likely. Mass Marxist parties, headed by the German Social Democrats, always had a rank-and-file who wanted only what they considered a more advantageous position within the existing market economy: they wanted political democracy, more leeway for trade unions, and more welfare-state provisions.

Marx and Engels themselves pioneered the view that what the workers actually thought about communism was less important than what the class struggle would make them do. The idea is that the workers find themselves inescapably thrown into a class struggle with the capitalists. The long-term chances are with the workers, since they are far more numerous and they are indispensable to the running of industry, whereas the capitalists increasingly become redundant coupon-clippers. The workers will eventually take political power, and they will naturally use it to organize society in their own interests—the interests of the great majority (white-collar workers are included in the working class). This, happening simultaneously with the inherent tendency of modern industry to form into ever larger administrative units, points to a democratically administered system planned on a society-wide scale.

Let us first consider a minor point: most workers are capitalists and most capitalists are workers. That's to say, most wage-workers receive interest income, for example from a savings account (the bank, of course, invests the deposits and receives income from stocks and bonds, which is then paid to the depositors as interest, so there's no dispute that anyone with a savings account is fully a capitalist in the sense described in *Capital*). Most capitalists, or at least most capitalists below the age of, say, 60, also receive payment for the sale of their labor services. This is not to deny that there are some people who are born so rich that they don't need to do paid work, and don't choose to. These people live on the contribution to current production of the assets they own, and therefore ultimately on the savings of other individuals, often ancestors, who donated them their wealth.

The relevant point here is that there is a huge overlap between workers and capitalists. The early Marxists expected that this overlap would dwindle, that there would be polarization. (Increasing inequality of wealth ownership would not be enough to guarantee the reduction of overlap. It appears that there has not been increasing inequality, and it is certain that there has not been reduction in the class overlap.) When the early Marxists were asked what the difference was between a worker and a capitalist, since most workers received some interest, a common reply was that a capitalist had sufficient capital to live without working. But there are many people whose savings are sufficient to enable them to live without working at an income below that of the average worker. A considerable portion of total capital represents workers' savings for retirement.

Though we should not forget the fact that the overwhelming majority of adults are simultaneously workers and capitalists, and may therefore be expected to have divided loyalties in the supposed class struggle, let us now imagine that this problem can be surmounted somehow. Assume that no capitalists work and no workers receive interest. It still remains the case that there never has been and never could be any *class* struggle between workers and capitalists. There are no issues which unite all workers, according to their interests, against all capitalists, according to their interests. There are, of course, struggles among competing interest-groups, but in such cases we observe struggles between sections of the same class, or more commonly, some capitalists and some workers on each side. Take the issue of tariff protection. Both workers and capitalists in protected industries, and perhaps a few closely-aligned industries, benefit from the introduction of protectionist legislation. Both workers and capitalists in the majority of non-protected industries suffer losses as a result of protection. Going by 'economic interests', the issue splits classes, with both workers and capitalists on each side. It's the same with most issues.

It is difficult even to consistently conceive of a measure which either benefits or is neutral to all workers and also harms or is neutral to all capitalists, or *vice versa*. Consider the nineteenth-century acts compulsorily improving factory conditions, for example by imposing maximum working-hours. These acts benefitted some workers and harmed some capitalists. But, as Marx points out, they also benefitted some capitalists and harmed some workers. In Marx's account, the big capitalists benefit because smaller competitors, who cannot comply and remain profitable, are driven out of business, and some workers lose their jobs because it no longer pays to employ them. Marx is delighted by both these developments, since they speed up the centralization of capital and remove a safety-valve for the desperate low-income workers (I, 453, 472). In our day, we might cite the example of a statutory minimum wage. This benefits some workers, who retain their jobs at a higher wage, benefits other workers who gain from the removal of low-cost competition, harms other workers, who lose their jobs, and harms a further round of workers, who suffer from the consequent fall in output.

The classic arena for the supposed class struggle is 'industrial action', but this is always primarily the struggle of one group of workers against another. One group of workers would like to be given jobs at a particular level of wages. Another group of workers is prepared to work for less. The employer, acting on behalf of consumers (mainly composed of yet other workers) who want goods at lowest cost and are not prepared to pay a higher price for goods made by union labor, prefers to hire the second group of workers. The first group of workers therefore endeavors to dissuade or prevent the second group of workers from working for that employer. The first group of workers demands that the second group of workers sacrifice their own palpable interests to those of the first group of workers. This is a struggle between two groups within a class. Spokesmen for the first group will, of course, sometimes claim that if they succeed in thwarting the second group of workers, the working class as a whole will benefit. But this claim is baseless, and not merely in the obvious and indisputable sense that the second group will suffer. There are no general benefits that redound to any major part of the working class as a result of the victory of the first group over the second group. There is a slight harm imposed on workers generally because of the consequent reduction in output—the second group has a better claim to stand for the interests of the working class in general, in the sense that the average worker's income will be slightly higher if the second group gets its way. But even here, the first group suffers an immediate loss in income, which they obviously value more highly than the long-term welfare of all workers.

The view that the second group of workers are 'traitors to their class' and ought altruistically to donate their jobs to the first group of workers may be termed 'class patriotism'. Interest-groups routinely present measures which benefit their members at the expense of other people as 'in the public interest', however far-fetched this claim may be. Marxists often attempt to expose the interest-groups who benefit from measures alleged to be in the national, or the public, interest, but whenever the Marxists uncover a group interest, they quite erroneously leap to the conclusion that they have uncovered a *class* interest. The irony is that class interests are usually just as chimerical as public or national interests. Class patriotism is just as deluded as territorial, linguistic, or ethnic patriotism—in fact it is more so, since gains can actually be made by one population, language-community, or ethnic group, at the expense of others. No gains can be made by workers as a whole at the expense of capitalists as a whole. This fact should arouse no surprise, for workers and capitalists are voluntary collaborators in common endeavors, sharing the gains of these common endeavors according to mutual agreements.

If there is no working class interest as against a capitalist class interest, it follows that there can be no such thing as a 'working class government', implementing measures which favor the working class and injure the capitalist class. One can conceive of a 'dictatorship of the proletariat', in the sense of a government composed of workers and answerable to workers. Such a government might, of course, attack the capitalists, much as some governments attack minority ethnic groups popularly supposed to be capitalists, but this cannot benefit the workers as a whole.

From the theory that government measures can be taken which benefit the workers and harm the capitalists, Marxists proceed to the theory that the workers have an interest in establishing communism. This abolishes both capitalists and workers, as classes, but it offers an increase in income to the former proletarians, and a decrease to the former capitalists. Although the working class is abolished, its former members are considered to benefit. This scenario presupposes that communism can exist, and is at least almost as efficient as capitalism.

Why don't the capitalists benefit from communism, as well as the workers? Presumably because communism raises most people's real incomes and lowers those of the rich. But, even leaving aside the fact that most workers are also capitalists, some workers have higher incomes than many capitalists. (Peter Falk gets paid more for his labor on one episode of *Columbo* than the savings of several typical elderly widows put together, and the elderly widow is the quintessential capitalist.) Thus, many capitalists must benefit from the introduction of communism, and some workers must suffer. (This effect would be even more marked if we considered a worker's interest income from his savings as an indirect yield from his wages, rather than counting it as simply an incident to his other role as a capitalist.)

Once again, there can be no such thing as a class struggle or a class issue between workers and capitalists.

There is a simple idea underlying the view that the class struggle will lead to communism. Workers want *more* from the employers, and employers or entrepreneurs are most often also capitalists. In wage negotiations, workers may seem to be pitted against capitalists, the one side striving for more wages, the other for less. Extrapolating the notion of 'more' beyond higher wages, ultimate success for the workers would appear to be to take over and displace the capitalists. A little observation and thought soon shows that merely taking what the richest ten percent of the population spend on their own personal consumption, and sharing this out among the remaining 90 percent (assuming that total output doesn't change as a result) cannot make a very great difference to that 90 percent. The same conclusion follows if we consider the whole sum of interest on capital (a large proportion of which is actually already destined for the pockets of the poorest 90 percent).[4]

Purely in terms of the arithmetic of 'more' and 'less', the workers cannot be made more than slightly better off by taking over industry and redistributing its output. Their incomes cannot rise much, and if we then countenance even a slight decrease in output for any reason associated with the workers taking over, they will be worse off than before: it would then be in their interests to pay the capitalists to come back. The ghost of the notion that the workers can effectively better their lot by looting the capitalists has persisted in the minds of many socialists, but in the writings of Marx, very little attention is paid to the personal consumption of the capitalists. All the emphasis is on increased output brought about by the abolition of the market and the introduction of society-wide planning. This proposal has to be evaluated independently of class.

V. IN DEFENSE OF RECIPES FOR FUTURE COOKSHOPS

All arguments against capitalism fail unless there is some feasible alternative which can do better. It seemed obvious and indisputable to the early Marxists that communism or some form of NFM socialism would do better than the market. This conviction was based on a misinterpretation of trends within capitalism and on a misconception of the role played by the market. The crucial misinterpretation was the centralization theory: capitalism could not last because the number of firms must become ever smaller, the ultimate limit being one big firm. The crucial misconception was the opposition to 'anarchy of production', seen as being wholly bad and manifestly inferior to 'conscious' planning.

Lying behind the hostility to anarchy of production was an almost total unawareness of the economic calculation problem, and lying behind this, perhaps, was a deeper misunderstanding: the theory that anything humans create they can and should completely understand and control (Bartley 1990). Although it may be premature to say that no one will ever find a replacement for the market, it is hardly premature to say that any such replacement, like the market, will have to be characterized by anarchy of production, as some anti-market socialists implicitly recognize (O'Neill 1989; Albert and Hahnel 1991).

According to Popper, the chief difference between Einstein and an amoeba is that the amoeba perishes along with its refuted theory, while Einstein can kill his theories and replace them with new ones. Tragically, Marxism fostered a partial regression to amoebic episte-mology. By elevating into a principle the notion that it was 'unscien-tific' to discuss the way in which socialism would work, Marxism ensured that millions would perish before we could all agree that Marxian socialism was an impossibility.

Many people now draw the conclusion that the problem with Marxism is its 'utopianism', and that utopias are dangerous. But if Marxism had been more unabashedly utopian, it would not have had the same motive to evade discussion of the mechanics of its proposed future society. The attempt to abstain from utopianism merely leads to unexamined utopias.

Critical utopianism could emerge as a legitimate branch of social science. In the freely creative and vigorously self-critical spirit of brainstorming, this discipline could scrutinize and evaluate pro-posed utopias, from both radical social theorists and speculative fiction, and could construct new utopias. Utopian proposals can be quite detailed, not because anyone seriously supposes that the details specified will ever come to pass, but as illustrations of possibilities— or perhaps, after examination, as demonstrations of impossibilities. This branch of enquiry would not immediately arrive at unanimous agreement on which utopias were out of the question, but there may be rapid convergence on some limited conclusions, along with an identification of those areas still open to investigation and debate.

There is no escape from utopianism, other than mute absten-tionism. But we can criticize our utopias, discard those convicted of unfeasibility, and replace them with better utopias. Wishful thinking is no vice, but openness to argument is a wonderful virtue.

BIBLIOGRAPHY

Entries are restricted to works which: 1. are cited in the text or notes; 2. were especially useful to me; or 3. are significant documents in the history of discussions of the economics of socialism. Some works are included for their importance as evidence of particular positions' being held rather than as intrinsically fine expositions of those positions.

ABBREVIATED REFERENCES

Capital I, II, and III. Volumes I, II, and III of Marx's *Capital*, in the edition listed below.
Capital IVa, IVb, and IVc. Volumes I, II, and III of Marx's *Theories of Surplus-Value* (Volume IV of *Capital*), in the edition listed below.
LCW. Lenin's *Collected Works*, as listed below.
MECW. *Karl Marx, Frederick Engels: Collected Works*, as listed below.

Akerloff, George A. 1970. The Market for 'Lemons': Qualitative Uncertainty and the Market Mechanism. *Quarterly Journal of Economics*, 84 (August).
Akin, William E. 1977. *Technocracy and the American Dream: The Technocrat Movement, 1900–1941*. Berkeley: University of California Press.
Albert, Michael, and Robin Hahnel. 1978. *Unorthodox Marxism: An Essay on Capitalism, Socialism, and Revolution*. Boston: South End Press.
———. 1981. *Socialism Today and Tomorrow*. Boston: South End Press.
———. 1991a. *The Political Economy of Participatory Economics*. Princeton: Princeton University Press.
———. 1991b. *Looking Forward: Participatory Economics for the Twenty-First Century*. Boston: South End Press.
Alchian, Armen A. 1977. *Economic Forces at Work*. Indianapolis: Liberty Press.
Alchian, Armen A., and Harold Demsetz. 1972. Production, Information Costs, and Economic Organization. *American Economic Review*, 62:5 (December). Reprinted in Alchian 1977.
Aristotle. 1992. *Politics*. Excerpts. In Michael L. Morgan (ed.), *Classics of Moral and Political Theory*. Indianapolis: Hackett.
Arnold, Scott. 1990. *Marx's Radical Critique of Capitalist Society*. New York: Oxford University Press.
Arrow, Kenneth. 1963. *Social Choice and Individual Values*. New York: Wiley.
Arrow, Kenneth J., L. Hurwicz, and H. Uzawa. 1958. *Studies in Linear and Non-Linear Programming*. Stanford: Stanford University Press.

Ashton, T.S. 1925. The Records of a Pin Manufactory, 1814–21. *Economica* (November).

Attewell, Paul A. 1984. *Radical Political Economy since the Sixties*. New Brunswick, NJ: Rutgers University Press.

Avineri, Shlomo. 1968. *The Social and Political Thought of Karl Marx*. Cambridge: Cambridge University Press.

Babbage, Charles. 1975 [1832]. *On The Economy of Machinery and Manufactures*. Works of Charles Babbage, Volume 8. New York: New York University Press.

Bailey, Thomas. 1990. Jobs of the Future and the Skills they will Require. *American Educator* (Spring).

Bain, Joe S. 1966. *International Differences in Industrial Structure: Eight Nations in the 1950s*. New Haven: Yale University Press.

Baldwin, Claude David. 1942. *Economic Planning: Its Aims and Implications*. Urbana: University of Illinois Press.

Ballod, Karl. 1919 [1898]. *Der Zukunftsstaat*. Second edition. Stuttgart: Stoccarda.

Baran, Paul A. and Paul M. Sweezy. 1966. *Monopoly Capital*. New York: Monthly Review Press.

Barltrop, Robert. 1975. *The Monument: The Story of the Socialist Party of Great Britain*. London: Pluto.

Barone, Enrico. 1908. Il ministerio della produzione nello stato collectivista. *Giornale degli Economisti e Rivista di Statistica,* 37 (September and October).

———. 1935. The Ministry of Production in the Collectivist State. Translation of Barone 1908. In Hayek 1935.

Barrot, Jean, and François Martin. 1974. *Eclipse and Re-Emergence of the Communist Movement*. Detroit: Black and Red.

Bartley, W.W., III. 1990. *Unfathomed Knowledge, Unmeasured Wealth: On Universities and the Wealth of Nations*. La Salle: Open Court.

Barzel, Yoram. 1989. *Economic Analysis of Property Rights*. Cambridge: Cambridge University Press.

Bauer, Otto. 1919. *Der Weg zum Sozialismus*. Vienna: Wiener Volksbuchhandlung Ignaz Brand.

Baumol, William J. 1958. Activity Analysis in One Lesson. *American Economic Review*, 48.

Baumol, William J., and Sue Anne Batey Blackman. 1980. Unprofitable Energy is Squandered Energy. *Challenge*, 23:3 (July–August).

Baumol, William J., Sue Anne Batey Blackman, and Edward N. Wolff. 1989. *Productivity and American Leadership: The Long View*. Cambridge, Ma: M.I.T. Press.

Baxter, W.T., and Sidney Davidson (eds.) 1977. *Studies in Accounting*. London: Institute of Chartered Accountants in England and Wales.

Beadles, Nicholas A., and L. Aubrey Drewry Jr. (eds.) 1968. *Money, the Market, and the State: Economic Essays in Honor of James Muir Waller*. Athens, Ga: University of Georgia Press.

Bebel, August. 1953 [1878]. *Die Frau und der Sozialismus*. Berlin: Dietz.

———. 1910. *Woman and Socialism*. Translated by Meta L. Stern. New York: Socialist Literature Company.

Becker, Gary S. 1976. *The Economic Approach to Human Behavior*. Chicago: University of Chicago Press.

———. 1971. *Economic Theory*. New York: Knopf.

Beckwith, Burnham Putnam. 1949. *The Economic Theory of a Socialist Economy*. Jericho, NY: Exposition.

———. 1955. *Marginal-Cost Price-Output Control: A Critical History and Restatement of the Theory*. New York: Columbia University Press.

———. 1974. *Liberal Socialism: The Pure Welfare Economics of a Liberal Socialist Economy*. Revised edition of Beckwith 1949. Jericho, NY: Exposition.

———. 1976. *Free Goods: The Theory of Free or Communist Distribution*. Palo Alto: Beckwith.

Bellamy, Edward. 1960 [1888]. *Looking Backward: 2000–1887*. New York: New American Library.

———. 1968 [1897]. *Equality*. Upper Saddle River, NJ: Gregg Press.

Benham, Lee. 1972. The Effects of Advertising on the Prices of Eyeglasses. *Journal of Law and Economics*, 15 (October).

Bennett, John. 1989. *The Economic Theory of Central Planning*. Oxford: Blackwell.

Bergson, Abram. 1949. Socialist Economics. In Ellis 1949.

———. 1967. Market Socialism Revisited. *Journal of Political Economy*, 75 (October).

Berkley, George E. 1988. *Vienna and its Jews: The Tragedy of Success, 1880s–1980s*. Cambridge, Ma: Abt.

Berliner, Joseph. Marxism and the Soviet Economy. *Problems of Communism*, 12:5 (September–October).

Bernardo, Robert M. 1971. The Theory of Moral Incentives in Cuba. University: University of Alabama Press.

Bestor, A. E. 1948. The Evolution of the Socialist Vocabulary. *Journal of the History of Ideas*, 9 (June), 259–302.

Bettelheim, Charles. 1965. Planning and the Market. *Monthly Review* (April).

———. 1975. *The Transition to Socialist Economy*. Hassocks, Sussex: Harvester.

———. 1976. *Economic Calculation and Forms of Property*. London: Routledge.

———. 1978. *Class Struggles in the USSR*. Two volumes. Hassocks: Harvester.

Bettelheim, Charles, and Paul Marlor Sweezy. 1971. *On the Transition to Socialism*. New York: Monthly Review Press.

Black, Bob. ca. 1985 (Undated). *The Abolition of Work and Other Essays*. Port Townsend: Loompanics.

Blaug, Mark. 1980. *The Methodology of Economics*. Cambridge: Cambridge University Press.

———. 1985. *Economic Theory in Retrospect*. Fourth edition. Cambridge: Cambridge University Press.

———. 1986 [1982]. Another Look at the Labour Reduction Problem in Marx. In *Economic History and the History of Economics*. New York: New York University Press.

———. 1990. *Economic Theories: True or False?* Aldershot: Elgar.

Bliss, C.J. 1972. Prices, Markets, and Planning. *Economic Journal*, 82.

Blodgett, Ralph H. 1979. *Comparative Economic Systems*. New York: Macmillan.

Bodington, Stephen. 1973. *Computers and Socialism*. Nottingham: Spokesman.

Boettke, Peter J. 1990. *The Political Economy of Soviet Socialism: The Formative Years, 1918–1928*. Boston: Kluwer.

Böhm-Bawerk, Eugen von. 1959 [1884–1921]. *Capital and Interest*. Three volumes published as one. South Holland, Il: Libertarian Press.

———. 1962. *Shorter Classics of Eugen von Böhm-Bawerk: Volume I*. South Holland, Il: Libertarian Press.

Bonin, John P., and Louis Putterman. 1987. *Economics of Co-operation and the Labor-Managed Economy*. Chur: Harwood.

Bookchin, Murray. 1971. *Post-Scarcity Anarchism*. San Francisco: Ramparts.

Boorstein, Edward. 1968. *The Economic Transformation of Cuba*. New York: Monthly Review Press.

Bornstein, Morris (ed.) 1974a. *Comparative Economic Systems: Models and Cases*. Homewood, Il: Irwin.

———. (ed.) 1974b. *Plan and Market*. New Haven: Yale University Press.

Boudin, Louis B. 1907. *The Theoretical System of Karl Marx in the Light of Recent Criticism*. Chicago: Kerr.

Bourgin, Maurice. 1933 [1904]. *Les Systèmes Socialistes*, Third edition. Paris.

Bradley, Robert, Jr. 1981. Market Socialism: A Subjectivist Evaluation. *Journal of Libertarian Studies*, 5:1.

Bradley, Keith, and Alan Gelb. 1983. *Worker Capitalism: The New Industrial Relations*. Cambridge, Ma: M.I.T. Press.

Brandow, Karen, and Jim McDonnell. 1981. *No Bosses Here! A Manual on Work-

ing Collectively and Co-operatively. Boston: Alyson/Vocations for Social Change.

Braverman, Harry. 1974. *Labor and Monopoly Capital: The Degradation of Work in the Twentieth Century.* New York: Monthly Review Press.

Brecher, Jeremy, et al. 1975. *Root and Branch: The Rise of the Workers' Movements.* Greenwich, Ct: Fawcett.

Brentano, Lujo. 1878. Die Arbeiter und die Produktionskrisen. *Jahrbuch für Gesetzgebung, Verwaltung, und Volkswirtschaft im Deutschen Reich,* 2:3.

Bresciani-Turroni, C. 1950. *Economic Policy for the Thinking Man.* London: Hodge.

Britan, Gerald M., and Ronald Cohen (eds.) 1980. *Hierarchy and Society: Anthropological Perspectives on Bureaucracy.* Philadelphia: Institute for the Study of Human Issues.

British and Irish Communist Organisation. 1970. *Marxism and Market Socialism.* Belfast: Atholl Books.

Brittan, Samuel. 1975. *Participation without Politics.* London: Institute of Economic Affairs.

Brown, J.A.C. 1980 [1954]. *The Social Psychology of Industry.* Harmondsworth: Penguin.

Brozen, Yale. 1982. *Concentration, Mergers, and Public Policy.* New York: Macmillan.

Brus, Włodzimierz. 1972. *The Market in a Socialist Economy.* London: Routledge.

———. 1973. *The Economics and Politics of Socialism.* London: Routledge.

———. 1975. *Socialist Ownership and Political Systems.* London: Routledge.

Brus, Włodzimierz, and Kazimierz Laski. 1989. *From Marx to the Market: Socialism in Search of an Economic System.* Oxford: Clarendon.

Brutzkus, Boris. 1935 [1921]. *Economic Planning in Soviet Russia.* London: Routledge.

Bryson, Phillip J. 1976. *Scarcity and Control in Socialism: Essays on East European Planning.* Lexington, Ma: Heath.

Buchanan, James McGill. 1969. *Cost and Choice: An Inquiry in Economic Theory.* Chicago: Markham.

Buchanan, James McGill, and G. F. Thirlby (eds.) 1973. *LSE Essays on Cost.* London: Weidenfeld and Nicholson.

Buick, Adam L. 1975. The Myth of the Transitional Society. *Critique,* 5.

———. 1978. Ollman's Vision of Communism. *Critique,* 9 (Spring–Summer).

———. 1987. Bordigism. In Rubel and Crump 1987.

Buick, Adam L., and John Crump. 1986. *State Capitalism: The Wages System under New Management.* New York: St. Martin's Press.

Bukharin, Nikolai Ivanovich. 1920. *Programme of the World Revolution.* Glasgow: Socialist Labour Press.

———. 1969 [1921]. *Historical Materialism: A System of Sociology.* Ann Arbor: University of Michigan Press.

———. 1971. *Economics of the Transformation Period: With Lenin's Critical Remarks.* New York: Bergman.

———. 1982. *Selected Writings on the State and the Transition to Socialism.* Edited and translated by Richard B. Day. New York: Sharpe.

Bukharin, Nikolai Ivanovich, and E Preobrazhensky. 1966 [1922]. *The ABC of Communism.* Ann Arbor: University of Michigan Press.

Campbell, Donald T. 1974. Evolutionary Epistemology. In Paul A. Schilpp (ed.), *The Philosophy of Karl Popper.* La Salle: Open Court.

Campbell, Robert W. 1961. Marx, Kantorovich, Novozhilov: Stoimost' versus Reality. *Slavic Review,* 20.

Cardan, Paul. 1972 [1957]. *Workers' Councils and the Economics of a Self-Managed Society.* London: Solidarity.

Carr, E.H. 1980 [1951–1953]. *The Bolshevik Revolution.* Three volumes. New York: Norton.

Carsten, F.L. 1972. *Revolution in Central Europe 1918–1919.* Berkeley: University of California Press.

Carver, Terrell. 1983. *Marx and Engels: The Intellectual Relationship.* Bloomington, In: Indiana University Press.

Case, J., and R.C.R. Taylor (eds.) 1979. *Co-ops, Communes, and Collective Experiments in Social Change in the 1960s and 1970s.* New York: Pantheon.

Cassel, Gustav. 1903. *The Nature and Necessity of Interest.* London: Macmillan.

Cave, Martin. 1980. *Computers and Economic Planning: The Soviet Experience.* Cambridge: Cambridge University Press.

Cave, Martin, and P. Hare (eds.) 1981. *Alternative Approaches to Economic Planning.* New York: Macmillan.

Chase, Stuart. 1971 [1934]. *The Economy of Abundance.* Port Washington, NY: Kenikat.

Chandler, Alfred D., Jr. 1962. *Strategy and Structure: Chapters in the History of the American Industrial Enterprise.* Cambridge, Ma: M.I.T. Press.

———. 1977. *The Visible Hand: The Managerial Revolution in American Business.* Cambridge, Ma: Harvard University Press.

Chandler, Alfred D., Jr., and Herman Daems (eds.) 1980. *Managerial Hierarchies: Comparative Perspectives on the Rise of the Modern Industrial Enterprise.* Cambridge, Ma: Harvard University Press.

Cherevik, E., and Y. Shvyrkov. 1982. *An ABC of Planning.* Moscow: Progress.

Cheung, Steven N.S. 1973. The Fable of the Bees: An Economic Investigation. *Journal of Law and Economics,* 16 (April).

———. 1978. *The Myth of Social Cost.* London: Institute of Economic Affairs.

———. 1982. *Will China go 'Capitalist'?* London: Institute of Economic Affairs.

———. 1983. The Contractual Nature of the Firm. *Journal of Law and Economics,* 26:1.

Chickering, A. Lawrence (ed.) 1976. *The Politics of Planning: A Review and Critique of Centralized Economic Planning.* San Francisco: Institute for Contemporary Studies.

Chiplin, Brian, et al. 1977. *Can Workers Manage?* London: Institute of Economic Affairs.

Claessen, H.J.M., and P. Skalnik (eds.) 1978. *The Early State.* The Hague: Mouton.

Clapham, J.H. 1924. *An Economic History of Modern Britain.* Cambridge: Cambridge University Press.

Clark, John Bates. 1914. *Social Justice without Socialism.* Boston: Houghton Mifflin.

———. 1956 [1899]. *The Distribution of Wealth: A Theory of Wages, Interest, and Profits.* New York: Kelley and Millman.

Clayre, Alasdair (ed.) 1980. *The Political Economy of Co-operation and Participation.* Oxford: Oxford University Press.

Cliff, Tony. 1970. *Russia: A Marxist Analysis.* London: International Socialism.

Coase, Ronald Harry. 1937. The Nature of the Firm. *Economica,* N.S. IV (November). Reprinted in Coase 1988.

———. 1945. Price and Output Policy of State Enterprise: A Comment. *Economic Journal* (April).

———. 1946. The Marginal Cost Controversy. *Economica,* N.S. 13 (August). Reprinted in Coase 1988.

———. 1973. Business Organization and the Accountant. In Buchanan and Thirlby 1973.

———. 1988. *The Firm, The Market, and the Law.* Chicago: University of Chicago Press.

Cohen, Gerald Allan. 1978. *Karl Marx's Theory of History: A Defence.* Princeton: Princeton University Press.

———. 1988. *History, Labour, and Freedom: Themes from Marx.* Oxford: Clarendon.

Cohen, Ronald 1978. State Origins: A Reappraisal. In Claessen and Skalnik 1978.

Cohn, Arthur Wolfgang. 1920. *Kann das Geld abgeschaft werden?* Jena: Gustav Fischer.

Cole, G.D.H. 1950. *Socialist Economics.* London: Gollancz.
―――. 1964 [1934]. *The Meaning of Marxism.* Ann Arbor: University of Michigan Press.
Coleman, Steve. 1988. Impossibilism. In Rubel and Crump 1988.
Conway, David. 1987. *A Farewell to Marx: An Outline and Appraisal of his Theories.* Harmondsworth: Penguin.
Conyngham, W.J. 1982. *The Modernization of Soviet Industrial Management.* Cambridge: Cambridge University Press.
Cowen, Tyler (ed.) 1988. *The Theory of Market Failure: A Critical Examination.* Fairfax, Va: George Mason University Press.
Creed, Thomas. 1987. Subliminal Deception: Pseudoscience on the College Lecture Circuit. *Skeptical Inquirer,* 11:4 (Summer).
Dahl, Robert, and Charles Lindblom. 1953. *Politics, Economics, and Welfare.* New York: Harper and Row.
Dawkins, Richard. 1986. *The Blind Watchmaker.* New York: Norton.
Demsetz, Harold. 1967. Toward a Theory of Property Rights. *American Economic Journal* 57 (May). Reprinted in Demsetz 1988.
―――. 1969. Information and Efficiency: Another Viewpoint. *Journal of Law and Economics,* 12 (March). Reprinted in Demsetz 1989.
―――. 1988. *Ownership, Control, and the Firm: The Organization of Economic Activity, Volume I.* Oxford: Blackwell.
―――. 1989. *Efficiency, Competition, and Policy: The Organization of Economic Activity, Volume II.* Oxford: Blackwell.
Deutscher, Isaac. 1954. *The Prophet Armed: Trotsky, 1879–1921.* New York: Oxford University Press.
Dickinson, Henry D. 1933. Price Formation in a Socialist Community. *Economic Journal* (June).
―――. 1939. *Economics of Socialism.* London: Oxford University Press.
Di Quattro, A. 1978. Alienation and Justice in the Market. *American Political Science Review,* 72.
Dobb, Maurice. 1933. Economic Theory and the Problems of a Socialist Economy. *Economic Journal,* 43.
―――. 1935a. Economic Theory and Socialist Economy: A Reply. *Review of Economic Studies,* 2.
―――. 1935b. Review of Brutzkus 1935 and Hayek 1935. *Economic Journal,* 45 (September).
―――. 1940 [1937]. *Political Economy and Capitalism.* London: Routledge.
―――. 1948. *Soviet Economic Development Since 1917.* London: Routledge.
―――. 1955. *On Economic Theory and Socialism: Collected Papers.* London: Routledge.
―――. 1969. *Welfare Economics and the Economics of Socialism: Towards A Commonsense Critique.* London: Cambridge University Press.
―――. 1970. *Socialist Planning: Some Problems.* London: Lawrence and Wishart.
Dolan, Edwin G. (ed.) 1976. *The Foundations of Modern Austrian Economics.* Kansas City: Sheed and Ward.
Domar, Evsey D. 1974. Poor Old Capitalism: A Review Article. *Journal of Political Economy* (November–December).
Dorfman, Robert. 1953. 'Mathematical' or 'Linear' Programming: A Non-Mathematical Exposition. *American Economic Review,* 43.
Drewnowski, Jan. 1961. The Economic Theory of Socialism: A Suggestion for Reconsideration. *Journal of Political Economy,* 64:4 (August).
―――. 1971. 'Drewnowski's Economic Theory of Socialism', by Paul Craig Roberts: A Reply. *Journal of Political Economy* (January–February).
―――. (ed.) 1982. *Crisis in the East European Economy.* London: Croom Helm.
Drucker, Peter. 1979. *Adventures of a Bystander.* London: Heinemann.
Durbin, Elizabeth. 1984. *The Fabians, Mr Keynes, and the Economics of Democratic Socialism.* New York: Routledge.

Durbin, Evan F. M. 1936. Economic Calculus in a Planned Economy. *Economic Journal*, 46 (December). Reprinted in Durbin 1949
———. 1937. A Note on Mr. Lerner's 'Dynamical' Propositions. *Economic Journal* (September).
———. 1940. *Politics of Democratic Socialism*. London: Routledge.
———. 1949. *Problems of Economic Planning*. London: Routledge.
Ebeling, Richard. 1991. Economic Calculation under Socialism: Ludwig von Mises and his Predecessors. In Herbener 1991.
Eckstein, Alexander (ed.) 1971. *Comparison of Economic Systems: Theoretical and Methodological Approaches*. Berkeley: University of California Press.
Edwards, R.S. 1973. The Rationale of Cost Accounting. In Buchanan and Thirlby 1973.
———. 1967. *Studies in Business Organization*. London: Macmillan.
Edwards, R. S., and Harry Townsend. 1961. *Business Enterprise*. London: Macmillan.
Eggertson, Thráinn. 1990. *Economic Behavior and Institutions*. Cambridge: Cambridge University Press.
Eidem, Rolf, and Staffan Viotti. 1978. *Economic Systems*. New York: Wiley.
Elliott, John E. 1976. Karl Marx and Contemporary Models of Socialism. *History of Political Economy* 8:2 (Summer 1976).
———. 1978. Marx's Socialism in the Context of his Typology of Economic Systems. *Journal of Comparative Economics* 2:1 (March 1978).
———. 1980. Marx and Engels on Communism, Scarcity, and Division of Labor. *Economic Inquiry* XVIII:1 (April 1980).
———. 1985. *Comparative Economic Systems*. Englewood Cliffs, NJ: Prentice-Hall.
———. 1987. Karl Marx: Founding Father of Workers' Self-Governance? *Economic and Industrial Democracy* 8:3 (August).
Ellis, Howard S. (ed.) 1949. *A Survey of Contemporary Economics*. Philadelphia: Blakiston.
Ellman, Michael. 1979. *Socialist Planning*. Cambridge: Cambridge University Press.
Elsner, Henry Jr. 1967. *The Technocrats: Prophets of Automation*. Syracuse, NY: Syracuse University Press.
Elster, Jon. 1983. *Explaining Technical Change: A Case Study in the Philosophy of Science*. Cambridge: Cambridge University Press.
———. 1985. *Making Sense of Marx*. Cambridge: Cambridge University Press.
———. 1989. From Here to There: Or, If Co-operative Ownership is so Desirable, Why Are There So Few Co-operatives? *Social Philosophy and Policy*, 6:2 (Spring).
Engels, Frederick. 1942. *Origin of the Family, Private Property, and the State, in the Light of the Researches of Lewis H. Morgan*. New York: International.
———. 1954. *Anti-Dühring: Herr Eugen Dühring's Revolution in Science*. London: Lawrence and Wishart (Moscow: Foreign Languages Publishing House).
Engels, Friedrich, and Karl Marx. See Marx and Engels.
Erlich, Alexander. 1960. *The Soviet Industrialization Debate, 1924–28*. Cambridge, Ma: Harvard University Press.
Espinas, A. 1890. Les Origines de la Technologie. *Revue Philosophique de la France et de l'étranger* (July–December).
Estrin, Saul, and Peter Holmes. 1983. *French Planning in Theory and Practice*. London: Allen and Unwin.
Eucken, Walter. 1948. On the Theory of the Centrally Administered Economy: An Analysis of the German Experiment. *Economica* (May–August).
Factor, Regis A. 1988. *Guide to the Archiv für Sozialwissenschaft und Sozialpolitik Group: A History and Comprehensive Bibliography*. New York: Greenwood.
Fama, Eugene F. 1980. Agency Problems and the Theory of the Firm. *Journal of Political Economy*, 88 (April).
Fama, Eugene F., and Michael Jensen. 1983. Separation of Ownership and Control. *Journal of Law and Economics*, 26 (June).
Farbman, Michael S. 1923. *Bolshevism in Retreat*. London: Collins.

Fayol, Henri. 1949 [1919]. *General Industrial Management.* London: Pitman.

Federn, Karl. 1939. *The Materialist Conception of History: A Critical Analysis.* London: Macmillan.

Feinstein, C. H. (ed.) 1967. *Capitalism, Socialism and Economic Growth: Essays Presented to Maurice Dobb.* Cambridge: Cambridge University Press.

Fetter, Frank A. 1977. *Capital, Interest, and Rent: Essays in the Theory of Distribution.* Ed. Murray N. Rothbard. Kansas City: Sheed, Andrews, and McMeel.

Fisher, Irving. 1906. *The Nature of Capital and Income.* New York: Macmillan.

———. 1930. *The Theory of Interest, as Determined by Impatience to Spend Income and Opportunities to Invest It.* New York: Macmillan.

Fox, R.M. 1938. *Smoky Crusade.* London: Hogarth Press.

Forde, C. Daryll. 1934. *Habitat, Economy, and Society: A Geographical Introduction to Ethnology.* London: Methuen.

Frank, Robert H. 1991. *Micro-Economics and Behavior.* New York: McGraw-Hill.

Freedman, Robert. 1961. *Marx on Economics.* New York: Harcourt, Brace.

———. 1968. *Marxist Social Thought.* New York: Harcourt, Brace.

———. 1990. *The Marxist System: Economic, Political, and Social Perspectives.* Chatham, NJ: Chatham House.

Friedman, David D. 1986. *Price Theory: An Intermediate Text.* Cincinnati: South-Western.

———. 1989 [1973]. *The Machinery of Freedom: Guide to a Radical Capitalism.* Second edition. La Salle: Open Court.

Friedman, Milton. 1947. Lerner on the Economics of Control. *Journal of Political Economy,* 55 (October). Reprinted in Friedman 1953.

———. 1953. *Essays in Positive Economics.* Chicago: University of Chicago Press.

———. 1962. *Capitalism and Freedom.* Chicago: University of Chicago Press.

———. 1976 [1962]. *Price Theory.* Chicago: Aldine.

Furubotn, Eirik G. 1976a. Worker Alienation and the Structure of the Firm. In Pejovich 1976.

———. 1976b. The Long-Run Analysis of the Labor-Managed Firm: An Alternative Interpretation. *American Economic Review,* 66.

Furubotn, Eirik G., and Svetozar Pejovich (eds.) 1974. *The Economics of Property Rights.* Cambridge, Ma: Ballinger.

Galbraith, John Kenneth. 1958. *The Affluent Society.* Boston: Houghton Mifflin.

Gambit, Jerzy. 1971. The Polish Economy: Models and Muddles. *Survey* (Summer).

Gilison, Jerome M. 1975. *The Soviet Image of Utopia.* Baltimore: Johns Hopkins Press.

Goldman, Marshall I. 1983. *USSR in Crisis: The Failure of an Economic System.* New York: Norton.

Goldschmid, Harvey J., et al. 1974. *Industrial Concentration: The New Learning.* Boston: Little, Brown.

Gordon, David. 1983. Miller on Market Neutrality, Co-operatives, and Libertarianism. *British Journal of Political Science,* 13.

———. 1990. *Resurrecting Marx: The Analytical Marxists on Freedom, Exploitation, and Justice.* New Brunswick: Transaction.

Gordon, David M., Richard Edward, and Michael Reich. 1982. *Segmented Work, Divided Workers: The Historical Transformation of Labor in the United States.* Cambridge: Cambridge University Press.

Gordon, David M., Samuel Bowles, and Thomas Weisskopf. 1983. *Beyond the Waste Land: A Democratic Alternative to Economic Decline.* New York: Doubleday.

Gorz, André. 1967 [1964]. *Strategy for Labor: A Radical Proposal.* Boston: Beacon.

Gossen, Hermann Heinrich. 1983. [1854]. *The Laws of Human Relations, and the Rules of Human Action Derived Therefrom.* Cambridge, Ma: MIT Press.

Graicunas, V.A. 1933. Relationship in Organization. *Bulletin of the International Management Institute* (March). Reprinted in Gulick and Urwick 1937

Grassl, Wolfgang, and Barry Smith (eds.) 1986. *Austrian Economics: Historical and Philosophical Background.* Croom Helm: London.

Gregory, Theodor E. 1933. *Gold, Unemployment, and Capitalism*. London: King.

Grossman, Gregory (ed.) 1960. *Value and Plan*. Berkeley: University of California Press.

———. 1967. *Economic Systems*. Englewood Cliffs, NJ: Prentice-Hall.

Guevara, Ernesto. 1969 [1964]. On the Budgetary System of Finance. In Rolando E. Bonachea and Nelson P. Valdes (eds.), *Che: Selected Writings of Ernesto Guevara*. Cambridge, Ma: MIT Press.

Gulick, Luther. 1937. Notes on the Theory of Organization. In Gulick and Urwick 1937.

Gulick, Luther, and L. Urwick (eds.) 1937. *Papers on the Science of Administration*. New York: Columbia University Press.

Gunn, Christopher Eaton. 1984. *Workers' Self-Management in the United States*. Ithaca: Cornell University Press.

Gunning, J. Patrick. 1991. *The New Subjectivist Revolution: An Elucidation and Extension of Ludwig von Mises's Contributions to Economic Theory*. Savage, Md: Rowman and Littlefield.

Haber, Franz. 1926. *Untersuchungen über irrtümer moderner Geldverbesserer*. Jena: Gustav Fischer.

Hackett, J., and A. Hackett. 1963. *Economic Planning in France*. London: Allen and Unwin.

Hahnel, Robin, and Michael Albert. 1990. *Quiet Revolution in Welfare Economics*. Princeton: Princeton University Press.

Hall, Robert Lowe. 1937. *The Economic System in a Socialist State*. London: Macmillan.

Hallpike, Christopher Robert. 1986. *The Principles of Social Evolution*. Oxford: Clarendon.

Halm, Georg N. 1935 [1928]. Further Considerations on the Possibility of Adequate Calculation in a Socialist Community. In Hayek 1935.

———. 1960 [1951]. *Economic Systems: A Comparative Analysis*. New York: Holt, Rinehart, and Winston.

———. 1968. *Economic Systems: A Comparative Analysis*. New York: Holt, Rinehart and Winston.

Hamilton, Ian. 1921. *The Soul and Body of an Army*. London: Arnold.

Hanke, Steve H. 1987. *Privatization and Development*. San Francisco: Institute for Contemporary Studies.

Harrington, Michael. 1972. *Socialism*. New York: Saturday Review Press.

———. 1976. *The Twilight of Capitalism*. New York: Simon and Schuster.

———. 1982. What Socialists Would Do in America—If They Could. In Irving Howe (ed.), *Beyond the Welfare State*. New York: Schocken, 1982.

Harris, A.L. 1958. *Economics and Social Reform*. New York: Harper and Row.

Hattiangadi, Jagdish. 1987. *How Is Language Possible? Philosophical Reflections on the Evolution of Language and Knowledge*. La Salle: Open Court.

Hayek, Friedrich August. 1932. *Prices and Production*. London: Routledge.

———. (ed.). 1935. *Collectivist Economic Planing*. London: Routledge.

———. 1937. Economics and Knowledge. *Economica*, 4. Reprinted in Hayek 1948.

———. 1940. The Competitive 'Solution'. *Economica*, 7:26, N.S. (May). Reprinted in Hayek 1948.

———. 1945. The Use of Knowledge in Society. *American Economic Review*, 35. Reprinted in Hayek 1948.

———. 1948. *Individualism and Economic Order*. Chicago: University of Chicago Press.

———. 1960. *The Constitution of Liberty*. Chicago: University of Chicago Press.

———. 1967. *Studies in Philosophy, Politics, and Economics*. Chicago: University of Chicago Press.

———. 1976. The New Confusion About 'Planning'. *Morgan Guaranty Survey* (January). Reprinted in Hayek 1978.

————. 1976 [1944]. *The Road to Serfdom*. Chicago: University of Chicago Press.

————. 1978a. *New Studies in Philosophy, Politics, and the History of Ideas*. Chicago: University of Chicago Press.

————. 1978b. Competition as a Discovery Procedure. In Hayek 1978a.

————. 1979 [1964]. *The Counter-Revolution of Science: Studies on the Abuse of Reason*. Indianapolis: Liberty Press.

————. 1984. *Money, Capital, and Fluctuations: Early Essays*. Chicago: University of Chicago Press.

————. 1988. *The Fatal Conceit: The Errors of Socialism*. The Collected Works of F.A. Hayek, Volume I. Chicago: University of Chicago Press.

————. 1992. *The Fortunes of Liberalism: Essays on Austrian Economics and the Ideal of Freedom*. The Collected Works of F.A. Hayek, Volume IV. Chicago: University of Chicago Press.

Hazlitt, Henry. 1951. *The Great Idea: A Novel about the Rediscovery of Capitalism*. New York: Appleton-Century-Crofts. (Later revised and republished as *Time Will Run Back: A Novel about the Rediscovery of Capitalism*. New Rochelle, NY: Arlington House, 1966.)

Heal, G.M. 1973. *The Theory of Economic Planning*. Amsterdam: North Holland.

Hearnshaw, F.J.C. 1929 [1928]. *A Survey of Socialism*. London: Macmillan.

Heilbroner, Robert L. 1970. *Between Capitalism and Socialism: Essays in Political Economics*. New York: Random House.

————. 1990. The Triumph of Capitalism. *The New Yorker* (23rd January).

Heimann, Eduard. 1918. Die Sozialisierung. *Archiv für Sozialwissenschaft und Sozialpolitik*, 45.

————. 1922. *Mehrwert and Gemeinwirtschaft: Kritische und positive Beiträge zur Theorie des Sozialismus*. Berlin: Robert Engelmann.

————. 1934. Planning and the Market System. *Social Research*, 1 (November).

————. 1939. Literature on the Theory of a Socialist Economy. *Social Research*, 6:1 (February).

————. 1945. *History of Economic Doctrines: An Introduction to Economic Theory*. London: Oxford University Press.

Heller, Michael, and Aleksandr Nekrich. 1985. *Utopia in Power: A History of the USSR from 1917 to the Present*. London: Hutchinson.

Herbener, Jeffrey (ed.) 1991. *The Meaning of Ludwig von Mises*. Boston: Kluwer.

Hicks, John. 1946 [1939]. *Value and Capital: An Inquiry into some Fundamental Principles of Economic Theory*. Oxford: Clarendon.

————. 1967. The Hayek Story. In Hicks, *Critical Essays in Monetary Theory*. Oxford: Clarendon.

Hilferding, Rudolf. 1981 [1910]. *Finance Capital: A Study of the Latest Phase of Capitalist Development*. London: Routledge.

Hirsch, Abraham, and Neil de Marchi. 1990. *Milton Friedman: Economics in Theory and Practice*. New York: Harvester Wheatsheaf.

Hirshleifer, Jack, 1984. *Price Theory and Applications*. Third edition. Englewood Cliffs: Prentice-Hall.

Hoebel, Edward Adamson. 1968 [1954]. *The Law of Primitive Man: A Study in Legal Dynamics*. Cambridge, Ma: Harvard University Press.

Hoff, Trygve J. B. 1949 [1938]. *Economic Calculation in the Socialist Society*. London: Hodge.

Hoffmann, Paul. 1988. *The Viennese: Splendor, Twilight, and Exile*. New York: Doubleday.

Horvat, Branko. 1982. *The Political Economy of Socialism*. New York: Sharpe.

House of Commons All-Party Select Committee on Science and Technology. 1978. *The Durability and Efficiency of Filament and Discharge Lamps* (3 vols.). London: HMSO.

Hunt, Richard N. 1974. *The Political Ideas of Marx and Engels, I: Marxism and Totalitarian Democracy, 1818–1850*. Pittsburgh: University of Pittsburgh Press.

——. 1984. *The Political Ideas of Marx and Engels, II: Classical Marxism, 1850–1895*. Pittsburgh: University of Pittsburgh Press.

Hurwicz, Leonid. 1960. Conditions for Economic Efficiency of Centralized and Decentralized Structures. In Grossman 1960.

——. 1972. On Informationally Decentralized Systems. In McGuire and Radner 1972.

——. 1973. The Design of Mechanisms for Resource Allocation. *American Economic Review*, 63 (May).

Hutchison, T.W. 1953. *A Review of Economic Doctrines, 1870–1929*. Oxford: Clarendon.

——. 1981. *The Politics and Philosophy of Economics: Marxians, Keynesians, and Austrians*. Oxford: Blackwell.

Iggers, Georg. 1958. *The Cult of Authority: The Political Philosophy of the Saint-Simonians: A Chapter in the Intellectual History of Totalitarianism*. The Hague: Nijhoff.

——. (ed.) 1972 [1958]. *The Doctrine of Saint-Simon: An Exposition. First Year, 1828–1829*. New York: Schocken.

Ireland, Norman J., and Peter J. Law. *The Economics of Labour-Managed Enterprises*. London: Croom Helm.

Jackall, Robert, and Henry M. Levin (eds.) 1984. *Worker Co-operatives in the United States*. Berkeley: University of California Press.

Jacobs, Daniel Norman. 1965 [1961]. *The New Communist Manifesto and Related Documents*. New York: Harper and Row.

Jasay, Antony de. 1989. *Social Contract, Free Ride: A Study of the Public Goods Problem*. Oxford: Clarendon.

——. 1990. *Market Socialism, A Scrutiny: 'This Square Circle'*. London: Institute of Economic Affairs.

Jay, Peter. 1984. *The Crisis for Western Political Economy and other Essays*. Totowa, NJ: Barnes and Noble.

Jencks, C. et al. 1979. *Who Gets Ahead? The Determinants of Economic Success in America*. New York: Basic.

Jerome, W., and Adam L. Buick. 1967. Soviet State Capitalism? The History of an Idea. *Survey*, 62 (January).

Jewkes, John. 1977. *Delusions of Dominance*. London: Institute of Economic Affairs.

Johnson, A.R. 1972. *The Transformation of Communist Ideology: The Yugoslav Case, 1945–1953*. Cambridge, Ma: M.I.T. Press.

Kant, Immanuel. 1983 [1793]. On The Proverb: That May be True in Theory But Is of No Practical Use. In Kant, *Perpetual Peace and Other Essays*. Indianapolis: Hackett.

Kautsky, Karl Johann. 1910 [1892]. *The Class Struggle (Erfurt Program)*. Chicago: Kerr.

——. 1902. *The Social Revolution*. Chicago: Kerr.

——. 1925 [1922]. *The Labor Revolution*. New York: Dial Press.

——. 1927. *Thomas More and his Utopia, with a Historical Introduction*. London: Black.

——. 1931. *Bolshevism at a Deadlock*. London: Allen and Unwin.

——. 1936. *The Economic Doctrines of Karl Marx*. New York: Macmillan.

——. 1988 [1929]. *The Materialist Conception of History*. Abridged. New Haven: Yale University Press.

Kawai, M. 1965. Newly Acquired Pre-Cultural Behavior of the Natural Troop of Monkeys on Koshima Islet. *Primates*, 6:1.

Kawamura, S. 1963. The Process of Sub-Cultural Propagation among Japanese Macaques. In C.H. Southwick (ed.), *Primate Social Behavior*. Princeton: Princeton University Press.

Key, William. 1973. *Subliminal Seduction*. Englewood Cliffs: Prentice-Hall.

――――. 1976. *Media Sexploitation*. Englewood Cliffs: Prentice-Hall.

Khudokormov, G. N., et al. 1967. *Political Economy of Socialism*. Moscow: Progress.

Kidron, Michael. 1974. *Capitalism and Theory*. London: Pluto.

Kirzner, Israel M. 1963. *Market Theory and the Price System*. Princeton: Van Nostrand.

――――. 1973. *Competition and Entrepreneurship*. Chicago: University of Chicago Press.

――――. 1976 [1960]. *The Economic Point of View*. Second edition. Kansas City: Sheed and Ward.

――――. 1979. *Perception, Opportunity, and Profit*. Chicago: University of Chicago Press.

――――. (ed.) 1982. *Method, Process, and Austrian Economics: Essays in Honor of Ludwig von Mises*. Lexington: Heath.

――――. 1985. *Discovery and the Capitalist Process*. Chicago: University of Chicago Press.

――――. 1988a. Some Ethical Implications for Capitalism of the Socialist Calculation Debate. *Social Philosophy and Policy*, 6:1 (Autumn).

――――. 1988b. The Economic Calculation Debate: Lessons for Austrians. *Review of Austrian Economics*, 2.

――――. 1989. *Discovery, Capitalism, and Distributive Justice*. Oxford: Blackwell.

――――. 1992. *The Meaning of Market Process: Essays in the Development of Modern Austrian Economics*. London: Routledge.

Kitcher, Philip. 1990. The Division of Cognitive Labor. *Journal of Philosophy*, 87:1 (1st January).

Knight, Frank H. 1936. The Place of Marginal Economics in a Collectivist System. *American Economic Review*, supplement to Volume 26 (March).

――――. 1938. Two Economists on Socialism. *Journal of Political Economy*, 46 (April).

――――. 1965 [1933]. *The Economic Organization*. New York: Harper and Row.

――――. 1971 [1921]. *Risk, Uncertainty, and Profit*. Chicago: University of Chicago Press.

――――. 1982 [1947]. *Freedom and Organization: Essays in Economics and Social Philosophy*. Indianapolis: Liberty Press.

Kolaja, Jiri. 1966. *Workers' Councils: The Yugoslav Experience*. New York: Praeger.

Kolakowski, Leszek, and Stuart Hampshire (eds.) 1974. *The Socialist Idea: A Re-Appraisal*. New York: Basic Books.

Kollontai, Alexandra. 1977. *Selected Writings of Alexandra Kollontai*. Translated and edited by Alix Holt. London: Allison and Busby.

Koopmans, Tjalling C. (ed.) 1956. *Activity Analysis of Production and Allocation*. New York: Wiley.

Kornai, János. 1959 [1957]. *Overcentralization in Economic Administration*. Oxford: Oxford University Press.

――――. 1971. *Anti-Equilibrium*. Amsterdam: North-Holland.

――――. 1980. *Economics of Shortage*. Amsterdam: North-Holland.

――――. 1986 [1983]. *Contradictions and Dilemmas: Studies on the Socialist Economy and Society*. Cambridge, Ma: MIT Press.

――――. 1990. *Vision and Reality, Market and State: Contradictions and Dilemmas Revisited*. New York: Routledge.

――――. 1992. *The Socialist System: The Political Economy of Communism*. Princeton: Princeton University Press.

Kowalik, Tadeuz, et al. 1965. *On Political Economy and Econometrics: Essays in Honour of Oskar Lange*. London: Pergamon/Warsaw: PWN.

Kropotkin, Peter A. 1907. *The Conquest of Bread*. New York: G.P. Putnam's Sons.

――――. 1968 [1890]. *Fields, Factories, and Workshops, Or: Industry Combined with Agriculture and Brain Work with Manual Work*. New York: Greenwood.

Kuusinen, O.W., et al. 1961. *Fundamentals of Marxism-Leninism: Manual*. Second Impression. Moscow: Foreign Languages Publishing House.

Lachmann, Ludwig M. 1978. *Capital and its Structure*. Kansas City: Sheed, Andrews, and McMeel.
——. 1986. *The Market as an Economic Process*. Oxford: Blackwell.
Lafargue, Paul. 1975 [1880]. *The Right to be Lazy*. Chicago: Kerr.
Lal, Deepak. 1985. *The Poverty of 'Development Economics'*. Cambridge, Ma: Harvard University Press.
Landauer, Carl. 1937. Value Theory and Economic Planning. *Plan Age*, 3 (October).
——. 1944. *Theory of National Economic Planning*. Berkeley: University of California Press.
——. 1959. *European Socialism: A History of Ideas and Movements from the Industrial Revolution to Hitler's Seizure of Power*. Two volumes. Berkeley: University of California Press.
Landes, David S. 1986. What Do Bosses Really Do? *Journal of Economic History* (September).
Lange, Oskar. 1937. Mr. Lerner's Note on Socialist Economics. *Review of Economic Studies*, 4.
——. 1938 [1936]. On the Economic Theory of Socialism. In Lippincott 1938.
——. 1967. The Computer and the Market. In Feinstein 1967. Reprinted in Nove and Nuti 1972.
Langlois, Richard N. (ed.) 1986. *Economics as a Process: Essays in the New Institutional Economics*. Cambridge: Cambridge University Press.
Lavoie, Donald C. 1982. The Development of the Misesian Theory of Interventionism. In Kirzner 1982.
——. 1985. *Rivalry and Central Planning: The Socialist Calculation Debate Reconsidered*. Cambridge: Cambridge University Press.
——. 1985. *National Economic Planning: What is Left?* Cambridge, Ma: Ballinger.
Lawton, Lancelot. 1927. *The Russian Revolution 1917–1926*. London: Macmillan.
Leibenstein, H. 1976. *Beyond Economic Man: A New Foundation for Micro-Economics*. Cambridge, Ma: Harvard University Press.
Leichter, Otto. 1923. *Die Wirtschaftsrechnung in der sozialistischen Gesellschaft*. Vienna: Wiener Volksbuchhandlung Ignaz Brand.
Leijonhufvud, Axel. 1986. Capitalism and the Factory System. In Langlois 1986.
Lenin, Vladimir I. 1960–. [Cited as LCW]. *Collected Works*. Moscow: Progress/ London: Lawrence and Wishart.
Leontief, Wassily. 1966. *Input-Output Economics*. New York: Oxford University Press.
Lepage, Henri. 1982. *Tomorrow, Capitalism: The Economics of Economic Freedom*. La Salle: Open Court.
Lerner, Abba P. 1934. Economic Theory and Socialist Economy: A Reply. *Review of Economic Studies*, 2 (October).
——. 1935. A Rejoinder to Mr Dobb. *Review of Economic Studies*, 2 (January).
——. 1936. A Note on Socialist Economics. *Review of Economic Studies*, 4:1 (October).
——. 1937. Statics and Dynamics in Socialist Economics. *Economic Journal*, 47 (June).
——. 1944. *The Economics of Control*. New York: Macmillan.
Leube, Kurt R., and Albert H. Zlabinger (eds.) 1985. *The Political Economy of Freedom: Essays in Honor of F.A. Hayek*. Munich: Philosophia.
Levin, Henry. 1987. Improving Productivity through Education and Technology. In Burke and Rumberger (eds.), *The Future Impact of Technology on Work and Education*. New York: Falmer.
Levin, Ira. 1970. *This Perfect Day*. New York: Random House.
Lewin, Moshe. 1991 [1974]. *Stalinism and the Seeds of Soviet Reform: The Debates of the 1960s*. New York: Sharpe.
Lewis, W. Arthur. 1949. *The Principles of Economic Planning*. London: Allen and Unwin.

Lindbeck, Assar. 1977. *The Political Economy of the New Left: An Outsider's View.* Second edition. New York: Harper and Row.

Lippincott, Benjamin E. (ed.) 1938. *On The Economic Theory of Socialism.* Minneapolis: University of Minnesota Press.

Little, Ian Malcolm David. 1950. *A Critique of Welfare Economics.* Oxford: Clarendon.

Loasby, Brian John. 1976. *Choice, Complexity, and Ignorance: An Enquiry into Economic Theory and the Practice of Decision-Making.* Cambridge: Cambridge University Press.

———. 1989. *The Mind and Method of the Economist: A Critical Appraisal of Major Economists in the Twentieth Century.* Aldershot: Elgar.

Lutz, Vera G. 1969. *Central Planning for the Market Economy.* London: Longmans.

Lydall, Harold. 1984. *Yugoslav Socialism: Theory and Practice.* Oxford: Clarendon.

———. 1989. *Yugoslavia in Crisis.* New York: Oxford University press.

McCloskey, Donald N. 1985. *The Applied Theory of Price.* New York: Macmillan.

MacDonald, J. Ramsay. 1924. *Socialism: Critical and Constructive.* Indianapolis: Bobbs-Merrill.

McFadzean, Frank S. 1970. The Economic Planners Viewed from Inside a Large Corporation. In Alec Cairncross (ed.), *The Managed Economy.* Oxford: Blackwell.

McGee, John S. 1958. Predatory Price Cutting: The Standard Oil (N.J.) Case. *Journal of Law and Economics,* 1 (October).

———. 1971. *In Defense of Industrial Concentration.* New York: Praeger.

McGuire, C.B., and R. Radner (eds.) 1972. *Decision and Organization.* Amsterdam: North-Holland.

Mackenzie, Richard B., and Gordon Tullock. 1978 [1975]. *The New World of Economics: Explorations into the Human Experience.* Homewood, Il: Irwin.

McLellan, David. 1973. *Karl Marx: His Life and Thought.* New York: Harper and Row.

Machlup, Fritz. 1940. *The Stock Market, Credit, and Capital Formation.* London: Hodge.

———. 1942. Competition, Pliopoly, and Profit. *Economica,* Part II, N.S., No. 34 (May).

———. 1967. Theories of the Firm: Marginalist, Behavioral, Managerial. *American Economic Review,* 57:1.

———. 1984. *Knowledge: Its Creation, Distribution, and Economic Significance. Volume III: The Economics of Information and Human Capital.* Princeton: Princeton University Press.

———. 1991 [1963]. *Economic Semantics.* Second edition. New Brunswick: Transaction.

Maddison, A. 1991. *Dynamic Forces in Capitalist Development.* Oxford: Oxford University Press.

Maksimović, I.M. 1965. Professor Oskar Lange on Economic Theory of Socialism, and Yugoslav Economic Thinking. In Kowalik 1965.

Malinvaud, Edmond. 1967. Decentralized Procedures for Planning. In Malinvaud and Bacharach 1967.

Malinvaud, Edmond, and Michael O.L. Bacharach. 1967. *Activity Analysis in the Theory of Growth and Planning.* London: Macmillan.

Malkiel, Burton G. 1973. *A Random Walk Down Wall Street.* New York: Norton.

Malle, Silvana. 1985. *The Economic Organization of War Communism, 1918–1921.* Cambridge: Cambridge University Press.

Mallock, W. H. 1907. *A Critical Examination of Socialism.* New York and London: Harper and Brothers.

Mandel, Ernest. 1968. *Marxist Economic Theory.* Two Volumes. New York: Monthly Review Press.

Manne, Henry G. 1965. Mergers and the Market for Corporate Control. *Journal of Political Economy,* 73 (April).

———. 1966. *Insider Trading and the Stock Market*. New York: Free Press.

Manove, Michael. 1971. A Model of Soviet-Type Economic Planning. *American Economic Review* (June).

Marglin, Stephen A. 1974. What Do Bosses Do? The Origins and Functions of Hierarchy in Capitalist Production. *Review of Radical Political Economy*, 6:2 (Summer).

Marschak, Jakob. 1923. Wirtschaftsrechnung und Gemeinwirtschaft: Zur Mises'schen These von der Unmöglichkeit sozialistischer Wirtschaftsrechnung. *Archiv für Sozialwissenschaft und Sozialpolitik*, 51.

Marshall, Alfred. 1919. Industry and Trade. London: Macmillan.

———. 1949 [1890, 1920]. *Principles of Economics*. London: Macmillan.

Marx, Karl Heinrich. 1963. [1862–63]. *Theories of Surplus Value (Volume IV of Capital)*. Three volumes, cited as IVa, IVb, IVc. Moscow: Progress.

———. 1970 [1859]. *A Contribution to the Critique of Political Economy*. New York: International.

———. 1973. *Grundrisse: Foundations of the Critique of Political Economy*. New York: Vintage.

———. 1974. [1867, 1885, 1894]. *Capital: A Critical Analysis of Capitalist Production*. Cited as Capital I, Capital II, Capital III. Three volumes (dates of first impressions apparently between 1954 and 1963). Moscow: Progress/London: Lawrence and Wishart.

Marx, Karl Heinrich, and Frederick Engels. 1975–. *Collected Works*. Cited as MECW. Fifty volumes planned. London: Lawrence and Wishart/New York: International/Moscow: Progress.

Meade, James Edward. 1936. *Economic Analysis and Policy*. Oxford: Oxford University Press.

———. 1949. *Planning and the Price Mechanism: The Liberal-Socialist Solution*. New York: Macmillan.

———. 1965. *Efficiency, Equality, and the Ownership of Property*. Cambridge, Ma: Harvard University Press.

———. 1970. *The Theory of Indicative Planning*. Manchester: Manchester University Press.

Meade, James Edward, and J. M. Fleming. 1944. Price and Output Policy of State Enterprise (Symposium). *Economic Journal* (December).

Meek, Ronald L. 1973. [1956]. *Studies in the Labour Theory of Value*. London: Lawrence and Wishart.

Menger, Carl. 1976. *Principles of Economics: First, General Part*. New York: New York University Press.

———. 1986. *Investigations into the Method of the Social Sciences with Special Reference to Economics*. New York: New York University Press.

Michels, Robert. 1962 [1910]. *Political Parties: A Sociological Study of the Oligarchical Tendencies of Modern Democracy*. New York: Free Press.

Milanovic, Branko. 1989. *Liberalization and Entrepreneurship: Dynamics of Reform in Socialism and Capitalism*. Armonk, NY: Sharpe.

Miller, David Leslie. 1989. *Market, State, and Community: Theoretical Foundations of Market Socialism*. Oxford: Clarendon.

Miller, Roger Leroy, and Roger E. Meiners. 1986 [1978]. *Intermediate Microeconomics: Theory, Issues, Applications*. New York: McGraw-Hill.

Mises, Ludwig Edler von. 1912. *Theorie des Geldes und der Umlaufsmittel*. Munich: Duncker and Humblot.

———. 1919. *Nation, Staat, und Wirtschaft: Beiträge zur Politik und Geschichte der Zeit*. Vienna: Manzsche.

———. 1920a. Die Wirtschaftsrechnung im sozialistischen Gemeinwesen. *Archiv für Sozialwissenschaften und Sozialpolitik*, 47:1 (April).

———. 1920b. Die Abschaffung des Geldes in Russland. *Neue Freie Presse* (17th November).

———. 1922. *Die Gemeinwirtschaft: Untersuchungen über den Sozialismus.* Jena: Gustav Fischer.

———. 1923. Neue Beiträge zum Problem der sozialistischen Wirtschaftsrechnung. *Archiv für Sozialwissenshcaften und Sozialpolitik,* 51:2.

———. 1927. *Liberalismus.* Jena: Gustav Fischer.

———. 1928. Neue Schriften zum Problem der sozialistischen Wirtschaftsrechnung. *Archiv für Sozialwissenschaft und Sozialpolitik,* 60:1.

———. 1929. *Kritik des Interventionismus: Untersuchungen zur Wirtschaftspolitik und Wirtschaftsideologie der Gegenwart.* Jena: Gustav Fischer.

———. 1932. *Die Gemeinwirtschaft: Untersuchungen über den Sozialismus.* Revision of Mises 1922. Jena: Gustav Fischer.

———. 1933. *Grundprobleme der Nationalökonomie.* Jena: Gustav Fischer.

———. 1935. Economic Calculation in the Socialist Commonwealth. Translation of Mises 1920. In Hayek 1935.

———. 1940. *Nationalökonomie: Theorie des Handelns und Wirtschaftens.* Geneva: Editions Union.

———. 1944. *Bureaucracy.* New Haven: Yale University Press.

———. 1956. *The Anti-Capitalistic Mentality.* Princeton: Van Nostrand.

———. 1957. *Theory and History: An Interpretation of Social and Economic Evolution.* New Haven: Yale University Press.

———. 1960. *Epistemological Problems of Economics.* Princeton: Van Nostrand.

———. 1962a. *The Free and Prosperous Commonwealth: An Exposition of the Ideas of Classical Liberalism.* Translation of Mises 1927. Princeton: Van Nostrand.

———. 1962b. *The Ultimate Foundation of Economic Science: An Essay on Method.* Princeton: Van Nostrand.

———. 1966. *Human Action: A Treatise on Economics.* Third revised edition. Revised translation of Mises 1948. Chicago: Regnery.

———. 1969a. *The Historical Setting of the Austrian School of Economics.* New Rochelle: Arlington House.

———. 1969b. [1944]. *Omnipotent Government: The Rise of the Total State and Total War.* New Rochelle: Arlington House.

———. 1971. *The Theory of Money and Credit.* Translation of Mises 1912. New York: Foundation for Economic Education.

———. 1978. *Notes and Recollections.* South Holland, Il: Libertarian Press.

———. 1981. *Socialism: An Economic and Sociological Analysis* Translation of Mises 1932. London: Cape.

———. 1983. *Nation, State, and Economy.* Translation of Mises 1919. New York: New York University Press.

———. 1977 [1929]. *A Critique of Interventionism.* Translation of Mises 1929. New Rochelle, NY: Arlington House.

———. 1990a. *Money, Method, and the Market Process: Essays by Ludwig von Mises.* Edited by Richard M. Ebeling. Dordrecht: Kluwer.

———. 1990b [1920]. *Economic Calculation in the Socialist Commonwealth.* Auburn: Ludwig von Mises Institute.

Mitchell, Margaret. 1973 [1936]. *Gone with the Wind.* New York: Avon.

Moore, Stanley. 1980. *Marx on the Choice between Socialism and Communism.* Cambridge, Ma: Harvard University Press.

Moore, Wilbert. 1966. The Utility of Utopias. *American Sociological Review,* 31.

Morris, William. 1970 [1890]. *News From Nowhere.* London: Routledge.

Morris, William T. 1968. *Decentralization in Management Systems: An Introduction to Design.* Columbus: Ohio State University Press.

Moss, Lawrence S (ed.) 1976. *The Economics of Ludwig von Mises: Towards a Critical Reappraisal.* Kansas City: Sheed, Andrews, and McMeel.

Mossé, R. 1937. The Theory of Planned Economy: A Study of Some Recent Works. *International Labour Review* (September).

Mueller, W. F., and L. G. Hamm. 1974. *Trends in Industrial Concentration, 1947 to 1970.* Review of Economics and Statistics, 56:513 (November).

Müller, Hans. 1967. *Ursprung und Geschichte des Wortes 'Sozialismus' und seiner Verwandten*. Hanover: Dietz.

Murrell, Peter. 1983. Did the Theory of Market Socialism Answer the Challenge of Ludwig von Mises? *History of Political Economy*, 15:1 (Spring).

Nell, Edward J. 1967. Automation and the Abolition of the Market. *New Left Notes* (*Praxis* supplement) (7th August).

Newman, K. 1980. Incipient Bureaucracy. In Britan and Cohen 1980.

Nimzowitsch, Aron. 1929. *My System*. London: Bell.

Nove, Alec. 1969. *Economic History of the USSR*. Harmondsworth: Allen Lane.

———. 1973. *Efficiency Criteria for Nationalized Industries: A Study of the Misapplications of Micro-Economic Theory*. Toronto: University of Toronto Press.

———. 1979. *Political Economy and Soviet Socialism*. New York: Allen and Unwin.

———. 1983. *The Economics of Feasible Socialism*. New York: Allen and Unwin.

———. 1991. *The Economics of Feasible Socialism Revisited*. London: Harper Collins.

Nove, Alec, and D.M. Nuti (eds.) 1972. *Socialist Economics*. Harmondsworth: Penguin.

Nozick, Robert. 1974. *Anarchy, State, and Utopia*. New York: Basic Books.

Nutter, G. Warren. 1968. Markets without Property: A Grand Illusion. In Beadles and Drewry 1968. Reprinted in Furubotn and Pejovich 1974 and in Nutter 1983.

———. 1983. *Political Economy and Freedom: A Collection of Essays*. Indianapolis: Liberty Press.

Nutter, G. Warren, and Henry Adler Einhorn. 1969. *Enterprise Monopoly in the United States, 1899–1958*. New York: Columbia University Press.

Oakeshott, R. 1973. Spain's Oasis of Democracy. *The Observer* (Colour Supplement, 21st January).

Okun, Arthur M. 1975. *Equality and Efficiency: The Big Trade-off*. Washington, DC: Brookings Institution.

Ollman, Bertell. 1979. *Social and Sexual Revolution: Essays on Marx and Reich*. London: Pluto.

O'Neill, John. 1989. Markets, Socialism, and Information: A Reformulation of a Marxian Objection to the Market. *Social Philosophy and Policy*, 6:2 (Spring).

Orwell, George. 1968. Review of Hayek, *The Road to Serfdom* and Burnham, *The Managerial Revolution*. In Sonia Orwell and Ian Angus (eds.) *The Collected Essays, Journalism, and Letters of George Orwell*, Volume 4. New York: Harcourt, Brace.

O'Shaughnessy, John. 1976. *Patterns of Business Organization*. London: Allen and Unwin.

Overbeek, Johannes. 1987. Nicolaas G. Pierson and Socialism. *Austrian Economics Newsletter* (Summer).

Owen, Robert. 1844. *The Book of the New Moral World, Part Fifth: The Elements of the Science of Society, Or of the Social State of Man*. London: Watson.

Packard, Vance. 1958. *The Hidden Persuaders*. New York: McKay.

———. 1960. *The Waste Makers*. New York: McKay.

Pannekoek, Anton. 1970. *Workers' Councils*. Detroit: Root and Branch.

Pareto, Vilfredo. 1969 [1909]. *Manual of Political Economy*. New York: Kelley.

Paul, Ellen Frankel et al. 1989. *Capitalism*. Oxford: Blackwell.

Pecqueur, Constantin. 1842. *Théorie nouvelle d'économie sociale et politique*. Paris: Capelle.

Pejovich, Svetozar. 1966. *The Market-Planned Economy of Yugoslavia*. Minneapolis: University of Minnesota Press.

———. (ed.) 1976. *Government Controls and the Free Market: The U.S. Economy in the 1970s*. College Station: Texas A&M University Press.

———. (ed.) 1978. *The Codetermination Movement in the West*. Lexington: Heath.

———. 1990. *The Economics of Property Rights: Towards a Theory of Comparative Systems*. Dordrecht: Kluwer.

——. (ed.) 1987. *Socialism: Institutional, Philosophical, and Economic Issues.* Dordrecht: Kluwer.

——. 1990. *The Economics of Property Rights: Towards a Theory of Comparative Systems.* Dordrecht: Kluwer.

Peltzman, Sam. 1976. Toward a More General Theory of Regulation. *Journal of Law and Economics,* 19:2 (August).

——. 1977. The Gains and Losses from Industrial Concentration. *Journal of Law and Economics* (October).

Perrin, Noel. 1980. *Giving Up the Gun: Japan's Reversion to the Sword, 1543–1879.* Boulder: Shambhala.

Petersen, Jørn Henrik. 1970. Some Further Comments on Drewnowski's Economic Theory of Socialism. *Journal of Political Economy* (March-April).

Pigou, A.C. 1937. *Socialism versus Capitalism.* London: Macmillan.

Pierson, Nikolaas Gerard. 1902. Het waardeproblem in een socialistische Maat-schappij. *De Economist,* 41.

——. 1935. The Problem of Value in the Socialist Community. Translation of Pierson 1902. In Hayek 1935.

Plekhanov, Georgii V. 1961. *Selected Philosophical Works, In Five Volumes.* London: Lawrence and Wishart/Moscow: Institute of Philosophy of the Academy of Sciences of the U.S.S.R.

Polanyi, George. 1967. *Planning in Britain: The Experience of the 1960s.* London: Institute of Economic Affairs.

Polanyi, Karl. 1922. Sozialistische Rechnungslegung. *Archiv für Sozialwissenschaft,* 49.

——. 1924. Die funktionelle Theorie der Gesellschaft und das Problem der sozialistischen Rechnungslegung. *Archiv für Sozialwissenschaft,* 52.

Polanyi, Michael. 1940. *The Contempt of Freedom: The Russian Experiment and After.* London: Watts.

——. 1951. *The Logic of Liberty: Reflections and Rejoinders.* London: Routledge.

Poole, Michael. 1989. *The Origins of Economic Democracy: Profit-Sharing and Employee-Shareholding Schemes.* London: Routledge.

Popper, Karl Raimund. 1968 [1934]. *The Logic of Scientific Discovery.* New York: Harper and Row.

——. 1961 [1957]. *The Poverty of Historicism.* London: Routledge.

——. 1971 [1962]. *The Open Society and Its Enemies.* Two volumes. Princeton: Princeton University Press.

Porter, Michael E. 1980. *Competitive Strategy: Techniques for Analyzing Industries and Competitors.* New York: Free Press.

Posner, Richard A. 1978. *Antitrust Law: An Economic Perspective.* Chicago: University of Chicago Press.

Progress Publishers. 1966. *Man's Dreams are Coming True.* Moscow: Progress.

Prychitko, David L. 1988. Marxism and Decentralized Socialism. *Critical Review,* 2:4 (Spring).

Pryor, Frederick L. 1973. *Property and Industrial Organization in Communist and Capitalist Countries.* Bloomington, In: Indiana University Press.

——. 1985. *A Guidebook to the Comparative Study of Economic Systems.* Englewood Cliffs: Prentice-Hall.

Radford, R.A. 1945. The Economic Organization of a P.O.W. Camp. *Economica,* 12 (November).

Rae, John. 1891. *Contemporary Socialism.* Second edition, revised and enlarged. New York: Scribner's.

Ramsey, James B. 1977. *Economic Forecasting: Models or Markets?* London: Institute of Economic Affairs.

Rawls, John. 1971. *A Theory of Justice.* Cambridge, Ma: Harvard University Press.

Read, Leonard E. 1958. I, Pencil: My Family Tree as Told to Leonard E. Read. *The Freeman* (December).

Redwood, John. 1980. *Public Enterprise in Crisis.* Blackwell: Oxford

Reed, John. 1977 [1919]. *Ten Days that Shook the World.* Harmondsworth: Penguin.
Reekie, W. Duncan. 1979. *Industry, Prices, and Markets.* New York: Wiley.
————. 1984. *Markets, Entrepreneurs, and Liberty: An Austrian View of Capitalism.* New York: St. Martin's.
Reekie, W. Duncan, and D.E. Allen. 1983. *The Economics of Modern Business.* Oxford: Blackwell.
Ricardo, David. 1951 [1817]. *Principles of Political Economy and Taxation.* The Works and Correspondence of David Ricardo, ed. Piero Sraffa. Cambridge: Cambridge University Press.
Richardson, G.B. 1960. *Information and Investment.* Oxford: Oxford University Press.
————. 1964. *Economic Theory.* London: Hutchinson.
Robbins, Lionel. 1934. *The Great Depression.* London: Macmillan.
————. 1935 [1932]. *An Essay on the Nature and Significance of Economic Science.* Second edition. London: Macmillan.
————. 1972 [1937]. *Economic Planning and International Order.* New York: Arno.
Roberts, Paul Craig. 1968. Drewnowski's Economic Theory of Socialism. *Journal of Political Economy,* 76:4 (July–August).
————. 1971a. *Alienation and the Soviet Economy.* Albuquerque: University of New Mexico Press.
————. 1971b. Review of Howard J. Sherman, *The Soviet Economy. Journal of Political Economy* (November–December).
————. 1972. Revealed Planners' Preferences Once Again: A Rebuttal to Drewnowski. *Journal of Political Economy* (May–June).
————. 1988. The Soviet Economy: A Hopeless Cause? *Reason* (July).
Roberts, Paul Craig, and Karen La Follette. 1990. *Meltdown: Inside the Soviet Economy.* Washington, DC: Cato Institute.
Roberts, Paul Craig, and Matthew A. Stephenson. 1983 [1973]. *Marx's Theory of Exchange, Alienation, and Crisis.* Stanford: Hoover Institution Press.
Robertson, D.H. 1928. *The Control of Industry.* London: Routledge.
Robertson, Edward Stanley. 1891. The Impracticability of Socialism. In Thomas MacKay (ed.) *A Plea for Liberty: An Argument against Socialism and Socialist Legislation.* New York: Appleton.
Robins, Philip K., and Richard W. West. 1980. Labor Supply Response over Time. *Journal of Human Resources,* 15 (Fall).
Robinson, E.A.G. 1958 [1931]. *The Structure of Competitive Industry.* London: Routledge.
Robinson, Joan. 1966 [1942]. *An Essay on Marxian Economics.* Second edition. London: Macmillan.
Robinson, Roland I., and Dwayne Wrightsman. 1974. *Financial Markets: The Accumulation and Allocation of Wealth.* New York: McGraw-Hill.
Roethlisberger, F.J., and William J. Dickson. 1939. *Management and the Worker.* Cambridge, Ma: Harvard University Press.
Roper, Brian, and Snowdon, Brian (eds.) 1987. *Markets, Intervention, and Planning.* London: Longman.
Roper, Willet Crosby, Jr. 1931. *The Problem of Pricing in a Socialist State.* Cambridge, Ma: Harvard University Press.
Rosen, Corey, and Karen M. Young (eds.) 1991. *Understanding Employee Ownership.* Ithaca, NY: ILR Press.
Rothbard, Murray Newton. 1962. *Man, Economy, and State: A Treatise on Economic Principles.* Two volumes. Princeton: Van Nostrand.
————. 1976. Ludwig von Mises and Economic Calculation under Socialism. In Moss 1976.
————. 1991. The End of Socialism and the Economic Calculation Debate. *Review of Austrian Economics,* 5:2.
Rothschild, J., and J.A. Whitt. 1986. *The Co-operative Workplace.* Cambridge: Cambridge University Press.

Rubel, Maximilien, and John Crump. 1987. *Non-Market Socialism in the Nineteenth and Twentieth Centuries*. New York: St. Martin's Press.

Russell, Bertrand. 1919 [1918]. *Proposed Roads to Freedom: Socialism, Anarchism, and Syndicalism*. New York: Holt.

Rutland, Peter. 1985. *The Myth of the Plan: Lessons of Soviet Planning Experience*. La Salle: Open Court.

Samuelson, Paul. 1964. Theory and Realism: A Reply. *American Economic Review* (September).

———. 1967. *Economics*. Seventh edition. New York: McGraw-Hill.

———. 1947. *Foundations of Economic Analysis*. Cambridge: Harvard University Press.

Schäffle, Albert E.F. 1877 [1874]. *Die Quintessenz des Sozialismus*. Gotha: Perthes.

———. 1881. *Bau und Leben des sozialen Körpers*. Gotha: Perthes.

———. 1889. *The Quintessence of Socialism*. Translation of Schäffle 1877. London: Swan Sonnenschein.

———. 1892. *The Impossibility of Social Democracy*. London: Swan Sonnenschein.

Schönfeld-Illy, Leo. 1982 [1924]. *Grenznutzen und Wirtschaftsrechnung*. Munich: Philosophia.

Schoeck, Helmut. 1966. *Envy: A Theory of Social Behavior*. New York: Irvington.

Schumpeter, Joseph Alois. 1950 [1942]. *Capitalism, Socialism, and Democracy*. Third edition. New York: Harper.

Schweickart, David. 1980. *Capitalism or Worker Control? An Ethical and Economic Appraisal*. New York: Praeger.

Scott, Howard, et al. 1933. *Introduction to Technocracy*. New York: John Day.

Scott, W. Richard. 1992 [1981]. *Organizations: Rational, Natural, and Open Systems*. Third edition. Englewood Cliffs, NJ: Prentice-Hall.

Selgin, George A. 1988. Praxeology and Understanding: An Analysis of the Controversy in Austrian Economics. *Review of Austrian Economics*, 2.

Selucký, Radoslav. 1985. *Marxism, Socialism, Freedom: Towards a General Democratic Theory of Labour-Managed Systems*. New York: Methuen.

Serge, Victor. 1963. *Memoirs of a Revolutionary, 1901–1941*. New York: Oxford University Press.

Shackle, George Lennox Sharman. 1955. *Uncertainty in Economics, and Other Reflections*. Cambridge: Cambridge University Press.

———. 1972. *Epistemics and Economics: A Critique of Economic Doctrines*. Cambridge: Cambridge University Press.

Shackle, George Lennox Sharman, and Alexander Shand. 1981. *Subjectivist Economics: The New Austrian School*. Oxford: The Pica Press.

Shand, Alexander. 1984. *The Capitalist Alternative: An Introduction to Neo-Austrian Economics*. New York: New York University Press.

Shapiro, Daniel. 1989. Reviving the Socialist Calculation Debate: A Defense of Hayek against Lange. *Social Philosophy and Policy*, 6:2 (Spring).

Sheehan, James J. 1966. *The Career of Lujo Brentano: A Study of Liberalism and Social Reform in Imperial Germany*. Chicago: University of Chicago Press.

Sherman, Howard J. 1970. The Economics of Pure Communism. *Soviet Studies*, 22:1 (July).

Sik, Ota. 1976. *The Third Way: Marxist-Leninist Theory and Modern Industrial Society*. White Plains: International Arts and Sciences Press.

———. 1985 [1979]. *For a Humane Economic Democracy*. New York: Praeger.

Simmons, John, and William Mares. 1985 [1982]. *Working Together: Employee Participation in Action*. New York: New York University Press.

Simon, Herbert A. 1947. *Administrative Behavior: A Study of Decision-Making Processes in Administrative Organization*. New York: Macmillan.

———. 1957. *Models of Man: Social and Rational*. New York: Wiley.

Simpson, David. 1975. *General Equilibrium Analysis: An Introduction*. Oxford: Blackwell.

Sinden, John A., and Albert C. Worrell. 1979. *Unpriced Values: Decisions without Market Prices.* New York: Wiley.

Singer, Max. 1987. *Passage to a Human World: The Dynamics of Creating Global Wealth.* Indianapolis: Hudson Institute.

Sirc, Ljubo. 1979. *The Yugoslav Economy under Self-Management.* New York: St. Martin's Press.

Smith, Adam. 1981 [1776]. *An Inquiry into the Nature and Causes of the Wealth of Nations.* Two volumes. Indianapolis: Liberty. Reprint of Oxford University Press, 1976.

Smith, Barry, and Wolfgang Grassl (eds.) 1986. *Austrian Economics: Historical and Philosophical Background.* New York: New York University Press.

Smith, Henry. 1962. *The Economics of Socialism Reconsidered.* London: Oxford University Press.

Smith, Ken. 1987. *Free is Cheaper.* London: John Ball Press.

Smith, Shirley J. 1986. The Growing Diversity of Work Schedules. *Monthly Labor Review*, 109 (November).

Snavely, William P. 1969. *Theory of Economic Systems: Capitalism, Socialism, and Corporatism.* Columbus: Merrill.

Sowell, Thomas. 1980. *Knowledge and Decisions.* New York: Basic Books.

Spadaro, Louis M. (ed.) 1978. *New Directions in Austrian Economics.* Kansas City: Sheed, Andrews, and McMeel.

Stalin, J.V. 1972 [1952]. *Economic Problems of Socialism in the U.S.S.R.* Peking: Foreign Languages Press.

Steedman, Ian. 1977. *Marx after Sraffa.* London: Verso.

Steedman, Ian, et al. 1981. *The Value Controversy.* London: Verso.

Steele, David Ramsay. 1986. Review of *Marxism: Philosophy and Economics* by Thomas Sowell. *International Philosophical Quarterly*, 36:2.

———. How We Got Here. *Critical Review*, 2:1 (Winter).

Steindl, J. 1965. Servomechanisms and Controllers in Economic Theory and Policy. In Kowalik 1965.

Steiner, Robert J. 1973. Does Advertising Lower Consumer Prices? *Journal of Marketing*, 37 (January).

Stephen, Frank H. (ed.) 1982. *The Performance of Labour-Managed Firms.* New York: St. Martin's Press.

———. 1984. *The Economic Analysis of Producers' Co-operatives.* New York: St. Martin's Press.

Stigler, George J. 1941. *Production and Distribution Theories.* New York: Macmillan.

———. 1971. The Theory of Economic Regulation. *Bell Journal of Economics and Management Science*, 2:1 (Spring). Reprinted in Stigler 1988.

———. 1987 [1942]. *The Theory of Price.* Fourth edition. New York: Macmillan.

———. 1983 [1968]. *The Organization of Industry.* Chicago: University of Chicago Press.

———. (ed.) 1988. *Chicago Studies in Political Economy.* Chicago: University of Chicago Press.

Strachey, John. 1936. *The Theory and Practice of Socialism.* London: Gollancz.

Streissler, Erich (ed.) 1969. *Roads to Freedom.* London: Routledge.

Ströbel, Heinrich. 1922. *Socialisation in Theory and Practice.* London: King.

Sugden, Robert. 1986. *The Economics of Rights, Co-operation, and Welfare.* Oxford: Blackwell.

Sweezy, A.R. 1936. The Economist's Place under Socialism. In *Explanations in Economics: Notes and Essays contributed in Honour of F.W. Taussig.* New York: McGraw-Hill.

Sweezy, Paul Marlor. 1949. *Socialism.* New York: McGraw-Hill.

———. 1968 [1942]. *The Theory of Capitalist Development.* New York: Monthly Review Press.

Sweezy, Paul Marlor, and Charles Bettelheim. 1971. *On the Transition to Socialism.* New York: Monthly Review Press.

Szamuely, László. 1974. *First Models of the Socialist Economic Systems: Principles and Theories*. Budapest: Akadémiai Kiadó.

Tagliacozzo, G. 1945. Croce and the Nature of Economic Science. *Quarterly Journal of Economics* (May).

Tamedly, Elizabeth. 1969. *Socialism and International Economic Order*. Caldwell, Id: Caxton.

Tarbuck, Kenneth J. (ed.) 1979. *The Politics and Economics of the Transition Period*. Boston: Routledge.

Taylor, Fred M. 1929. The Guidance of Production in a Socialist State. *American Economic Review*, 19:1 (March). Reprinted in Lippincott 1938.

Temkin, Gabriel. 1989. On Economic Reform in Socialist Countries: The Debate on Economic Calculation under Socialism Revisited. *Communist Economies*, 1:1.

Thimm, Alfred L. 1980. *The False Promise of Codetermination: The Changing Nature of European Workers' Participation*. Lexington, Ma: Heath.

Thirlby, G. F. 1946a. The Subjective Theory of Value and Accounting 'Cost'. *Economica* (February). Reprinted in Buchanan and Thirlby 1973.

——. 1946b. The Ruler. *South African Journal of Economics* (December). Reprinted in Buchanan and Thirlby 1973.

——. 1952. The Economist's Description of Business Behaviour. *Economica* (May). Reprinted in Buchanan and Thirlby 1973

——. 1960. Economists' Cost Rules and Equilibrium Theory. *Economica* (May). Reprinted in Buchanan and Thirlby 1973

Thomas, H., and C. Logan. 1982. *Mondragon: An Economic Analysis*. London: Allen and Unwin.

Thomas, P. 1980. *Karl Marx and the Anarchists*. Boston: Routledge.

Tisch, Kläre. Wirtschaftsrechnung und Veteilung im zentralistisch organisierten sozialistischen Gemeinwesen. Ph.D. dissertation, University of Bonn.

Tschayanoff, Alexander D. 1923. Zur Frage einer Theorie der nichtkapitalistischen Wirtschaftssysteme. *Archiv für Sozialwissenschaft und Sozialpolitik*, 1:51.

Tugan-Baranowsky, Michael I. 1966 [1908]. *Modern Socialism in its Historical Development*. New York: Russell and Russell.

Untermann, Ernst. 1907. *Marxian Economics: A Popular Introduction to the Three Volumes of Marx's 'Capital'*. Chicago: Kerr.

Urwick, L. 1937. Organization as a Technical Problem. In Gulick and Urwick 1937.

Vanek, Jaroslav. 1970. *The General Theory of Labor-Managed Economies*. Ithaca: Cornell University Press.

——. 1971. *The Participatory Economy*. Ithaca: Cornell University Press.

——. (ed.) 1975. *Self-Management, Economic Liberation of Man: Selected Readings*. Harmondsworth: Penguin.

Vaughn, Karen Iverson. 1980a. Does it Matter that Costs are Subjective? *Southern Economic Journal*, 46.

——. 1980b. Economic Calculation under Socialism: The Austrian Contribution. *Economic Inquiry*, 18.

Veblen, Thorstein. 1963 [1919]. *The Engineers and the Price System*. Introduction by Daniel Bell. New York: Harcourt, Brace.

Walicki, Andrzej. 1988. Karl Marx as Philosopher of Freedom. *Critical Review*, 2:4 (Fall).

Walras, Léon. 1954 [1874, 1926]. *Elements of Pure Economics, Or The Theory of Social Wealth*. Homewood, Il: Irwin.

Ward, Benjamin N. 1958. The Firm in Illyria: Market Syndicalism. *American Economic Review*, 48.

——. 1960. Kantorovich on Economic Calculation. *Journal of Political Economy*, 68.

——. 1967. *The Socialist Economy: A Study of Organizational Alternatives*. New York: Random House.

Webb, Sidney, and Beatrice. 1935. *Soviet Communism: A New Civilization?* Two volumes. London: Longmans, Green.

Weber, Max. 1978. [1922] *Economy and Society: An Outline of Interpretive Sociology.* Two volumes. Berkeley: University of California Press.

Weil, Felix. 1924. Gildensozialistische Rechnungslegung. Kritische Bemerkungen zu Karl Polanyi: 'Sozialistische Rechnungslegung' in diesem *Archiv,* 49:2, S.377 ff. *Archiv für Sozialwissenschaft und Sozialpolitik,* 52.

Weizsäcker, Carl Christian von. 1984. Rights and Relations in Modern Economic Theory. *Journal of Economic Behavior and Organization,* 5:2 (June).

Wells, Herbert George. 1913. *New Worlds for Old.* New York: Macmillan.

Whyte, William Foote, and Kathleen King Whyte. 1991 [1988]. *Making Mondragòn: The Growth and Dynamics of the Worker Co-operative Complex.* Ithaca, NY: ILR Press.

Wicksteed, Philip Henry. 1933 [1910]. *The Common Sense of Political Economy.* Two volumes. London: Routledge.

Wieser, Friedrich von. 1956 [1889]. *Natural Value.* New York: Kelley and Millman.

Wiles, Peter. 1962. *The Political Economy of Communism.* Oxford: Blackwell.

Wilczynski, J. 1970. *The Economics of Socialism: Principles Governing the Operation of the Centrally Planned Economies in the USSR and Eastern Europe under the New System.* London: Allen and Unwin.

———. 1973. *Profit, Risk, and Incentive under Socialist Economic Planning.* New York: Harper and Row.

Williams, George C. 1966. *Adaptation and Natural Selection: A Critique of Some Current Evolutionary Thought.* Princeton: Princeton University Press.

Williams, Henry Fortson. 1950. *The Writings of Ludwig von Mises on Socialism.* Chicago: M.A. Dissertation, University of Chicago.

Williamson, Oliver E. 1975. *Markets and Hierarchies.* New York: Free Press.

———. 1976. The Modern Corporation as an Efficiency Instrument. In Pejovich 1976.

———. 1985. *The Economic Institutions of Capitalism: Firms, Markets, Relational Contracting.* New York: Free Press/Macmillan.

Williamson, Oliver E., and Sidney G. Winter (eds.) 1991. *The Nature of the Firm: Origins, Evolution, and Development.* New York: Oxford University Press.

Wilson, Edward O. 1975. *Sociobiology: The New Synthesis.* Cambridge, Ma: Harvard University Press.

Wilson, T. 1945. Price and Output Policy of State Enterprise. *Economic Journal,* 55:220 (December).

Winiecki, J. 1988. *The Distorted World of Soviet-Type Economies.* Pittsburgh: University of Pittsburgh Press.

Wiseman, Jack. 1953. Uncertainty, Costs, and Collectivist Economic Planning. *Economica* (May). Reprinted in Buchanan and Thirlby 1973.

———. 1957. The Theory of Public Utility Price: An Empty Box. *Oxford Economic Papers,* 9. Reprinted in Buchanan and Thirlby 1973.

———. 1989. *Cost, Choice, and Political Economy.* Aldershot: Edgar.

Wolfe, Bertram David. 1964 [1948]. *Three Who Made a Revolution: A Biographical History.* New York: Dell.

———. 1965. *Marxism: One Hundred Years in the Life of a Doctrine.* New York: Dial.

———. 1981. *Revolution and Reality: Essays on the Origin and Fate of the Soviet System.* Chapel Hill: University of North Carolina Press.

Wolfe, Tom. 1987. *The Bonfire of the Vanities.* Farrar, Straus, and Giroux.

Wootton, Barbara. 1934. *Plan or No Plan.* New York: Farrar and Rinehart.

———. 1945. *Freedom Under Planning.* Chapel Hill: University of North Carolina Press.

Zaleski, Eugene. 1980. *Stalinist Planning for Economic Growth.* London: Macmillan.

Zassenhaus, H. 1934. Über die ökonomische Theorie der Planwirtschaft. *Zeitschrift für Nationalökonomie,* 5 (September).

NOTES

1. A QUICK LOOK AT THE MISES ARGUMENT

1. Mises was born in Lemberg (now Lviv) in 1881. His younger brother, Richard, became a leading probability theorist. Mises's step-daughter is the writer, Gitta Sereny. Mises and his student F.A. Hayek were both born into families with the unusual combination, in the Dual Monarchy, of being aristocratic (as shown by the 'von') and Jewish. Among illuminating accounts of Mises's central European milieu are Berkley 1988; Drucker 1979; Factor 1988; Hayek 1992, Part I; Hoffmann 1988; and Mises 1978.

2. For instance, Samuelson 1967, 617n; Schumpeter 1950, 173; Smith 1962, 93.

3. For example, Lal 1985, 72–73.

4. Beckwith (1976) says that factors should be priced, "even in a communist state which distributes all consumers" goods free of charge" (95). Beckwith may not accept that prices entail markets, and opposes free distribution of *all* consumer goods.

5. I have read somewhere, in the writings of followers of Bordiga, that there will be no 'enterprises' under communism. I don't think this was meant to deny the possibility of any decisions about production being made by local organizational units—which is all that is implied by my use of the term 'enterprise'. But if it was, the argument can easily be reformulated to avoid such an assumption.

6. There are several sound and entertaining accounts of price theory, among which I have found especially engrossing: Frank 1991; Friedman 1986, Hirshleifer 1984; McCloskey 1985; Miller and Meiners 1986; and Stigler 1987. Somewhat more advanced and harder going are Becker 1971; Friedman 1976; and Samuelson 1958. Useful background reading includes Becker 1976; Blaug 1985; Kirzner 1976; Knight 1965; McKenzie and Tullock 1978; Marshall 1949; Mises 1966; Stigler 1941; and Wicksteed 1933.

7. Kirzner (1988, 4) includes a third aspect, "the role of discovery", which I subsume under information.

8. Factories seem to be useful as vivid examples, although not many people now work in factories. The same principle applies to a restaurant, a hospital, a publishing house, or an airline.

2. THE ABOLITION OF THE MARKET

1. The term 'market socialist', which was originated by German writers in the early 1920s, but can be applied to some of the earliest, pre-Marxian socialists, is liable to obscure the precise scope of the market in socialism. Most of the self-styled 'market socialists' have written in a milieu where *some* role for the market under socialism was taken for granted, and have argued that there should be markets for factors (means of production). But those who have called themselves 'non-market socialists' (Rubel and Crump 1987) have generally opposed any role for trade, seeing the absence of money as a defining condition of socialism.

3. THE ECONOMIC ORGANIZATION OF POST-CAPITALIST SOCIETY

1. For example: "where production is under the actual, predetermining control of society" (III, 187); "a society, in which producers regulate their production according to a preconceived plan" (III, 261). Roberts and Stephenson are wrong to concede that planning "was never specially emphasized" (1973, 25) in Marx's writings.

2. For a readable though naive introduction to these issues, see Brown 1980.

3. Braverman holds that workers *don't like* "degraded" (unskilled and fragmented) work (148–49). If this dislike reduced workers' productivity it would give capitalists a special incentive to favor non-degraded work (though it might yet be true that workers' dislike of degradation does reduce their productivity, but that degradation still pays in net productivity, sufficient for the workers to prefer the higher wages it gives them to lower wages with less degraded work.) Braverman has a vision of all workers "assuming the scientific, design, and operational prerogatives of modern engineering" (445); this he assumes, without argument, to be feasible and desirable; he never spells out why, in that case, it wouldn't benefit the capitalists. He is appalled by the drive to ever-increasing productivity, which he discusses in indignant terms (206–212), without mentioning that this is the prerequisite to improvement in workers' living standards. Capitalism's magnificent improvement in real incomes for the mass of workers, utterly dwarfing what has been achieved, or credibly imagined, in any other social order, is shyly referred to as "a certain enlargement of the customary bounds of subsistence for the working class" (151). The key to Braverman's approach is that he sees work as pure recreation, and ignores the fact that work is also a means to the production of goods for consumers. He therefore feels free to play around in his imagination with the organization of work, comparing the actual with his ideal and treating the repercussions on output as non-existent. He never perceives any need to explain how the disliked aspects of modern work could prevail unless they were efficient.

4. Albert and Hahnel (1991, 33–34) take the example of doctors changing bedpans and contend that: 1. the Babbage approach assumes only a

tiny proportion of the population can become doctors; 2. quite a lot of people could be trained to be doctors; 3. training to become a doctor could be made more enjoyable; 4. if everyone received "ample training in some relevant area for which they had relevant talent", then "there would be no significant opportunity costs no matter who changed bed pans", so doctors might as well do it. Comments: 1. It might be that 80 percent of the population could be trained to become good doctors, but these same 80 percent, and only they, could be trained to become good architects, programmers, or managers. This might indicate it would be cheaper to hire bedpan changers from the remaining 20 percent. A more detailed analysis would look at degrees of trainability in different tasks, though most valuable abilities seem to be positively correlated. 2. The actual non-M.D. bedpan changer might be trainable but not trained—for example, might have chosen to work as a musician in the evenings, rather than go through medical school. 3. There's no reason to suppose that if everyone had "ample training" the opportunity costs of their labor would become equal. 4. One of the main reasons some people aren't trained more is that their productivity wouldn't benefit sufficiently from it. 5. Training isn't a free good.

5. Marx held the expression 'value of labor' to be absurd (since he defined value as a quantity of labor). Readers may substitute some such phrase as 'that part of the value of the product which derives from living labor' for my expression "value of labor".

6. It might be argued that there is 'unused capacity', especially in large, immobile plants. (On the possible wastefulness of this, see below, 12.ii.c.) Such unused capacity could be taken up at existing technical coefficients only by adding labor, raw materials, and mobile equipment, which are currently more fruitful in other employments. Alternatively, the existing labor, raw materials, and mobile equipment could be 'spread out' over the existing fixed plant. But if this could be done without reducing output, it would be done within the market. More generally, unused capacity exists either because mistakes were made in the past or because of the need for flexibility in output. If both of these are assumed away, there would be no unused capacity of produced equipment. But Marx's argument for the "greater scope", based on his theory that s should not be attributed to c, would be unchanged.

7. "Capital is dead labour that, vampire-like, only lives by sucking living labour, and lives the more, the more labour it sucks" (I, 224). Marx conceals from himself and from his readers that 'capital' has no free-floating urge to 'self-expansion' for its own sake: the point of accumulating capital is to increase future output for consumers. Ironically, 'capital' was accumulated as an end in itself, without benefit to consumers, in Soviet Russia and in various Third World countries under the influence of Marxist ideas (unless the real consumers were bureaucrats contemplating reports of gross output of steel, cement, and so forth).

8. By the First World War there had been a major convergence among socialists, in their conception of post-capitalist society. Socialism came to mean the nationalization, municipalization, or acquisition by state-backed co-operatives, of at least the bulk of industry, with the retention of a money system and payment of money wages to workers, supplemented by increased

provision of 'free' services. This view was shared by Marxists and Fabians—there is little disagreement, for instance, between Kautsky 1902 and Wells 1913. This description leaves open whether state enterprises will buy their non-labor inputs from other state enterprises and will be obliged to make a profit, and such questions were indeed often not clearly addressed—though most often tacitly answered in the negative. Psychologically, there remained an important division among socialists, between those who would readily accept that the above were a fair description of socialism and those who (though they in fact had little else to suggest) would have indignantly rejected it as a travesty. The psychological dilemma arose because all the elements of this 'socialism' had long since been extensively tried and found less than delightful. Really radical spirits were therefore bound, if they wanted to be socialists, to come up with a 'socialism' which either a. was quite different from this; or b. had vitally important additional features.

9. Kautsky was no longer a member of the 'Majority' Social Democrats, having split from them because of his opposition to the War, which the SPD supported.

10. An exception was the then Menshevik Trotsky.

11. Lenin seems to have noticed that what he attributes to Marx is not actually stated by Marx, and he therefore offers an argument that it is implicit in Marx. He points out (476) that Marx uses the term 'law' to describe distribution in the first phase of communism, and claims that the existence of law implies the existence of a state. However, the term used by Marx is not *Gesetz* ('law') but *Recht*, which, according to context, can mean 'right' (entitlement), 'justice', or 'law'. The term *Recht* doesn't imply a state.

12. At least one of these preconditions, universal literacy, was absent in Russia. Doubtless Lenin would have explained what difference this might make, in his unwritten final chapter. The only interpretation consistent with Lenin's later behavior and statements is that he would have argued for a more prolonged period of centralization and education before the whole population could become state employees at equal wages, rather than "immediately, overnight".

13. Early writings on Bolshevik Russia, friendly or hostile, depicted the abolition of the market as the implementation of Marxist ideas. When the 'makeshift' story became the Moscow line in the late 1920s, it was given an early, and brilliantly perceptive, challenge by Michael Polanyi (1940). More recently, the story has been attacked in detail by Roberts (1971a) and Boettke (1990).

14. See in particular Bukharin 1971, an edition which includes Lenin's marginal comments. See also the popular Bukharin and Preobrazhensky 1966. For a general account see Szamuely 1974. The 'left' communists expressed no satisfaction with the actual progress of War Communism. They demanded more radical and rapid measures. For example see Kollontai 1977, 159–200.

15. According to Serge (1963, 115), "the social system in these years was later called 'War Communism'. At the time it was called simply 'Communism', and anyone who, like myself, went so far as to consider it purely temporary was looked upon with disdain."

16. LCW v33, 63, 69, 93, et passim. The Bolshevik leaders undoubtedly knew of Mises 1920 and must have discussed it either before or shortly after they abandoned War Communism, though I don't know of any direct evidence of its precise influence on their views. See Erlich 1960, 10. Trotsky saw the need to abandon War Communism earlier than Lenin (Deutscher 1954, 495-98), and for the rest of his life argued with unusual clarity for the absolute necessity of retaining the market (until the 'higher phase of communism', which Trotsky came to see as extremely remote).

17. Nearly 43 years after the abandonment of War Communism, the Cuban Industries Minister, Ernesto Guevara, produced an article (Guevara 1969) whose ideas guided Cuban government thinking. Recalling Lenin's 'retreat' from War Communism to NEP, Guevara states that it was "a tactic closely tied to the historical situation" and without "universal validity": because of the level of administrative technique in 1964 Cuba, there is no need to repeat Lenin's retreat. Guevara's "budgetary system" is a conscious imitation of War Communism. Enterprises have no independent legal existence and no funds of their own; they are "part of the single great enterprise that is the state". Moral incentives are to be used wherever possible to prepare people for the end of money, and 'prices' must be assigned on the basis of labor-time. There was no civil war and Cuba was not isolated. Vast sums were poured by the Soviet Union into Cuba, already one of the richest countries in Latin America, and hundreds of Marxist experts from East and West arrived in Havana to offer their fraternal assistance. Cuba's industrialization program collapsed, with numerous expensive investments wasted because of the absence of prices. Rebounding from this fiasco, Cuba embarked on the 'Ten Million Ton Sugar Harvest', also a colossal waste of resources.

4. THE DISCOVERY OF THE ECONOMIC CALCULATION PROBLEM

1. Of all these writers, Schäffle is the least antagonistic to socialism, and despite the fact that most of his writing on socialism was purely in opposition, in his 1881 he made suggestions for a moderate kind of market socialism. He argues that for allocative purposes labor-hours would have to be adjusted by a system of 'social taxes'. This was quoted in a treatise by Adolf Wagner, on which Marx made comments in a set of posthumously published 'notes'. Marx's caustic comments on Wagner and Schäffle are disingenuous. Marx denies indignantly that he, Marx, has advocated 'social taxes', and points out that his theory of value is designed to explain capitalism, not to serve as a proposal for socialism (MECW v24, 536-37). However, Schäffle had accurately interpreted Marx's references to the way socialism would operate using labor-hours, and Schäffle did not claim that Marx had originated the 'social taxes'. See Moore 1980, 87-89. Forty years later, Cohn (1920, 122) replied to the Mises argument by citing Schäffle's 'social taxes'. Mises replied that the socialist administration would not be

able to accurately determine the appropriate "social taxes" (Mises 1924, 489–490).

2. Brutzkus's name is sometimes transliterated 'Brutskus'. His 1935 book comprises the 1921 articles based on his 1920 lecture, plus a 1934 analysis of Russian development through Stalin's first five-year plan.

3. Mises's failure to get an academic post has been attributed both to antisemitism and to the socialism of Viennese Jewish intellectuals. "A Jewish intellectual who advocated socialist ideas had his respected place . . . But a Jewish intellectual who justified capitalism appeared to most as some sort of monstrosity, something unnatural, which could not be categorised and with which one did not know how to deal" (Hayek 1992, 157; and see 128n).

4. The fact that there were capable liberals in Europe after World War II is mainly due to the influence of *Die Gemeinwirtschaft* during the inter-war years. There might not have been any West German 'economic miracle' without the existence of a handful of active people converted from socialism by Mises. Hayek, a socialist before he read *Die Gemeinwirtschaft*, recalls: "We felt that the civilization in which we had grown up had collapsed. We were determined to build a better world, and it was this desire to reconstruct society that led many of us to the study of economics. Socialism promised to fulfil our hopes for a more rational, more just world. And then came this book. Our hopes were dashed. *Socialism* told us that we had been looking for improvement in the wrong direction" (Hayek 1992, 136).

5. RE-READING MISES ON ECONOMIC CALCULATION

1. The term 'praxeology', which Mises took from Espinas (1890), should not be confused with Kotarbiński's 'praxiology'. Praxiology is concerned with efficient action, praxeology with any goal-directed action, no matter how ill-considered. (Of course, some amount of *prima facie* effectiveness may be necessary for us to recognize a case of action, however minimally conceived.)

2. The closest thing to an argument which might be mistaken for such a proof is that 1. all human action presupposes means and ends; 2. the use of means to attain ends presupposes scarcity of factors; 3. therefore, abolition of scarcity of factors would mean abolition of human action; 4. Hence, since socialism is usually conceived as permitting human action, socialism is impossible (see Mises 1966, 234–36). Aside from the fact that the inferiority of socialism at coping with scarce factors is not provable on aprioristic grounds alone, we can suppose a society in which automated factories turn out plenty of goods and people spend their days playing table tennis, all their other wants having been sated. While playing table tennis they are acting, and their shots may be analyzed in terms of scarcity, especially scarcity of time. Thus the requirement for scarce factors can be trivially fulfilled, while the land and capital employed in producing all people's non-table-tennis wants is not scarce.

3. Lavoie (1982) shows how Mises's definition of 'interventionism' evolved and how it always remained inconsistent. As Lavoie points out, Mises excludes piecemeal nationalization from both socialism and capitalism.

4. Extreme subjectivists might try to save price determination from any influence on the part of 'objective' stocks of materials by pointing out that such stocks can influence behavior only insofar as they are known about. This is true, but without assuming some influence of what actually exists on what is known, no interesting conclusions about any real or imagined states of affairs would be possible.

6. USING LABOR-HOURS TO PLAN PRODUCTION

1. See Capital III, 187, 851. The idea that all allocational decisions would be made by balancing useful effects against labor-time was advanced in Engels's *Outline* of 1843, which made a powerful impression on Marx, and there is no sign that either of them departed from this idea thereafter. Even in his discussion of Robinson Crusoe (I, 81), Marx implies that Crusoe could conveniently do all his book-keeping in terms of labor, which of course is mistaken.

Yet it never occurred to Marx, Engels, Bebel, and others that a socialist society might face a serious problem in choosing among production methods (at least, it never occurred to them in their early, formative periods), so it's anachronistic to think of them as offering labor-time-units to solve such a problem. They do see the broader 'problem' (they conceive it to be a transparently simple one) of allocating the available resources to the production of different kinds of desirable goods, and they suppose that labor-time would play a special role in this planning process. The underlying assumption is that market influences on production techniques are arbitrary, hence, absent prices, the correct techniques are obvious. Even this simple problem, however, would involve some measure of consumer demand in general units, as well as labor-time.

2. Neurath is even better known as an instigator of Logical Positivism. There is an obvious, if very rough, parallel between denial of the existence of 'metaphysical' entities and denial of the need for economic value or price.

3. Some confusion has been generated by a failure to perceive that Marx's terminology and his methodology were transformed around 1860. Earlier, as in the *Grundrisse* of 1858 and the *Critique of Political Economy* of 1859, Marx is essentially a Ricardian, and he uses the terms 'exchange-value' and 'value' interchangeably; especially, he often uses 'exchange-value' where he means what he would later strictly define as 'value'. In the manuscript of 1861–63, from which *Theories of Surplus-Value* is taken (designed to be Volume IV of *Capital* though written before Volume I), a new conception of value and a new terminology appear. Now 'value' and 'exchange-value' are strictly separated, with 'value' *defined* as socially-necessary labor-time. Other changes appear at around the same time: the

theory of surplus-value, with its distinction between labor and labor-power; the terms 'constant' and 'variable' capital and 'organic composition of capital' (previously just 'composition of capital'). From his new theoretical standpoint, suggested by the example of natural science, Marx sees Ricardo as methodologically naive and muddled.

4. Marx confines the term 'value' to quantities of abstract labor-time *as they manifest themselves by governing market prices*. 'Value' to Marx is inherently fetishistic. Thus, Marx does not employ the term 'value' in discussing allocation of labor-time in non-commodity societies.

5. This is missed by Cohen (1988, 225) who rhetorically asks for the theoretical difference between Ricardo and Marx, given that both admit divergence of actual equilibrium prices from quantities of labor-time. The most obvious difference is that since in Marx prices are nothing but transformed values, if one price is above or below value, other prices must be below or above values by a corresponding amount. In Ricardo, if one price is above or below value, this can be accepted without further repercussions.

6. What follows is a restatement of the argument as given by Mises (1981, 114–15).

7. Marx does *also* attempt to show that capital was originally accumulated by robbery rather than voluntary saving (Capital I, 667ff), since he could hardly fail to notice that in his theory machines increase physical output (though not its labor-value), and that therefore anyone might argue that the capitalist is entitled to some reward for having saved. Marx's account here is a preposterous misrepresentation of history. In actuality, most early capitalists practiced frugality and thrift, often starting as low-income workers. Cases of looting and pillage as the formation of investible fortunes form a minute part of the total picture. One might as well characterize workers' wages as theft from the capitalist, because some workers pilfer from their employers.

8. Contrary to a legend, Böhm-Bawerk and other leading critics of Marx never claimed that Marx only noticed the great contradiction when he got to Volume III. Marx knew, when writing Volume I, the broad lines of the 'solution' he would give in Volume III, and Böhm-Bawerk himself pointed this out in advance of the appearance of Volume III. However, it does seem quite likely that the reason for Marx's failure to do any work on *Capital* in his final years was his awareness of the impasse he had reached. It's an intriguing possibility (Hayek 1988, 150) that the new marginalist thinking helped convince Marx his own theory was doomed.

9. Capital I, 44–46. The fallacies in this argument were pointed out by Wicksteed (1933, 705–724) and Böhm-Bawerk (1962, 256–278).

10. Böhm-Bawerk (1962, 229–230) lists four counters by Marx to this obvious charge. Of these, I think the one Marx relies on is the fourth—his contention that, without the derivation of prices from values, the amount of surplus-value or 'profit' becomes indeterminate (Capital III, 157, 313, 865). Aside from the later development of the theories of Clark, Fisher, and others, which provide a better explanation of the rate of return on capital, Marx's own theory cannot easily escape the charge of indeterminacy. Marx's theory is compatible with any positive magnitude of s. The 'value of labor-power' incorporates a "historical and moral element", making it only very loosely

determinate. And there is no convincing theory of how the forces of market competition 'know' where to bid prices to, to preserve the 'right' amount of s. As Budge points out, the classical theory differs from the Marxian in that we can see why prices would tend towards the classical 'natural price' or 'cost price', but we are in the dark as to why prices would tend towards Marxian prices of production, carefully preserving the total mass of surplus-value.

11. Strictly, this works only if the 'small quantities' are infinitesimal, but that has no practical significance. With small quantities like five minutes of labor, the result is very close to the infinitesimal—closer than we would normally be able to calculate in industry.

12. A reader new to this may wonder what I mean by 'following this method', since my illustration doesn't offer any guidance on what combination of factors to choose. The efficiency rule is that each factor must be so allocated to all its possible uses that its marginal product is the same in every use. This condition tends to be fulfilled automatically in a competitive market.

13. There are still a few economists who deny this way of putting it, but I think their objection is purely semantic (as well as being wrong). The sense in which one's marginal product means what one's resources contribute to output captures *something* but not *everything* in the vernacular notion of 'contribution to output'. If we want to cling to the element of that notion which is not preserved in marginal product, we have to say that the concept of individual contribution to co-operative output becomes meaningless. Marginal productivity still excludes surplus-value.

14. Hardly anyone refers to the great achievement of John Bates Clark without lamenting his naivety in deriving an ethical defense of the market's distribution of incomes from his theory. It's true that such a defense requires the premiss that individuals are entitled to the full value of what the resources they own contribute to output, but Clark is quite explicit that he accepts this by no means bizarre premiss, so his sketchy ethical argument is quite consistent and not at all naive. Clark began as a socialist sympathizer on the basis of his judgment that workers did not get the full fruits of their labor, but changed his mind when his own analysis convinced him that workers did in point of fact get precisely that.

Rawls (1971, 308) voices a common objection to marginal productivity as a basis for distributive justice, when he comments that the marginal product of labor depends upon supply and demand, and that, for instance, an individual's contribution "is also affected by how many people offer similar talents. There is no presumption, then, that following the precept of contribution leads to a just outcome unless the underlying market forces, and the availability of opportunities which they reflect, are appropriately regulated." However, supply and demand are not external disturbances, but the way in which the tendency to payment by marginal product is manifested in the market. If I have valuable skills and the availability of people offering those skills increases, then my income falls *because my contribution to output falls* (if the supply of any factor increases, the 'last' unit of that factor is moved to a less-highly-valued use). Rawls attributes to Clark a "mistake" and asserts that "Marxian exploitation is compatible with perfect competition, since it is the outcome of a certain structure of property relations" (309 n35). That "certain structure" is very broad. According to Marx, all interest arises from unpaid labor, so that exploitation occurs whenever anyone receives income as a result of having saved.

15. In the early years, certain stock objections were repeatedly raised to the marginal product idea, but these were all satisfactorily laid to rest. See Knight 1971, 110–14.

16. By stipulating that labor does not 'count' as labor unless it is useful, and 'counts' only to the extent that it is useful, Marx undermines his argument for labor as the source of value, and inadvertently points to the theory that things have labor bestowed upon them because they have value, rather than *vice versa*. See Wicksteed 1933, 258–260.

17. Opportunity cost can be illustrated by the acute remark of Aron Nimzovitsch that key squares should always be protected by pawns rather than pieces, because a pawn "works for least wages" (Nimzovitsch 1929, 36). The wages are implicit, but the cost is real. The cost of using a piece is greater than that of using a pawn because a piece is worth more than a pawn: that part of the piece's contribution (to the weighted probability of winning and drawing) which would have to be given up by tying the piece down to protecting a square is greater than that part of a pawn's contribution which would have to be given up using it to protect a square.

18. Engels also tries to elucidate the 'roundabout' nature of market prices by adding: "Just as little as it would occur to chemical science to express atomic weights in a roundabout way, relatively, by means of the hydrogen atom, if it were able to express them absolutely, in their adequate measure, namely in actual weights, in billionths or quadrillionths of a gramme." Roundabout and relative to compare with a hydrogen atom, but direct and absolute to compare with a piece of platinum located in Paris?

7. FROM MARKET SIMULATION BACK TO MARKET SOCIALISM

1. Lange 1938 cites Heimann 1932 and 1934 in his bibliography. Dickinson 1939 cites Heimann 1931 and 1932. Neither cites any of the debate from the 1920s. These are typical. However, Heimann 1939 gives a summary of the discussion, linking his own earlier contributions to the recent English-language discussion.

2. The marginal cost is the cost, at a given output, of a slight increase in output (or the cost saved by a slight decrease). The idea is that a firm will keep on increasing output as long as the revenue from a slight increase exceeds the cost, and will stop increasing it when these are equal.

3. Brus and Laski (1989, 55) count three, but this doesn't affect my point here.

4. In the body of his essay Lange claims (61–62) that Mises confuses two notions of price, exchange ratios on a market, and "the terms on which alternatives are offered". Every society, says Lange, needs to pay attention to prices in the second sense, but not necessarily in the first sense. This view of

Lange's is strange, since Mises unswervingly maintains that prices are necessary specifically in the first sense (in other words, Mises claims that prices in the first sense are necessary to get at prices in the second sense, in a technologically complex system). In his appendix, Lange cites quotations to show that leading Marxists "were and are quite aware of the necessity of the price system in a socialist economy" (141). All the quotations refer unmistakeably to actual market prices, prices in the first sense, which Lange has claimed are *not* necessary under socialism.

5. The term 'accounting prices' has more recently come to be used as an alternative to 'shadow prices'. But shadow prices are quite different from Lange's 'accounting prices': shadow prices are prices divergent from market prices, used in the evaluation of some government projects; they are not determined by the method of watching surpluses and deficits in stocks, but by calculating adjustments to market prices with the idea of compensating for externalities.

6. My remarks in the next two subsections draw upon many sources critical of schemes like Lange's, notably Hayek 1940; Hoff 1948; Mises 1966, 705–710; Robbins 1937; Roberts 1971a; Buchanan 1969; Coase 1946; Nutter 1968; Thirlby 1946; 1952; Wiseman 1953; Machlup 1984, 190–203.

7. Perfect competition is an illustrative construction. It assumes that all firms are complete 'price takers'; if a firm asks a price even slightly above the market price, it makes no sales, and if it asks a price even slightly below the market price, it captures the entire market (but makes losses). The definition of the model normally includes a specification of all the conditions considered necessary to ensure that result (many firms producing identical products in each industry, 'perfect information', and so forth). The essential idea of perfect competition, that sellers have no control over price, was often utilized by economists before perfect competition was defined. It is habitually employed by Marx in *Capital*.

8. In some discussions, a system somewhat like Lange's system is modified by supposing that each enterprise is allocated some 'liquid funds'. This is a big move away from the Lange system to something closer to a conventional market economy. To make the complete transition, substantially free financial markets are needed. Any entrepreneur with an idea may be able to persuade savers or their agents to devote funds to a particular enterprise. Such a system is not compatible with state ownership of industry.

9. Further, if we make an empirical prediction from static analysis, and this turns out to be approximately correct, that corroborates the theory that the adjustment processes are highly efficient. This is what we do generally observe in free-market situations.

10. To take one example, the valuation of inventory helps to determine the cost of sales figure on an income statement. Inventory is often valued at historical cost or replacement cost. Intrinsically, both of these figures are irrelevant to the true cost, the opportunity cost. Suppose that this morning the inventory became worthless, in the sense that it has no other possible use except to fulfill the next month's orders. Strictly, the cost of sales from inventory should be immediately adjusted to zero, which may show a handsome profit from now on, while re-interpreting the past, perhaps to show that huge losses were made when profits appeared to be made. Accounting tries to cope with such changes by periodic write-downs, but these are

necessarily crude and infrequent. Sensitivity is sacrificed to caution, and accuracy to professional objectivity. (A mean that deviates substantially from the ideally accurate magnitude, but with a small scatter, may be preferable to a mean that deviates slightly, with a larger scatter.)

8. PROPERTY RIGHTS AND THE LIMITS OF MARKET SOCIALISM

1. The appeal to Soviet experience as demonstrating beyond question that there can be no incongruity between socialist planning and factor markets is made, for instance, by Durbin (1949, 52).

2. The conception of property I defend in this chapter is similar to that developed by many writers on the economic theory of property rights. For example, see Furubotn and Pejovich 1974; Demsetz 1967. I do not see these recent writings as being at odds with the property theories of Grotius and, more especially, Pufendorf, which were well-known to eighteenth-century writers like Locke, Ferguson, Hume, Millar, and Smith. To avoid several pages of intellectual history here, I neither want to claim the slightest originality for anything I say in this chapter about property, nor to attribute any one of these views to any other writer.

3. It's sometimes claimed that prior to the modern period there was no concept of 'rights'. Even if 'rights' is given a very strict meaning, this is controversial. However, rights can be understood without being analyzed or identified by a special term, just as logic or grammar undoubtedly existed for thousands of years without being identified as distinct conceptual systems.

If it be true that there was no ancient notion of 'rights', as an abstract entity which could constitute an object of enquiry in general terms, this is a curiosity on a par with the fact that there is no occurrence of a word for 'religion' in the Old Testament (or in the chief scriptures of many religions). Rights are implicit in any culture which features litigation, and litigation is recorded from the very dawn of history, as well as being observed by anthropologists in many primitive societies.

My discussion assumes that not all property rules need be property rights, though generally most are. Jan Lester argues (personal communication) that all rules can be viewed as rights: a tribe's rule that 'no one shall touch the sacred tree' can be seen as the right of each individual not to have anyone else touch the sacred tree. I'm unconvinced that this dissolves all distinction between rules and rights. It doesn't affect the argument in the text.

4. Slavery has not been abolished, for people in prison are slaves. This would be more obvious if prisons leased their inmates for outside contracting, a point noted by that great defender of slavery, Margaret Mitchell (1936). The main reason why 'slavery' rather than imprisonment (slavery plus internment) was popular prior to recent times was that populations were too poor to be prepared to bear the expense of special buildings with numerous full-time staff, merely to house offenders. What most people today rightly object to is not slavery *per se*, but the custom of consigning adults to slavery for life because of their status at birth.

5. This must not be taken to suggest that individual rights morally

derive from the entity 'society'. But any actually prevailing rights derive from 'society' in a purely factual sense: they would not prevail without widespread acquiescence.

6. The line of division between capital and money markets is not sharp; both convey immediate command over real resources, through intermediaries, from those whose saving enables those resources (or their equivalent) to be available, to entrepreneurs who have ideas for using those resources productively, and both give the savers, in return, some kind of claim on the assets of the entrepreneurs. The convention is that capital markets deal in securities with maturities of more than one year; money markets, securities of less than one year. Capital markets include corporate stocks and bonds; money markets include commercial paper and bankers' acceptances.

7. Writers on history often assume, for instance, that if credit and banking develop, new productive ventures can be funded out of the formerly idle savings of those who kept their savings under the mattress. However, keeping money under the mattress is part of the demand for cash balances, and will (compared with the alternative of lending it) lower prices. It doesn't, by any simple and immediate mechanism, decrease the stock of capital goods or the opportunities for profitably combining them. Moving money from under the mattress into the bank does not *ipso facto* increase real output, any more than an increased money supply increases real output (in both cases, it may seem that some additional projects are enabled to go ahead, but this must be because resources have been bid away from other employments, thus curtailing other projects). On the other hand, the fact that it becomes easier to lend money at interest may encourage a greater volume of saving. The benefits of a more developed credit system lie chiefly in more accurate tracking, better co-ordination of production, which indirectly leads to increased output.

8. Here I use the term 'investment' as it's used in economics. Building a restaurant, laying a road, ploughing a field are examples of investment. Paying $1,000 into a money market account is not an example of investment (even if we define it as investment, it is not net investment for the economy as a whole, since the institution disinvests $1,000 just as the depositor invests it).

9. This laconic explanation will have to do here. Those unconvinced should read Machlup 1940. Those convinced should also read this fascinating work. (It is possible to construct 'dynamic' scenarios by which 'hoarding' could lead to reduced investment—although most economists now view these scenarios as less likely than they did during the Keynesian period. Even if accurate, however, such scenarios would not contradict my cautiously worded text.)

10. Does this mean that we cannot do without a stock exchange? The quick answer is: If a government simply outlawed stock exchanges, there would be increased use of non-exchange trading (in the so-called 'third market'). If the government outlawed stock trading *per se*, there would be black-market stock trading. If the government ruled out all of these, alternative means of conveying savings to entrepreneurs (bonds, merchant banking and so forth) would expand. There would be some drop in output and living standards. If the government were not satisfied with this, and determined to go further in outlawing anything which looked like a close

substitute for stock trading, the impoverishment would be greater *pari passu* with the scope of the government's aggression. The evil effects of all such measures are mitigated if the government implementing them exists in a world where most countries do not follow suit.

9. MOTIVATION AND INFORMATION

1. Durbin (1949, 89) claims that the economic calculation debate is really about motivation, and Buchanan (1969, 96–97) maintains that it should have been. Both are wrong.

2. For other remarks on incentives, see Rae 1891, 402–410; Hearnshaw 1929, 355–59. In his critical survey of socialism, Hearnshaw cites and praises Mises 1922, but Hearnshaw's own criticisms betray no awareness of the economic calculation problem.

3. Throughout this book, I conform to the fashion for randomly alternating female and male pronouns—except that I refer to workers as male and to capitalists as female, since this reflects the reality that most wealth is produced by men and most wealth is owned by women.

4. Some differences in money income are immediately due to people's preferences. We can imagine two people with identical money-making opportunities choosing to make very different amounts of money. Such measurable income differences are due to individuals acting in different ways to maximize their psychic incomes (that is, their total incomes, pecuniary and nonpecuniary). Forcing these two individuals to have the same post-tax incomes would make their psychic incomes (the incomes that really matter) unequal.

5. Bellamy (1960; 1968) proposes a system in which paid incomes are equal and everyone is obliged to work a certain number of hours, though with free choice of occupation. This raises the problem that people will crowd into the more enjoyable jobs and leave the more irksome posts unfilled. Bellamy therefore proposes to raise or lower the obligatory hours for each job, to equalize supply and demand for every kind of work. But this means, for instance, that someone working few hours in an unpleasant job is deprived of the opportunity to increase his hours and his pay, a move that would benefit himself and others. (The proposal also overlooks the fact that each worker can do many jobs, and requires differences in pay to inform him of the value of each of those jobs to consumers.)

6. Carens, 96. With these words Carens is attributing a view to Merton, but clearly Carens agrees with it.

7. To mention one simple example, in every large human population that has been studied enough to yield a finding on the matter, the majority of people are predominantly heterosexual in their inclinations and a minority of people are predominantly homosexual. No one knows how to 'socialize' a population so that all its members are a. heterosexual, b. homosexual, c. bisexual, or d. asexual. An individual's sexual orientation includes some goals and values, and it also influences the formation of other goals and values.

It shouldn't be supposed, however, that genetic or congenital drives are the only alternative to 'socialization'. Many of our desires owe little to genetic or congenital drives or to socialization. For example, as rational creatures we will, if the opportunity is there, conceive a desire for versatile instruments which could help us to achieve a wide range of possible goals. Telephones, cars, cameras, and guns are not popular because people are socialized into using them. People are socialized into using them because they are popular, and they are popular because they are so obviously and enormously useful in achieving a vast array of possible objectives. Hence, different people often want these machines to pursue entirely different objectives; it is their pursuit of these objectives, plus their knowledge that the machines will help them pursue those objectives, which explains the prevalence of the machines, and therefore explains the fact that people are socialized into using these machines.

Even if it were true that all goals and values were determined by the culture, no one knows precisely how they are so determined, so no one is able to devise a culture that will guarantee everyone a given set of goals.

Carens suggests that people will do what is required in the ESM in order to gain the approval of others. This weakens his case in two ways: 1. It admits that there is, after all, a limit to what socialization can achieve—why else bother to socialize people to seek approval, if they could be socialized to directly value social duty? 2. It affords unbounded scope for cheating, since the ESM is essentially self-policing: no one can ever prove that I am not making the decision I would have made in the PPM.

8. (Wicksteed 1933, 163–65; Robbins 1932, 12–17; Kirzner 1976, 51–66). What is characteristic of market behavior is that each person pursues her own self-chosen purposes, and these purposes *may* be selfish, though they may consist entirely of her own view of the common good. Some of people's behavior in the PPM is altruistic. But 'altruism' is not the name for a single goal. Everyone pursuing their own view of altruism does not lead to any more agreement about the allocation of resources than everyone's pursuing their own selfish interest.

9. Carens suggests that, even under the PPM, people don't reduce their offers of labor if they are guaranteed an income independent of their labor. This claim runs counter to every piece of evidence that exists on the matter, and the evidence is not slender (Robins and West 1980).

10. DIVISION OF KNOWLEDGE

1. It may be objected that neither Walras nor Muth are known as advocates of *laissez faire*. But Walras arrived at an unprecedented understanding of the complex interaction of many markets, which led to a new vindication of competition. Walras's 'socialist' views are largely hold-overs from his earliest notions, mainly absorbed from his father. Walras's brilliant apprehension of the possibility of general equilibrium equations was suggested by reading Poinsot on mechanics. Muth's work led to the

'rational expectations' school, which has provided a mathematically sophisticated theoretical foundation for the judgment that much government intervention of the 'macro-economic' sort associated with post-
Keynesianism is self-defeating.

2. The ancient Germans had an interesting technique. They would
discuss all important issues twice—once drunk and once sober.

3. A random example of the sort of objectionable assertions I have in
mind is Simpson 1975, xvi, under "*i. Institutions*".

4. See Alchian and Demsetz 1972. The existence of the price system,
with its definitive test of profit and loss, affords a fertile area for the
operation of what I have called "cumulative rational selection", a mechanism whose importance in human cultural evolution I hold to be immense.
See Steele 1988.

5. The possible existence of serious defects in the market cannot be
refuted on *a priori* grounds alone. Among candidates are some public goods
arguments and such scenarios as that analyzed in Akerloff 1970. If any of
these were shown to be problems, the superiority of a coercively imposed
solution could not be demonstrated on *a priori* grounds alone.

6. In most cases, NFM socialists who say that they reject 'central
planning' tacitly argue as though their socialism *would* have the benefit of a
'central plan'. O'Neill claims that Marx has been misrepresented as holding
that production can anticipate demand instead of adapting to it. Yet,
summarizing Marx, O'Neill says that "the possibility of crises . . . is a
consequence of the spatial and temporal gap between the processes of
production and sale of commodities" (202). With the possible substitution
of some other term for "sale", this gap automatically exists in any system
where production adapts to manifested demand instead of perfectly anticipating it. O'Neill (206) approvingly quotes Engels as saying that supply and
demand are never in balance "because in this unconscious condition of
mankind no one knows how big supply and demand is [sic]". As Engels, but
apparently not O'Neill, is able to see, this must be true of any economic
system not governed by a single great plan.

7. We could conjecture that this would occur more often in industries
with a few firms, in which each firm's products were far from being perfect
substitutes for those of the other firms. Withholding information in this
context might be a source of inefficiency, though not of any systematic
tendency to overproduction.

It would be possible to formulate a more direct defense of rivalrous
withholding of information, for instance by focussing on the conjectural
benefits of pursuing a hypothesis undistracted by alternatives. But such
arguments would be subtle, uncorroborated, and supererogatory.

11. PLANNING AND THE MARKET

1. It's possible to imagine a trade which doesn't involve property titles,
but merely actual possession. Such are the exchanges one sees in adventure

movies, where two objects—sometimes human hostages—are laid on the ground at the same time, and the exchangers warily circle each other. Here there is not necessarily any presumption that anyone recognizes anyone else's legal or moral right to anything, so that either party might at any moment abruptly decide to take back the object given up and keep the object received. Such exchanges are difficult to conduct but possible in a limited range of circumstances.

2. The new era of British planning was introduced by a Conservative government in 1961, at the instigation of the then Federation of British Industries (F.B.I., the employers' pressure group, now the Confederation of British Industries), cheered on by the *Times* and *Economist*. Attempts at national planning have now been abandoned in Britain and France, and in the U.S., the Humphrey-Javits planning bill failed to be adopted after considerable public debate. See Jewkes 1977; Polanyi 1967; Lutz 1969; Hayek 1976.

3. In economic terminology, 'natural' often means 'abstracting from monetary influences' (as in 'natural rate of interest'). There is no implication that the 'natural' phenomenon is natural in the sense of being dictated by non-cultural forces of nature.

4. Polanyi was evidently no chessplayer. By "places" he apparently means squares, and by "castles", rooks.

5. See the "survey" of the cotton industry in *Financial Times*, 1976.

6. From its foundation in 1904, the Socialist Party of Great Britain advocated a strictly marketless form of socialism on traditional Marxist grounds (see Barltrop 1975). Beyond a few generalities, the party discouraged discussion of the workings of socialism, but there was little reason to suspect that its members rejected the Marxian view that the market would be replaced by society-wide planning. In the 1980s, the party began to sporadically attack the very idea of 'central planning'. In 1988, the party began to call itself 'The Socialist Party' (dropping 'of Great Britain') and subsequently expelled the remaining Marxist 'planners', who promptly constituted themselves "The Socialist Party of Great Britain".

7. Friedman (1962, 122–23) gives reasons why people tend to believe in the prevalence and growth of high concentration or monopoly. Other reasons are: 1. that folk theories of how the market works don't supply any explanation why bigger size isn't always advantageous; and 2. that people tend to compare conspicuous concentration in some industries today with an imagined degree of 'atomism' that did not in fact prevail in the nineteenth century, if ever.

8. Throughout this book I use the general term 'industry' to encompass all production, including services.

9. More explicitly, if the market is seen as an arena where competing theories of the best way to do things are pitted against one another, then even though it were true that the whole of industry would be best run as a single organization, supposing that organization to have as close an approximation to the best theories as the one that prevails in the market, it becomes untrue once we recognize that the prevailing array of theories could not have been generated by one organization.

10. "The rate of profit . . . is above all important to all new offshoots of

capital seeking to find an independent place for themselves. And as soon as formation of capital were to fall into the hands of a few established big capitals, for which the mass of profit compensates for the falling rate of profit, the vital flame of production would be altogether extinguished" (III, 259).

11. Economists refer to the combining of productive processes and firms conducting those processes as 'integration'. Horizontal integration occurs when two or more units are combined which do the same thing, such as two paper mills. Vertical integration occurs when two successive stages are combined, as when a paper mill is combined with a lumber company or a printing press.

12. Coase points out that taxation or government regulation will increase firm size, by making it less costly to move some transactions from the market into the firm. Judgments vary on whether this effect is large or small. See Stigler 1968, 136; Williamson 1985, 127–28.

12. ABUNDANCE AND THE PRICE SYSTEM

1. Socialists have persistently claimed that the market is so wasteful that socialism would be able to double output, and they take this as a license to make all sorts of generous assumptions about socialism. At a very modest annual growth rate of 2 percent, output will double in 35 years; at 5 percent, in 15 years. On the most optimistic plausible assumption, it would take socialism a while to double output. Thus, to say that socialism will double output is to say that socialism will more quickly give us the same output we could get without socialism by waiting 15–35 years.

2. The economic problem is sometimes explained in the following way. Suppose that everyone makes a list of precisely what they would like to have for, say, the coming year, ignoring cost. Then, as a matter of fact, the resources of society do not permit the production of all the goods on all these lists. Choices have to be made to sacrifice some of those goods to others. While this is correct, it should be noted that even if the resources of society were adequate to produce all the listed goods, it's possible that these resources might be misallocated and output might fall short of that objective. The economic problem, and the concomitant economic calculation problem, therefore don't require that satiety of final goods be unattainable.

Although it may be counter-intuitive, it seems to follow that even if complete satiety were achieved for all consumer goods, there would still need to be consumer good prices (if factors still had to be economized).

3. In the technical terms of price theory, both the 'income effect' and the 'substitution effect' are very small. *Both* must be very small for the amount consumed to be insensitive to price changes.

The absence of close substitutes is the crucial point for the distinctiveness of salt. If the government provides bread free and pays for this by taxation, then for consumers as a whole (or for the average person), there is no income effect, since people's incomes are reduced by the taxation just as they would be by buying the bread. But for each individual there will be misallocation unless that person's tax-for-bread were exactly what they would have spent on the bread. But if this intricate adjustment were in fact arranged for everyone, they would in effect be paying the market price for the bread.

All the arguments in the text apply to any subsidy for a consumer good, whether this makes it free or merely cheaper than the market price. (There are specific arguments, quite different from those discussed here, for subsidies of some goods. I don't address these arguments in this work.)

4. An 'inferior good' is one which is consumed less as income rises. The opposite relationship characterizes 'normal goods'.

Mandel suggests that goods can be provided free where their elasticity of demand has "become negative" (1968, 659). He probably means the *income* elasticity of demand—the case of an inferior good. But people will increase their consumption of an inferior good if its price falls—including a fall to zero. An inferior good *ipso facto* has close substitutes.

5. Beckwith advocates an expansion of free provision, but argues that this should be restricted to certain goods, and in many cases should extend only to a limited ration of the good. I think that his arguments for free provision are fallacious, but I have not discussed them all in this chapter, since Beckwith doesn't support the 'abundance argument' for communism, and criticizes some of the arguments in that vein.

Beckwith claims that free distribution is best, for goods such as "uncongested highways", where marginal cost equals zero. This seems to be factually incorrect: each car-mile adds to maintenance costs. But it is in any case a *non sequitur*, since if all the people who use a road receive its services at zero marginal cost, this can hardly be an argument for making people pay for the road who don't use it at all. Further, road providers cannot correctly gauge the urgency of demand for various roads, helping them to decide which roads to expand and which to close, without the information provided by purchases of road use at a price (see Demsetz 1988, 39).

Beckwith favors free provision as a means to income redistribution, but (aside from ethical objections to any coercive redistribution), free distribution of some goods will usually be a very inexact way (compared with taxation) of accomplishing redistributive goals: there will be many unintended redistributive consequences.

6. The impossibility of general satiety does not imply the impossibility of satiety with respect to each good. As income rises, one could become satiated with respect to one good but still unsatiated with respect to others. However, the impossibility of general satiety along with the possibility of satiety of some goods implies either: a. that there is an infinite number of possible goods or, b. that there is at least one good (wisdom? longevity?) for which satiety is not possible.

7. This chapter doesn't argue that the actual representation of want-satisfaction costs as financial costs in any particular market is perfectly accurate; there are arguments for the shortcomings of some markets which I do not evaluate here. The chapter restricts itself to a particular type of argument related to scarcity, abundance, and waste.

8. If business or accounting profits are equal to the rate of interest, then there is no profit, in the strict economic sense. True profit is a return above interest; loss, a return below interest. Particular profits (like losses, but unlike interest) disappear rapidly in a competitive market. Under competition, a

profit shows that the recipient has temporarily been able to outguess the market, and thereby to benefit society by an unusually percipient or lucky allocation of resources. Interest is payment for the use of factors: buildings, raw materials, machines, and so forth. It goes to people who have placed their savings at the disposal of businesses, to produce goods consumers most urgently want.

9. Two qualifications: 1. Although I speak of "the" interest-rate, we always observe a variety of interest-rates. However, these are clustered together and tend to move together. Safer investments have lower rates than riskier investments. Allowing for risk, the average rate of return on all types of investment tends to be the same. 2. Observable interest rates include an allowance for anticipated inflation, and may seem to fluctuate quite rapidly, mainly in response to the disturbing actions of governments. The underlying real interest rate is, apart from catastrophes like major wars, stable. In and around major commercial centers, this real rate has been about two to four percent for centuries.

10. The conceptual problems in the theory of interest are uncommonly subtle, and it would not be surprising if mainstream theory had overlooked important insights of Fetter's. But as far as I have been able to discover, the Fetter-Mises proponents have been unable to make a clear and convincing reply to Fisher's arguments, notably his use of the "hard tack", "figs", and "sheep" examples.

11. See Hutt 1977 for a clarification of the circumstances in which observable 'idleness' of resources may be objectionable or unobjectionable. Unused capacity may appear in restriction of output by cartels, but not all unused capacity indicates the existence of such restriction.

12. Packard's best-selling book was successful in giving the impression that it had proved what in fact it did nothing to substantiate. Gorz (1967, 79) refers to "motor vehicles, which are *deliberately* built with parts which will wear out rapidly (and cost as much as longer-lasting parts would have)", and in support cites Packard, "which contains numerous examples of this type". Packard contains no examples of this type drawn from real life.

13. Further consequences of the trade-off: 1. If the price of a light bulb falls in relation to the price of a unit of electricity, the planned life of the bulb ought to be shortened. 2. People who want bulbs to last longer are advocating greater consumption of electricity. Planned obsolescence, in this instance, is an energy conservation measure. 3. In a region where electricity is comparatively cheap, lamp lives ought to be longer. The report mentions that in Norway at the time (a country with low population density and excellent conditions for hydro-electric generation) bulbs were made to last longer than elsewhere.

14. Baran and Sweezy refer to advertising as "brainwashing" (1962, 121). Here we have apologists for regimes which practice actual brainwashing (keeping people confined, pounding their feet with rifle butts, urinating in their food, and so forth, until they say whatever their captors want to hear) who object to the 'brainwashing' of 'Good To The Last Drop!'. Such insensitivity to the reader's sense of irony would make any advertising copywriter blush.

15. Or too little. Many ads involve a substantial free-rider effect: one

can't advertise a brand of toothpaste without simultaneously promoting toothpaste in general, from which other brands will benefit. According to a commonly accepted rule of welfare economics, this presents a case that advertising is underproduced, and should be subsidized out of taxes. (I don't agree with that conclusion.)

16. Schweickart also however suggests that nonrational appeals are very common, which is not true of the kind of misleading appeals he instances. He has a footnote referring to Packard 1958, Packard 1960, Key 1973, and Key 1976, so presumably Schweickart endorses the fanciful notions of 'depth psychology' and 'subliminals'. Key's claims about subliminals have been debunked in Creed 1987.

If a cigarette ad announces 'It's toasted!', some cigarette consumers may buy the advertised brand because they wrongly conclude that other brands are not toasted. *Prima facie* those consumers have made a suboptimal judgment, and this effect of that ad is in a sense inefficient. That much has to be conceded to Schweickart, though the slogan 'It's toasted!' has a largely different function, more akin to that of slogans like 'It's the real thing!' or 'Fahrvergnügen', which no plausible exegesis can render as misleading.

17. In 1985, 46 percent of U.S. non-farm workers worked other than the standard 40-hour week, and 26 percent worked considerably more or less than this standard—over 48 or under 30 hours (Smith 1986).

18. All words possess a family of associated meanings, and here I'm merely pointing to some implications of one common cluster of usages of 'waste'. My remarks have no relevance to usages which lack any suggestion that 'waste' ought to be minimized.

13. ANARCHY, STATE, AND COMMUNISM

1. A recent scholarly legend holds that Engels did not refer to the 'withering away' but to the 'dying out' of the state. This seems to be based on little more than the fact that the German verb 'absterben' (to wither away) includes the stem 'sterben' (to die) along with the separable prefix 'ab'. The normally solid Marxologist Richard N. Hunt (*not* to be confused with the notoriously inaccurate R.N. Carew Hunt) gets this exactly wrong, contending that while 'absterben' in a figurative sense can mean 'atrophy', 'wither', or 'fade away', its "primary and literal meaning" is "die out" (Hunt 1984, 242). In fact the primary and literal meaning is 'wither away' or 'shrivel up', as used of plant leaves. Hunt refers to the fact that recent editions of *Anti-Dühring* translate Engels's "*Er stirbt ab*" as "It dies out" (Engels 1954, 389). But this is an unfortunate mistranslation; a correct rendering is 'It withers away'. Hunt also points out that this term was used only once by Engels, and never by Marx. But it appears in what was intended as a comprehensive statement of the Marxist position, placed by Engels in italics for emphasis, and it occurs unchanged in that part of *Anti-Dühring* which was excerpted as a popular pamphlet, edited anew by Engels with additions and amendments. Elsewhere Hunt argues that *Anti-Dühring* must have been in harmony with Marx's views. (Despite all this, I agree with Hunt

that Marx and Engels saw the disappearance of the state as being a more rapid process than most of their later followers have done.)

2. The surprising part of Ricardo's insight is that it pays both (or all) 'sides' (nations, regions, or individuals) to specialize and trade even where one side is clearly inferior to the other in every activity. Ricardo took the example of Portugal sending wine to Britain in exchange for wool, to show that total output of wine and wool would be greater by this specialization, even though Portugal were more efficient at producing both goods (Ricardo 1951, 134–141). Both the populations of Portugal and Britain would benefit from trade. Ricardo's theory has been completely borne out by almost two centuries of rigorous investigation.

14. PROSPECTS FOR WORKERS' SELF-MANAGEMENT

1. The expected consequence would be that co-ops would hire the services of outside suppliers in cases where comparable non-co-ops would hire employees, but I don't know if this has been looked at in the case of Mondragón. It would also be worth investigating whether some of the non-member employees are among the lowest paid, and how this affects the 6:1 ratio.

2. "The CLP [co-operative bank] is unwilling to subsidize co-ops indefinitely. This is not simply a response to the law of survival of the capitalist jungle, but a recognition that it is not desirable to use scarce social resources and energy to maintain an unproductive enterprise" (Morrison, 126), in other words, exactly the law of survival of the capitalist jungle.

3. I use the term 'end-product' to refer to the 'external' product. Work-satisfaction is also a product of the work.

4. I refer to *all* the features of a job which might appeal to the worker as a 'package' of 'benefits'. This should not be confused with 'fringe benefits' (paid vacations, retirement and health plans, and so forth). For the purposes of this discussion, these can be included among money wages.

5. Some people reject this well-substantiated theory on the grounds that lower-paid jobs are often among the more unpleasant. But that's irrelevant. To see the effects of compensation we have to look at alternative jobs that could be done by the same individuals. Coal miners tend to be paid more than they could get in the less unpleasant occupations open to people with their abilities. They get paid less than many lawyers, but they generally lack the ability or motivation to become passable lawyers. If all individuals were completely interchangeable among jobs, then the *only* differences in wages would be higher pay for the more disliked jobs. If all individuals were interchangeable and all jobs were equally liked or disliked, then all wages would be equal.

6. If the government doesn't tax a co-op's 'surplus' on the same basis as a conventional firm's 'profits', this can amount to a substantial privilege for co-ops. See Mises 1990a, 265–276.

7. Law firms and physicians' group practices are often operated as partnerships. Presumably this is related to the fact that these firms sell services primarily performed by individual members, and that therefore,

though there is some gain from association, it is not derived from team organization.

8. There is a large and controversial technical literature on this question. See Ward 1958; 1967; Vanek 1970; Furubotn and Pejovich 1974. A possible misapprehension should be pointed out. It is sometimes stated that models show that the short-run inefficiency of co-ops' investment decisions 'will disappear in the long run'. Some readers may mistakenly conclude that this means that co-ops will actually converge on the same optimum as conventional firms, that things will come out all right in the end. But 'short-run' and 'long-run' don't mean 'short-term' and 'long-term'. In changing conditions, a short-run inefficiency leads to a permanently worse outcome.

15. IN DEFENSE OF SCIENTIFIC UTOPIANISM

1. My advocacy of utopias as bold conjectures which can then be criticised and possibly rejected is an obvious application of Popper's theory of science to social policy. Popper's espousal of piecemeal as against utopian engineering is reminiscent of the instrumentalist conception of scientific theories, which he rejects, while the utopian approach is more in keeping with the rationalist and metaphysical-realist conception of science which he defends.

2. In some places (for instance I, 477; IVa, 396) Marx emphatically declares that all labor is productive under capitalism if anyone makes a profit out of it. In other places (for instance III, 281), he insists that it makes no difference if 'unproductive' services (such as book-keeping) are provided on the market at a profit. A curiosity of Marx's approach is that he identifies a definition of productive labor which he claims belongs to capitalism— although only Marx, not the bourgeois economists, apply this definition. Hence such oddities as Marxist feminists of the 1970s bitterly denouncing the theory that housework is 'unproductive', a theory maintained in this century only by Marxists. Three comments are worth adding: 1. Purely as a matter of correct price theory, Marx is wrong to claim that some activities represent mere 'deductions from surplus-value'. Book-keeping is priced according to its marginal product, no less than planting potatoes. 2. If it really were tenable that a large and growing body of workers were paid out of surplus-value, then it would be inescapable, within Marx's theory, that these workers, like the capitalists, would be exploiting the productive workers. 3. Marx engages in an elaborate display of sarcasm against the view that 'all labor' is productive by affecting to laud the virtues of theft, robbery, fraud, and so forth (IVa, 387–88). These activities are *ex ante* productive for the individuals engaged in them, but there are victims who lose (usually by more than the thieves gain). In voluntary market transactions, by contrast, all participants are willing, and gain *ex ante*.

3. This point is often misunderstood. Marx's famous statement that "the emancipation of the working-class must be the work of the working-class itself" was made precisely because he did not think it true of all revolutions that they are necessarily made by the rising class. Hence, also,

the early Marxists foresaw the possibility that political revolutions led by representatives of the working class might occur in backward countries like Russia. These proletarian-led revolutions would necessarily be bourgeois, even if members of the bourgeoisie played little or no role in them.

4. Socialists are often impressed by such statistics as that ten percent of the population own 90 percent of the wealth, one percent owns 50 percent, and so forth. Though such extreme figures represent incomplete or misconstrued data (omitting life-cycle effects, for example), wealth ownership is certainly not equally distributed among the population, nor could it be. However, most such 'wealth' consists of productive assets; its 'redistribution', therefore, should not be viewed as the redivision of an immediate supply of consumable goods. If we hypothetically suppose that wealth can be redistributed without affecting output, then what the poorest 90 percent would gain in income by an equalitarian redistribution would be a few percentage points of the value of their newly acquired wealth, per year thereafter. Total income from labor is almost three times the size of total income from 'property', and much of the property income represents income from retirement investments of workers.

Index

Kirzner, Israel M., 401 n6, n7; on
history of economic calculation
debate, 120; on rationality of all
action, 98; on role of discovery,
401 n7; on scope of economics,
283, 415 n8
Kitcher, Philip, 240
Knight, Frank Hyneman, 95, 255,
401 n6
knowledge. *See* division of
knowledge.
Kollontai, Alexandra, 71, 404 n14
Kotarbiński, Tadeusz, 406 n1
Kropotkin, Prince Peter Alexeivich:
on anarchocommunist society,
317–18; on international spread of
manufacturing, 318–320, 322; on
Marxian labor-vouchers, 31; on
Ricardianism, 319–320, 322
Krushchev, Nikitia S., 268

labor: employed where comparatively
cheap, 289–290, 298–99; supply of
falls in response to welfare
payments, 224–25, 415 n9. *And
see* labor-power; labor-time.
labor theory of value (LTV). *See*
value, labor theory of.
labor unions, 63, 372; and
co-operatives, 343
labor-power, 55–56, 408–09 n10
labor-time: as lying behind
exchange-value, 26–27; in Marx's
view the only true cost, 55–56,
124; proposals to make prices
correspond with, 29–30, 37, 148;
405 n17; proposed for planning
production under socialism, 56,
123–24, 127–131, 405 n17, n1;
socially necessary, 129–130,
144–46. *And see* heterogeneity of
labor.
labor-value. *See* value, labor theory
of.
labor-vouchers (labor certificates) as
advocated by Marx, 29–33, 45,
282; metamorphosis into money,
33–36, 80–81, 89; not money,
29–30, 31–33

Lachmann, Ludwig, 97
Lafargue, Paul, 295
laissez-faire. *See* market, free;
liberalism; libertarianism.
Lal, Deepak, 401 n2
Landauer, Carl, 50, 75, 109, 115–117
Lange, Oskar: account of history of
economic calculation debate, 89,
109, 112, 410 n1, n4; adherence to
NFM socialism, 154–56; assumes
information available to socialist
managers, 242; on gratuitous
provision of consumer goods, 286;
proposal for socialist calculation,
126, 151–54, 190, 271, 411 n5, n6,
n8; reputation as refuter of Mises,
2–3, 88, 153–54
Laski, Kazimierz, 3, 166–67, 410 n3
Lassalle, Ferdinand, 58
Lausanne School, 82, 114. *See also*
Pareto, Vilfredo; Walras, Léon.
Lavoie, Donald C., 3, 49, 105, 114,
120, 122, 154, 407 n3
leisure, 224–25, 301–03
Leijonhufvud, Axel, 273
Lenin, Vladimir Ilyich, 29, 36, 43,
44–45, 64, 66–69, 70–71, 93, 190,
270, 312–13, 354, 355, 404 n11,
n12, n14, 405 n16, n17
Lerner, Abba P., 170–71
Lester, Jan Clifford, 412 n3
Levin, Henry, 53
Levin, Ira, 9
liberalism, 22–23, 73–74, 106, 317,
406 n4
libertarianism, 22–23. *And see*
liberalism.
light bulb, myth of the everlasting,
300–01, 420 n13
Lippincott, Benjamin E., 152
Little, Ian Malcolm David, 112, 154
living labor, 87–91, 137–38, 403 n5,
n7
living standards: dependence of high
l.s. upon functioning market, 3–4,
93
Locke, John, 412 n2
logical positivism, 407
Looking Backward (Bellamy), 46, 47,
218, 274, 414 n5